MW00636887

Contractors Guide to Business, Law and Project Management

South Carolina Residential Builders
8th Edition

Supplemental forms and links are available at **NASCLAforms.org** using access code **SCR129354**.

NASCLA®
NATIONAL ASSOCIATION OF STATE CONTRACTORS LICENSING AGENCIES

National Association of State Contractors Licensing Agencies (NASCLA)
23309 N. 17th Drive
Building 1, Unit 110
Phoenix, Arizona 85027
(623) 587-9354
(623) 587-9625 fax
Visit our web site:
www.nascla.org

NASCLA Contractors Guide to Business, Law and Project Management

South Carolina Residential Builders 8th Edition

Previously published as *Construction Management Guide, South Carolina Residential Builders' Commission Edition* and *Business Management and Law for Residential Builders, South Carolina Residential Builders' Commission Edition*

National Association of State Contractors Licensing Agencies (NASCLA)
23309 North 17th Drive, Building 1, Unit 110
Phoenix, Arizona 85027

ISBN-10 1-948558-06-8

ISBN-13 978-1-948558-06-8

INTRODUCTION

The construction industry is one of the strongest industries in America. To keep the construction industry thriving and to be a successful construction contractor, you must be knowledgeable in both your trade and managing a business.

Thorough business planning and good management skills are the keys to success in today's market. A solid business plan lays the foundation for your financial, marketing, and management strategies and helps you maximize your potential. Competition can be fierce in the construction industry. In developing a business plan, you analyze your market and competition and understand where you can gain an edge.

Good management skills entail applying knowledge from all aspects of the business to create a successful operation. Effective managers know how to win customers, satisfy employees, meet all legal obligations, and increase the bottom line. If this is where you want to take your business, this book can help you get there.

About This Book

This book is organized into three sections. Part 1 focuses on planning and starting your business. This section will help you formulate a business plan, choose a business structure, understand licensing and insurance requirements and gain basic management and marketing skills.

Part 2 covers fundamentals you will need to know in order to operate a successful construction business. This section covers estimating, contract management, scheduling, project management, safety and environmental responsibilities, and building good relationships with employees, subcontractors, and customers.

Part 3 provides valuable information to assist you in running the administrative functions of your business. Financial management, tax basics, and lien laws are covered. Effective management of these areas of business is vital and can cause serious problems if you do not give them proper attention.

Part 1: Getting Your Business Off the Ground

- ✓ Chapter 1 covers tips for writing a business plan and discusses key characteristics of entrepreneurship. A sample business plan is provided in Appendix B and at **NASCLAforms.org** using access code **SCR129354**.
- ✓ Chapter 2 describes each type of business entity and summarizes their advantages and disadvantages.
- ✓ Chapter 3 reviews the licensing process and the requirements for getting a license.
- ✓ Chapter 4 discusses insurance and bonding options to protect your business against unmitigated risk.
- ✓ Chapter 5 is your business toolbox with tips on time management, delegation, business ethics, and technology. It also provides information on resources available to assist small businesses.
- ✓ Chapter 6 helps you execute your marketing plan through promotional materials, public relations and effective selling skills.

Part 2: Fundamentals for the Field

- ✓ Chapter 7 shows you how to formulate estimates and evaluate bid opportunities.
- ✓ Chapter 8 takes you through the key elements of contracts and what is needed to make them enforceable.
- ✓ Chapter 9 covers scheduling techniques and the fundamental skills needed to effectively manage construction projects.
- ✓ Chapter 10 explains the importance of understanding customer expectations and handling change orders effectively. The basics of successful negotiation are also addressed.
- ✓ Chapter 11 is your resource for employment law, hiring and retaining of good employees, and discipline and termination of employees if unfortunate employment circumstances arise.
- ✓ Chapter 12 gives you the fundamentals for understanding OSHA laws and setting up a safety program for your company. Environmental considerations and possible permitting situations are covered in the event you are creating or working with environmental hazards.
- ✓ Chapter 13 covers the basics of finding and hiring good subcontractors and establishing good working relationships with them.

Part 3: Office Administration

- ✓ Chapter 14 takes you through the accounting cycle, the preparation and analysis of financial statements and payroll procedures.
- ✓ Chapter 15 gives you federal and state tax basics and helps you understand the forms you need to file.
- ✓ Chapter 16 covers lien law regulations and the process for filing a lien.

Supplemental forms and links are available at **NASCLAforms.org** using access code **SCR129354**.

Whether you are studying for the contractors' licensing exam or need an ongoing reference manual for managing your business, the *NASCLA Contractors Guide to Business, Law and Project Management* will serve as a valuable resource. We hope you find this reference useful in your daily operations and that the concepts discussed give you the tools for running a successful business.

TABLE OF CONTENTS

PART I
Getting Your Business Off the Ground

PART III
Office Administration

PART 1
Getting Your Business Off the Ground

Chapter 1
THE PLAN

Chapter Survey...

- ⇨ *Being an Entrepreneur*
- ⇨ *The Benefits of a Business Plan*
- ⇨ *Elements of a Business Plan*
- ⇨ *Business Plan Pitfalls*

Just as you need trade tools to successfully complete contracting jobs, you need business tools to successfully manage your business. As a business owner you go from being an expert in your trade to requiring expertise in project management, marketing, employee management, financial management, contract management and much more.

Success Factors: It takes an organized, consistent approach to achieve success in today's market. Businesses fail every day. The top reasons businesses fail are

- ✓ poor sales,
- ✓ competitive weakness,
- ✓ high operating expenses,
- ✓ difficulty collecting on invoices,
- ✓ inventory problems,
- ✓ too many fixed assets,
- ✓ poor location, and
- ✓ fraud.

To Sum It Up...
Poor planning and management are overriding factors in business failure.

From this point forward, we will build your business management expertise so you can identify and understand these obstacles, there by, increasing your chances of building and operating a successful business.

Being an Entrepreneur

Understanding Entrepreneurship: As a business owner, you may be referred to as an entrepreneur. There are many definitions of "entrepreneur." For our purposes, an entrepreneur is a person engaged in strategic activities that involve the initiation and development of a new business, created to build long-term value and steady cash flow streams.

Risk Taking: Entrepreneurs are often regarded as risk takers. There is risk involved with any venture, but entrepreneurs understand the importance of taking calculated risks. A calculated risk is a risk that is well-thought through where all outcomes are considered. This chapter will introduce the business planning process and help you understand the risks and opportunities involved with business ownership and how to manage them.

Something to Consider...
Entrepreneurship has its rewards as well as its drawbacks. Before embarking on any business venture, an entrepreneur must weigh all of these factors carefully.

Rewards and Challenges: Rewards of owning your own business include

- ✓ being your own boss;
- ✓ flexibility of time;
- ✓ having more freedom and independence;
- ✓ ability to make your own decisions; and
- ✓ receiving personal satisfaction from completing a job.

Entrepreneurship also has many frustrations and challenges, including

- ✓ long working hours;
- ✓ managing cash flow and payroll;

- ✓ high potential for overwhelming responsibility;
- ✓ finding and keeping qualified employees;
- ✓ paying taxes; and
- ✓ knowing and following government regulations.

Entrepreneurs need to decide if the rewards of entrepreneurship outweigh the challenges.

The Benefits of a Business Plan

Preparing a business plan that outlines strategies and goals for your business is useful for a newly-formed or early-stage business. It can also be a helpful tool for a company that is making major strategic changes (i.e., providing additional product or service offerings). A business plan should be a living document that changes as your business and the market change.

Think of the business plan as a blueprint for your business. Just as you would not perform your trade without a blueprint or plan from the customer, you should not operate your company without a business plan.

Key Functions: A business plan serves three key functions:

- ✓ **Planning Tool:** Your business plan is a road map for the growth of the business. Putting together the plan helps you think through all possible scenarios for growth in the market.
- ✓ **Loan or Investor Document:** If you are planning to seek loan financing or approach an investor, you will need a business plan. Investors or loan officers will review this document for many reasons, including the qualifications of your management team, your projected growth, and your competitive advantage.
- ✓ **Benchmarking Tool:** Your business plan should also serve as a base to measure and monitor the company's performance. If your company underperforms or over-performs compared with your projections, you can investigate the reasons for the difference.

A business plan will allow you to think through all aspects of your business, thus providing you with a competitive edge.

Elements of a Business Plan

The following are the typical elements found in a business plan:

- ✓ **Cover Page:** Contact information and a confidentiality statement are stated on the cover page.
- ✓ **Executive Summary:** Placed after the cover page at the beginning of the business plan, the executive summary is usually written last. It should include highlights of the plan and gain the interest of the reader.
- ✓ **Company Summary:** The company vision, legal structure, management personnel, business location, and facilities are outlined in the company summary section.
- ✓ **Products and Services:** Your specific products and services, primary subcontractors and suppliers, the effect of technology on your business, and expansion opportunities are all covered in the products and services section.
- ✓ **Market Analysis:** Your target market, market trends, and major competitors are defined under market analysis.
- ✓ **Marketing Strategy:** Your marketing strategy outlines the uniqueness of your product or service as well as your pricing, advertising, and promotional strategies.
- ✓ **Financial Plan:** If you already have financial statements, you should include a balance sheet, an income statement, and a cash flow statement as part of your business plan. New and existing businesses can put together financial projections as additional documentation.

A business plan template that can be customized for your company is located in Appendix B. The template provides specific guidance for completing each section.

Samples: The websites listed below are among several that offer sample business plans:

- ✓ www.allbusiness.com
- ✓ www.bplans.com
- ✓ www.inc.com
- ✓ www.sba.gov

- ✓ www.americanexpress.com/us/small-business/openforum
- ✓ www.bizmove.com/small-business/business-plan.htm

Business planning software packages that provide a step-by-step guide to creating a business plan are also available for purchase.

Your business plan is the blueprint for your business.

Business Plan Pitfalls

Before you start creating your business plan, there are guidelines you should follow to make sure you are giving customers an accurate and honest picture of your business.

- ✓ Make sure your assumptions are realistic.
- ✓ Keep the language simple. Don't use technical terminology or jargon.
- ✓ Cover the risks as well as the opportunities.
- ✓ Analyze your competition thoroughly.

By applying these simple guidelines, your business plan will have a solid foundation.

Final Inspection...

Being an Entrepreneur: Entrepreneurs should take calculated risks and weigh all factors when making business decisions.

The Benefits of a Business Plan: A business plan is sometimes required by bank loan officers or by investors. It can also be used as a planning and benchmarking tool.

Elements of a Business Plan: A business plan typically contains a cover page, an executive summary, a company summary, a listing of products and/or services, a market analysis, an explanation of the marketing strategy, and a financial plan.

Business Plan Pitfalls: It is important to portray an accurate picture of your business when formulating your business plan.

Supplemental Forms

Supplemental forms and links are available at **NASCLAforms.org** using access code **SCR129354**. The following forms can be found in the Business Planning section.

Business Plan Template	This template gives an outline for the business plan, including questions that help create detailed assumptions for each section of the plan.
Profit and Loss Pro Forma	This spreadsheet automatically calculates your totals when you enter the profit and loss numbers. You can adjust your numbers to determine your revenue and expense break-even point.

Chapter 2
CHOOSING YOUR BUSINESS STRUCTURE

Chapter Survey...

- ⇨ *Sole Proprietorships*
- ⇨ *Partnerships*
- ⇨ *C Corporations*
- ⇨ *S Corporations*
- ⇨ *Limited Liability Company (LLC)*
- ⇨ *Summary of Business Legal Structures*
- ⇨ *Joint Ventures*
- ⇨ *Naming Your Business*
- ⇨ *Reserving Your Name in South Carolina*
- ⇨ *Contacting the South Carolina Secretary of State*

When starting a business, one of the first things you need to decide is the legal structure your business will take. Each form of business has its advantages and disadvantages. The right choice depends on the nature of your business, plus various tax and liability issues. To ensure you are making the appropriate choice, it is best to consult with an attorney and an accountant.

Sole Proprietorships

Getting Started: Many businesses begin as sole proprietorships, because it is the simplest ownership form to set up. In a sole proprietorship, you are the sole owner of the company. If the sole proprietorship does business under a name different than your own, typically, a fictitious name certificate needs to be filed at a local or state government office.

If you are doing any type of significant business, a sole proprietorship may be a risky legal business structure, because it exposes you to unlimited liability for the business debt.

Key Characteristics of Sole Proprietorships:

- ✓ ***Existence:*** You own the assets of the company. If you decide to sell your sole proprietorship business, in actuality you are selling the assets of the business. You would have to close out your business license and the new buyer would have to obtain all appropriate licenses and accounts in his or her name. A sole proprietorship is terminated upon the owner's death.
- ✓ ***Financial Management:*** Business and personal expenses must be separated and careful records must be kept, because the IRS may question the handling of these funds and you may be asked to provide documentation.
- ✓ ***Liability:*** You bear personal liability for all actions undertaken in the name of the business.
- ✓ ***Taxes:*** Your net income from the business is reported as ordinary income. Sole proprietors do not pay corporate income taxes.

Advantages of a Sole Proprietorship:

- ✓ Minimal legal restrictions
- ✓ Simple ownership form
- ✓ Low startup costs
- ✓ Sole ownership of profits
- ✓ Freedom in decision-making process

Disadvantages of a Sole Proprietorship:

- ✓ Unlimited personal liability
- ✓ Less available capital
- ✓ Possible difficulty in obtaining long-term financing
- ✓ Dissolution of the business in the event of the owner's death

Sole proprietorships are easy to form but are risky because the owner has unlimited personal liability.

Partnerships

Partnering Up: A partnership is a relationship between two or more persons who join to carry on a trade or business. Each person contributes money, property, labor, or skill, and each partner expects to share in the profits and losses of the business. A partnership may be considered when neither partner can operate the business alone. Each partner should bring specific advantages to the business. There are two types of partnerships—general and limited. The differences are outlined in the following key characteristics.

Key Characteristics of Partnerships:

- ✓ ***Existence:*** A general partnership can be formed through an oral agreement, but it is recommended that a written partnership agreement be made. General partners own the assets of the company, just as an individual owns assets in a sole proprietorship. A limited partnership consists of one or more general partners and one or more limited partners. Limited partners have limited liability in the company. A partnership exists as long as the partners agree it will and as long as all of the general partners remain in the partnerships. If a general partner leaves the partnership or dies, the partnership dissolves and the assets of the partnership must be sold or distributed to first pay the creditors and then the partners.
- ✓ ***Financial Management:*** The partnership should keep separate bank accounts and financial records for the business so that partners know whether there are profits and losses and the distribution of these amounts. The use of an outside accountant for record-keeping is recommended to prevent suspicion or doubt among partners.
- ✓ ***Liability:*** All owners in a general partnership have personal and unlimited liability for all actions undertaken in the name of the business, including all debts. Each partner is responsible for the acts of other partners when they act in the name of the business. Limited partners have no personal liability for the business of the partnership. Limited partners are liable only for the previously agreed-upon contribution or investment to the business.
- ✓ ***Taxes:*** Business, income, and sales taxes are the responsibility of every partner. For federal income taxes, partners must file returns on IRS Form 1065.

Advantages of a General Partnership:

- ✓ Ease of formation
- ✓ Direct profit rewards
- ✓ Larger management base than that of a sole proprietorship

Disadvantages of a General Partnership:

- ✓ Unlimited personal liability of general partners
- ✓ Multiple decision makers
- ✓ Limited life of the business
- ✓ Changes of partners or partnership agreement may be difficult
- ✓ Partnership dissolves in the event of a general partner's death

Use Caution: Partnerships should be entered into carefully. Potential partners should discuss their expectations of the business before deciding to go into business together.

Questions to ask include these:

- ✓ Do the partners want to grow and operate a company long-term?
- ✓ Do the partners want to grow a short-term company to sell?
- ✓ How will profits be distributed: 100 percent to partners, or a part to the business, the rest to partners? What are the profit distribution percentages?
- ✓ Do the partners agree on the nature of the business, including the types of jobs the business will accept?

Also, be sure to define each partner's individual responsibilities as well as the group responsibilities.

- ✓ Who can sign debt instruments, such as notes, bonds, and leases for the partnership?
- ✓ Who determines the amount and frequency of compensation, salaries, draws, or profit-sharing for the partners?
- ✓ Who will handle record-keeping?
- ✓ If required, who oversees recruitment of additional partners or dissolution of the partnership?

- ✓ Who can make amendments to the partnership agreement?

South Carolina Limited Partnership Registration: To register a South Carolina limited partnership, you must file the Certificate of Limited Partnership with the South Carolina Secretary of State. The filing fee is $10.

Foreign Limited Partnership Registration: To register a foreign (not formed in South Carolina) limited partnership, you must file the Registration of Foreign Limited Partnership with the South Carolina Secretary of State. A certificate of existence not more than 30 days old from the jurisdiction in which the business is located must accompany the application. The filing fee is $10.

South Carolina Limited Liability Partnership Registration: To register a South Carolina limited liability partnership, you must file the Application for Registration of a Domestic Limited Liability Partnership with the South Carolina Secretary of State. The filing fee is $100.

Foreign Limited Liability Partnership Registration: To register a foreign (not formed in South Carolina) limited liability partnership, you must file the Application by a Foreign Limited Liability Partnership for a Certificate of Authority to Transact Business with the South Carolina Secretary of State. A certificate of existence not more than 30 days old from the jurisdiction in which the business is located must accompany the application. The filing fee is $100.

Carefully examine business expectations and responsibilities before entering into a partnership.

C Corporations

Your Corporate Identity: If you decide to do business under a corporate identity, you will have to comply with the formal requirements of state law to create the corporation. A business assumes a corporate identity in South Carolina when it files as a corporation with the South Carolina Secretary of State.

Key Characteristics of Corporations:

- ✓ ***Existence:*** Incorporation gives your business a legal existence. That is, the business can own assets and conduct business in its own name. A corporation lasts as long as the stockholders determine it should.
  A corporation continues to exist even if one or more of the shareholders die.
- ✓ ***Financial Management:*** The corporation needs separate bank accounts and separate business records. The corporation, not the shareholders, owns the money that the shareholders pay to buy the corporation's stock, all the assets, and the money earned by the corporation.
- ✓ ***Liability:*** The owners of the corporation, known as stockholders, are not personally liable for the losses of the business. Generally speaking, the corporate entity is responsible for business debts.
- ✓ ***Taxes:*** The corporation must file income tax returns and pay taxes on the profits. Dividends paid to shareholders by the corporation are also taxed to each shareholder individually. That is why there is said to be a "double tax" on corporations.

Other requirements for a corporation include

- ✓ a board of directors and corporate officers;
- ✓ stockholders as owners of the company;
- ✓ periodic board meetings, maintenance of board minutes, and approval of corporate resolutions; and
- ✓ a board empowered to authorize certain actions such as borrowing money, entering into contracts, and allocating corporate resources beyond routine business transactions.

Advantages of a C Corporation:

- ✓ Separate legal entity
- ✓ Limited liability for stockholders
- ✓ Unlimited life of the business
- ✓ Availability of capital resources
- ✓ Transfer of ownership through sale of stock

Disadvantages of a C Corporation:

- ✓ Complex and expensive organization
- ✓ Limitations on corporate activities and decisions by the corporate charter
- ✓ Extensive regulation and record-keeping requirements
- ✓ Double taxation (one on corporate profits and again on dividends)

South Carolina Corporation Registration: To register a South Carolina corporation, you must file Articles of Incorporation with the South Carolina Secretary of State. The Initial Report of Corporations (Department of Revenue Form CL-1) must accompany the Articles of Incorporation. The filing fee is $135.

Foreign Corporation Registration: To register a foreign (not formed in South Carolina) corporation, you must file the Application by a Foreign Corporation for a Certificate of Authority to Transact Business with the South Carolina Secretary of State. The Initial Report of Corporations (Department of Revenue Form CL-1) and a certification of existence not more than 30 days old from the jurisdiction in which the business is located must accompany the Articles of Incorporation. The filing fee is $135.

If the corporation's name is unavailable in the State of South Carolina, then it must file a certified copy of the board of directors' resolution approving a fictitious name. This document must accompany the application with a $10 fee.

Corporations are more complex to form and operate but reduce personal liability of the owners.

S Corporations

If your business is an eligible domestic corporation, you can avoid double federal taxation (corporate and shareholder taxes on the same earnings as in a C corporation) by electing to be treated as an S corporation under the rules of Subchapter S of the Internal Revenue Code. In this way, the S corporation passes its items of income, loss, deduction, and credits through to its shareholders to be included on their separate returns.

Requirements for an S Corporation:

- ✓ Domestic corporation with one class of stock
- ✓ No more than 100 shareholders who are citizens or legal residents of the U.S.
- ✓ All shareholders must consent to S corporation status
- ✓ Use of a permitted tax year
- ✓ Filing of IRS Form 2553

S corporations have special tax considerations. Consult with the appropriate financial and legal professionals to find out if this option is right for you.

Limited Liability Company (LLC)

A Hybrid Structure: This legal arrangement shares characteristics of both sole proprietorship and corporate identities. LLCs must consist of at least one member. The ownership in your LLC is invested in memberships rather than shares of stock.

Limited liability companies offer some protection from liability for actions taken by your company or by other members of your company. It does not protect from liability for personal actions. In this way, it resembles a sole proprietorship rather than a corporation.

Like an S corporation, federal income taxes are paid only on income distributed to members as ordinary income. A limited liability company can be expensive to organize and requires more administrative work. This form of organization is useful to professionals and general partnerships.

Advantages of a Limited Liability Company:

- ✓ Limited disclosure of owners
- ✓ Limited documentation
- ✓ No advance IRS filings
- ✓ No public disclosure of finances
- ✓ Limited liability for managers and members
- ✓ Ability to delegate management to a non-member

Tax Implications: LLCs are not taxed at an entity level. Depending on the number of business owners, the LLC is taxed differently.

- ✓ An LLC with one owner is taxed as a sole proprietorship.
- ✓ An LLC with more than one owner may elect to be taxed as a partnership or as a corporate entity.

South Carolina Limited Liability Company Registration: To register a South Carolina limited liability company, you must file Articles of Organization with the South Carolina Secretary of State. The filing fee is $110.

Foreign Limited Liability Company Registration: To register a foreign (not formed in South Carolina) limited liability company, you must file the Application for Authority by a Foreign Limited Liability Company to Transact Business with the South Carolina Secretary of State. A certificate of existence not more than 30 days old from the jurisdiction in which the business is located must accompany the application. The filing fee is $110.

Summary of Business Legal Structures

	Ownership	Liability	Formation Documents	Taxation	Management
Sole Proprietorship	One Owner	Unlimited personal liability	Doing Business As (DBA) Filing	Entity not taxed; profits and losses claimed on personal taxes	Owner
General Partnership	Unlimited number of general partners	Unlimited personal liability	General Partnership Agreement	Entity not taxed; profits and losses claimed on personal taxes of general partners	General partners
Limited Partnership	Unlimited number of general and limited partners	Unlimited personal liability of the general partners; limited partners generally have no personal liability	Limited Partnership Certificate Limited Partnership Agreement	Entity not taxed; profits and losses claimed on personal taxes of general and limited partners	General partners
Limited Liability Company (LLC)	Unlimited number of members	Generally no personal liability of the members for obligations of the business	Articles of Organization Operating Agreement	Entity not taxed (unless chosen to be taxed); profits and losses are passed through to the members	Manager or members designated in Operating Agreement
C Corporation	Unlimited number of shareholders	Generally no personal liability of the shareholders	Articles of Incorporation Bylaws Organizational Board Resolutions Stock Certificates Stock Ledger IRS and State S Corporation Election	Corporation taxed on its earnings at the corporate level and the shareholders may have a further tax on any dividends distributed ("double taxation")	Board of Directors
S Corporation	Up to 100 shareholders allowed	Generally no personal liability of the shareholders	Articles of Incorporation Bylaws Organizational Board Resolutions Stock Certificates Stock Ledger IRS and State S Corporation Election	Entity generally not taxed, as profits and losses are passed through to the shareholders ("pass-through" taxation)	Board of Directors

Joint Ventures

Complement Your Strengths: A joint venture is a special business arrangement that exists when two or more companies join to undertake a specific project. The management of a joint venture is often assigned to one individual or company. This arrangement brings together companies with complementary resources and strengths. When forming this type of venture, it is important to consult an attorney to ensure that all aspects of risk are covered.

Naming Your Business

Choose Wisely: Selecting a name is an important part of forming your business. The name you choose affects your customers' impression of your company. The individuality of the name affects future trademarks and service marks. It is important to select a name that is distinctive.

Do your homework before you decide on a name for your company. A search can be conducted using the following sources:

- ✓ U.S. Patent and Trademark Office (800) 786-9199 or at www.uspto.gov
- ✓ Secretary of State Office in the state where you intend to do business
- ✓ Internet search engines such as www.yahoo.com or www.google.com

Reserving Your Name in South Carolina

In order to reserve a corporate or limited liability company name in South Carolina, domestic corporations must submit an Application to Reserve a Corporate Name form and a $10 filing fee to the Secretary of State's office. Foreign corporations must submit an Application to Register a Corporate Name and required documentation.

You can research business names through the Online Business Filings Database located on the Secretary of the State website. If you file a name that is too similar to another registered business name, your application will be rejected and you will need to re-file with another unique name.

Contacting the South Carolina Secretary of State

For questions about registering your business in South Carolina or obtaining forms, contact the South Carolina Secretary of State.

State of South Carolina
Secretary of State
Business Filings Division
Edgar Brown Building
1205 Pendleton Street, Suite 525
Columbia, South Carolina 29201

General Phone: (803) 734-2170
Business Filings Phone: (803) 734-2158
Corporations Phone: (803) 734-2158

Website: www.scsos.com

The Secretary of the State website also offers other valuable information, such as business forms, fee schedules, and filing guidelines.

Final Inspection...

Sole Proprietorships: This business structure offers easy formation and operation. However, unlimited personal liability is a concern because the business and owner are considered the same legal entity.

Partnerships: Partnerships can bring together two or more people with strengths and resources in different areas but also allow for unlimited personal liability of general partners. To reduce conflicts among partners, responsibilities and business goals must be clearly outlined at the beginning of the business arrangement.

C Corporations: C corporations offer liability protection to the owners and easy ownership transfer through stock sales. This business structure is more complex to operate and shareholders may be "double-taxed" on their earnings.

S Corporations: S corporations are similar to C corporations but offer special tax considerations. S corporation status can be filed with the IRS, if companies meet the specified criteria.

Limited Liability Company (LLC): LLCs have characteristics of both sole proprietorships and corporations.

Summary of Business Legal Structures: Each type of business entity has unique ownership, liability, taxation, and management characteristics. Required formation documents differ for each business structure.

Joint Ventures: Joint ventures are generally formed on a project basis in order to integrate positive attributes and resources of two or more companies.

Naming Your Business: An appropriate business name is important and defines how your customers perceive you.

Reserving Your Name in South Carolina: A corporate or limited liability company name can be reserved through the Secretary of State. All names must be distinguishable from other registered business names.

Contacting the South Carolina Secretary of State: The Secretary of State can be contacted about registering your business in South Carolina, obtaining various business forms, and filing guidelines for businesses.

Supplemental Forms

Supplemental forms and links are available at **NASCLAforms.org** using access code **SCR129354**. The following forms can be found in the Business Entities section.

Summary of Business Legal Structures	Table showing the primary features of each type of business entity (featured earlier in the chapter).
IRS Form 2553	IRS form to elect S corporation status

Chapter 3
BECOMING A LICENSED CONTRACTOR

Chapter Survey...

- *Purpose of Licensing*
- *South Carolina Residential Builders Commission*
- *When is a Contractor's License Needed?*
- *Licensing Process*
- *Complaints Against Licensed Contractors*
- *Notice and Opportunity to Cure Construction Dwelling Defects*

Purpose of Licensing

A major purpose of contractor licensing is to protect the health, safety, and welfare of the public. Licensing also defines the work that a contractor is allowed to do under a particular license.

Licensing establishes entrance requirements, standards of practice, and disciplinary authority to protect the public from unqualified, incompetent, and unethical contractors.

Entrance Requirements: Licensing ensures that those practicing a trade or occupation have met a minimum set of qualifications, such as experience, training, and required examination.

Standards of Practice: Contractors are required to adhere to standards of practice established by law. The workmanship standards ensure an appropriate level of quality is given to the public. Continuing education may be required for certain trades.

Disciplinary Authority: Statutes and regulations define illegal and prohibited activities. The law provides licensing authorities with a mechanism to conduct investigations and to administer discipline to problem contractors. Violations can result in penalties, including fines and loss of license.

South Carolina Residential Builders Commission

The Commission authorizes persons to practice residential home building and home inspecting by qualifying and issuing a license to homebuilders, specialty contractors (including electrical, plumbing, and HVAC), and to home inspectors. Additionally, the Commission receives and processes complaints against those persons authorized to practice. The Commission also responds to complaints concerning unlicensed contractors.

The Residential Builders Commission has eight members appointed by the Governor with the advice and consent of the Senate. Two members must be consumers, not engaged in the business of residential building, and four members must have been actively engaged in residential building for at least five years prior to their appointment and one of whom has been actively engaged in residential specialty contracting for a period of at least five years before the date of appointment.

Of the eight, one must be appointed from the state at large. Members are appointed for a term of four years or until their successors are appointed.

For more information, contact:

South Carolina Department of Labor, Licensing and Regulation
Residential Builders Commission
Synergy Business Park
Kingstree Building
110 Centerview Drive
Columbia, South Carolina 29210

Telephone: (803) 896-4696
Fax: (803) 896-4814

Website: www.llr.sc.gov/pol/ResidentialBuilders

When is a Contractor's License Needed?

Homebuilder's License: If an individual wishes to engage in residential building from the ground up, the individual is required first to obtain a residential builder's license if the total cost of the construction exceeds $5,000. The applicant must pass a residential builder's examination administered by the Commission's examination service, Psychological Services, Inc. (PSI). The Commission also requires a licensed residential builder to provide a surety bond in the amount of $15,000, with the Commission being the bondholder, or provide proof of financial responsibility acceptable to the Commission. There is no monetary limitation for residential work performed by the licensee.

Specialty Contractor: Anyone engaging in residential specialty work over $200 must complete a specialty registration form. The Commission will allow an individual to choose up to three specialty registration classifications from a list of nine specialty classifications (defined in Appendix F). If the individual is engaging in more than three classifications, the Commission requires the individual to apply for a residential builder license. The residential specialty registration also limits the individual to $5,000 per residential project unless he or she secures a surety bond in an amount not less than $5,000 and approved by the Commission. The Commission is the bondholder. Once bonded, there is no dollar limitation for the residential specialty work performed. The residential specialty registration is issued to an individual, not a business entity. A specialty contractor cannot build a residential structure or make an addition to a residential structure from the ground up.

Home Inspector License: Home inspectors must meet certain requirements as required by the South Carolina Home Builders' Commission to obtain a home inspector license. Licensed general contractors holding a building classification, licensed home builders, architects, and engineers are not required to obtain a home inspector's license and may perform home inspections using their respective licenses.

Specialty Electrician, HVAC, or Plumbing License: Anyone engaging in residential specialty Electrical, HVAC, or Plumbing work over $200 must complete a residential specialty contractor license form. The residential specialty contractor license also limits the individual to $5,000 per residential project unless he or she secures a surety bond in an amount not less than $10,000 on a form approved by the Commission. The Commission is the bondholder. Once bonded, there is no dollar limitation for the residential specialty contractor license for work performed. The residential specialty contractor license is issued to an individual, not a business entity.

Licensing Process

Homebuilder's License and Specialty Electrician, HVAC or Plumbing License: To become licensed as a home builder, specialty electrician, HVAC or plumber in South Carolina you are required to:

- ✓ file a written application as required by the Commission;
- ✓ submit a credit report;
- ✓ submit a certified check, cashier's check, or money order for $100 for the application fee;
- ✓ submit an affidavit showing proof of at least one year of actual experience under the supervision of a licensed builder;
- ✓ pass an examination given by PSI; and
- ✓ pay $160 for a two-year license; if license is issued for 12 months or less, the fee is $80.

A license may be granted without examination to those builders in good standing in other states deemed by the Commission to have comparable exams.

The homebuilder's license must be renewed July 1 of each EVEN year at a cost of $160.

The specialty electrician, HVAC, or plumbing license must be renewed July 1 of each ODD year at a cost of $160.

Home Inspector License: A home inspector is a person who engages in the business of inspecting a home and preparing a written or oral report, in exchange for compensation of any sort. The report explains the condition of the construction or improvements to the home. A report can include but is not limited to: structural problems or conditions, damage, safety problems or deterioration, and equipment and systems that are visible and readily accessible.

Home inspection does not include a contract or proposal for repair, renovation, or remodeling of the improvements to a residence.

The parties to a home inspection agreement may limit or expand the scope of the inspection.

A person desiring to be licensed as a home inspector must submit an application to the Commission along with the appropriate fee. After approval, the applicant must take the home inspector licensing examination. Upon successful completion of the exam, the Commission will issue a license authorizing the applicant to engage in the business of home inspection in South Carolina. The home inspector license must be renewed by July 1 of each EVEN year.

The following persons are not required to be licensed as home inspectors in order to perform home inspections:

- ✓ A person licensed as a homebuilder
- ✓ A person licensed as a general contractor holding a building classification
- ✓ A professional engineer
- ✓ An architect

See Appendices E and F for statutory requirements relating to licensing of home inspectors.

Specialty Contractor Registration: The Commission also registers specialty contractors in the following classifications at a cost of $100 for a two-year registration ($50 if the license is issued for 12 months or less) and upon approval of the applicant's credit report:

- ✓ Vinyl and aluminum siding installers
- ✓ Insulation installers
- ✓ Roofers
- ✓ Floor covering installers
- ✓ Masons
- ✓ Dry wall installers
- ✓ Carpenters
- ✓ Stucco installers
- ✓ Painters/Wall paper hangers
- ✓ Solar panel installers

A residential specialty contractor is an independent contractor who is not a licensed residential builder. The specialty contractor contracts with a licensed residential builder, general contractor, or individual property owner to do construction work, repairs, improvements, or re-improvements requiring special skills and involving the use of specialized construction trades or craft when the undertakings exceed $200.

Complaints Against Licensed Contractors

The board responds to complaints concerning licensees and unlicensed contractors. Consumers, local or state jurisdictions, or other contractors may submit a complaint for regulated construction work or actions that are in violation of the licensing statutes. Complaints pertaining to regulated construction work may be related to code violations, failure to comply with manufacturer's recommendation for installation instructions, failure to comply with Residential Standard Guidelines for Construction as adopted by the board, or other violations of the contracting statutes. Unjustified nonpayment of monies owed to subcontractors or suppliers may also result in possible sanctions against a licensee. Contractual disputes and money matters are otherwise not addressed and should be resolved by independent arbitrators or within the judicial system.

Notice and Opportunity to Cure Construction Dwelling Defects

The Notice and Opportunity to Cure Construction Dwelling Defects Act requires homeowners to serve a notice of claim on contractors and subcontractors 90 days prior to filing a court action.

The notice of claim must contain the following:

- ✓ a statement that the claimant asserts a construction defect;
- ✓ a description of the claim or claims in reasonable detail sufficient to determine the general nature of the construction defect; and
- ✓ a description of any results of the defect, if known.

The contractor or subcontractor must notify the claimant within 15 days if the construction defect is not sufficiently described.

From receipt of the notice of claim, the contractor has 30 days to respond. The contractor can either serve a notice to inspect, offer to remedy, offer to settle, or deny the claim. If a response is not given within 30 days, it is considered a denial of claim.

The claimant has ten days to serve a response to the contractor's offer. If an agreement cannot be reached, the matter will proceed to litigation.

Final Inspection...

Purpose of Licensing: A major purpose of licensing is to protect the health, safety, and welfare of the public.

South Carolina Residential Builders Commission: The South Carolina Residential Builders Commission regulates contracting activities through examination, licensure, and disciplinary action.

When is a Contractor's License Needed?: The South Carolina Residential Builders Commission issues a homebuilder's and home inspector license, and specialty contractor license/registration.

Licensing Process: You must complete the licensing process in order to obtain a contractor license/ registration.

Complaints Against Licensed Contractors: The Board investigates complaints against licensed and unlicensed contractors and determines the proper disciplinary action.

Notice and Opportunity to Cure Construction Dwelling Defects: Homeowners must notify contractors or subcontractors with a notice of claim 90 days prior to filing a court action for construction defects.

Chapter 4
MANAGING RISK

Chapter Survey...

- ⇨ *Risk Management Benefits*
- ⇨ *Insurance*
- ⇨ *Property Insurance*
- ⇨ *Liability Insurance*
- ⇨ *Business Owner's Policies (BOPs)*
- ⇨ *Automobile Insurance*
- ⇨ *Burglary and Theft Insurance*
- ⇨ *Key Man Life Insurance*
- ⇨ *Coverage Gaps and Overlaps*
- ⇨ *Employment-Related Insurance*
- ⇨ *Insurance Coverage for Subcontractors*
- ⇨ *What is a Bond?*
- ⇨ *Bond Language*
- ⇨ *Types of Bonds*
- ⇨ *Qualifying for a Bond*
- ⇨ *Bond Claims*
- ⇨ *Laws Governing Bonding of Federal Construction Projects*
- ⇨ *Laws Governing Bonding of South Carolina State Public Construction Projects*

Managing risk can be one of the biggest challenges you'll face in the construction industry. The weather, site conditions, customer changes, and employees can be just a few of the unpredictable factors in a job. Some of the risks that you face are preventable and others can be mitigated.

Risk assessment is one of the most important steps in the risk management process. You must determine the probability of loss occurring and the consequences if the loss occurs. Your approach to a risk with the potential for a large loss and a low probability of occurring is handled differently from a risk with a potential for minimum loss but a high likelihood of occurring.

Degrees of risk must be examined on a project and overall business basis. Future chapters will focus on the skills you need to assess, manage, and ultimately protect yourself against risks for certain situations such as environmental and safety risks.

Risk Management Benefits

Unmanaged risk can harm your business, resulting in financial loss, lower profit margins, and unnecessary liabilities. Risk management involves assessing all areas of your business from operations to administrative functions. Good risk management provides several benefits that can affect your reputation and bottom line:

- ✓ Lower business and liability insurance premiums
- ✓ Reduce chances of being sued
- ✓ Improve chances of prevailing in a lawsuit

Risk is managed in several ways. There may be provisions added into a contract to reduce your risk (discussed in Chapter 8), or you may put safety or operating programs and procedures in place. Other risks are mitigated through insurance coverage and bonding, which will be discussed in this chapter.

Insurance

While some risks can be mitigated, others are uncontrollable. Insurance is a way to supplement your risk management program to protect your business against unforeseen events, such as accidents and theft. Without it, you could lose your business in a lawsuit as a result of one bad accident. The less coverage your business has, the more risk you assume. As you increase coverage, you reduce your risk.

Insurance Defined: Insurance is a protective measure in which coverage is obtained for a specific risk (or set of risks) by a contract. In this contract or policy, one party indemnifies another against specified loss in return for premiums paid. Indemnity is a way to transfer risk and exemption from loss incurred by any course of action. Sometimes an insurance payout is called an indemnity.

An insurance policy outlines the specifics of the contract between your business and the insurance company. At a minimum, the policy lists the policy term, coverage, premiums, and deductibles.

Finding the Right Insurance Company and Agent: Large companies often employ full-time risk managers. Most small business owners do not have this benefit, and this makes finding the right insurance company and agent important to the risk management process. There are two types of agents: those who work with only one insurance company and independent agents who can shop around for policies with competing companies. Regardless of which type of agent you choose, it is important to find a professional you can trust. Your agent will provide you with a wealth of knowledge on insurance and risk management topics and help you assess your insurance needs.

Required Coverage: The law may require you to carry a certain level of coverage, such as workers' compensation, unemployment, and vehicle insurance.

Many construction contracts require a contractor to maintain certain types of insurance and coverage levels. The following chart gives an example of how insurance coverage requirements might be outlined in a contract.

Type of Insurance	**Minimum Insurance Coverage (Combined Single Limit Per Occurrence / Aggregate)**
Commercial General Liability including Premises - Operations Products / Completed Operations Contractual Insurance Property Damage Independent Contractors Bodily Injury	$3,000,000 / $3,000,000
Automobile Liability Owned, Non-owned, or Rented	$3,000,000 / $3,000,000
Workers' Compensation and Occupational Diseases	As Required by Applicable Laws
Employer's Liability	$3,000,000

It is important to conduct a site survey to assess any special conditions that may cause added risk to a project. You should also consider the nature of each project to be sure you have adequate coverage for the work you are performing. You may want to talk this over with your insurance agent and add supplemental coverage when necessary.

In this chapter, we will focus on policies that apply to the construction industry, but you should consult with your insurance carrier for a plan that is right for you and provides your business with the best protection.

Property Insurance

Property insurance typically covers your business and personal property when damage, theft, or loss occurs. You can buy property insurance to cover specific risks such as fire or theft or you can purchase a broad-based policy to cover a variety of risks (including fire, theft, vandalism, and "acts of God" such as lightning strikes). In considering property insurance, evaluate your physical location and the region in which you do business to determine which risks are likely to occur, such as hurricanes or floods.

Types of Property You May Want to Cover:

- ✓ Buildings and other structures (owned or leased)
- ✓ Furniture, equipment, and supplies
- ✓ Inventory
- ✓ Machinery
- ✓ Computers/tablets
- ✓ Intellectual property (i.e., books and documents)
- ✓ Automobiles, trucks, and construction equipment
- ✓ Intangible property (i.e., good will, trademarks, etc.)
- ✓ Leased equipment

All-Risk Builders' Risk Insurance

All-risk builders' risk insurance is a form of property insurance that covers property owners and builders for buildings under construction. This type of insurance typically covers machinery, equipment, materials, supplies, and fixtures that are part of the structure or will become part of the structure. Additional coverage can be added for items, such as temporary structures and scaffolding, used during construction. In general, major construction defects such as poor workmanship and faulty design are not covered. Your tools also may not be covered under this type of policy. You should talk to your insurance agent about getting separate coverage for these items.

All-risk coverage provides for direct loss by those perils that are not specifically excluded by the policy. It generally provides coverage for almost all risks, including theft, vandalism, accidental losses, and damage or destruction. Construction must be in progress for coverage to exist.

The American Institute of Architects (AIA) and the Associated General Contractors of America (AGC) publish contract documents useful for owners and contractors (for AIA documents, see www.aiacontracts.org; for AGC documents, see the organization's website at www.agc.org). These standard documents require the purchase of all-risk coverage. An owner has the option of giving the responsibility of purchasing all-risk coverage to the general contractor. If this is the case, the owner is required to notify the general contractor in writing. General contractors may prefer to purchase the insurance because they may have a deeper understanding of the project and the potential risk. The cost of the insurance is then passed on to the owner.

The standard AIA and AGC documents require replacement cost coverage for losses that occur. Replacement cost coverage replaces damaged property without any allowances or deductions, such as depreciation.

If you use documents other than the AIA and AGC standard forms, carefully examine the insurance obligations for both you and the owner and discuss any concerns with your insurance agent.

A subrogation clause is generally located within the builders' risk insurance policy. Subrogation typically occurs when the insurance company pays the insured for damage or loss and then sues the negligent third party to pay for the loss. This can lead to a situation where the contractor is sued by the owner's insurance company for a loss that occurred.

To avoid this situation between the owner, contractor, and subcontractors, the contract may contain a clause waiving the parties' right to sue one another.

Named Peril Builders' Risk Insurance

Named peril builders' risk insurance policies have narrower coverage than all-risk insurance and specify what perils are covered. Typical named peril policies are written for fire and lightning but can also include events such as wind damage, explosion, water damage, terrorism, or earthquake.

Inland Marine/Equipment Theft Insurance

Inland marine insurance is a type of property insurance that you can purchase for your tools and equipment. It provides coverage for goods in transit and projects under construction. The cost of the insurance may be more than the cost of putting preventive measures in place to deter theft. It is important to secure your equipment by using the proper locks, creating limited access through fencing and locked storage areas, and removing keys from the ignition of all vehicles. Equipment theft increases the cost of insurance premiums, and if it happens often, you might find it difficult to obtain coverage.

Equipment Floater Policy

An equipment floater policy is a type of inland marine insurance. Coverage for equipment is available on an all-risk or specified-peril basis. The coverage provided is for direct physical loss to the equipment and is designed to cover mobile equipment while it is stored on premises, in transit, or at temporary locations or jobsites. An endorsement can be added for rented or leased equipment. Normal wear and tear is generally not covered by the equipment floater policy.

Transportation Floater and Motor Truck Cargo Insurance

Both transportation floater and motor truck cargo insurance are types of inland marine insurance. A transportation floater policy protects the transporter against damage that occurs to freight during transport. Motor truck cargo insurance protects the transporter in the event of damaged or lost freight. This protection also applies to contractors who transport equipment or materials to and from the jobsite.

Liability Insurance

Liability insurance is designed to protect against third-party claims that arise from alleged negligence resulting in bodily injury or property damage. Payment is not typically made to the insured but rather to someone suffering loss who is not a party to the insurance contract.

Commercial General Liability (CGL)

Commercial general liability (CGL) insurance offers basic liability coverage. CGL covers four types of injuries, including

- ✓ bodily injury that results in actual physical damage or loss for individuals who are not employees;
- ✓ damage or loss to property not belonging to the business;
- ✓ personal injury, including slander or damage to reputation; and
- ✓ advertising injury, including charges of negligence that result from promotion of goods or services.

Most businesses in the construction industry will need to supplement their CGL policy with other types of insurance, such as a vehicle insurance policy.

Umbrella Liability Insurance

An umbrella liability insurance policy can supplement your CGL policy. The umbrella policy provides additional coverage in the areas that are not covered in the CGL policy. This type of insurance takes effect once a certain deductible or self-insured retention level is met. Umbrella insurance coverage can be customized to meet the needs of your business.

Director's and Officer's (D and O) Liability Insurance

Director's and officer's liability insurance protects directors and officers from liability due to actions connected with their corporate positions. These actions include such things as misstatement of financial reports, misuse of company funds, and failure to honor an employment contract. This insurance does not cover intentional or illegal acts.

Other Types of Liability Insurance

Other types of liability insurance may be purchased in order to cover exclusions that exist in your CGL policy. Examples of additional liability coverage include:

- ✓ **Contractual liability insurance** provides contractors with protection for damages that result from their negligence while under written contract.
- ✓ **Completed operations liability insurance** provides coverage for loss arising out of completed projects.
- ✓ **Contractor's protective public and property damage liability insurance** protects contractors who supervise and subsequently are held liable for actions of subcontractors from claims for personal injury and property damage.
- ✓ **Professional liability insurance** (sometimes called errors and omissions insurance) protects contractors from negligence resulting from errors or omissions of designers and architects.
- ✓ **Construction wrap-up liability insurance** bundles liability and workers' compensation insurance for general contractors and subcontractors on large construction projects. This type of insurance helps eliminate gaps in coverage. To qualify for this type of insurance, certain contract cost requirements must be met. These requirements vary by state.

Business Owner's Policies (BOPs)

Business owner's policies (BOPs) bundle property and liability coverage together. This type of coverage can eliminate gaps or overlaps between separate property and liability policies. Small and mid-sized companies usually qualify for this type of policy. A business selects the amount of liability coverage it needs based on its assets and you can purchase additional coverage depending on the particular risks of the company.

Automobile Insurance

If you have a company vehicle or a fleet of vehicles, auto insurance provides coverage for liability and physical damage associated with vehicles owned by your company. All states require vehicle owners to carry some level of liability insurance covering bodily injury and property damage incurred in a vehicle accident. Physical damage coverage pays for the damage to the insured vehicle. Different types of automobile insurance are available. Various options include coverage for only vehicles owned; vehicles owned, leased or hired; and for all automobiles, including those not owned, leased, or hired.

Burglary and Theft Insurance

Burglary and theft insurance covers loss or damage by burglary, theft, larceny, robbery, forgery, fraud, and vandalism. However, this type of insurance generally does not cover employee acts.

A fidelity bond or employee theft insurance is used to cover criminal acts of burglary and theft by employees.

Key Man Life Insurance

This type of coverage is beneficial if your company depends on specific individuals for the continuing success. For example, if your legal structure is a partnership, the success or ongoing existence of the company would not continue if one of the partners died or became incapacitated. Key man insurance is available as life insurance, disability insurance, or both.

Coverage Gaps and Overlaps

It is important to understand the coverage that each of your policies provides. You must be aware of gaps and overlaps that may exist between policies. Differences in coverage can cause difficulties in claim settlement, particularly when a claim falls in the gray area between coverages. For example, if a claim involves both an automobile and property, there may be a conflict between which policy covers the damage. To minimize these conflicts, you may want one insurer for all policies. If you have overlapping coverage, make sure that each policy has fairly equal reimbursement levels. This will ensure that you receive equal coverage in the case where more than one policy covers a claim.

Carefully evaluate your risk management program and supplement it with the appropriate insurance coverage.

Employment-Related Insurance

Workers' Compensation Insurance

Workers' compensation insurance provides coverage for employees who are injured on the job. The insurance is purchased by the employer; no part of it should be paid for by employees or deducted from their pay.

South Carolina Program: The South Carolina program is administered through the Workers' Compensation Commission. For more information, contact:

South Carolina
Workers' Compensation Commission
P.O. Box 1715
1333 Main Street, Suite 500
Columbia, South Carolina 29202-1715

Phone: (803) 737-5700

Website: wcc.sc.gov

Chapter 11, Employee Management, covers workers' compensation insurance in more detail.

Follow the Law...

Workers' compensation insurance coverage may be required by law for your business. It is 100 percent employer-paid and premiums cannot be deducted from the employee's pay.

Employer's liability insurance can be purchased to supplement your workers' compensation insurance in the event you are sued for negligence as a result of an employee injury or death.

Unemployment Insurance

Unemployment insurance (UI) programs provide unemployment benefits to eligible workers who become unemployed through no fault of their own and meet certain other eligibility requirements. This program is jointly financed through federal and state employer payroll taxes (federal/state UI tax).

Generally, employers must pay both state and federal unemployment taxes if

- ✓ they pay wages to employees totaling $1,500 or more in any quarter of a calendar year; or
- ✓ they had at least one employee during any day of a week during 20 weeks in a calendar year, regardless of whether or not the weeks were consecutive.

South Carolina Program: The South Carolina Unemployment Compensation Law provides workers with benefits during periods of total or partial unemployment.

An *Employer Handbook* is available on the South Carolina Department of Employment and Workforce website at www.dew.sc.gov/Documents/EmployerHandbook.pdf.

Chapter 11, Employee Management, covers unemployment insurance in more detail.

Social Security Insurance

The Social Security Administration (SSA) is a federal agency responsible for paying retirement, disability, and survivors benefits to workers and their families. The SSA is also responsible for administering the Supplemental Security Income program. The SSA issues Social Security numbers, which are required for employees to legally work in the United States.

Chapter 15, Tax Basics, explains how to submit Social Security tax for employees.

Insurance Coverage for Subcontractors

When hiring subcontractors, you should verify their insurance coverage to ensure it is adequate enough to cover any liability arising from their work.

There are a few simple questions that you can ask to assess proper coverage.

- ✓ **Does the subcontractor carry the appropriate insurance?** Determine what type of insurance is needed. For example, you may require the subcontractor to carry commercial general liability (CGL) insurance.
- ✓ **Is the coverage adequate for the type of work being performed?** You can be held responsible for damages not covered by the subcontractor's insurance. Make sure their coverage limits are large enough to cover your project.
- ✓ **Is the insurance coverage current?** You can check with the insurance company listed on the insurance certificate to verify that the subcontractor's insurance coverage is current and that it will cover your project.

If insurance coverage is required, it is prudent to write the requirements into the contract. Chapter 8, Contract Management, talks about indemnification clauses as a contract provision to limit risk. This provision can also be included in your contract with the subcontractor. Indemnification absolves your company of any losses or damages incurred by the subcontractor.

What is a Bond?

A surety bond is a risk transfer mechanism between a surety, the contractor, and the project owner. The agreement binds the contractor to comply with the terms and conditions of a contract. Typically, if the contractor can not perform the contract, the surety assumes the contractor's responsibilities and ensures that the project is completed. In South Carolina, a surety bond can only be called on to cover codes and standards violations.

Statutory and Common-Law Bonds: The federal government uses surety bonds on construction projects as a way to pre-qualify prospective construction firms. A surety bond many times is required by law for public projects. It is referred to as a statutory bond. The owner of a private construction project may also opt to require a bond as an added guarantee that a project will be completed on-time, on budget, and within specified requirements. These private construction bonds are sometimes referred to as common-law bonds.

Surety Bonding Companies: When selecting a surety bonding company, check with the U.S. Department of the Treasury or a similar state agency (i.e., Department of Insurance) to ensure that the company is licensed for bonding. The surety company is the primary risk-taker in a bonding agreement, so it is important that it complies with all the applicable laws and regulations.

Bond Language

Bonds generally contain four basic requirements:

- ✓ **Total dollar amount required for the bond**
  The bond amount is generally set as a percentage of the estimated cost. This number can vary and can be up to 100 percent of the estimated cost of construction. Maintenance bonds often use a figure of 10 percent of construction cost as the required amount.

- ✓ **Length of the bond**
  Bond lengths are typically required for a fixed rate of time following a project milestone, after which the bond is released. For construction performance bonds, this is usually after completion and final approval of the project.
- ✓ **Requirements for notice of defect or lack of maintenance**
  A period for completion of corrections is generally outlined after a notice of defect. The bond also establishes a time period for response from the bonding company, if the contractor fails to meet the obligations of the contract.
- ✓ **Bond enforcement**
  If the contractor does not successfully complete all required work or violates any requirement of the bond, enforcement measures are outlined to ensure project completion and proper maintenance.

Types of Bonds

A **bid bond** guarantees that the contractor, if awarded the job, will do work at the submitted bid price, enter into a contract with the owner, and furnish the required performance and payment bonds. Bid bonds serve as a deterrent against frivolous or unqualified bidders. If the contractor defaults on the bid agreement, the bid bond can be used to make up the pricing difference with the next lowest bidder.

A **performance bond** guarantees that the contractor will complete a contract within its time frame and conditions.

A **payment bond** guarantees subcontractors and suppliers that they will be paid for work if they perform properly under the contract.

A **maintenance bond** guarantees that for a stated period, typically for one year, no defective workmanship or material will appear in the completed project.

A **completion bond** provides assurance to the financial backers of a construction project that it will be completed on time.

A **fidelity bond** covers business owners for losses due to dishonest acts by their employees.

A **lien bond** guarantees that liens cannot be placed against the owner's property by contractors for payment of services. This type of bond allows someone to "bond around" a labor or materialmen's lien.

Just as the owner may require the general contractor to obtain a performance bond, a payment bond, or both, the general contractor may require the same of the subcontractor. The **subcontractor's bond** protects the general contractor in the event that the subcontractor does not fully perform the contract and/or pay for labor and materials.

A **bank letter of credit** is not a bond but is a cash guarantee to the owner. It is not a guarantee of performance but can be converted to a payment to the owner by a bank or lending institution. The letter of credit typically does not cover 100 percent of the contract but customarily 5 percent to 10 percent of the contract.

Various types of bonds are issued as a protective measure in the event that contractual obligations are not met.

Qualifying for a Bond

Before issuing a bond, a surety company will examine your business thoroughly to make sure it is established, profitable, and well-managed. Some of the items the surety company will evaluate to make this determination include

- ✓ good references;
- ✓ ability to meet current and future obligations;
- ✓ experience matching contract requirements;
- ✓ necessary equipment to complete the work;
- ✓ financial stability;
- ✓ good credit; and
- ✓ established bank relationship and line of credit.

A surety's underwriting process consists of an extensive prequalification process in order to guarantee to the project owner that the contractor will fulfill the terms of the contract.

Bonds are priced on the basis of a percentage of the contract amount. Market conditions and prevailing industry practices set the percentage. Bond premiums vary among surety companies, but typically range from a half percent to two percent of the contract amount.

Bond Claims

Filing Process: Construction law and the contractual relationships govern the bond claims process. The filing process is outlined in the bond language for common-law bonds. Government statutes outline the filing process for statutory bonds.

Project Changes: Unless specifically outlined in the bond agreement, the surety company will not cover changes to the original contract. In most cases, a request for additional coverage must be made and the bonding company must be notified of the contract changes.

Payment in the Event of Default: In the event of contractor default, the surety has several options. The surety may

- ✓ provide additional financing for the contractor to finish the project;
- ✓ arrange for a new contractor or hire subcontractors to complete the work; or
- ✓ pay out the amount of the bond.

Laws Governing Bonding of Federal Construction Projects

Miller Act: As a result of the high failure rate for completion of public construction projects, the Heard Act was enacted in 1894, allowing the use of surety bonds for federally funded projects. In 1935, the Miller Act replaced the Heard Act. The Miller Act is the current law requiring performance and payment bonds on all federal construction projects valued at greater than $100,000.

The surety amounts are defined as follows:

- ✓ A performance bond is required in an amount that the contracting officer regards as adequate. The bond is normally 100 percent of the contracted price.
- ✓ A separate payment bond is required for the protection of the suppliers of labor and materials. The sum of the payment bond varies, based on the size of the contract. These amounts include:
- ✓ Fifty percent of the contract amount for projects less than $1 million
- ✓ Forty percent of the contract amount for projects between $1 million and $5 million
- ✓ $2.5 million payment bond for contracts in excess of $5 million

Little Miller Acts: Most states and local governments also have similar surety laws on public works projects that are referred to as "Little Miller Acts."

Construction Industry Payment Protection Act of 1999: The Construction Industry Payment Protection Act of 1999 makes several amendments to the Miller Act of 1935. Its purpose is to improve payment bond protections for persons who furnish labor or material for use on federal construction projects. This law was passed because the bonding amounts specified in the Miller Act may not provide subcontractors with adequate protection.

The Construction Industry Payment Protection Act of 1999 outlines three specific requirements:

- ✓ The general contractor of a project generally must obtain a payment bond in an amount that is equal to the total value of the federal contract, unless a lesser amount is specified by the contracting officer. The payment bond cannot be less than the performance bond.
- ✓ Subcontractors are permitted to notify contractors of intent to sue by any means which provides written, third-party verification of delivery.
- ✓ Waivers of Miller Act payment bond protections are void before the work begins. Any waiver of a subcontractor's right to sue on a payment bond must be in writing, signed, and executed after the subcontractor has first furnished labor or materials for use in the project.

Laws Governing Bonding of South Carolina State Public Construction Projects

The South Carolina Consolidated Procurement Code specifies bond requirements for South Carolina public construction projects.

Bid Bonds: A bid bond in the amount of 5 percent of the amount of the bid must accompany all proposals for public construction contracts over $50,000. The purpose of this bond is to ensure that the contractor will enter into the contract according to the plans, specifications, and conditions set forth. The bid bonds are returned to the unsuccessful bidders. The successful bidder gets the bid bond back after execution of the contract and bonding of the project.

Performance and Payment Bonds: The following bonds are required before executing contracts over $50,000 funded by the state for the construction, alteration, or repair of public works:

- ✓ A performance bond for the full contract amount. The purpose of this bond is to protect the state by guaranteeing performance according to the plans, specifications, and conditions of the contract.
- ✓ A payment bond for the full contract amount. The purpose of this bond is to protect material suppliers and subcontractors in the event of non-payment by the prime contractor. If payment is not made within 90 days after last furnishing materials or labor, the material supplier or subcontractor has the right to sue against the payment bond. A person contracting with a subcontractor to the bonded contractor must give notice of the amount owed to the bonded contractor within 90 days after last furnishing labor, rental equipment or materials on the project in order to preserve the right to sue the payment bond. A suit on the payment bond must be brought within one year after last furnishing the labor, rental equipment or materials on the project.

All bonds must be issued by a surety company authorized to do business in South Carolina.

Final Inspection...

Risk Management Benefits: Managing risk is challenging but is important to your reputation and bottom line.

Insurance: Insurance should supplement your risk management program. It provides protection against unforeseen events and is sometimes required by law. Several different types of insurance coverage are available to fit the needs of your business.

Property Insurance: Property insurance typically covers your business and personal property when damage, theft, or loss occurs. All-risk builders' risk, named peril builders' risk, inland marine/equipment theft, equipment floater, transportation floater, and motor truck cargo policies are types of property insurance that may benefit your business.

Liability Insurance: Liability insurance is designed to protect against third-party claims that arise from alleged negligence resulting in bodily injury or property damage. Several types of liability insurance policies are available, such as commercial general, umbrella, and director's and officer's liability insurance.

Business Owner's Policies (BOPs): Property and liability coverage are bundled under business owner's policies.

Automobile Insurance: Liability and physical damage associated with vehicles owned or leased by your company are covered under automobile insurance. Several types of coverage are available.

Burglary and Theft Insurance: Loss or damage by burglary, theft, larceny, robbery, forgery, fraud, and vandalism is covered under burglary and theft insurance.

Key Man Life Insurance: This type of insurance is available as life insurance or disability insurance, or both, to protect the continuing success of the business.

Coverage Gaps and Overlaps: It is important to evaluate all of your insurance coverage. Using one insurer may minimize gaps and overlaps in coverage.

Employment-Related Insurance: Workers' compensation, unemployment, and social security are employment-related insurance regulated by the state and/or federal government.

Insurance Coverage for Subcontractors: When hiring subcontractors, ensure that they carry the proper insurance coverage. These requirements should be outlined in the construction contract.

What is a Bond? Bonds provide protection in the event that contractual obligations are not met.

Bond Language: At a minimum, bonds should contain the total dollar amount, length of the bond, requirements for notice of defect or lack of maintenance, and bond enforcement.

Types of Bonds: Several types of bonds are available depending on the desired coverage.

Qualifying for a Bond: Before issuing a bond, the surety company will review your business to ensure it is established, profitable, and well-managed.

Bond Claims: The bond claim filing process is outlined in the bond language for common-law bonds and in the government statutes for statutory bonds.

Laws Governing Bonding of Federal Construction Projects: The Miller Act and Construction Industry Payment Protection Act of 1999 outline bonding requirements for federal construction projects.

Laws Governing Bonding of South Carolina State Public Construction Projects: State public construction projects require a payment bond for contracts exceeding $50,000.

Chapter 5
YOUR BUSINESS TOOLBOX

Chapter Survey...

- ⇨ *Time Management*
- ⇨ *Delegation*
- ⇨ *Business Ethics*
- ⇨ *Technology*
- ⇨ *Small Business Assistance and Loans*
- ⇨ *Small Business Certifications*

Just as you need a toolbox filled with tools to accomplish jobs in your trade, as a businessperson you need tools of resources and skills that help you run your business. This chapter will introduce a few of these tools and will lay a foundation for tools covered in future chapters.

Time Management

Time Is Money: This familiar phrase holds special meaning for business owners. Your ability to manage time effectively can make the difference between completing a job successfully and failing to meet customer expectations. Time is one of your most important tools. Use it wisely.

Four Time Management Tips: These habits will help you organize and manage your time.

- ✓ Prioritize tasks daily.
- ✓ Delegate when possible.
- ✓ Use checklists and calendars.
- ✓ Do not procrastinate.

Competitive Edge: Effective time management gives you a competitive edge and helps you to anticipate problems before they occur. You can focus on being proactive and minimize time spent "putting out fires." Your professionalism will be appreciated by your customers, subcontractors, and suppliers.

Time is money.
Use it wisely.

Delegation

You Can't Do It All: When you become a business owner, you go from a tradesperson to a manager of many jobs and a business administrator. Delegation is a key tool and will ensure that you get all tasks accomplished. You simply cannot do it all and be efficient.

Preparing to Delegate: Learning to delegate is often difficult because you are giving up control of certain tasks. You may feel that a task won't be done correctly or that it takes longer to explain a task than just doing it yourself.

Delegation is a way of developing your employees and building a solid team. Giving your employees increased responsibility builds their confidence and motivation, making them more productive and loyal. Delegation gives you the chance to concentrate strategically on running your business.

How to Delegate: Here are simple steps on how to delegate:

1. Identify a person for the task.
2. Explain the task clearly and make sure you are understood. You may want to ask the person to repeat their understanding of the task back to you.
3. Follow up with the person throughout the process.
4. Give positive feedback and any guidance on how the task can be improved, if necessary.

Effective delegation increases your efficiency.

Business Ethics

Your Reputation: Good business ethics are a must if you want to safeguard your reputation in the industry. Practicing good business ethics, when dealing with customers, employees, subcontractors, and suppliers, is not only the right thing to do, it is the best way to avoid litigation.

Defining Ethics: You may ask, "What are ethics?" In general, the term as it applies to business means behaving in a trustworthy, fair, honest, and respectful manner toward everyone with whom you have dealings. Your core values serve as your moral compass and guide this standard.

> ***Studies Say...***
> Top management has the strongest influence on employees' ethical behavior. If top managers demonstrate unethical behavior, employees are likely to do the same.

Establishing a code of conduct is a good first step to ensuring that good ethics are practiced throughout your company. A code of conduct is a documented way that an organization should operate.

This document can include

- ✓ guidelines for employees, management, subcontractors, and suppliers;
- ✓ standards for doing business; and
- ✓ commitment to the community.

You may want to provide your customers with your code of conduct. It will reinforce your commitment to good ethics and demonstrate professionalism.

> ***Make the right ethical choices to protect your reputation and avoid litigation.***

Technology

Technology as an Essential Tool: Technology is an essential tool for communicating and keeping your business competitive. Purchasing technology is becoming increasingly cost-effective. There are many technological tools specifically designed for the construction industry. These tools increase efficiency and aid in various tasks, such as

- ✓ estimating and bidding,
- ✓ accounting,
- ✓ job costing,
- ✓ scheduling, and
- ✓ construction management.

If you have not jumped into the technology age, here are a few basics to start with:

Computer/Laptop/Tablet For a business owner, a computer can serve many uses in streamlining administrative functions. This is the basic tool you will need to operate any programs you need for applications such as writing, accounting, scheduling, estimating, and email. Some builders opt to have laptop computers or tablets to perform these functions on the jobsite.

Phone: Cell phone, or smart phone, technology has advanced in the area of communications, use of email, photography, text messaging, and calendar management. Regardless of the features you choose for your business cell phone, it is important that you are always accessible to your customers and employees.

Fax Machine: Although email has become a prevalent means for communications, it is still important for businesses to have a fax machine so that copies of important documents can be transmitted quickly and efficiently.

Printer: A printer allows you to produce hard copies of the files you have on your computer. A printer will come in handy when creating customer correspondence and contracts. Portable printers that are small enough to bring to the jobsite are also available.

Scanner: Documents and small objects can be copied or scanned in a form that can be stored on a computer and then these files can be manipulated and printed for use.

Multifunction Hardware: You can purchase a single machine that works as a photocopier, fax, printer, and scanner. This type of hardware can be convenient and cost-effective if your business uses such functions frequently. However, bear in mind that if the unit breaks, you may lose several or all of the functions until it is repaired or replaced.

Digital Camera or Smart Phone: A digital camera or a smart phone with a camera are great ways to store photos on a computer or cloud server. It is important for you to document your work every step of the way, and digital pictures are a cost effective way to organize that information. Your pictures can be stored on a drive or cloud server with project files and emailed or shared as necessary.

Internet: The Internet is a powerful tool. It can be used for research, communication, or marketing your company. It is also the foundation for a growing number of social media platforms (i.e., Facebook, LinkedIn, Instagram, etc.). Social media allows you to connect with customers in new and unique ways. Most businesses these days have a social media presence on multiple platforms.

Word Processing Software: Word processing can save you a lot of time because the information you need is stored in a computer. Handwritten documents need to be rewritten each time, while documents entered in a computer can be modified and reused. Many word processing programs have templates of commonly used business documents which can be used, modified, and reused at any time. Word processing programs are available as both software and web-based.

Spreadsheet Program: This type of software gives you the flexibility to create financial worksheets on the computer. You can set up the worksheet to automatically calculate figures, reducing mathematical errors. Spreadsheet programs are available as both software and web-based.

A Warning about Software: Although software is designed to streamline your processes, you must still understand the basics. For example, if you purchase accounting software but do not understand the fundamentals of accounting, the software is useless to you. In future chapters, we will cover basic skills that will help you utilize software packages.

Once you become comfortable with technology, you may want to purchase other advanced tools and software.

Using technology can increase your efficiency and keep you competitive.

Small Business Assistance and Loans

Various federal, state and local resources can help you with small business services or education you might need. Many of these services may be free or at a minimal cost to business owners. Below are some of the resources available to you:

State of South Carolina Department of Commerce

This division of the South Carolina state government has business development and business services resources. It publishes the *Starting a Business in South Carolina Guide*, which can be downloaded off the Internet. The guide covers areas such as business planning, financial assistance, regulations, and taxes.

State of South Carolina
Department of Commerce
1201 Main Street, Suite 1600
Columbia, South Carolina 29201-3200

Phone: (803) 737-0400

Website: www.sccommerce.com

Local Community Colleges & Universities

Business education opportunities are available through local community colleges and universities. Seminars, workshops, and courses are offered on business skills and small business management.

Small Business Administration (SBA)

The Small Business Administration's mission is to counsel, assist, and protect the interests of small business. The SBA provides training and online help for small businesses. The SBA Headquarters is located in Washington, D.C., but you can check the website at www.sba.gov or call 1-800-U-ASK-SBA to find an office near you.

Columbia District Office
1835 Assembly Street, Suite 1425
Columbia, South Carolina 29201

Phone: (803) 765-5377
Fax: (803) 765-5962

Website: www.sba.gov/offices/district/sc/columbia

Service Corps of Retired Executives (SCORE)

SCORE is a national volunteer organization of retired executives who can provide counseling and training to you if you are an entrepreneur and/or business owner. There are several SCORE offices located throughout the state. You can find the SCORE office nearest to you on the website.

SCORE Association
1175 Herndon Parkway
Suite 900
Herndon, VA 20170
1-800-634-0245

Website: www.score.org

USA.gov Website

The website at www.usa.gov/business provides several online resources to Federal, state, and local information for business owners. Resources include:

- ✓ Starting a Business
- ✓ Registrations, Licenses, and Permits
- ✓ Finance and Taxes
- ✓ Expanding Your Business
- ✓ Legal Compliance
- ✓ Industry Specifics
- ✓ State and Local Resources

A partnership program through Business.gov links business owners from across the nation to create a social network and provide access to experts.

Appendix C contains additional references and website links on topics covered in this book.

Small Business Certifications

Federal and state governments often have opportunities for businesses to bid on contracts. These contracts are highly sought after for a number of reasons. To level the playing field, the government has established certifications for small, minority-owned, and women-owned businesses. If your company fits the criteria, you can obtain one or more certifications, which can provide additional opportunities for you to bid on government contracts.

The U.S. Small Business Administration has a Small Disadvantaged Business (SDB) certification. Information on this certification is found on the SBA website at www.sba.gov/federal-contracting or by calling 1-800-U ASK SBA. The website contains helpful links about government contracting and business development.

Certifications are also available at the state and local level. The South Carolina Office of the Governor has a Small and Minority Business Assistance Program. Certification information is available on their website at osmba.sc.gov or by calling (803) 734-5044.

Final Inspection...

Time Management: Effective time management gives you a competitive edge and helps you to anticipate problems before they occur.

Delegation: Effective delegation increases your efficiency and helps to develop your employees.

Business Ethics: The right ethical choices help to protect your reputation and avoid litigation.

Technology: Technology is an essential tool for communicating and keeping your business competitive.

Small Business Assistance and Loans: Several organizations are available to help small businesses with a variety of functions.

Small Business Certifications: Certifications for small, minority, and women-owned businesses are available through the government. If your company qualifies, certifications can provide additional opportunities for you to bid on government contracts.

Chapter 6
MARKETING AND SALES

Chapter Survey...

⇨ *Executing Your Marketing Plan*
⇨ *Logos, Stationery, and Business Cards*
⇨ *Promotional Materials*
⇨ *Public Relations*
⇨ *Effective Selling Skills*
⇨ *Organizing the Sales Process*
⇨ *Your Sales Presentation*

Start Off on the Right Foot: First impressions can tell your potential customers a lot about your business. Customers may judge your professionalism or reputation on this initial contact. Marketing, in some cases, may be the first impression of your business, and you want to make sure customers feel comfortable with you and your company from this point on.

The purpose of marketing is to bring in new customers and retain current customers. A good marketing program helps ensure a steady flow of leads and customers and, more important, a steady flow of incoming cash.

First impressions are lasting ones. Make your company's first impression a positive one.

Executing Your Marketing Plan

Maximize Your Marketing Potential: When developing your market analysis and marketing strategy (featured in the business plan template in Appendix B), you should answer questions such as these:

- ✓ Who are my customers?
- ✓ What is the best way to reach these customers?
- ✓ What is my competitive advantage?
- ✓ What growth opportunities exist in my industry?

Now it is time to put these thoughts into action. Developing a promotion plan will help you bring these ideas to life.

Logos, Stationery, and Business Cards

Create Your Identity: A simple start to developing your promotion plan is to create a logo. Not only will your name distinguish you in the market but a logo will set you apart from your competitors. Logos become part of your company identity and convey a professional look, which is important for that first impression.

A good logo design should be

- ✓ simple and easy to remember;
- ✓ attractive in color and black and white;
- ✓ limited to one or two colors;
- ✓ representative of your company identity; and
- ✓ scalable up or down and attractive in any size.

Money Saving Tip...

A local print shop or graphic designer can design a logo for your company. You may also be able to approach a graphic arts class at a local community college to develop your logo. One of the students may be able to use this as a class project and save you a few dollars.

Once your logo is created, you should include it on your business cards and stationery.

Promotional Materials

You may also apply your logo to several different promotional items. These items include

- ✓ brochures,
- ✓ direct mailings,
- ✓ jobsite signs,
- ✓ truck signs,
- ✓ yellow pages,
- ✓ social media sites, and
- ✓ websites.

Using promotional materials will give you name recognition. When potential customers have an upcoming job, they may be more likely to approach your company to put in a bid because your name is out in the market.

Business promotion through social media has become a prevalent means of marketing. You can create a business account on social media websites, such as Facebook, Twitter, and LinkedIn, to advertise your services, post updates on your business, and gain name recognition. Participation in social media can be an inexpensive way to market and increase traffic to your business website. In addition to creating a business page on social media sites for promotion, these sites have areas where you can buy advertising space.

A good marketing program is an investment that can help you gain customers and strengthen your reputation.

Public Relations

Benefits of Networking: Public relations are an inexpensive but effective marketing tool. It is important to build name recognition; good public relations constantly keep your business in the eye of the public—your potential customers. The downside to public relations is its labor-intensive nature, but your time invested will give you great rewards. You may use this approach to not only get potential customers but as a way to get referrals to good subcontractors, suppliers, or employees.

In the Public Eye: Here are some ideas to get you started.

- ✓ ***Join local trade associations***
  This is a good opportunity to meet new people in your industry. You can also volunteer to speak at meetings and conferences to showcase your knowledge and expertise.
- ✓ ***Participate in a local non-profit initiative (for example, be a volunteer Habitat for Humanity worker).*** High-profile projects will put you in a positive light in the public eye and also may get some press coverage.
- ✓ ***Volunteer for local leadership opportunities***
  Leadership positions in organizations such as schools or the local Chamber of Commerce may give you time with other influential people in the community who can make good referrals about you and your business.
- ✓ ***Sponsor community events***
  When you sponsor community events, your business name is often featured in event brochures, signage, and media promotions such as newspapers and radio advertisements.
- ✓ ***Send press releases to the local media***
  This public relations technique offers exposure to a broad audience and gives you credibility because it is communicated through a third-party. Press releases can report your involvement in the local community, new construction trends, or any ideas that might be interesting to the public and will promote your company.
- ✓ ***Hold an open house***
  You can hold an open house at your office or at a job where you can showcase your work. An open house gives you a chance to reinforce current business relationships and make new ones.

Effective Selling Skills

Don't Underestimate Your Selling Skills: Selling is often perceived as a salesperson pitching a product or service and the customer saying yes or no. Many people don't feel comfortable with the process of selling, because it makes them feel pushy and overbearing. Selling should be the simple process of matching your company's skills and expertise with what the customer needs.

Listen Up: Active listening is the golden rule to effective selling. Without listening, you cannot clearly understand what your customer needs. You may ask yourself, "What exactly is active listening?" Here are a few simple rules:

- ✓ Maintain good eye contact.
- ✓ Be attentive.
- ✓ Keep an open mind.

- ✓ Don't interrupt.
- ✓ Ask clarifying questions.
- ✓ Put yourself in the "shoes" of the other person.
- ✓ Pay attention to body language (i.e., facial expressions).

Using these simple guidelines, you will gain a more thorough understanding of your potential customers and be able to target your response to their needs.

A Word of Caution...

Be careful not to make unrealistic or inaccurate statements just to make a sale. You will hurt your business in the long run and potentially leave yourself open to a lawsuit. All advertising and marketing claims must be truthful and not deceptive. Individual state contractor licensing boards may have specific guidelines regarding licensed contractor advertising such as including a licensing number and specific verbiage required by law.

Organizing the Sales Process

Put It in Writing: Selling is a process. Generally speaking, higher-value sales have a longer selling process than a lower-value sale. To manage this selling process and provide the best service possible, you must be organized. Tracking potential customers is made simple by developing a sales tracking sheet for each contact you make. Your tracking sheet should contain the contact information for the potential customer, the type of work the customer wants, a summary of communication, the source of referral for that customer, and any other information you feel is necessary.

The next step is to prioritize your sales leads. Prioritizing leads is a way to manage your time in the sales process and can give you key insights into the effectiveness of your marketing program. You want to concentrate most of your time on the strong leads.

Tracking and prioritizing leads makes the sales process most effective.

Your Sales Presentation

Present Your Best Side: Once you have determined your strongest sales leads, you should schedule time to make a sales presentation. This is your opportunity to show customers how your company can meet their needs; in the sales presentation you try to gain a commitment to perform the work.

Presentation materials are important visuals and give the customer something concrete to take away and read after the meeting. These materials can include

- ✓ a company information sheet,
- ✓ brochures,
- ✓ business cards,
- ✓ past customer testimonials,
- ✓ warranty information, and
- ✓ photographs of past projects.

To avoid any awkward stumbling in the presentation, have materials prepared ahead of time. This demonstrates your professionalism and ensures that you have thought through the presentation.

Overcoming "No": Handling objections is one of the more difficult parts of the sales process. This is the time to use your active listening skills and overcome the objection.

- ✓ Repeat the objection to ensure that you completely understand the potential customer's reservation.
- ✓ No question is a stupid question. The person with the objection may just not understand the process.
- ✓ Give an example of a customer with the same question and how you effectively fulfilled his/her needs.

Communication Is Key: Closing the sale is a very important part of the process. Try to gain a commitment from the potential customer, whether it is hiring your company to do the work or even just scheduling another appointment to follow up.

Follow up on all sales presentations. This may be as simple as making a phone call or sending a card or small gift. Consistent follow-up ensures that you are at the top of your potential customer's mind and gives you an advantage over competitors.

Clearly understanding your potential customer's needs is imperative.

Final Inspection...

Executing Your Marketing Plan: Once you develop your marketing plan, the next step is implementing it.

Logos, Stationery, and Business Cards: These simple marketing tools can help establish your company's identity.

Promotional Materials: You can extend your marketing program by using various promotional materials.

Public Relations: This is an inexpensive but effective way to market your company.

Effective Selling Skills: Effective selling involves carefully listening to your potential customer's needs.

Organizing the Sales Process: Tracking potential sales leads can help you organize the process of selling.

Your Sales Presentation: Preparation and follow-up are important when presenting to potential customers.

PART 2
Fundamentals for the Field

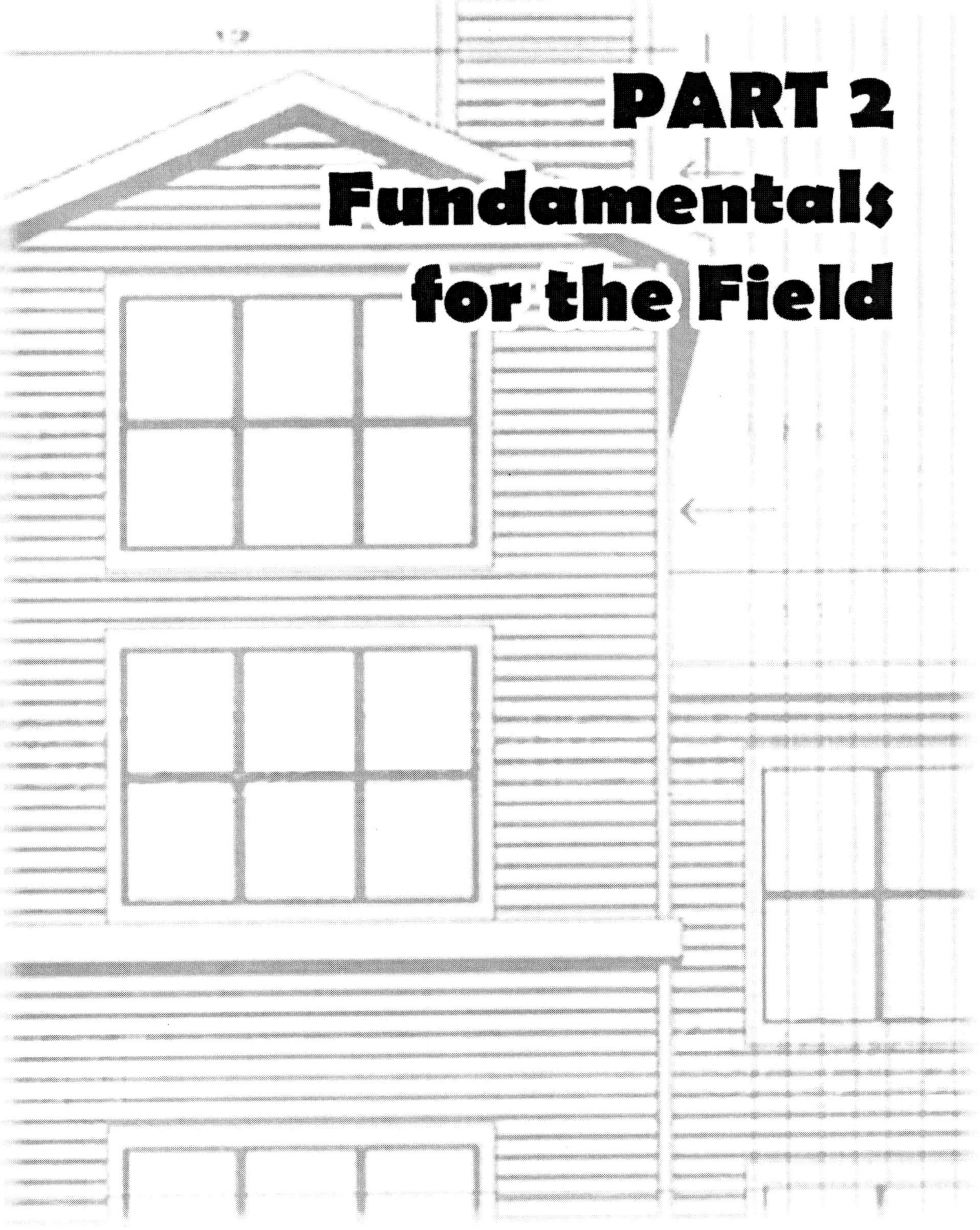

Chapter 7
BIDDING AND ESTIMATING

Chapter Survey...

- ⇨ *Bid Documents*
- ⇨ *Ethics in Bidding*
- ⇨ *Estimate Planning*
- ⇨ *Estimating Framework*
- ⇨ *Determining Estimated Costs*
- ⇨ *Other Methods of Estimating*
- ⇨ *Estimating Pitfalls*
- ⇨ *Using an Estimator*
- ⇨ *Submitting Your Bid*
- ⇨ *Job Cost Recording System*
- ⇨ *Technology Tools for Estimating*

Accurate estimating is important to the profitability of a construction company. If a job is estimated correctly, the contractor has a good chance at getting the job and making money. If the job is poorly estimated, the contractor may lose the bid or win the bid and lose money on the project.

The estimator must ask these questions when assessing whether to bid or not bid a project.

- ✓ ***Company Resources and Type of Work:*** Does our company have the resources to perform this work? Is this project consistent with the type of work we do?
- ✓ ***Site Considerations:*** Are there any special site considerations that we need to consider? Do the site conditions create any additional costs for our company?
- ✓ ***Location and Cost Effectiveness:*** How can we do the work efficiently and in the most cost effective manner? Does the location present special considerations and added cost through travel time and limited accessibility?
- ✓ ***Risk Assessment:*** What are the risks and how will we manage them?
- ✓ ***Profitability of Project:*** What is our profit margin on this work?

If you know you cannot complete the job on time or there is a chance you could lose money on the project, we recommend that you do not bid the job. The jobs you choose should contribute to your long-term goals and the reputation you want your company to have in the market.

Bid Documents

In a competitive bid situation, a bid package is often put together that includes

- ✓ **an invitation to bid** that gives a brief overview of the project, deadlines, and general requirements;
- ✓ **bid instructions** that contain specifics of how the bid should be completed and submitted;
- ✓ **bid forms**, including but not limited to items such as a bid sheet, bid schedule, bidder's questionnaire on experience, financial responsibility and capability, and a copy of the contract; and
- ✓ **supplements**, including items important to the overall bid process such as a property survey and soil analysis.

It is important to follow all the instructions in the bid package carefully and submit all documents according to the required specifications. The bidder can be found unresponsive if information is incorrectly submitted or omitted altogether.

Pre-bid meetings may also be scheduled, especially for larger projects. In a pre-bid meeting, the project specifications and any changes to the bid package are discussed.

If changes are made to a bid package before it is due, an **addendum** is issued. The addendum becomes part of the bid documents and, ultimately, part of the contract when awarded. It is important to carefully review all addenda to evaluate the impact on your bid. Changes in plans and specifications may affect your bid pricing or even your decision to bid at all.

Carefully evaluate whether bidding on a project is the right decision for your company.

Ethics in Bidding

Good ethical conduct is necessary to maintain the integrity of the bidding process. The situations listed below are not only a poor way to do business, but some state statutes forbid these practices on public projects.

- ✓ **Bid Shopping**
  Bid shopping occurs when the general contractor approaches subcontractors other than those who have submitted bids to seek a lower offer than what was quoted in original bids. In this situation, the general contractor reveals the original bids submitted and tries to reduce the price.
- ✓ **Bid Peddling**
  Bid peddling occurs when the subcontractor approaches the general contractor after the project was awarded with the intent of lowering the original price submitted on bid day.
- ✓ **Bid Rigging**
  Bid rigging is a form of collusion where contractors coordinate their bids to fix the award outcome of a project.

Estimate Planning

Once you have determined that you want to submit a bid, you must prepare your estimate. An estimate is the sum of the costs to complete the project, plus your added overhead and profit margin. Before you start putting numbers down on paper, you should understand all the factors that impact the cost of the job. A good estimate will fall within 1 percent to 2 percent of actual construction costs.

Project Documents

A complete set of project documents is required to prepare an accurate cost estimate. These documents include the following:

- ✓ **Construction or architectural drawings** that show a schematic diagram of the job. The drawings may illustrate many different views or elevations of the job.
- ✓ **Specifications** are details that determine the type of materials or methods to be used in construction. If there is a conflict between the specifications and applicable codes, you must follow the stricter of the two. The codes are the minimum requirements by law. You always must meet or exceed the applicable codes.
- ✓ The **contract** is the agreement between you and your customer to complete the specified work. The conditions outlining the obligations of each party, such as the owner and contractor, are included in the contract. If your bid is accepted, the construction drawings and specifications become part of the contract package. Contracts are covered in more detail in Chapter 8.
- ✓ **Bonds** may be required as part of the bid submittal (discussed in Chapter 4). Bonds commonly required are bid and performance bonds.

You should carefully review these documents to understand the project and the expectations of the customer.

Site Visit

There may be specifics about the site that influence the cost estimate. These details cannot always be determined from the construction documents. It is important that you go to the actual site and look at any factors that may bear on the project. Soil type, grading, vehicle access, and availability to electricity and water are some of the variables that could affect the cost of the project. You want to anticipate as many of these problems as you can before beginning work.

During this time, you should consider the environmental aspects of the project. If you need to obtain environmental permits, this process will affect your estimated costs. Your project may also require special equipment and processes that should be factored into your estimate. Chapter 12, Jobsite Safety and Environmental Factors, discusses environmental impacts in more depth.

Estimating Framework

Estimating should be a systematic process. Approaching the estimate in an organized way will help you avoid errors or omissions. Taking the extra time to construct a framework for the estimate will increase your accuracy.

Your estimating framework essentially lists the process for completing the job. This can be accomplished by

- ✓ defining the phases of the project; and
- ✓ listing each task and materials needed within each phase.

Once your framework is established, you can enter the time and cost for each task. If you are awarded the job, you can easily convert your estimating framework into your job schedule.

Define the Phases

The first thing you need to consider when you build your estimate is the phases of the project that you are working on. For example, you might list the phases as preconstruction, construction, and post-construction. The order of tasks will drive your scheduling process.

List Each Task and Materials Needed

Once you list the phases of the project, then you need to develop a list of tasks and materials for each phase. Be very specific in this step. If you omit an item or add an unnecessary item, your estimate will be inaccurate. The task and material list should also include labor time needed and material amounts. By identifying these items early in the process, you may also determine the need for items such as overtime to meet certain project deadlines and temporary storage. All of these items play a part in the cost estimate.

Estimating Checklist

The Construction Specifications Institute publishes a classification system called MasterFormat. This system includes numbers and job tasks grouped by major construction activities. This is a helpful tool when setting up your estimating framework to ensure that you have accounted for all aspects of materials and labor. After you become familiar with the estimating process, you may develop your own estimating checklist customized for your needs.

Determining Estimated Costs

Quantity Take-off Method

One accurate method of estimating is the quantity take-off method. Using this method, you individually estimate units of materials and labor that you listed for each task in your estimating framework.

After estimating materials and labor, the following items are added:

- ✓ subcontractor fees,
- ✓ labor burden,
- ✓ project overhead costs,
- ✓ project equipment,
- ✓ contingencies,
- ✓ allowances,
- ✓ company overhead, and
- ✓ profit.

By going through the items on an individual basis, you can adjust your estimate to accommodate the unique aspects of the project that you may have uncovered when reviewing the construction documents or during your site survey.

STEP 1

Determine Labor Cost for Each Task

Using your estimating framework, you can begin to enter your labor cost. Information from previous jobs can help you determine accurate job costs. There are also published costs available through books such as the RSMeans cost data series, but this is no substitute for your knowledge of the industry. Your experience with your local labor market and wages should be factored into your estimated costs.

For each listed labor item on your estimating framework list, use the following formula to determine the labor cost.

Required Labor Hours per Task x Labor Rate = Labor Cost per Task

The required labor hours can vary based on several different factors, such as employee skill level, size of crew, and weather conditions. These factors must be taken into account when determining the required labor hours. Hours spent planning and scheduling must also be figured into the labor cost equation.

Another helpful tool when determining labor cost is your historical cost data. Determining your final labor cost from past projects will help you put together more accurate estimates for future jobs. Developing a cost-tracking system is discussed later in this chapter.

STEP 2

Add Labor Burden

As an employer, you incur costs such as mployment taxes and insurance. These obligations add approximately 30 percent to your labor cost. This additional amount is referred to as labor burden.

Labor burden includes items such as

- ✓ Medicare and social security (discussed in Chapter 15),
- ✓ federal unemployment insurance (discussed in Chapter 15),
- ✓ workers' compensation,
- ✓ liability insurance,
- ✓ state unemployment insurance, and
- ✓ company benefits (such as medical insurance, vacations, etc.).

Labor burden must be factored into your total labor cost.

STEP 3

Determine Materials Cost

Just as you plugged in the labor cost into your estimating framework, you can do the same with the materials cost. For each listed material item on your estimating framework, you need to obtain a cost.

Your suppliers can provide you with the materials price per unit or a lump sum. The cost of materials can fluctuate according to the availability of raw materials and demand, so it is important to keep current cost data. In addition to tracking wage, earnings, employment, and benefit statistics, The Bureau of Labor Statistics (www.bls.gov) tracks the prices of major groups of construction materials as part of its Producer Price Index (PPI) program. Periodically reviewing this resource can help you to understand potential increases and decreases in materials cost.

You may receive the materials cost as a unit cost. If necessary, use the following formula to determine the total material cost per unit for each of the materials categories on your take-off sheet.

Price per Unit x Number of Units Needed = Total Material Unit Cost

To make sure you are receiving the best price, obtain at least three bids from suppliers. You should also add a small contingency for waste. Depending on the type of material and the job specifications, your waste contingency will vary.

STEP 4

Determine Project Equipment Costs

Equipment needed to complete the job is figured as a direct cost to complete the project and added to your estimate.

For example, if you need a crane to set an air handling unit on the top of a building as part of a HVAC project, it is considered a direct cost.

Small tools and pickup trucks are considered an indirect cost and not part of project equipment. These indirect costs are figured into project overhead.

Figuring the direct cost of equipment differs depending if you rent or own the equipment.

Owned Equipment: To estimate owned equipment, you must arrive at a unit cost for the equipment. To calculate unit cost, consider the following factors:

- ✓ actual value of equipment factoring in its age and amount of depreciation from the original purchase price;
- ✓ maintenance and operating costs;
- ✓ taxes and fees;
- ✓ labor to operate equipment, including any training or licensing costs; and
- ✓ insurance.

Unit cost is calculated by estimating the number of hours you will use the equipment per year and dividing this number by the total yearly cost of the equipment calculated by considering the operational factors.

For example, if you figure the total cost of the equipment for the year is $30,000 and you plan to use the equipment for a total of 1,000 hours, your unit cost to operate the equipment is $30 an hour.

If you estimate using the equipment for 40 hours on a project, your estimated project equipment cost for that project is $1,200.

Rental Equipment: The following items are considered when figuring the cost of rental equipment:

- ✓ equipment rental rate;
- ✓ labor cost to pick up and return equipment or delivery fees;
- ✓ labor cost to operate equipment; and
- ✓ other costs associated with operating the equipment (e.g., cost of fuel).

Subcontracting: You may decide that neither option is cost effective or feasible and subcontract the work. In this case, this line item would appear under subcontractor fees.

Rent, Lease, or Buy? Construction equipment is vital to the completion of construction projects. Equipment can range from cranes to computers. The decision to rent, lease, or purchase this equipment is a challenging one, and there are many considerations to each option.

Leasing is a long-term rental agreement that provides the benefits of using the equipment without purchasing. Lease payments are made to the owner of the equipment in exchange for the use of the equipment. At the end of the lease term, the owner takes possession of the equipment.

Leasing equipment has many advantages. One of the biggest is the ability to use the equipment with a limited capital expenditure. Other advantages compared to purchasing include

- ✓ no down payment;
- ✓ duration of payments over a longer period making them lower;
- ✓ lease payments (as defined by the IRS) deductible as operating expenses; and
- ✓ obsolete equipment is returned to the owner at end of the lease.

Equipment ownership allows you to take advantage of certain tax benefits and usually costs less than leasing in the long run. Leases are long-term contractual agreements that generally cannot be cancelled. If you no longer need the equipment, you must still make payments for the full term of the lease.

Purchasing equipment is advantageous when the equipment has a long and useful life and will not become obsolete in the short-term. You gain ownership of the equipment after the purchase is made but you should consider how the equipment will hold value over a long-term period. For this reason, salvage value is a benefit to purchasing equipment.

Renting equipment may be an alternative to purchasing or leasing. Although renting equipment is usually the costliest, it is the best option in certain circumstances. These include

- ✓ short-term, specialized projects;
- ✓ replacement for equipment being repaired;
- ✓ equipment with high maintenance costs; and
- ✓ jobs that require transportation and storage to distant locations.

The decision to rent, purchase, or lease is one that should be analyzed carefully to provide the most cost-effective solution for your company.

STEP 5 Add Subcontractor Fees

Subcontractors will be a consideration if you need to outsource work that your company does not have the resources to complete. Chapter 13 covers hiring and working with subcontractors. You should get at least three bids from subcontractors, so you have a good measure of comparison. Carefully evaluate your subcontractors to determine that they have the proper qualifications, licensure, and insurance coverage. The subcontractor fees must be added to the estimate that you give your customer.

STEP 6 Add Allowances

There may be items that are not specified in the project plans, such as finish materials (carpeting, fixtures, lighting, etc.). For these items, you can specify an allowance in your estimate. This is the owner's budget for these items. If the owner's choices exceed or fall short of the allowance amount, the contract should clearly address who is responsible for the difference. Typically, a change order is created, in this case, stating the amount under or over what is stated in the contract. Change orders are discussed in Chapter 8.

STEP 7 Add Contingencies

A contingency percentage is sometimes added to an estimate to protect the contractor if an unanticipated problem or condition arises during the course of the project. Contingency markups are generally based on the risk level of the project.

For example, a low risk level project might have a 2 percent contingency markup, but a project that has more unknown factors would have a higher markup.

STEP 8

Add Project Overhead

Project overhead costs are items that are necessary to completing the project but are not directly associated with labor and materials. These costs typically account for 5 percent to 10 percent of the total bid, but these costs should be itemized as much as possible to achieve the most accurate result.

Examples of project overhead costs include

- ✓ bonds,
- ✓ temporary storage,
- ✓ temporary office,
- ✓ security guard,
- ✓ utilities,
- ✓ dumpsters, and
- ✓ portable toilets.

Project overhead differs from company overhead. Company overhead cannot be directly linked with a project.

STEP 9

Add Company Overhead

Company overhead is the cost of doing business. These expenses are necessary to keeping the operation running. Examples of these expenses are

- ✓ office rent,
- ✓ accounting fees,
- ✓ taxes,
- ✓ telephone,
- ✓ legal fees, and
- ✓ administrative labor.

Calculating an Overhead Percentage

Using historical information from the past year is the best way to predict overhead for the following year. Overhead percentages generally average between 5 percent and 20 percent, so it is best to calculate the overhead rates specific to your company.

Company Overhead: To arrive at a company overhead percentage, you can make the following calculations.

- ✓ Add up all of your overhead costs from the previous year. These numbers may also be found on your income statement as part of your administrative expenses.
- ✓ Divide your overhead costs by your revenues (also found on your income statement) to arrive at your overhead percentage.

Project Overhead: Project overhead is a similar calculation.

- ✓ Add up all of your project overhead costs from the previous year.
- ✓ Divide your project overhead costs by your revenues (found on your income statement) to arrive at your overhead percentage.

Adding Overhead to the Bid: You must add these overhead percentages to your estimate to cover your overhead costs.

For example, let's say you calculated the direct costs for your bid at $100,000, your project overhead at 9 percent, and company overhead percentage at 11 percent. Your direct costs are then 80 percent of your total bid price. Since overhead is a percentage of revenue, you should divide the direct costs of your bid by 80 percent (.80).

Here is what the calculation should look like:

$100,000 ÷ .80 = $125,000

After adding in overhead, the bid price with direct costs and overhead is $125,000.

STEP 10

Add Markup and Determine Profit Margin

Considerations for properly pricing a job include

- ✓ cost estimate,
- ✓ customer needs and expectations,
- ✓ local market and competition, and
- ✓ expected profit margin.

Determining the right pricing based on these factors is important to maximizing your profit and satisfying your customers.

Cost-based pricing is one of the most common ways to price a bid. Essentially, the cost of the project is determined through the cost estimate and an overhead percentage, plus a markup percentage. The markup percentage is divided into the direct costs of the project, just like the overhead costs in the previous example. If you estimated correctly, you will achieve your internal profit margin goals.

The standard industry markup is 15 percent, but you should consider the market and competition. You must be careful to keep your estimate in line with your competition and understand how much your customers are willing to pay for your work.

In your estimate, markup is applied to the direct costs of the project, such as labor, material, project equipment, project overhead, and subcontractors.

If your markup is too low, you may not cover your costs to complete the project, causing you to break even, or you may lose money on the job. To get the work, you may decide to bid low by lowering your profit markup and make it up on future projects, but this should not be a common practice. You will eventually go out of business if an insufficient amount of profit is achieved over time.

On the flip side, if your markup is too high, you may bid yourself out of jobs. Typically, the higher the markup, the fewer jobs you receive. The lower the markup, the more jobs you receive. You must estimate and choose your markup carefully to ensure a steady flow of jobs and profits for your company.

Attention to detail is important to preparing an accurate estimate.

Other Methods of Estimating

Quantity take-off is generally the most accurate way to estimate, but there are other estimating methods you can use.

- ✓ A **conceptual estimate** is generally prepared by the architect using cost models from previous projects. The contractor may arrive at a much different cost because of the project's unique characteristics.
- ✓ Using the **square-foot method** of estimating, the project cost is a calculation of the square footage of the project multiplied by a unit cost. This is a quick way to arrive at an estimated cost, but this method does not account for project specifics that affect cost. Another variation of this method is putting together an estimate using cubic feet of the project multiplied by a unit cost.
- ✓ The **unit price method** of estimating bundles all of the cost factors such as labor, materials, equipment, and subcontractors to come up with a unit price for the entire task. For example, let's say you are placing and finishing a 2,000-square-foot concrete slab and you determined that your unit price is $2.00 per square foot for this task. The total unit price is $4,000.

Estimating Pitfalls

Accurate estimating is a vital function for construction businesses and can make the difference between getting the right jobs and making a profit on a job. There are pitfalls that are detrimental to the estimating function that you want to avoid.

Preliminary Estimates

Your customers may be eager to determine what their project will cost, and they ask you for an estimate on the spot. Quoting a price before you have a chance to make accurate calculations is a risky practice. If you quote a price too high, it is possible that you could lose the bid. If you quote a price too low, the potential customer may be disappointed and feel you were dishonest in your initial contact.

Inaccurate Estimates

Inaccuracies occur when you make errors and omissions in your estimate. To avoid inaccuracies, you should always check your estimates. Errors to look for:

- ✓ ***Mathematical errors:*** Always check your work and if possible, have someone else check the mathematical accuracy of the estimate.
- ✓ ***Omissions in labor or materials:*** Be as thorough as possible when setting up the framework for your estimate. The use of a standard format, such as MasterFormat, will help you avoid this mistake.
- ✓ ***Non-standard abbreviations:*** Non-standard abbreviations may be interpreted as a different measurement or material. Spell out the actual word rather than inventing an abbreviation that is unclear or vague.
- ✓ ***Units of measure:*** Define linear, square, and cubic measure accurately. The difference between these measures can make a drastic difference in cost.

The more accurately you prepare your estimates, the better chance you have to make your expected profit.

Accurate estimates help you get the right jobs and make a profit.

Using an Estimator

Estimators develop the cost information that business owners or managers need to make a bid for a contract. Small business owners or managers may perform this function without the use of a professional estimator. Larger companies or a larger project may need to use an estimator.

Estimators follow the same estimating process: performing the quantity take-off, analyzing subcontractor bids, determining equipment needs and sequence of operations, analyzing physical constraints at the site and contingencies, and determining allowances and overhead costs. The estimator may also have a say in setting the profit for the project and the terms and conditions of the contract. The estimator's job is solely to perform the estimating function and, if used, is an important part of the project team.

Submitting Your Bid

Once your estimate is complete and you are ready to submit your bid, you must make sure that you follow all of the instructions in the bid package. These instructions include submitting all of the required documents and the exact information requested by the bid submittal deadline. Even though you may have a template put together for the estimating process, you may need to customize your bid so as to respond to the specifications of the bid. Once your bid is submitted, it is reviewed by the owner. Bid review is generally a 30- to 90-day process. You are notified of the acceptance or rejection of your bid after this review process is complete.

Job Cost Recording System

A job cost recording system provides many benefits to the estimating and project management process.

- ✓ Current projects are monitored more closely with a cost tracking system. Cost overruns are identified and corrective action is taken sooner.
- ✓ Information from a job cost recording system helps with future estimates by creating more accurate unit costs.
- ✓ Many analytical reports can be generated from the cost data to review performance by project, activity, year, etc. Using this data can help you make more strategic decisions.

There are many ways to set up a job cost recording system, but to ensure accuracy, it must remain consistent for all projects.

The first step is to develop a cost code system. A cost code system includes the following components.

- ✓ ***Project Number:*** A project numbering system could be as simple as starting with the number one (1) and consecutively numbering subsequent projects. A more complex project numbering system might also include a code for the type of project and the year it was started. For example, let's say you are working on a remodel project (R) that started in 2016 (16) and was the first (01) project of the year. Your project number could be R-16-01.
- ✓ ***Activity Classification Code:*** You may want to develop your own system or use a classification system such as the CSI MasterFormat. For example, for a finish carpentry job you could use MasterFormat number 16200. If you use the same classifications on your estimate, it will be easier to compare estimated to actual costs.
- ✓ ***Distribution Code:*** These are items such as material, labor, equipment, and project overhead. For example, coding might be as simple as one-letter abbreviations:
  Material = M
  Labor = L
  Equipment = E
  Project Overhead = P
- ✓ This code can be placed behind the activity classification code. For example, the labor for finish carpentry could be classified as 16200L and materials as 16200M.

Once your system is set up, you can begin entering the cost data. Materials, equipment, and project overhead costs can be gathered from purchase orders, receipts, and invoices. Labor costs can be taken from timecards. It is important that employees fill out timecards completely and with enough detail so you can accurately record labor costs. A sample time card is located in Chapter 14.

Technology Tools for Estimating

Many computer tools are available to help streamline the estimating process. This technology can provide many benefits:

- ✓ shorter time to prepare the estimate;
- ✓ improved accuracy; and
- ✓ professional presentation to the customer.

Estimating software ranges from a basic spreadsheet format to complex databases. However, the programs share some common features:

- ✓ databases for unit cost items, such as material and labor;
- ✓ multiple estimate report formats to present to the customer (hard copy and electronic);
- ✓ a tracking method for historical information;
- ✓ ability to recall and modify past projects; and
- ✓ job costing capabilities.

As with any software, you must understand the fundamentals. If you do not know how to estimate, the software available will provide limited benefits to the process.

Final Inspection...

Bid Documents: All bid documents should be completed according to the specific requirements of the bid.

Ethics in Bidding: Good ethical practices are important to maintaining the integrity of the bid process.

Estimate Planning: Careful review of construction documents and a site visit are important first steps to creating an accurate estimate.

Estimating Framework: An estimate framework includes the project phases and the labor and materials needed for each phase.

Determining Estimated Costs: The quantity take-off method is one of the more accurate estimating methods. All direct and indirect costs must be added to ensure the estimate is complete.

Other Methods of Estimating: Estimates can be put together using different methods with varying degrees of accuracy.

Estimating Pitfalls: It is important to be accurate and detailed when estimating a job. You may not make your expected profit if you make mistakes in your estimate.

Using an Estimator: An estimator is used to perform the estimating function on a project. The estimator may also make recommendations on the project profit margin and terms of the contract.

Submitting Your Bid: All instructions in a bid package must be followed or the bid may be rejected. There is typically a 30- to 90-day bid review process.

Job Cost Recording System: Monitoring of current projects, creating more accurate future estimates, and providing reports for analysis are benefits of implementing a job cost recording system.

Technology Tools for Estimating: There are several computer tools to help you create your estimate, but it is still important to fully understand the process.

Chapter 8
CONTRACT MANAGEMENT

Chapter Survey...

- ⇨ *Required Contract Elements*
- ⇨ *Contract Provisions*
- ⇨ *Breach of Contract*
- ⇨ *Boilerplate Provisions*
- ⇨ *Provisions to Limit Risk*
- ⇨ *What Are Recitals?*
- ⇨ *Types of Construction Contracts*
- ⇨ *Contracting Methods*
- ⇨ *Sources of Contracts*
- ⇨ *Making Changes to the Contract*
- ⇨ *Resolving Claims*
- ⇨ *Alternative Dispute Resolution*
- ⇨ *Making Substitutions*
- ⇨ *Contract Documents and Project Manual*
- ⇨ *Are Oral Agreements Legally Binding?*
- ⇨ *Legal Interpretation*
- ⇨ *Subcontracting*

Legally Speaking: Contracts are legally binding agreements between two or more parties. The main purpose of contracts is to prevent disputes between parties entering into an agreement. Many times, agreements are made verbally, but it is best to get a contract in writing.

Contracts also serve many purposes including

- ✓ **defining the obligations of the agreement;**
- ✓ **outlining payment terms; and**
- ✓ **limiting the liability of the parties invol**ved.

Contracts need to be worded carefully to protect your company. It is recommended you consult with an attorney experienced in construction law to ensure you have a legally enforceable contract.

Required Contract Elements

Make it Binding: You may have reached an agreement to do work for a customer, but that does not mean that you have a contract. There are four key elements that must be in effect to make a contract binding.

- ✓ **Offer and Acceptance**
- ✓ **Consideration**
- ✓ **Competent Parties**
- ✓ **Legal Purpose**

Offer and Acceptance

The Offer is on the Table: An offer specifically outlines the obligations of the contract, including the work to be done and compensation for this work. When you submit an estimate or bid for work, this is considered an offer. All parties must be clear on the essential details and obligations of the contract to have a valid offer. Once an offer is made, you are bound to what you have agreed to do.

An offer generally has a specific amount of time in which an acceptance needs to be made. This time frame is typically 30 days, but it should be stated in the offer. If a deadline for acceptance is not outlined in the offer, it expires in a "reasonable time." Reasonable time is up to court interpretation and is considered on an individual case basis.

Negotiation: Negotiation is the process where the owner and contractor come to an agreement on the contract price and terms of the contract. Chapter 10 discusses negotiation techniques that helps guide you through the negotiation process. An offer is usually the outcome of a negotiation, but parties are not bound to the contract terms until an offer is made and acceptance is achieved. It is important to be clear when a communication is for negotiation purposes so it is not misconstrued as an offer.

Acceptance: The next step of the process is acceptance. Acceptance is agreeing to the offer made and generally is done by signing the offer. In some cases, a counteroffer is made. A counteroffer is not considered acceptance. It is only when both parties agree to the contract terms that you obtain acceptance.

Offer Checklist: Your offer should contain certain components because, if accepted, you are contractually bound to it:

- ✓ Date of offer
- ✓ Names and contact information of contracting parties
- ✓ Name and location of project
- ✓ Description of the work to be performed
- ✓ Contract time or start and completion date
- ✓ Payment terms, including progress payment schedule and final payment
- ✓ Conditions for schedule delays
- ✓ List of contract documents, including general conditions, drawings, and specifications
- ✓ Contract sum, including contract type such as lump sum, unit price, or cost plus (discussed later in this chapter)
- ✓ Expiration date of offer

Once accepted, this agreement becomes part of the contract's Standard Form of Agreement.

Consideration

An Exchange: Both parties must give up something of value to have consideration. Most likely this will be money, but it could be anything of value. Payment terms should be clearly outlined in the contract. Typically, the contractor provides services and in exchange, the owner provides monetary compensation.

Competent Parties

Legal Capacity: The parties in agreement should have the legal capacity to enter into a contract. Simply put, the parties must both be of sound mind in order for the contract to be valid. A situation where parties may not have legal capacity might be if you contracted with someone who is heavily under the influence of drugs or alcohol. The courts may rule someone incompetent if they are mentally disabled. Minors are prohibited from entering into contracts without parental consent.

Legal Purpose

Contracts must be possible to perform, not intended to harm anyone, and cannot require any illegal activity. For example, a contract that requires the contractor to build a house that does not comply with building codes does not have legal purpose and is invalid.

Consult with an attorney to ensure your contracts are legally enforceable.

Contract Provisions

Make it Clear: Contracts should be clear and concise. It is important that both parties understand the terms of the contract. There are provisions that you need to include in your contracts to ensure that all details are clearly outlined. Provisions are simply clauses that outline the stipulations of the contract.

Key Contract Provisions: Contracts are full of provisions, but a few key ones you will want to include:

- ✓ **Contract Price and Payment Terms**
- ✓ **Obligation of the Parties**
- ✓ **Supplemental Conditions**
- ✓ **Breach of Contract**

Contract Price and Payment Terms

Getting Paid: The contract should specify how the contract price is calculated. Whether you choose to use a lump-sum, unit-price or cost-plus method, include all fees the customer is expected to pay.

Payment terms should be very specific and include

- ✓ who is issuing payment,
- ✓ amount of the payment,
- ✓ form of payment, and
- ✓ when the payment will be issued.

Progress Payments: Progress payments are partial payments made after specified phases of construction are complete. Payments are generally calculated by taking the difference between the completed work and materials delivered and a predetermined schedule of unit costs.

Requirements for the schedule of progress payments should be clearly outlined in the construction contract including

- ✓ number of payments,
- ✓ amount of each payment,
- ✓ stage of progress between payments, and
- ✓ date or stage when each one is due.

It is important to monitor the progress payment schedule to ensure timeliness. You may be required to submit a partial payment estimate to the project architect or engineer prior to the payment due date. The partial payment estimate outlines the work performed and proof of materials and equipment delivery required for the next stage of construction. The architect or engineer certifies each progress payment by confirming the information in the partial payment estimate.

Progress payments have two functions: one, to protect the owner by holding the contractor responsible for following the planned schedule and two, to allow the contractor to pay for labor and material expenditures as they occur. This method of payment also protects both parties in the event of a contract breach on either side.

Retainage: Retainage is used by the owner to ensure completion of the construction project and provide protection against liens, claims, and defaults. It is calculated as a percentage (generally 10 percent) withheld from each progress payment. The retainage amount may be reduced further after substantial completion of the project (for example, retainage amounts may drop to 5 percent after 75 percent completion of the project). Retainage amounts must be clearly stated in the construction contract. Prime contractors generally hold the same percentage of retainage for their subcontractors.

The architect or engineer certifies when the project is complete and the work meets the conditions of the contract documents.

The retained amounts are generally due to the contractor upon completion and acceptance of the work.

Final Payment: Once the structure can be used for its intended purpose, the architect issues a certificate of substantial completion. A certificate of occupancy, issued by a building inspector, deems the structure meets all applicable codes and is safe for occupancy.

Final payment is generally due when all punch list items are complete as agreed between the owner and contractor, proper approvals are obtained, and all paperwork is complete.

To receive a final payment, the following documentation should be prepared and delivered to the owner upon completion of the project:

- ✓ Completion certificates issued by the architect
- ✓ Inspection certificates
- ✓ Guaranties and warranties
- ✓ Affidavits that all subcontractors and project bills have been paid
- ✓ Equipment operation manuals
- ✓ Final lien waivers for those who submitted preliminary notices
- ✓ Final project drawings
- ✓ Any other documents as required by contract

It is important to organize paperwork throughout the construction process. A delay in putting the final paperwork together can consequently delay the final payment.

Obligation of the Parties

Contract Conditions: The obligation of the parties should be specifically outlined in the contract and include both the contractor's obligations and the owner's obligations. The obligations of the parties are the contract conditions.

Contractor's obligations include but are not limited to

- ✓ having proper licensure;
- ✓ securing building permits;
- ✓ ordering all materials and supplies and arranging for site delivery;
- ✓ furnishing all labor, including obtaining required subcontractors to complete the job;
- ✓ completing all work in compliance with all applicable codes and scheduling inspections on a timely basis;
- ✓ completing all work according to plans and specifications; and
- ✓ keeping the construction site clean and removing all debris during and upon completion of construction.

Owner's obligations include but are not limited to

- ✓ ensuring prompt approval of all plans and specifications;
- ✓ ensuring project meets zoning specifications;
- ✓ issuing payments according to the specified progress payment schedule;
- ✓ paying for all required permits, assessments, and charges required by public agencies and utilities;
- ✓ furnishing all surveys and recording plats and a legal description of the property; and
- ✓ providing access to the construction site in a timely manner.

Each list of obligations must be customized according to the agreement reached and the individual job being performed. Most contracts require agreement by both parties if obligations are assigned to another party.

Supplemental Conditions

The supplemental conditions modify the general conditions of the contract and are often prepared in a separate document. Supplemental conditions are tailored specifically to each project. They may outline items such as specific insurance requirements, project procedures, and local law requirements.

Be very specific when outlining the obligations of both parties.

Breach of Contract

A breach of contract occurs when one of the parties involved fails to perform in accordance with any of the terms and conditions of the contract.

A breach may occur when a party

- ✓ **refuses to perform the contract;**
- ✓ **performs an act prohibited by the contract; or**
- ✓ **prevents the other party from performing its obligations.**

There are two types of breaches: **material** and **immaterial**.

A **material breach** is a serious violation of the contract. For example, if a contractor refuses to perform or complete a job or if an owner refuses to pay for completed or partial jobs, this is considered a breach of contract. This type of breach may void the contract and will most likely end up in litigation.

The injured party can seek monetary damages for the loss suffered as a result of the breach. Sometimes the damages are written into the contract. These are called **liquidated or stated damages**.

Breach of contract can occur if contracts are not completed within the time frame specified in the contract. If a time is not specified in the contract, the project must be completed in a "reasonable time." If the project has an unexcused delay, the owner may be entitled to liquidated damages for the "loss of use." Some contracts specify a per-day rate for liquidated damages. For example, if a contract specifies a $400 per day assessment and the contractor finished 30 days late, $12,000 in liquidated damages is assessed to the contractor. An owner who sues for liquidated damages cannot sue for actual damages.

If you sue for breach of contract, you must do so within the statute of limitations. Statutes of limitations are laws that set a maximum period of time within which a lawsuit or claim may be filed. The deadlines vary depending on the circumstances of the case and the type of claim. If a claim is not filed before the statutory deadline, you may lose the right to file a claim.

An **immaterial** or **partial breach** is a less serious violation and usually does not result in termination of the contract. The injured party may only sue for the value of the damages.

Boilerplate Provisions

Standard Language: The term "boilerplate" refers to standard language or clauses used in a legal contract. Sometimes they are referred to as "miscellaneous" clauses. They generally appear at the end of the contract and their purpose is to protect the business in the event of a lawsuit. Attorney's fees, arbitration, and consent to jurisdiction (meaning where the disputes will be settled) are a few examples of boilerplate provisions. When dealing with contracts, make sure to draft and read the boilerplate provisions carefully. These provisions affect your legal rights just as much as the other parts of the contract.

Provisions to Limit Risk

Allocating Risk: As mentioned at the beginning of the chapter, one of the purposes of a contract is to limit the liabilities of the parties involved. Your contract should address the allocation of risk among parties. Examples of risk allocation provisions are listed below:

- ✓ **Force majeure** addresses "acts of God" and other external events such as war or labor strikes. This provision is written to either absolve the owner or contractor of costs associated with these occurrences.
- ✓ **Indemnification** absolves the indemnified party from any payment for losses and damages incurred by a third party. Simply put, it is a way to shift payment or liability for any loss or damage that has occurred. Indemnification clauses must be examined carefully to ensure the proper liability is distributed between the contractor and owner.
- ✓ **Differing site conditions** provision allocates the responsibility for extra costs due to unexpected site conditions. As discussed in Chapter 7, the site conditions must be investigated and taken into consideration when putting together the bid. The owner is responsible for disclosing all site information during the bid process. If errors or omissions occur, the owner may be responsible for incurring the extra construction cost.
- ✓ **Warranties or guarantees** define the contractor's responsibility for the repair of defects to the construction project after the completion of work. Warranties are often set forth for a defined time period.
- ✓ **Delays and extensions of time** provide a contingency in the case that the completion deadline is not met. Delays at no fault of the contractor, such as changes by the owner or architect and environmental or severe weather delays, are generally not considered breach of contract. These types of delays are considered excusable and are granted time extensions. This contingency needs to be clearly outlined in the contract.
- ✓ **Schedule acceleration** provides assignment of costs incurred to complete a project ahead of schedule. In general, if the owner requires the contractor to accelerate the schedule, the owner is responsible for all associated costs. If the owner requests the schedule be accelerated due to project delays caused by the contractor, the contractor is generally liable for additional costs incurred.
- ✓ **Artistic changes** clause addresses changes made by the architect or design professional during the course of the project for artistic or creative purposes. The drawings and specifications outline the technical aspects of the project, but may not show the artistic objectives of the project. Including an artistic changes clause will put a limit on the number of changes that can occur as a result of artistic decisions.

Standard legal language must be used when specifying risk assignments to make the contract enforceable. Since legal language is often difficult to understand, it is recommended that you consult with legal counsel when drafting and/or interpreting these provisions.

What Are Recitals?

Background Information: Recitals are language at the beginning of the contract that provides background to the contract, such as the parties entering into the contract, the contract contents, and reasons for the parties' entering into the contract. Recitals cannot always be enforced by law, so it is important to provide specific terms throughout the contract.

Types of Construction Contracts

The differences in the types of contracts are primarily

- ✓ **who takes the risk that the work will be performed for the estimated cost;**
- ✓ **who pays for cost overruns; and**
- ✓ **who keeps the cost savings if the project performed is less than the estimate.**

Contracts between the owner and primary contractor may differ from contracts between the primary contractor and the subcontractors.

Lump-Sum Contract

In a lump-sum contract, the contractor agrees to complete the project for a predetermined, specified price. The contractor essentially assumes all of the risk under this contract agreement because the contractor is responsible for additional costs associated with unforeseen circumstances. For example, if extra cost is incurred due to inclement weather, the contractor must absorb these costs. Conversely, the contractor gets to keep any cost savings incurred.

If you use this type of contract, you may be required to formally submit a specific schedule and your quality assurance program, so your customer knows that you are completing the project to the highest standards. You should avoid this type of contract unless plans and specifications are detailed enough that a final cost can be determined in advance.

Unit-Price Contract

A unit-price contract may be used for jobs where the extent of work cannot be fully determined, or the actual quantities of required items cannot be accurately calculated in advance. A price per unit is calculated for each item and the contractor is paid according to the actual quantities used.

Cost-Plus Contract

Using the cost-plus contract method, the contractor is reimbursed for the actual cost of labor and materials and is paid a markup fee for overhead and profit. The cost-plus contract can be calculated different ways. The owner may pay the actual costs, plus a percentage markup or a fixed fee markup.

Contracting Methods

Single Prime

The single prime method is the traditional form of contracting. The project owner typically hires an architectural firm to design the project. The contractor then performs the work according to the specifications of the project and is responsible for the costs of all materials and labor to obtain project completion.

Design/Build

Using the design/build method of construction, the owner contracts with one company to complete the process from start to finish. The company awarded the design/build contract puts together a team of construction professionals, which may include designers, architects, engineers, and contractors that take a project from design through completed construction. The team works closely to satisfy the owner's needs within a predetermined budget.

Construction Management

Under the construction management method, the project owner contracts with a professional construction manager to coordinate and manage the project. The construction manager generally receives a fee to manage, coordinate, and supervise the construction process from the conceptual development stage through final construction. Work must be performed in a timely manner and on an economical basis.

Turnkey

Turnkey construction is similar to the design/build construction model. In addition to managing the construction and design team, the contractor also obtains financing and land. Under the turnkey model, the construction firm is obligated to complete a project according to pre-specified criteria but with expanded responsibilities and liability. A price is generally fixed at the time the contract is signed.

Fast-Track Construction

Under fast-track construction management, the construction process begins before completion of the contract documents. Fast-track construction involves a phased approach to the project. A contract may be drawn up for each phase. Generally, the cost is not fixed until after construction documents are complete and some construction commitments have already been made.

Multiple Prime Contracts

Large construction projects may involve multiple prime contracts. The owner may contract with two or more prime contractors to complete the same project. This contracting method may integrate elements of the construction management and fast-track construction models. The owner takes on a more active role in managing the different prime contractors. Contractor and owner obligations must be clearly defined in the contract.

Partnering

Partnering starts with setting common objectives and goals for a construction project. All parties involved, such as the owner, design professionals, engineers, and contractors, work together to achieve these objectives and goals. Several meetings are held throughout the bid and construction process to evaluate the decisions made by all parties and adjustments occur when necessary. Partnering increases communication and trust, consequently reducing potential litigation and claims.

Sources of Contracts

Standard forms for contracts are readily available through many sources. There are numerous books available that provide sample contracts and forms. Associations such as the American Institute of Architects (AIA) or the Associated General Contractors (AGC) also have standard forms for contracts.

In situations where the form of the contract is not written by you, it is important to

- ✓ read the contract very carefully;
- ✓ highlight anything that is vaguely worded for further clarification;
- ✓ make necessary additions;
- ✓ review changes with the other party;
- ✓ make sure any requested changes have been added prior to signing; and
- ✓ review the contract again, prior to signing.

Always make sure you keep a signed copy of every contract that you sign, in case you need to refer to it in the future.

Making Changes to the Contract

A **change order** is a written agreement between the owner and contractor to change the contract. Change orders add to, delete from, or otherwise alter the work set forth in the construction documents. Change orders are standard in the construction industry as a legal means for making changes to the contract.

Common reasons for generating a change order include

- ✓ change in scope (for example, owner requests a design change or owner exceeds allowance amount);
- ✓ unforeseen conditions when site conditions differ from the expected; and
- ✓ errors or omissions in the construction plans or specifications.

The AIA and AGC have standardized forms that you can use to execute change orders. Change orders are legally binding and it is important that all of the provisions are clear to both parties. Change orders should include

- ✓ date of change order;
- ✓ description of the change in work;
- ✓ reason for change;
- ✓ change in contract price;
- ✓ change, if any, in contracted time; and
- ✓ signatures from both parties.

Chapter 10 also discusses how to handle change orders from a customer relations perspective.

Changes prior to the contract award are called **addenda**. Changes made after the contract is signed and executed are called **modifications**.

Resolving Claims

The claims resolution process provides a way for the owner and contractor to resolve disputes about additional amounts owed as a result of contract changes. As discussed in the previous section, the purpose of written change orders is to avoid disputes. If a change is made to the contract without a change order, claims may arise.

Claims Procedure: The contract may stipulate specific procedures for handling claims. Many times, the contract defers to the architect to initially resolve claims. If claims cannot be resolved by the architect, the contractor and owner may proceed to mediation. If mediation fails, the next step is arbitration. The contract should outline the time allowed to request arbitration. A typical deadline for an arbitration request is 30 days from the time the architect makes a decision on the claim.

Project Schedule: During the claims resolution process, the project cannot be delayed. All schedules and deadlines must be followed. The only exception is disputes involving safety. Work must cease on the disputed activities until all safety issues are resolved.

Alternative Dispute Resolution

Alternative dispute resolution (ADR) involves settling legal disputes by avoiding the often costly and time intensive process of a government judicial trial. The most common forms of ADR are: negotiation, mediation, collaborative law, and arbitration.

Negotiation: Negotiation is a dialogue entered into for the purpose of resolving disputes or producing an agreed upon course or courses of action. Negotiation is inexpensive and generally the first step in ADR. Negotiation allows for an unstructured discussion between both parties and generally does not involve anyone other than the affected parties. If an agreement is not reached, more formal methods of dispute resolution are required.

Mediation: In mediation, the parties themselves set forth the conditions of any agreement with dialogue facilitated by an independent, third party mediator. The mediator is not a judge or arbitrator who sets forth the terms of an agreement, rather a mediator is a trained professional in negotiations and the process of mediation. The goal of mediation is to find areas of agreement between the parties involved by using strategies and techniques designed to allow the parties to work towards a mutual and fair agreement. If a settlement is not reached, the dispute may go through mediation again or sent to litigation arbitration. The option to take legal disputes to mediation is desirable from a cost perspective because it is generally less expensive and allows for a quicker resolution than going to trial.

Collaborative Law: Collaborative law is a facilitative process wherein all parties agree at the onset to work to identify a solution that is beneficial to all parties involved. In collaborative law, the parties use their advocates, most often their lawyers, to facilitate a mutually beneficial result through the process of negotiation. There is no neutral mediator or arbitrator involved and the parties are expected to reach a settlement without using further methods of ADR or litigation.

Arbitration: Arbitration uses a third-party arbitrator or arbitrators to act as a judge or judges to render a decision by which all parties are legally bound. Arbitration is held in a format less formal than a trial. The arbitrator(s), unlike a mediator, is not involved in the negotiation discussion towards a settlement. Arbitrators may be attorneys or retired judges who serve individually or as a panel. They are either chosen by the parties involved in the dispute or appointed by the court according to the terms of the contract. Arbitrators with industry-specific experience (such as construction litigation experience) may be appointed to certain types of disputes. The decision or arbitral award made by the arbitrator(s) is legally binding unlike in mediation. Many times, contracts call for disputes to be resolved through arbitration over taking matters to a costly trial. Arbitration may be required by law for certain types of disputes. Nearly all states have adopted the federal Uniform Arbitration Act making arbitral awards binding by both state and federal law.

Making Substitutions

When bidding on a project, many contractors bid from their normal manufacturers and suppliers and not the manufacturer that appears on the plans. When bidding, you need to make sure that you can pay for the cost of all items and products as specified. Failure to do so may cost you a lot of money.

Substitution Approval Process: The best way to ensure a specific substitution is by the "prior approval" process. A "prior approval" occurs during the bid stage only. If a particular product or item is desired other than the specified item, you must submit a request while the project is being bid. If approved, all bidders will be allowed to use that item or product in their bids. That is why the "prior approval" is done in the bidding stage. It keeps the playing field level for all competitors.

Substitutions After the Bid Process: A substitution may be made after the bid has been accepted. Nevertheless, any substitution must meet certain criteria to even be considered. The specifications should describe the conditions for such substitutions. Usually there are only four reasons that a substitution would be entertained:

- ✓ the specific item or product is no longer available;
- ✓ a cost savings;
- ✓ a time savings; or
- ✓ combination of cost and time savings.

Discontinued Products: A product no longer available is the only event, generally speaking, that will not require a change order reducing cost and/or time, unless it was approved under the "prior approval" process. Do not forget to note those reductions in the substitution request. The reason a reduction of cost and/or time is required is due to the fact that it is understood that the bid was based on the item or product that was specified. To make a change, the result must be a benefit to the owner; otherwise, there is no reason to make the substitution.

Substitution Specifications: If there is a basis for the substitution, the next trial is that the item or product must be equal to that which was specified. Just as the reference of a 2 x 4 to contractors is not measured as 2" x 4", its nomenclature is referred to as "nominal." Many other products are referred to as "nominal" sizing. HVAC systems are especially that way. Just because one manufacturer references a unit as five-tons, it does not mean that it produces the same capacity as a five-ton unit from another manufacturer under the same conditions.

The specifications must be analyzed carefully before submitting the substitution request. Be sure to cover the cost of the specified item, as a substitution may not be granted, not even in the "prior approval" process.

Contract Documents and Project Manual

The project manual is a central location for bid documents, contract provisions, technical specifications, and addenda. This bound manual is a useful tool easily referenced on the jobsite. It can be reproduced and distributed to contractors, subcontractors, and suppliers. The following is a detailed summary of the documents contained in a typical project manual.

Bid Documents:

- ✓ Invitation to bid
- ✓ Bid instructions
- ✓ Bid forms
- ✓ Supplements
- ✓ Addenda

Contract Provisions:

- ✓ Form of agreement
- ✓ General conditions or obligation of parties
- ✓ Supplemental conditions
- ✓ Change orders
- ✓ Index of drawings

Supplemental Forms:

- ✓ Required bonds
- ✓ Certificate of insurance

Technical Specifications are generally organized by a classification system, such as the CSI MasterFormat.

The **construction drawings** are also part of the contract documents. For larger projects, the drawings are divided by design discipline and trades. Drawings may include but are not limited to:

- ✓ architectural,
- ✓ structural,
- ✓ plumbing,
- ✓ electrical,
- ✓ mechanical,
- ✓ landscape, and
- ✓ civil.

The drawings are kept separate but can be indexed in the project manual.

Are Oral Agreements Legally Binding?

Under most circumstances, oral agreements are just as binding as written agreements with a few exceptions. Exceptions include contracts which have a high risk of fraud such as the sale or purchase of land. Oral agreements present a challenge because it is difficult to prove what terms were agreed upon if a dispute arises. Needless to say, it is a risky way to do business and it is best to get everything in writing.

Sometimes parties enter into agreements that are partially oral and partially written. For example, you may have carefully put together a written contract to do work. The customer then verbally gives you a change order. Now you are in a situation where you have an oral agreement for the change. To protect yourself, it is best to follow up with a written change order. In a legal judgment, written agreements always take precedence over oral agreements.

Oral agreements are not a good way to do business. Get it in writing!

Legal Interpretation

Clarity of language and meaning is one of the most important aspects of interpreting contracts and avoiding disputes. It is strongly recommended that you use an attorney when drafting contracts to ensure that the contract will stand up in a dispute. There are also necessary provisions that should be included in a contract. A contract lawyer can advise you on this matter.

The use of plain language is important when establishing intent in a contract. If a dispute arises, the contract will be interpreted using the plain meaning of the words in the contract. If your contract goes to litigation, the judge may not have a background in the construction industry. This is why it is important to clearly state the terms in the contract using plain language.

Using technical terminology in contracts between parties who understand their technical meaning may be used. However, many customers may not understand technical jargon so you may want to use caution putting these terms in a contract. Rather, you should express your intentions in layman terms. Disputes may arise when parties do not understand undefined technical language and contract interpretation may not end up in your favor.

If the provision being disputed is vague, the actions of the parties will be examined first. If the parties conducted themselves consistently with what they thought the provision meant at that time, the provision would likely take that meaning. If the contract cannot be clarified based on this method, the interpretation will go against the party who wrote it.

Subcontracting

Subcontractors contract with the general contractor or other subcontractors to complete a portion of a larger project. The same principles that apply to owner/contractor contracts also apply to subcontracts.

Subcontracts should include similar content as owner/contractor contracts, such as

- ✓ Date
- ✓ Names and contact information of contracting parties
- ✓ Name and location of project
- ✓ Description of the work to be performed
- ✓ Subcontract time or start and completion date
- ✓ Payment terms, including progress payment schedule and final payment
- ✓ Conditions for schedule delays
- ✓ Drawings and specifications
- ✓ Contract sum
- ✓ Any general and supplemental conditions that apply
- ✓ Signatures from both parties

Depending on the stipulations in the owner/contractor agreement, the owner may need to approve subcontractors.

It is also important to get subcontracts in writing to avoid disputes. In providing a written contract, both parties have a clear understanding of the agreement. Oral contracts can lead to ambiguity and one party may interpret the agreement differently than the other.

Clarity is very important to an enforceable contract.

Final Inspection...

Required Contract Elements: Required contract elements include offer and acceptance, consideration, competent parties, and legal purpose.

Contract Provisions: Your contract should contain provisions that clearly outline the terms of the contract. A few key provisions you want to include are contract price and payment terms, obligation of the parties, and breach of contract.

Breach of Contract: A breach of contract occurs when one of the parties involved fails to perform in accordance with any of the terms and conditions of the contract.

Boilerplate Provisions: These provisions contain standard language designed to protect you in the event of a lawsuit.

Provisions to Limit Risk: These provisions limit the liability of the contracting parties by addressing allocation of risk.

What Are Recitals? This language appears at the beginning of the contract and is intended to give background information.

Types of Construction Contracts: Different types of contracts address who is responsible for cost savings and overruns for estimated work.

Contracting Methods: Depending on the level of involvement in a construction project, different types of contracting methods are used.

Sources of Contracts: Contracts are available through several different sources, including associations such as the American Institute of Architects (AIA) or the Associated General Contractors (AGC).

Making Changes to the Contract: To change the contract, a change order is written and agreed upon by the owner and contractor.

Resolving Claims: The claims resolution process provides a way for the owner and contractor to resolve disputes about additional amounts owed as a result of contract changes.

Alternative Dispute Resolution (ADR): This process involves settling legal disputes by avoiding the process of a government judicial trial. The most common forms of ADR are: negotiation, mediation, collaborative law, and arbitration.

Making Substitutions: The specifications must be analyzed carefully before submitting the substitution request. Substitutions may be granted if products are discontinued or to provide a cost or time savings.

Contract Documents and Project Manual: The project manual is a central location for bid documents, contract provisions, technical specifications, and addenda.

Are Oral Agreements Legally Binding? Oral agreements can be binding, but it makes good business sense to get a contract in writing.

Legal Interpretation: Clarity of language and meaning in contracts is important to avoid disputes and ensure proper legal interpretation in the event of a lawsuit.

Subcontracting: The same principles that apply to owner/contractor contracts also apply to subcontracts. Similar language is used to ensure that each party is clear on terms and conditions of the contract.

Chapter 9
SCHEDULING AND PROJECT MANAGEMENT

Chapter Survey...

- ⇨ *Scheduling Process*
- ⇨ *Scheduling Methods*
- ⇨ *Scheduling and Cash Management*
- ⇨ *What is Project Management?*
- ⇨ *Who is the Project Manager?*
- ⇨ *Project Supervisory Team*
- ⇨ *Project Life Cycle*
- ⇨ *Tracking the Progress of the Project*
- ⇨ *Budget and Cost Controls*
- ⇨ *Quality Assurance*
- ⇨ *Value Engineering*

Many construction jobs are performed every day without using a formal scheduling method. Knowing how to schedule and organize your tasks helps you complete projects on time, which increases your customer satisfaction and ultimately your competitive edge.

Using the quantity take-off method, as explained in Chapter 7, you developed the basis for your project schedule. Each task was assigned the number of labor hours for completion to determine labor cost. Scheduling takes the list of tasks and labor hours and assigns an order of completion.

Scheduling Process

Planning is a key element to formulating an accurate schedule and effectively managing the project. Planning allows you to visualize the project and anticipate potential conflicts and challenges. The project start and completion dates are outlined in the contract. It is the job of the scheduler to fit in all necessary tasks within this time frame in the most efficient manner.

Sequence of Tasks: Understanding the correct sequence of tasks is critical to completing your project on time. As you created your estimate (discussed in Chapter 7), you probably listed your tasks in the order of completion. This determination is particularly important when scheduling subcontractors. Be sure to review the tasks outlined in the estimate and make any corrections, if necessary, to the sequence of tasks.

Some tasks may be completed at the same time while other tasks must come before starting the next task. For example, interior and exterior paint may be applied at the same time but drywall must be completed before paint is applied.

Activity Duration: When creating your estimate, you determined the number of labor hours it takes to complete each task on the project. Using this estimate, you need to make a determination on the duration of the task. The duration of each task depends on a few factors:

- ✓ size of the project;
- ✓ labor hours estimated; and
- ✓ length of time dedicated to the task each day. For example, if a task is estimated at four hours but your crew only has two hours per day to work on the task, the activity duration is two working days.

When determining activity duration, it is important to have input from your subcontractors and the experienced members of your crew.

Once the duration is determined for each activity, you can compare the total time against the project completion time outlined in the contract. If the total time exceeds the project completion time, adjustments must be made. Consideration must be given to increasing labor resources, requiring overtime, or extending the project completion date. These options must be weighed carefully due to added costs and possible timeline conflicts with the owner.

Contingency Time: Contingency time is used as a buffer between tasks to protect against unforeseen task delays. To determine contingency time, the task is analyzed to determine the likelihood of a delay occurring. A few general rules apply to determine contingency time.

- ✓ Tasks subject to weather delays require more contingency time.
- ✓ Standard work requires less contingency time than custom work.
- ✓ Tasks performed in areas with limited access require more contingency time.

With contingency time in place, the likelihood of a delayed task impacting the entire schedule is reduced.

Task Time Ranges: After completing the sequence of tasks, activity duration, and contingency time, the earliest and latest start date and earliest and latest end date are calculated. If the task completion falls outside these dates during the construction process, the project manager has an accurate calculation of the amount of time the project is ahead or behind.

Float Time: Float time is the remaining time after a task is complete and before the next task begins.

- ✓ The amount of time an activity can be delayed without impacting the early start of the next activity is called free float time.
- ✓ Total float time refers to the amount of leeway allowed in starting or completing an activity without delaying the project completion date.
- ✓ Activities with "zero float" are considered critical activities.

Scheduling Methods

A schedule is your blueprint to finishing the project on time. There are three main types of scheduling methods used in the construction industry:

- ✓ **Calendar Scheduling**
- ✓ **Bar Chart Scheduling**
- ✓ **Critical Path Method**

The type of schedule you use depends on factors such as project size, complexity, and location.

Calendar Scheduling

Calendar scheduling is a simple method and can be done on a regular desk calendar. The primary advantage to this method is that you can link project tasks to specific dates, such as

- ✓ dates of other projects,
- ✓ delivery dates of materials,
- ✓ payment schedules, and
- ✓ employee vacations and holidays.

To create a calendar schedule, you need to know the sequence of tasks and activity duration. After these factors are determined, you can plug the activities into the calendar.

The following is a sample calendar schedule. Calendar scheduling works for smaller, less complex projects but is not recommended for large ones.

SAMPLE CALENDAR SCHEDULE

Project Name: ____________ Start Date: ____________ End Date: ____________

Sunday	Monday	Tuesday	Wednesday	Thursday	Friday	Saturday
1 Off	2 Excavation	3	4 Layout Slab Foundation Forms	5 Under-ground Plumbing	6 Pour Concrete	7 Concrete Cure Time
8 Concrete Cure Time	9	10	11 Frame Exterior Walls	12	13	14 Off
15 Off	16 Frame Roof	17 Install Doors & Windows	18	19 Lay Roofing Materials	20	21
22 Off	23 Electrical Rough-In Plumbing Rough-In	24	25 HVAC	26 Siding	27	28 Off
29 Off	30 Siding Insulation	31	1 Install Drywall Paint Exterior	2	3	4 Off
5 Off	6 Install Wood/Tile Flooring	7	8	9 Install Trim	10	11 Off
12 Off	13 Paint Interior	14	15 Finish Electrical Finish Plumbing	16	17 Install Carpeting	18 Site Clean-up

Bar Chart Scheduling

Just as the calendar scheduling method, the bar chart schedule also shows the activity duration and sequence of tasks to be completed. It is an easy-to-read visual showing a graphical depiction of the schedule in its entirety.

One of the main weaknesses of the bar chart and calendar scheduling methods is that they do not show the interdependencies of the activities.

For example, if there is a delay in a task, the bar chart does not show the impact it has on the other tasks. The following is a sample bar chart schedule.

SCHEDULE BAR CHART FOR RETAIL STORE CONSTRUCTION

Description of Tasks	March				April				May				June			
	W1	W2	W3	W4	W1	W2	W3	W4	W1	W2	W3	W4	W1	W2	W3	W4
Contract Award	■															
Field Survey		■														
Documents Reviewed		■														
Building Permit			■	■												
Pre-Meeting				■												
Demolition				■												
Door & Windows					■											
Electrical Rough In					■	■										
Plumbing Rough In					■	■										
Lighting						■	■									
HVAC						■										
Fire Protection						■										
Ceiling					■	■										
Drywall						■	■									
Plumbing Fixtures							■									
Caulking & Sealants							■									
Flooring								■	■							
Cash Wrap										■	■	■				
Product Racks										■	■	■				
Electrical Fixtures												■				
Painting												■	■			
Signage												■	■			
Construction Cleaning														■		
Project Closeout															■	

Critical Path Method

The critical path method (CPM) of scheduling illustrates the interdependent relationships of tasks. To develop a CPM schedule, you start by determining the sequence of tasks and activity duration as you would with bar chart or calendar scheduling. In addition, you need to outline the following:

- ✓ Relationship between tasks
- ✓ Simultaneous events
- ✓ Critical path

Relationship between Tasks: Most construction tasks are interrelated. For example, you can't start framing until you pour the foundation. A CPM schedule graphically shows which tasks are related and which ones are not. When you create your CPM schedule, you need to determine how each task impacts another.

Simultaneous Events: If you know which tasks can be performed simultaneously, you can shorten project completion time. When creating the CPM schedule, you must show when simultaneous tasks are possible.

Critical Path: The critical path is the sequence of tasks that determines the duration of the project. If a task on the critical path is delayed by one week, the project is delayed by one week. You must know which subsequent tasks cannot begin until a critical path item is completed.

The following diagram illustrates a simple critical path example.

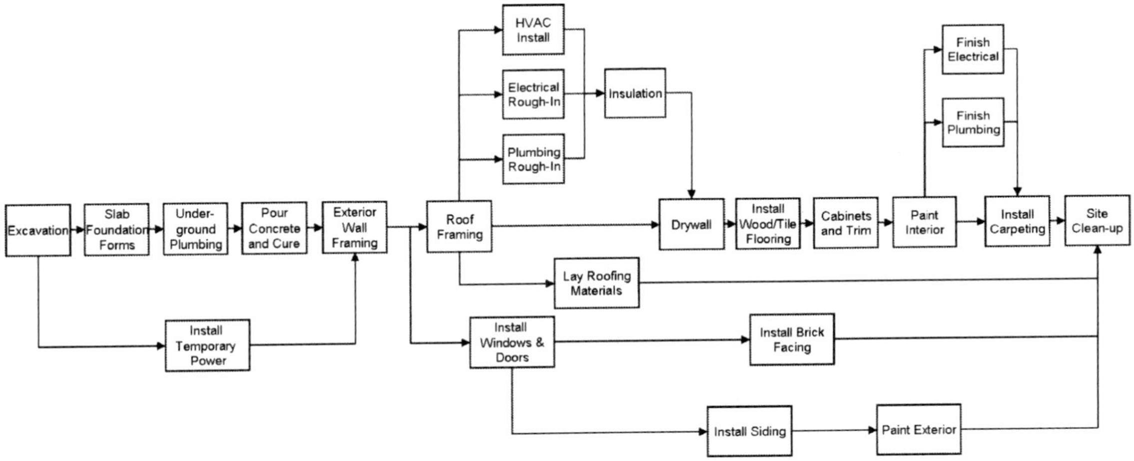

Adding Activity Duration to the CPM Schedule: The CPM schedule can be placed against a timeline. An example of this is illustrated in the bar chart schedule earlier in the chapter. Another alternative is to place the activity duration with each task. You can also put a code with the activity to correlate it to your estimate. If you use your estimating format, you could use the CSI MasterFormat to code the tasks in your schedule. For example, let's say the task of painting the interior has a three-day duration and you use MasterFormat code 09900. Your task might look like this on the CPM chart.

Paint Interior	
09900	3

Many different types of software are available to help you create schedules. You want to choose a program that is right for your needs whether they are simple or more complex. Some programs allow you to adjust the timelines if, for example, you experience a delay in the project. Scheduling software also facilitates the tracking function of a project schedule, which is a key project management tool.

Scheduling and Cash Management

It is important to track your incoming cash and expenditures during the construction project to ensure you have enough working capital to complete the job. "Working capital" refers to the amount of cash available after the liabilities or debts are paid. Balancing incoming progress payments and outgoing expenditures is important to manage the project effectively and should be a consideration when preparing your schedule.

If you have more expenditures than incoming cash in any stage of construction, you may not have enough money to proceed to the next stage of construction or pay your debts.

A preliminary cash flow budget, outlining stages of construction with anticipated revenues and expenditures, should be completed during the scheduling phase to anticipate any cash shortages. Cash flow should be tracked through the duration of the project.

What is Project Management?

Effective project management is a challenging task on a construction project. It involves a carefully balanced combination of management skills with an understanding of the design and construction process. Project managers may manage several projects at the same time with projects at different stages of the process. A project manager not only has to manage time through the scheduling process but must also consider many other factors:

- ✓ Budget constraints
- ✓ Quality standards
- ✓ Project plans and specifications
- ✓ Resource management such as labor, materials, etc.

Project management has applications that are unique in nearly every industry, including construction.

The ability to effectively manage significantly contributes to the success or failure of the project.

Who is the Project Manager?

Construction project managers plan and coordinate construction projects to meet the overall goals of the project and serve as the main contact with the owner. Responsibilities generally include but are not limited to

- ✓ preparing budgets;
- ✓ reviewing shop drawings to determine appropriate construction methods;
- ✓ determining labor requirements and preparing schedules;
- ✓ monitoring overall progress of the project and preparing job records;
- ✓ monitoring compliance with building and safety codes;
- ✓ ensuring proper handling of change orders; and
- ✓ regularly meeting with owners, trade contractors, architects, and other design professionals on project progress.

Construction project managers work closely with the project superintendent who manages the daily site operations.

Construction managers may be owners or salaried employees of a construction management or contracting firm, or they may work under contract or as a salaried employee of the owner, developer, contractor, or management firm overseeing the construction project. They may plan and direct a whole project or just a part of a larger project.

What Qualities Does a Good Manager Need?

A good manager must possess several qualities to effectively lead a team.

- ✓ Good communication skills
- ✓ Honesty and integrity
- ✓ Positive attitude
- ✓ Effective delegation skills
- ✓ Team and morale building skills

Project Supervisory Team

While the project manager has a high level understanding of the project, supervisors coordinate and monitor the daily aspects of the project. Depending on the size of the project, the number of supervisory team members may vary.

Superintendent: The superintendent is the onsite supervisor responsible for the daily operations. Depending on the size of the project and amount of responsibility the project manager wants to delegate, the superintendent's duties may include

- ✓ coordinating the project activities and serving as a liaison with subcontractors, architects, utilities, and others;
- ✓ participating in the project construction development and planning;
- ✓ processing utility requests for construction projects;
- ✓ representing the company regarding onsite construction quality control reviews;
- ✓ making recommendations and processing change order requests;
- ✓ reviewing punch lists;
- ✓ assuring construction specifications are met;
- ✓ tracking deviations from project schedules and costs; and
- ✓ maintaining project records and reports.

Communication between the project manager and superintendent is important to keeping the project on-time and within budget and providing a quality product.

Foreman: The foreman assists the superintendent in the daily project operations. The superintendent generally oversees all of the daily operations, but the foreman usually supervises specific areas by trade. For example, a carpentry foreman may supervise rough and finish carpentry while the masonry foreman supervises formwork and concrete installation.

The foreman assists the supervisor by

- ✓ reviewing project plans and blueprints;
- ✓ providing input to estimated time, material, equipment and supplies needed;
- ✓ developing schedules and crew assignments;
- ✓ inspecting work areas;
- ✓ evaluating employee and subcontractor performance;
- ✓ completing time sheets, accident reports, and work orders; and
- ✓ training employees.

Materials Expediter: Timely delivery of materials is important to keeping a project schedule on track.

A materials expediter supervises the materials procurement process to ensure accurate and timely delivery of materials.

Later in the chapter, we will discuss the importance of effective materials management.

Architect and Owner's Representative: The owner will sometimes defer to an appointed representative to oversee a project. In this case, the owner's representative and/or architect will deal with the project manager. The owner's representative and architect usually do not have supervisory authority over the employees and subcontractors but they may communicate with the project manager in order to express any concerns with the project work.

In general, the owner's representative and architect have access to the jobsite and work records and can contribute to the quality control on the project. The architect (or sometimes the engineer) must certify each progress payment, so it is in the best interest of the project manager to work closely with the architect and owner's representative.

Project Life Cycle

Each project has a start point, project life cycle, and end point. Through each phase of the project life cycle, you must manage each aspect of the project such as customer relations, materials, budget, and subcontractors. Using the customer relations category, the following example illustrates various management aspects in the project life cycle.

Contract Award

After you are successfully offered the job, you should get a contract signed as soon as possible. A few weeks before the job starts, schedule a pre-construction meeting with your customer and any other relevant parties (i.e., architect, subcontractors, etc.).

Pre-Construction Phase

During the pre-construction meeting, you should go over customer expectations. Chapter 10 discusses creating realistic expectations for your customer to avoid disappointment. At this time, you should have a preliminary schedule prepared, so potential scheduling conflicts can be discussed. Be sure to follow up with written notes taken at the meeting and distribute to those in attendance as well as those who could not attend.

Construction Phase

As the project progresses, you should carefully monitor the budget, schedule, and project quality. Regularly meet with your customer to discuss the progress of the project and any issues or questions that arise. If you are billing in progress payments, make sure that you are invoicing regularly and collecting payments within the defined terms.

Job Completion and Closeout

After the job is complete, you must do a walkthrough and develop a punch list of follow-up items. Discuss any warranties contained in your contract and how the customer can request warranty repairs. Send a customer satisfaction survey to gather feedback for future improvements.

Key Elements for a Successful Project Outcome

Many elements go into a successful project outcome:

- ✓ Project manager who understands the total project as a big picture
- ✓ Early preparation and planning
- ✓ Good management and front-line supervision
- ✓ Effective responses to problems and changes
- ✓ Active customer involvement
- ✓ Good communication skills

Tracking the Progress of the Project

Daily Reports

Many contractors find that keeping a daily log is a useful project tool. You can use a log to track the progress of a project and as a legal back up in case any disputes arise.

The daily log can list:

- ✓ Project name and location
- ✓ Date
- ✓ Weather conditions
- ✓ Personnel on the job
- ✓ Description of work
- ✓ Hours worked on each task
- ✓ Change orders
- ✓ Progress of the job
- ✓ Other relevant information

Personal comments should not be made in the daily report. It should just contain factual information.

There are specific guidelines you should follow to increase the credibility of the daily report, if a legal dispute arises.

- ✓ The report should be completed daily. If there was no work completed, note that fact and the reason for it.
- ✓ Writing should be in ink and not altered.
- ✓ Pages should be in consecutive order and in a bound book.

Photos are a good way to document the progress of a project and can serve as a supplement to the daily log. Photos should be taken of the site prior to starting work and at critical points during the project to document any problem areas of the project. Digital cameras make photo-taking easy with instant results. You also have the flexibility to store photos on your computer and send them through email.

Status Reports

Status reports are a summary of project highlights that address items completed, in progress, and outstanding. This report is a helpful communication tool to send to your customer, managers, subcontractors, and suppliers periodically throughout the project.

To support your status reports, you should have work records easily accessible for review. These work records include

- ✓ daily reports,
- ✓ project photographs,
- ✓ previous status reports,
- ✓ safety and accident reports,
- ✓ change orders,
- ✓ shop drawings,
- ✓ purchase orders,
- ✓ receiving documentation, and
- ✓ relevant written correspondence.

You should solicit feedback on any anticipated problems or concerns and encourage two-way communication throughout the project. Status reports are a good way to initiate this communication.

Tracking the Schedule

A good project manager makes sure that deadlines are met on time. As discussed earlier, the first step is to develop the schedule. Next, you want to make sure you communicate the schedule to anyone who is impacted by it, such as your crew, subcontractors, and suppliers. You need to make sure that they understand the deadlines and their assignments. You may want to present the schedule in a graphical format so team members can get a visual snapshot of the timeline.

Budget and Cost Controls

Project management involves working with budget constraints. A good project manager will control costs and make sure that the project comes in on budget.

If the budget is not monitored carefully, a job that was estimated correctly can turn into a loss for the company.

Materials

Just-In-Time (JIT): Just-in-time deliveries will keep your inventory cost low. This process will allow you to time deliveries to arrive as you need the materials in the construction process. Using your schedule, you can closely predict when you need the materials according to the work being completed and then coordinate this timing with your suppliers. Less inventory onsite will also cut down the risk of theft or vandalism.

Purchase Orders: Using a purchase order system can help you organize and document your materials purchases. If you prepare your purchase orders in advance, you can review these with your customers. This process can potentially reduce change orders by allowing customers to make decisions and sign off on them in advance. Your purchase orders can also serve as your delivery date documentation so you can organize your just-in-time deliveries.

Receiving: You can control material costs through proper receiving. When materials are delivered, someone should check the materials against the purchase order to confirm the correct quantity and items ordered were received. If there are discrepancies, follow up with the supplier as soon as possible to ensure you receive the proper credits or replacements.

To the best of your abilities, you want to estimate and order the correct amount of materials. If you have an excess of materials, check with your supplier for a return policy. Excess materials should be stored correctly to preserve their condition. Some suppliers charge a restocking fee, but it is generally nominal and worth your time to receive a materials credit.

Budget Tracking

The easiest way to track your budget is to use the cost estimate and a job cost system to determine if you have any cost overruns.

Cost overruns occur when you exceed the budgeted amounts in your estimate. These overruns can happen in many areas of the project such as exceeding the amount of labor through improper scheduling and excessive materials waste. Chapter 8, Contract Management, summarizes types of contracts that address who is responsible for cost overruns.

It is important to track costs as the project progresses because cost overruns can indicate a possible problem. The sooner these problems are identified, the easier it will be to take corrective action.

Cost overruns may occur because you have a bad estimate. Tracking your budget will help you or your estimator prepare more accurate estimates in the future.

Cost overruns reduce the amount of profit you make on the job. If you are not making a profit or you are losing money on your projects, you will eventually go out of business.

Quality Assurance

Ensuring the customer receives a quality built product is one of the most important aspects of project management. You may find ways to cut corners, but neglecting quality can cost you in the long run. You may also run into ethical considerations when neglecting quality. Concealing defective work and design flaws can leave you open to a lawsuit and ruin your reputation.

Accurate and Detailed Specifications and Plans

Accurate and detailed specifications and plans are important to setting the quality standards of the project. These items will help you put together a more accurate estimate and should be part of the contract documents. If details are vague, your decisions on material quality and construction methods may differ from the owner's. This misunderstanding can cause conflict and disappoint your customer. It is best to set expectations and obtain agreement from the customer early in the project.

Detailed Shop Drawings

In addition to the specifications and plans, shop drawings are often required to detail specific aspects of a project. Shop drawings may outline specific details, materials, dimensions, and installation for specific items. Product data and samples may accompany shop drawings to provide additional information. Shop drawings are produced by the material supplier, contractor, subcontractor, or manufacturer. As part of the quality control process, the architect and contractor must review and approve shop drawings.

Quality Assurance Program

Setting up a quality assurance program is a good way to let your employees and customers know the importance of producing a high quality product. Internal inspections should take place at different stages of the construction process to review the completed work and confirm that it meets your quality standards.

Your company philosophy should stress quality. You want your employees to take pride in their work. As an employer, you can create a positive work atmosphere and provide the tools employees need to be successful. Providing ongoing training for employees so they can expand their knowledge base can help improve the quality of their work. Employees should know the standards they are expected to follow. Documenting work standards and conducting regular performance reviews are good ways to create a mutual understanding of the level of quality you expect.

Customer Satisfaction Surveys

Customer satisfaction surveys are also a good tool to receive feedback about the quality of your work. Customer surveys are good for asking about the professionalism of your employees, quality of work, and overall service. Potential customers may be interested that you have a continuous improvement program. Positive feedback from your current or former customers can serve as a good marketing tool to gain new business.

Value Engineering

Value engineering is a project management approach. The objective is to understand the owner's cost, quality, and time priorities to deliver a product of the highest value. Many owners will provide incentives to contractors to meet these objectives. For example, an owner may provide a bonus for a contractor who can cut costs without sacrificing quality while meeting all deadlines. If value engineering bonuses exist, it is important that they are included in the construction contract.

The Society of American Value Engineering International (SAVE) publishes a methodology for the construction industry. The purpose of this methodology is to reduce costs, improve productivity, and develop innovative ways to solve problems.

Final Inspection...

Scheduling Process: During the project scheduling process, the sequence of tasks, activity duration, contingency time, task time ranges, and float time are determined.

Scheduling Methods: The three main types of scheduling are calendar scheduling, bar chart scheduling, and critical path method (CPM).

Scheduling and Cash Management: Effective cash management helps ensure that you have enough working capital to complete your project.

What is Project Management? Project management involves managing several different factors including budgets, quality controls, project plans and specifications, and resource management.

Who is the Project Manager? The ability to manage effectively contributes significantly to the success or failure of a project.

Project Supervisory Team: Depending on the size of the project, the supervisory team may consist of a superintendent, foreman, materials expediter, architect, and owner's representative.

Project Life Cycle: Through each phase of the project life cycle, you must manage each aspect of the project such as customer relations, materials, budget, and subcontractors.

Tracking the Progress of the Project: A good project manager makes sure that deadlines are met on time. Daily reports and status reports are tools you can use to track your progress.

Budget and Cost Controls: A good project manager will control costs and make sure that the project comes in on budget.

Quality Assurance: Ensuring that the customer receives a quality built product is one of the most important aspects of project management.

Value Engineering: Balancing the owner's cost, quality, and time priorities while delivering the highest value product are objectives of the value engineering approach.

Chapter 10
CUSTOMER RELATIONS

Chapter Survey...

- ⇨ *Communication with Customers*
- ⇨ *Handling Customer Change Orders*
- ⇨ *Negotiation Basics*

Understanding Expectations: You will find customers have specific expectations of the outcome of your work. If those expectations are not satisfied, your customers will be disappointed, which will reflect poorly on your company. Instead of promising your customers an unrealistic outcome, it is easier to be honest and bring expectations to a realistic level. If customers have a realistic picture of the project, you can avoid disappointing them. The best way to accomplish this is through consistent and effective communication with your customers.

Communication with Customers

It is important for customers to understand the status of their project and have all the information needed to make informed decisions. This communication will not only keep the customer's expectations realistic but also build a trusting relationship with you and your company.

Communication Opportunities: You have several opportunities to communicate with your customers and keep their expectations at a realistic level, including

- ✓ contract negotiations,
- ✓ contract acceptance,
- ✓ weekly meetings,
- ✓ punch list and final walkthrough, and
- ✓ post-job follow-up.

Establishing communication at these times will ensure that your customer is aware of your progress and of issues that arise during any step of the process.

Communication Basics: Now that we have established when to communicate with customers, let's go over a few basics on how to communicate.

- ✓ Understand that your customer may not have the same level of technical knowledge as you. Avoid using technical terminology and clarify when necessary.
- ✓ Give your customer a chance to ask questions and express any concerns. Use active listening skills, and remember that all questions are important to the customer.
- ✓ When dealing with difficult customers, always remain professional.
- ✓ Use email or written communication as a follow-up to verbal conversations to document key items discussed and any changes agreed to.
- ✓ Don't forget the personal touch. Email and fax are great tools, but schedule time to talk to the customer in person.
- ✓ Return phone calls promptly.

Good communication can build customer trust and help you understand customer expectations.

Handling Customer Change Orders

Proper handling of customer change orders is very important. This is a critical point in the customer-contractor relationship that can result in a positive or negative outcome. If you do not follow through with the change order as the customer expects, it will result in disappointment and mistrust. If you follow through to the customer's specifications, you will reinforce that you are responsive and understand the importance of customer service.

You should always apply a few general rules when change orders arise:

- ✓ Always obtain a signed change order for significant amounts of change work.
- ✓ Small changes done with verbal approval should be followed up with a written and signed change order.
- ✓ Invoice for change order work promptly.
- ✓ Include any complimentary work done without charge on the invoice.
- ✓ Show labor and quantity details when pricing change orders as you would when creating your initial estimate.

Negotiation Basics

Good negotiation skills can benefit you personally and in all areas of your business. When a successful negotiation occurs, both parties are satisfied with the outcome.

Preparing to Negotiate: Negotiation is a process and it is important to prepare ahead of time to get the most out of the negotiation. Considering these questions will help:

- ✓ What are you negotiating (i.e., money, time, conditions, etc.)?
- ✓ What is the ideal outcome?
- ✓ How much are you willing to compromise?
- ✓ What is the other person trying to achieve?

A negotiation may not always involve price. Consider what is valuable to your business. For example, if time is a critical factor to completing your current projects, you may want to negotiate on project timelines. It is important not to compromise your reputation in a negotiation. You don't want to lose your best customer or future referrals.

Confident Negotiations: Now that you are prepared, you can come to the negotiation confident in knowing what you want. Aim high in your negotiation and you will get more. If you ask for more than you want, people will tend to meet you in the middle. It is important to be flexible during the negotiation. Even though you have prepared ahead of time, the other party may change the direction of the negotiation to different terms. For example, you may have prepared to negotiate on price, but your counterpart may want to deal on the timeline of the work.

When possible, it is important to get the final outcome of your negotiation in writing. Once it is in writing, both parties can sign off on what they agreed to, which will help avoid any disappointment or confusion.

Final Inspection...

Communication with Customers: Good communication helps you build trust and understand customer expectations.

Handling Customer Change Orders: Change orders should be handled carefully and accurately documented.

Negotiation Basics: Come to a negotiation prepared, and, when possible, make sure you get any agreement in writing.

Chapter 11
EMPLOYEE MANAGEMENT

Chapter Survey...

- *Interviewing and Hiring Employees*
- *New Hire Reporting*
- *Hiring Minors for Construction Work*
- *Employee Documentation*
- *Key Employment Laws*
- *Fair Labor Standards Act (FLSA)*
- *Immigration and Nationality Act*
- *Americans with Disabilities Act (ADA)*
- *Other Labor Laws*
- *South Carolina Payment of Wage Laws and Recordkeeping Requirements*
- *Required Postings*
- *Employee Handbook and Policies*
- *Employee Satisfaction*
- *Providing Benefits*
- *Disciplining Employees*
- *Terminating Employees*
- *Sample I-9 Form*

Finding good, hardworking employees can sometimes mean the difference between success and failure in business. It is easier to delegate to good employees and produce high-quality work from employees who care about their job. Bad employees can cost a company wasted time and ultimately money. The first step to finding good employees is taking the extra time to hire the right people for the job.

Employees should start off with a few fundamental qualities. They should be

- ✓ qualified for the position;
- ✓ motivated to do the job and show initiative;
- ✓ responsible for their work and actions;
- ✓ dependable to show up on time and keep work commitments; and
- ✓ open to learning new skills.

These basic qualities will result in an employee who is capable of performing their present job responsibilities and taking on more tasks in the future.

Interviewing and Hiring Employees

Asking Questions: Asking the right interview questions is a key aspect in finding the right employees. The wrong interview questions can get you into trouble. You must convey that you are a fair and non-discriminatory employer. If you ask questions implying otherwise, you will open yourself to a lawsuit. Some questions could lead to legal action and are strictly off-limits, especially the following:

- ✓ How old are you?
- ✓ Do you have any disabilities?
- ✓ Are you pregnant?
- ✓ Are you married?
- ✓ Do you have children?
- ✓ What is your religious affiliation?
- ✓ What is your sexual orientation?
- ✓ What ethnic background are you?

Your interview should focus on the skills, experience, and qualities the candidate has and how these fit with the job position and your company culture.

Hiring the right people for the job is the first step to finding good employees.

New Hire Reporting

Reporting Requirements: You are required to report all new employees to the South Carolina New Hire Reporting System no later than 20 days from the date of hire or rehire. There are several reporting methods you can use:

Internet: South Carolina has a reporting system that will allow you to register and report online. There are two methods of reporting through this website: newhire.sc.gov.

- ✓ Smaller employers (i.e., those reporting fewer than 20 new employees per session) and those reporting for a small number of employers (i.e., fewer than five different employers) register using the online form.
- ✓ Employers with a large number of employees and those reporting for a large number of different employers should use the file transfer method. Usually, this method requires a great deal of technical knowledge and may prove to be too time-consuming for smaller employers.

Mail: A South Carolina New Hire form may be found on the following websites: dss.sc.gov/child-support/employer-resources/ or newhire.sc.gov.

The South Carolina Form, a copy of an employee W-4 form, or any form that contains the data elements listed below can be used:

- ✓ Employer Name
- ✓ Employer Address
- ✓ Employer Federal Identification Number
- ✓ Employer Phone Number (optional)
- ✓ Employee Name
- ✓ Employee Address
- ✓ Employee Social Security Number
- ✓ Employee Date of Birth (optional)
- ✓ Employee Date of Hire (optional)

The completed form can be mailed to:

South Carolina Department of Social Services
Financial Institution Data Match Program
Child Support Services Division
New Hire Reporting Program
P.O Box 1469
Columbia, South Carolina 29202-1469

(803) 898-9314 or 1-888-454-5294

Fax: You may fax completed forms to (803) 898-9100.

Tape and Diskette Reporting: You may also submit your data by diskette or tape. If an employer chooses to report by magnetic media or by electronic means, the employer is required to report newly-hired or rehired employees twice a month. If you need any assistance with reporting by diskette or tape, call New Hire Reporting at 1-888-454-5294.

- ✓ ***Purpose of New Hire Reporting:*** New hire information submitted by employers is used to establish and enforce child support orders and detect fraud in unemployment benefits, workers' compensation, and in other government programs, such as welfare and food stamps.

Penalties: The penalty for failing to report newly-hired or rehired employees is:

- ✓ $25 for the second offense and $25 for each offense thereafter; or
- ✓ $500 for each and every offense, if the failure to report is the result of a conspiracy between the employer and the employee not to supply the required information or to supply false or incomplete information.

Hiring Minors for Construction Work

The State of South Carolina and the U.S. Department of Labor have strict rules about the hiring of minors. The state statutes and regulations are not intended to be stricter than the federal laws. Employment of minors under the age of 14 is the most restricted.

Working Hours:

- ✓ When school is in session, a minor 14 or 15 years of age may not begin work before 7 a.m., work later than 7 p.m., or more than three hours a day, or more than 18 hours a week. Work is prohibited during school hours.
- ✓ A minor 14 or 15 years of age may not begin work before 7 a.m., work past 7 p.m. (9 p.m. during summer months when school is not in session), or more than eight hours a day, or more than 40 hours a week on non-school weeks.
- ✓ A minor 16 years of age or older does not have any time or scheduling restrictions.

Prohibited Tasks: Minors ages 14 or 15 years of age may work in office, clerical, and sales jobs. They are prohibited from performing certain job tasks, including the use of ladders or scaffolding and warehousing and storage. All minors are prohibited from employment in occupations considered hazardous. Specific tasks outlined as hazardous or detrimental that apply to the construction industry (with the exception of apprentices as defined by law) include

- ✓ operating power-driven woodworking machines or power-driven circular saws, band saws, or guillotine shears;
- ✓ operating a power-driven hoisting apparatus;
- ✓ operating power-driven metal-forming punching and shearing machines;
- ✓ driving any motor vehicle and being an outside helper;
- ✓ manufacturing brick, tile, and related products;
- ✓ roofing operations; and
- ✓ excavation operations.

Investigations: State or federal investigators may conduct investigations at any time, tour the business establishment or worksite, review employment records, and interview employees. If violations of child labor laws occur, the Department of Labor, Licensing and Regulation may assess penalties. First-offense violators are subject to a written warning and fines of up to $1,000. Second and subsequent offenses are subject to fines of up to $5,000.

Further Information: For further information on South Carolina Child Labor Law, contact:

South Carolina Department of Labor,
Licensing and Regulation
Wages and Child Labor
110 Centerview Drive
P. O. Box 11329
Columbia, South Carolina 29211-1329

Phone: (803) 896-4470

Fax: (803) 896-7680

Website: www.llr.state.sc.us

Employee Documentation

Once you hire an employee, you should make sure you set up an employee file.

These items should be included in your employee files:

- ✓ **Form I-9**: The United States Customs and Immigration Service requires this form. It shows that the worker has legal immigration status in the United States. (For more information on I-9s, see the following section on the Immigration and Nationality Act.)
- ✓ **IRS Form W-4**: This form is required to determine the appropriate level of federal tax withholding. Employees can change the amount of federal tax withholding at anytime by completing a new W-4 form.
- ✓ **State Tax Form**: This form is required to determine the appropriate level of state tax withholding, if applicable. South Carolina has adopted the use of the federal IRS W-4 form. In Chapter 15, Tax Basics, state income tax withholding will be covered in more detail. Additional information is also available at dor.sc.gov.
- ✓ **Employment Application**: All employees should complete an application before being hired. It should contain basic information such as the employee's name, address, and phone number. The application should also be signed, giving your company authorization to check references on the employment history section.
- ✓ **Policy Signoffs**: If you have written policies or an employee handbook, have your employees sign a receipt that the employee has received and reviewed it.
- ✓ **Emergency Notification Form**: It is important that you know who to contact in the event of an emergency. Make sure to update this information periodically.

The employee file should be maintained throughout employment and other relevant documentation can be added, such as disciplinary action forms or insurance enrollment forms.

Setting up employee files will help keep you organized.

Key Employment Laws

There are several key laws governing equal employment opportunities and prohibiting discrimination in employment. It is important to understand and abide by these laws, not only to protect your company from a lawsuit but also to safeguard your reputation as a good employer.

Fair Labor Standards Act (FLSA)

The Fair Labor Standards Act, which prescribes standards for the basic minimum wage and overtime pay, affects most private and public employment. It applies to employers who have one or more employees. Individual states may also have additional minimum wage requirements.

- ✓ Effective July 24, 2009, federal minimum wage increased to $7.25 per hour. Minors under 20 years of age may be paid a minimum wage of not less than $4.25 per hour during the first 90 consecutive calendar days of employment. Employers may not displace any employee to hire someone at the youth minimum wage.
- ✓ Employers must pay overtime compensation of one-and-one-half-times the regular rate after 40 hours of work in a workweek.
- ✓ Wages must be paid on the regular payday for the pay period covered.
- ✓ The act restricts the hours that children under age 16 can work and forbids the employment of children under age 18 in certain jobs deemed too dangerous.

FLSA is administered by the Employment Standards Administration's Wage and Hour Division within the U.S. Department of Labor.

Determining Exemption Status: Some employees are exempt from the overtime pay provisions or both the minimum wage and overtime pay provisions as defined under the Fair Labor Standards Act (FLSA). This rule would apply to the following examples of employees who might be employed in the construction industry:

- ✓ Executives
- ✓ Administrative personnel
- ✓ Professional employees
- ✓ Outside sales employees
- ✓ Employees in certain computer-related occupations as defined in the Department of Labor regulations

Workweek Defined under FLSA: A workweek is a period of 168 hours during seven consecutive 24-hour periods. It may begin on any day of the week and at any hour of the day established by the employer. Generally, for purposes of minimum wage and overtime payment, each workweek stands alone; you may not average two or more workweeks. Employee coverage, compliance with wage payment requirements, and the application of most exemptions are determined on a workweek basis.

Work Hours Defined Under FLSA: Work hours ordinarily include all time during which an employee is required to be on the employer's premises, on duty, or at a prescribed work place.

Bona fide meal periods (typically 30 minutes or more) generally need not be compensated as work time. The employee must be completely relieved from duty for the purpose of eating regular meals. The employee is not relieved if he or she is required to perform any duties, whether active or inactive, while eating.

Employment Practices Not Covered: While FLSA does set basic minimum wage and overtime pay standards and regulates the employment of minors, there are a number of employment practices that FLSA does not regulate.

FLSA does not require

- ✓ vacation, holiday, severance, or sick pay;
- ✓ meal or rest periods, holidays off, or vacations; or
- ✓ premium pay for weekend or holiday work.

Also, FLSA does not limit the number of hours in a day or days in a week an employee may be required or scheduled to work, including overtime hours, if the employee is at least 16 years old.

These matters not covered by FLSA are left for agreement between the employer and the employees or their authorized representatives. Individual state labor departments may have specific regulations separate from FLSA regarding these requirements.

For more information, contact:

South Carolina Department of Labor, Licensing and Regulation
Wages and Child Labor
110 Centerview Drive
P. O. Box 11329
Columbia, South Carolina 29211-1329

Phone: (803) 896-7756

Fax: (803) 896-7680

Website: www.llr.state.sc.us

Recordkeeping under the FLSA

The FLSA requires employers to keep records on wages, hours, and other items as specified in Department of Labor recordkeeping regulations. Most of this information is maintained by employers in ordinary business practice and in compliance with other laws and regulations. The records do not have to be kept in any particular form, and time clocks need not be used.

Required Information: For employees subject to the minimum wage provisions or both the minimum wage and overtime pay provisions, the following records must be kept:

- ✓ personal information, including employee's name, home address, occupation, sex, and birth date (if under 19 years of age);
- ✓ basis on which employee wages are paid;
- ✓ hour and day when workweek begins;
- ✓ total hours worked each workday and each workweek;
- ✓ total daily or weekly straight-time earnings
- ✓ regular hourly pay rate;
- ✓ weekly overtime earnings;
- ✓ total overtime pay for the workweek;
- ✓ deductions from or additions to wages;
- ✓ total wages paid each pay period; and
- ✓ date of payment and pay period covered.

Special information is required for home workers, for employees working under uncommon pay arrangements, for employees to whom lodging or other facilities are furnished, and for employees receiving remedial education.

Chapter 14, Financial Management, covers the basics of payroll accounting and how to process the listed information.

Penalties

Enforcement of FLSA is carried out by investigators stationed across the U.S. They conduct investigations and gather data on wages, hours, and other employment conditions or practices in order to determine compliance with the law. Where violations are found, they may also recommend changes in employment practices to bring an employer into compliance.

Retaliation against an employee for filing a complaint or for participating in a legal proceeding under FLSA is against the law.

Willful violations of employment under FLSA may be prosecuted criminally, and the violator fined up to $10,000. A second conviction may result in imprisonment.

Employers who willfully or repeatedly violate the minimum wage or overtime pay requirements are subject to a civil money penalty of up to $1,100 for each violation.

Immigration and Nationality Act

The employment eligibility provisions of the Immigration and Nationality Act require employers to verify the employment eligibility of all individuals hired. Immigration and Naturalization Service forms (I-9) must be kept on file for at least three years after the date of hire or for one year after the date employment ends, whichever is later.

I-9 forms must be completed with required documentation within three days of hire. A sample I-9 form is located at the end of this chapter.

Unlawful Discrimination: Discrimination based on national origin or citizenship status is prohibited. If an Office of Special Counsel for Unfair Employment-Related Discrimination (OSC) or Equal Employment Opportunity Commission (EEOC) investigation reveals employment discrimination covered by the

Immigration and Nationality Act, the employer will be ordered to cease the prohibited practice and may be ordered to take one or more of the following steps:

- ✓ hire or reinstate, with or without back pay, individuals directly injured by the discrimination;
- ✓ lift any restrictions on an employee's assignments, work shifts, or movements;
- ✓ post notices to employees about their rights and about employers' obligations;
- ✓ educate all personnel involved in hiring and in complying with the employer sanctions and anti-discrimination laws; and
- ✓ remove a false performance review or false warning from an employee's personnel file.

Employers may also be ordered to pay civil monetary penalties of $250 to $2,000 per individual discriminated against for the first offense, $2,000 to $5,000 per individual discriminated against for the second offense, and $3,000 to $10,000 per individual discriminated against for subsequent offenses.

Completing the I-9 Form for New Hires

A sample of the I-9 form is located at the end of this chapter and is available for download on the U.S. Citizenship and Immigration Services website at www.uscis.gov or by calling (800) 870-3676. The National Customer Service Center at (800) 375-5283 can answer questions on USCIS forms and information on immigration laws, regulations and procedures. The following gives step-by-step instructions on how to complete the form properly.

Section One

The employee completes section one of the I-9 form at the start of employment. The employee's name, address, date of birth, and social security number, certification of legal status, and expiration for temporary work authorization are required. Permanent aliens and authorized aliens must fill in either their alien number or authorization number. The employee must sign and date the form.

Section Two

An authorized employee representative completes section two by examining one document from list A or by examining one document from list B and one document from list C (a summary of approved documents is listed in the following section and a complete list is on the back of the I-9 form). The representative must view original documentation and keep copies of the front and back of this documentation on file.

Acceptable Documentation: The purpose of providing documentation is to establish identity and employment eligibility. Listed below are common forms of identification used when completing the I-9 form. A complete list is included on the back of the I-9 form located at the end of this chapter. I-9 forms must be updated when identity and employment eligibility documents are changed or renewed.

Employees can provide one of the following documents that establishes both identity and employment eligibility:

- ✓ U.S. passport
- ✓ Certificate of U.S. citizenship
- ✓ Certificate of naturalization
- ✓ Unexpired foreign passport with I-551 stamp or attached I-94 form indicating current employment authorization
- ✓ Permanent resident card or alien registration receipt with photograph

Employees also have the option of providing two documents—one to establish identity and the other to establish employment eligibility.

Documents that establish identity include

- ✓ state-issued driver's license with photo;
- ✓ ID card with photo issued by federal, state or local government agencies;
- ✓ voter's registration card; and
- ✓ U.S. military card.

Documents that establish employment eligibility include

- ✓ U.S. Social Security card issued by the Social Security Administration;
- ✓ original or certified birth certificate;
- ✓ U.S. citizen ID card (form I-197);
- ✓ resident ID card; and
- ✓ Native American tribal document.

Certification

The date to be used in the certification section must correspond with the current employment date. The authorized employee representative must sign and date this section.

Americans with Disabilities Act (ADA)

This law prohibits discrimination against persons with disabilities and applies to employers with 15 or more employees. In general, the employment provisions of the ADA require

- ✓ equal opportunity in selecting, testing, and hiring qualified applicants with disabilities;
- ✓ job accommodation for applicants and workers with disabilities when such accommodations would not impose "undue hardship;" and
- ✓ equal opportunity in promotion and benefits.

Employment Discrimination: ADA prohibits discrimination in all employment practices, including job application procedures, hiring, firing, advancement, compensation, training, and other terms, conditions, and privileges of employment. It applies to recruitment, advertising, tenure, layoff, leave, fringe benefits, and all other employment-related activities.

Qualified Individuals with Disabilities: Employment discrimination is prohibited against "qualified individuals with disabilities" including applicants for employment and employees. An individual is considered to have a "disability" if that individual has a physical or mental impairment that substantially limits one or more major life activities or has a record of such an impairment, or is regarded as having such an impairment.

Conditions Covered: The ADA applies to persons who have impairments that substantially limit major life activities such as seeing, hearing, speaking, walking, breathing, performing manual tasks, learning, caring for oneself, and working.

Examples include an individual with

- ✓ epilepsy,
- ✓ paralysis,
- ✓ HIV infection,
- ✓ AIDS,
- ✓ substantial hearing or visual impairment,
- ✓ mental retardation, or
- ✓ specific learning disability.

An individual with a minor, non-chronic condition of short duration, such as a sprain, broken limb, or the flu, generally would not be covered by the ADA.

Reasonable Accommodations: An employer is required to accommodate a "known" disability of a qualified applicant or employee unless it imposes an "undue hardship" on the operation of the employer's business. A reasonable accommodation is any modification or adjustment to a job or the work environment that will enable a qualified applicant or employee with a disability to participate in the application process or to perform essential job functions. Reasonable accommodations also include adjustments to assure that a qualified individual with a disability has rights and privileges in employment equal to those of employees without disabilities.

Additional Resources: The Equal Employment Opportunity Commission has developed several resources to help employers and people with disabilities understand and comply with the employment provisions of the ADA. Resources include

- ✓ a technical assistance manual that provides "how-to" guidance on the employment provisions of the ADA as well as a resource directory to help individuals find specific information; and
- ✓ a variety of brochures, booklets, and fact sheets.

For more information about the ADA, contact:

U.S. Equal Employment Opportunity Commission
131 M Street, NE
Fourth Floor, Suite 4NWO2F
Washington, D.C. 20507

Phone: (202) 663-4000

TTY: (202) 663-4494

Website: www.eeoc.gov

Other Labor Laws

Many other labor laws protect the rights of employees.

- ✓ The **Davis-Bacon Act** requires payment of prevailing wage rates and fringe benefits on federally-financed or assisted construction.
- ✓ The **Walsh-Healey Public Contracts Act** requires payment of minimum wage rates and overtime pay on contracts that provide goods to the federal government.

- ✓ The **Service Contract Act** requires payment of prevailing wage rates and fringe benefits on contracts to provide services to the federal government.
- ✓ The **Contract Work Hours and Safety Standards Act** sets overtime standards for service and construction contracts on federal projects.
- ✓ The **Wage Garnishment Law** limits the amount of an individual's income that may be legally garnished and prohibits firing an employee whose pay is garnished for payment of a single debt.
- ✓ The **Employee Polygraph Protection Act** prohibits most private employers from using any type of lie detector test, either for pre-employment screening of job applicants or for testing current employees during the course of employment.
- ✓ The **Family and Medical Leave Act** entitles eligible employees of covered employers to take up to 12 weeks of unpaid job-protected leave each year, with the maintenance of group health insurance, for the birth and care of a child, for the placement of a child for adoption or foster care, for the care of a child, spouse, or parent with a serious health condition, or for the employee's serious health condition.
- ✓ **Title VII of the Civil Rights Act of 1964** prohibits discrimination on the basis of race, color, religion, national origin, and sex. Sexual harassment is considered a form of sex discrimination and is a violation of Title VII. An amendment to Title VII provides protection against sex discrimination on the basis of pregnancy, childbirth, and related medical conditions.
- ✓ The **Equal Pay Act of 1963** prohibits employers from paying different wages to men and women who perform essentially the same work under similar working conditions.
- ✓ The **Age Discrimination in Employment Act (ADEA)** prohibits discrimination against individuals who are age 40 or older. It applies to employers with 20 or more employees.
- ✓ The **Worker Adjustment and Retraining Notification Act (WARN)** offers protection to workers, their families, and communities by requiring employers to provide notice 60 days in advance of covered plant closings and covered mass layoffs.
- ✓ **Title III of the Consumer Credit Protection Act (CCPA)** protects employees from being discharged by their employers because their wages have been garnished for any one debt and limits the amount of employees' earnings that may be garnished in any one week.
- ✓ The **Uniformed Services Employment and Reemployment Rights Act (USERRA)** protects service members' reemployment rights when returning from a period of service in the uniformed services, including those called up from the reserves or National Guard, and prohibits employer discrimination based on military service or obligation.
- ✓ **Numerous labor organizing, collective bargaining and dispute resolution acts** give employees the right to organize, join labor unions, bargain collectively, and strike.
- ✓ **Right-to-work laws** secure the right of employees to decide for themselves whether or not to join or financially support a union. South Carolina is a right-to-work state.

South Carolina Payment of Wage Laws and Recordkeeping Requirements

The South Carolina Department of Labor, Licensing and Regulation is the regulating agency for the state wage and hour laws.

Listed below is a summary of the rules that may apply to your business.

- ✓ **Payment on Termination:** The employer shall pay an employee who is voluntarily or involuntarily terminated within 48 hours or the next regular payday, provided that the payment period does not exceed 30 days.
- ✓ **Withholding of Wages:** No employer may withhold or divert any portion of an employee's wages unless required or empowered by state or federal law, or unless the employer has written authorization from the employee on an approved form. Employers must give employees an itemized statement reporting his or her gross pay and deductions for each pay period.
- ✓ **Employer to Furnish Certain Information:** State law requires an employer of five or more

employees to notify each employee in writing at the time of hiring of the wages agreed upon, the time and place of payment, and the deductions that will be made from wages, including insurance programs. The employer has the option of giving individual notification of this information or posting the terms conspicuously at or near the place of work. Any changes in these terms must be given to the employee in writing at least seven calendar days before they become effective.

- ✓ **Wage Disputes:** If an employer fails to pay wages due to an employee, the employee may recover in a civil action an amount equal to three times the full amount of the unpaid wages, plus costs and reasonable attorney's fees as the court allows. The employee must bring the suit within three years. The Department of Labor, Licensing and Regulation will, upon complaint, investigate wage complaints to determine if any violations have occurred.
- ✓ **Recordkeeping Requirements:** Records of names and addresses of all employees and the wages paid and deductions made each pay period must be kept for three years.

Be aware of the labor laws that apply to your business.

Required Postings

Some of the statutes and regulations enforced by agencies within the U.S. Department of Labor require that posters or notices be posted in the workplace. A complete list of postings can be found at www.dol.gov. Postings that may apply to you are listed below:

Poster	Description of Employers Required to Post Notice
Safety and Health Protection on the Job	Employers located in states with OSHA-approved state plans should obtain and post the state's equivalent poster.
Equal Opportunity is the Law	Businesses holding federal contracts or subcontracts or federally assisted construction contracts of $10,000 or more.
Employee Rights for Workers with Disabilities/Special Minimum Wage Poster	All employers having workers employed under special minimum wage certificates must post this notice.
National Labor Relations Act (NLRA) Poster (effective January 31, 2012)	All private-sector employers (excluding agricultural, railroad and airline employers) must post this notice.
Your Rights Under the Family and Medical Leave Act	Public agencies (including state, local, and federal employers), public and private elementary and secondary schools, as well as private sector employers who employ 50 or more employees in 20 or more work weeks and who are engaged in commerce or in any industry or activity affecting commerce, including joint employers and successors of covered employers.
Fair Labor Standards Act (FLSA): Minimum Wage Poster	All private, federal, state and local government employers subject to the FLSA.
Uniformed Services Employment and Reemployment Rights Act	The full text of the notice must be provided by each employer to persons entitled to rights and benefits under USERRA.
Notice to All Employees Working on Federal or Federally Financed Construction Projects	Any contractor/subcontractor engaged in contracts in excess of $2,000 for the actual construction, alteration/repair of a public building or public work or building or work financed in whole or in part from federal funds, federal guarantee, or federal pledge.
Notice to Employees Working on Government Contracts	Every contractor or subcontractor engaged in a contract with the United States or the District of Columbia in excess of $2,500 the principal purpose of which is to furnish services in the U.S. through the use of service employees.
Notice: Employee Polygraph Protection Act	Any employer engaged in or affecting commerce or in the production of goods for commerce. Does not apply to federal, state and local governments, or to circumstances covered by the national defense and security exemption.
Notification of Employee Rights Under Federal Labor Laws	Federal contractors and subcontractors are required to post the prescribed employee notice conspicuously in plants and offices where employees covered by the National Labor Relations Act (NLRA) perform contract-related activity, including all places where notices to employees are customarily posted both physically and electronically.

Free posters are available by contacting:

Department of Labor, Licensing and Regulation (LLR)
PO Box 11329
Columbia, South Carolina 29211-1329

Phone: (803) 896-4300

Website: www.llr.sc.gov

LLR also distributes two posters required by the South Carolina Employment Security Commission and one required by the South Carolina Workers' Compensation Commission. These posters include:

- ✓ Employment Discrimination,
- ✓ Workers' Compensation, and
- ✓ Unemployment Compensation.

Other state agencies may also require display of specific documents in the workplace. Contact the appropriate agencies directly to verify any poster display requirements.

Employee Handbook and Policies

Having clear and well-documented policies helps employees understand the rules of the workplace and protects you if a disgruntled employee files a lawsuit or complaint against you.

Enforcing Policies and Procedures: An employee handbook is a document you put together that lists company policies and employee benefits and rights. It is important for employees to sign a receipt that they have read and understood the contents in the handbook. This documentation is helpful in enforcing the policies and procedures of your company.

Changing Your Handbook: An employee handbook is not a static document. You can add items to the handbook but make sure that you distribute these amendments to employees and have them sign off on the changes.

Writing Your Employee Handbook

It may be difficult to determine where to start when writing your employee handbook and policies. Consider the following sections when putting your handbook together:

- ✓ Company history
- ✓ Compensation guidelines (i.e., introductory period, full-time status requirements, etc.)
- ✓ Payroll distribution dates and times
- ✓ Benefits
- ✓ Normal working hours
- ✓ Overtime pay
- ✓ Vacation time
- ✓ Sick days
- ✓ Policy on sexual harassment
- ✓ Policy on the use of illegal drugs or alcohol
- ✓ Non-discrimination policy
- ✓ Rules of conduct (i.e., disciplinary action for insubordination, fighting, etc.)
- ✓ Safety policies
- ✓ Equipment and tool policies
- ✓ Disciplinary action procedures

You may want to have an attorney review your employee handbook. In many states, the employee handbook is considered an employment contract. There may be certain wording and disclaimers contained in your employee handbook to protect you against legal action.

Employee Satisfaction

Benefits of Employee Satisfaction: Keeping your employees happy and motivated can have a tremendous effect on the performance of your work teams. Your company can benefit from satisfied employees in several ways:

- ✓ Stronger company loyalty and corporate culture
- ✓ Higher quality work and customer satisfaction
- ✓ Lower employee turnover
- ✓ Increased productivity

Maintaining employee satisfaction is not as easy as it sounds. Even though employers may have good intentions, when faced with tight deadlines and day-to-day operations, employee satisfaction sometimes drops to the bottom of the priority list.

Motivating Employees: The following checklist includes simple ways you can motivate your employees and give them a feeling of achievement:

- ✓ Provide informal and formal training opportunities for employees to learn new skills.
- ✓ Empower employees to make decisions and give positive and constructive feedback.

- ✓ Provide clear expectations for your employees.
- ✓ Conduct performance reviews on a regular basis.
- ✓ Mentor your employees and tell them about the advancement opportunities in your company and the industry.
- ✓ Recognize and reward employees for good work.

The Value of Job Descriptions

Job descriptions give employees a guideline for the responsibilities of their job. Job descriptions benefit the employee because employees understand your expectation for their performance. It also makes it easier for you to monitor their performance, give reviews, and conduct disciplinary action if necessary.

Job descriptions should contain a few basic elements:

- ✓ Job title
- ✓ Job description, including who the position reports to and summary of job purpose
- ✓ Key responsibilities
- ✓ Required licenses and/or certifications
- ✓ Skills and knowledge needed

Sample Job Description: Listed below is a sample job description for a construction superintendent position using the above categories. All job descriptions must be carefully reviewed and modified to fit the individual company's requirements.

Job Title: Construction Superintendent

Description: Under general direction of the company owner, the construction superintendent serves as a member of the construction management team with broad authority over assigned projects, participating in all phases of construction from project planning to completion. Emphasis is on quality control, evaluation of change order requests, and timely completion of construction schedules.

Key Responsibilities: The duties listed below are intended only as illustrations of the various types of work that may be performed by the construction superintendent:

- ✓ Coordinates activities associated with the company's construction projects.
- ✓ Serves as liaison with subcontractors, architects, utilities, and others.
- ✓ Participates in project construction development and planning.
- ✓ Processes utility requests for construction projects.
- ✓ Represents the company regarding onsite construction quality control reviews.
- ✓ Makes recommendations and processes change order requests.
- ✓ Reviews punch lists.
- ✓ Assures construction specifications are met.
- ✓ Notes deviations from project schedules and costs.
- ✓ Maintains records and prepares reports.

The omission of specific statements of duties does not exclude them from the position if the work is similar, related, or a logical assignment to this class.

Required Licenses or Certifications: Requires a valid driver's license

Skills and Knowledge Needed:

- ✓ Principles and practices of construction management, building operation and maintenance, quality assurance programs and systems, budget administration, construction specifications, and bidding processes.
- ✓ Ability to plan, organize, and manage time to track progress and elements of assigned construction projects effectively.
- ✓ Establish and maintain effective working relationships with coworkers, employees of subcontractors, and outside entities.
- ✓ Prepare or participate in the development of construction and other budgets and monitor performance against the approved budget.
- ✓ Communicate effectively, both orally and in writing.
- ✓ Ability to lift up to 50 pounds.

Providing Benefits

Offering benefit plans can be an effective means of attracting and retaining good employees, keeping up with the competition, and boosting employee morale. Traditional employee plans include

- ✓ health insurance,
- ✓ dental insurance,
- ✓ vision insurance,
- ✓ long-term disability,
- ✓ life insurance, and
- ✓ 401(k) or other retirement plan.

Some employers also opt to offer more creative benefit options, such as tuition reimbursement, gym subsidies, and child care referral services.

However you decide to package your benefits plan, a few key laws are important.

Workers' Compensation Laws provide monetary compensation to employees who are injured or disabled on the job. These laws also provide benefits for dependents of those workers who are killed because of work-related accidents or illnesses. Some laws protect employers by limiting the amount an injured employee can recover from an employer and by eliminating the liability of coworkers in most accidents. Workers' compensation laws and programs are established at the state level for most employment.

Workers' compensation fraud is committed when an individual willfully intends to provide false or inaccurate information to receive workers' compensation benefits. Examples of fraud include

- ✓ reporting an injury as work-related when it was not;
- ✓ continuing to work and receive benefits at the same time; and
- ✓ misrepresenting an injury.

Employers are in the best position to identify workers' compensation fraud. Workers' compensation fraud is illegal. Your workers' compensation administrator should be notified if you suspect fraud.

Workers' compensation insurance is purchased by the employer; no part of it should be paid for by employees or deducted from their pay.

South Carolina Program: The South Carolina program is administered through the Workers' Compensation Commission.

For more information, contact:

> ***South Carolina***
> ***Workers' Compensation Commission***
> ***P.O. Box 1715***
> ***1333 Main Street, Suite 500***
> ***Columbia, South Carolina 29202-1715***
>
> ***Phone: (803) 737-5700***
>
> ***Website: wcc.sc.gov***

Coverage Requirements: In general, employers who have four or more full-time or part-time employees must carry workers' compensation coverage. Workers' compensation carriers determine employer premiums by analyzing the number of employees, total employee wages, type of work, and history of accidents and claims.

Subcontractor Coverage: The South Carolina workers' compensation law also requires that a contractor who sublets any part of contract work to a subcontractor may be liable for coverage for the employees of the subcontractor, if the subcontractor has not obtained workers' compensation insurance coverage.

To protect your business, confirm that your subcontractors have the appropriate workers' compensation coverage.

Employee Compensation: Employers are required to report injuries needing medical treatment to their insurance carrier. The insurance carrier reports the injury to the Workers' Compensation Commission.

The employee is compensated for the necessary medical treatment and loss of wages. Coverage also includes compensation for permanent disability or disfigurement.

Unemployment Compensation programs provide unemployment benefits to eligible workers who become unemployed through no fault of their own and meet certain other eligibility requirements. This program is jointly financed through federal and state employer payroll taxes through the federal/state unemployment insurance tax.

Generally, employers must pay both state and federal unemployment taxes if

- ✓ they pay wages to employees totaling $1,500, or more, in any quarter of a calendar year; or
- ✓ they had at least one employee during any day of a week during 20 weeks in a calendar year, regardless of whether or not the weeks were consecutive.

South Carolina Program: The South Carolina Unemployment Compensation Law provides workers with benefits during periods of total or partial unemployment.

Funds for the payment of unemployment benefits are provided by employers through a quarterly payroll tax. All employers must submit Form UCE, Employer Status Report to the Unemployment Compensation Commission. The Commission will determine the liability or non-liability of the employing unit. Liable employers must submit the Quarterly Contribution and Wage Report (Form UCE 101/120) each quarter.

Chapter 15, Tax Basics, covers unemployment compensation rates.

SUTA Dumping: SUTA dumping is a transfer of employees between businesses for the purpose of obtaining a lower unemployment compensation tax rate. SUTA dumping is prohibited and subject to criminal and/or civil penalties according to state law. The state agency responsible for the state unemployment program investigates suspicious activity in the transfer or acquisition of a business or shifting of employees to identify SUTA dumping.

The **Consolidated Omnibus Budget Act of 1985 (COBRA)** includes provisions for continuing health care coverage. These provisions apply to group health plans of employers with 20 or more employees on 50 percent of the typical working days in the previous calendar year. COBRA gives "qualified beneficiaries" (a covered employee's spouse and dependent children) the right to maintain, at their own expense, coverage under their health plan that would be lost due to a "qualifying event," such as termination of employment, at a cost comparable to what it would be if they were still members of the employer's group.

Health Insurance Portability and Accounting Act of 1996 (HIPAA) provides for improved portability and continuity of health insurance coverage connected with employment. These provisions include rules relating to exclusions of preexisting conditions, special enrollment rights, and prohibition of discrimination against individuals based on health status-related factors. HIPAA also addresses an employee's right to privacy concerning their health information. As an employer, you need to be aware of this act and keep records concerning any employee's medical conditions in a confidential file.

Disciplining Employees

Corrective action may be necessary from time to time for employees who are not following employment policies and procedures properly. Employers need to administer discipline fairly to promote a respectful work environment and to avoid trouble later.

Progressive Discipline: Progressive discipline is a method of corrective action where the consequences of the improper behavior become more significant if it continues. Progressive discipline gives the employee a chance to take corrective action to prevent future disciplinary action. There are certain offenses that may be cause for immediate termination (i.e., theft, endangering the safety of others, etc.) that are not subject to progressive discipline.

The employee manual is a good place to have written disciplinary policies and a comprehensive list of offenses that lead to immediate dismissal.

Terminating Employees

At one time or another, most employers run into circumstances where they need to terminate employees. It is not a fun or rewarding task but sometimes a necessary one. When terminating an employee, you want to make sure that you have followed the proper procedures to minimize your risk of a wrongful termination lawsuit.

Employment relationships are either contractual or at-will; the definition of the relationship influences the procedures for termination.

Contractual Employees

Union employees and some executives have employment contracts. When terminating a contractual employee, it is important to comply with the terms of the contract. If the contract is breached, you may be subject to a lawsuit.

At-Will Employees

"At-will employment" means that either the employer or the employee may terminate employment at any time without notice or cause. It is not exactly that easy, and there are restrictions that you should be aware of as an employer. These restrictions include:

- ✓ An employer may not terminate an employee for discriminatory reasons (i.e., race, gender, etc.).
- ✓ An employer cannot terminate an employee for taking time off to serve on a jury.
- ✓ Reporting health and safety violations and abuses of power cannot lead to termination. There are "whistle-blower laws" that protect employees if this circumstance does occur.
- ✓ All employers should use good faith and fair dealing throughout employment. This is why documenting poor performance is strongly recommended. Without documentation, the termination may be perceived as a breach of good faith.

These are all general guidelines, and it is recommended you consult with an expert in Human Resources or an attorney regarding specific situations.

Proper documentation is important when disciplining and terminating employees.

Final Inspection...

Interviewing and Hiring Employees: Your interviews should focus on skills, experience, and qualities. There are certain questions you should avoid because they are not legal to ask.

New Hire Reporting: South Carolina has mandatory new hire reporting requirements.

Hiring Minors for Construction Work: The State of South Carolina and U.S. Department of Labor have strict rules for hiring minors, such as restricted working hours and prohibited tasks.

Employee Documentation: Employee files should be maintained throughout employment with relevant documents, such as tax forms and disciplinary forms.

Key Employment Laws: There are several employment laws that you must comply with, such as the Fair Labor Standards Act (FLSA), Immigration and Nationality Act, and the Americans with Disabilities Act (ADA).

Fair Labor Standards Act (FLSA): Standards for basic minimum wage and overtime pay are outlined in the Fair Labor Standards Act. The Act applies to most private and public employers who have one or more employees.

Immigration and Nationality Act: Employers are required to verify the employment eligibility of all individuals hired through I-9 forms. These forms must be kept on file for at least three years after the date of hire or for one year after the date employment ends, whichever is later.

Americans with Disabilities Act (ADA): This law prohibits discrimination against persons with disabilities. It applies to employers with 15 or more employees.

Other Labor Laws: Several other labor laws protect the rights of employees. Specific laws exist that set guidelines for federal contractors, wage garnishment, and an employee's right to join a union. Other laws provide protection against the discriminatory actions of employers.

South Carolina Payment of Wage Laws and Recordkeeping Requirements: The South Carolina Department of Labor, Licensing and Regulation regulates payment of wage laws, including payment on termination, withholding of wages, employer furnishing of certain information, and wage disputes. Employers must also follow specific recordkeeping requirements.

Required Postings: Employers must post certain notices for employees under federal and state law.

Employee Handbook and Policies: An employee handbook is a useful document for communicating your policies and procedures.

Employee Satisfaction: Your company can benefit in several ways from putting employee satisfaction programs in place.

Providing Benefits: There are some mandatory benefits you must provide employees. Other benefits, such as health insurance, may also be offered to attract and retain employees.

Disciplining Employees: Discipline should be administered in a fair manner and documented appropriately.

Terminating Employees: Using proper termination procedures will help minimize your risk of a wrongful termination lawsuit.

Supplemental Forms

Supplemental forms and links are available at **NASCLAforms.org** using access code **SCR129354**. The following forms can be found in the Employee Management section.

IRS Form W-4	IRS form to determine federal income tax withholding
Form I-9	Required form to confirm legal immigration status
Fair Labor Standards Act (FLSA)	Copy of the FLSA law from the U.S. Department of Labor
Americans with Disabilities Act (ADA)	ADA guide for small businesses published by the U.S. Department of Justice
Job Description Template	Form featured earlier in the chapter that shows a sample job description
Employer's Tax Guide (Circular E)	Publication used to determine federal income tax withholding for employees

Employment Eligibility Verification
Department of Homeland Security
U.S. Citizenship and Immigration Services

USCIS
Form I-9
OMB No. 1615-0047
Expires 08/31/2019

►START HERE: Read instructions carefully before completing this form. The instructions must be available, either in paper or electronically, during completion of this form. Employers are liable for errors in the completion of this form.

ANTI-DISCRIMINATION NOTICE: It is illegal to discriminate against work-authorized individuals. Employers **CANNOT** specify which document(s) an employee may present to establish employment authorization and identity. The refusal to hire or continue to employ an individual because the documentation presented has a future expiration date may also constitute illegal discrimination.

Section 1. Employee Information and Attestation *(Employees must complete and sign Section 1 of Form I-9 no later than the **first day of employment**, but not before accepting a job offer.)*

Last Name *(Family Name)*	First Name *(Given Name)*	Middle Initial	Other Last Names Used *(if any)*

Address *(Street Number and Name)*	Apt. Number	City or Town	State	ZIP Code

Date of Birth *(mm/dd/yyyy)*	U.S. Social Security Number	Employee's E-mail Address	Employee's Telephone Number
	☐☐☐ - ☐☐ - ☐☐☐☐		

I am aware that federal law provides for imprisonment and/or fines for false statements or use of false documents in connection with the completion of this form.

I attest, under penalty of perjury, that I am (check one of the following boxes):

☐ 1. A citizen of the United States

☐ 2. A noncitizen national of the United States *(See instructions)*

☐ 3. A lawful permanent resident (Alien Registration Number/USCIS Number): ____________

☐ 4. An alien authorized to work until (expiration date, if applicable, mm/dd/yyyy): ____________
Some aliens may write "N/A" in the expiration date field. *(See instructions)*

Aliens authorized to work must provide only one of the following document numbers to complete Form I-9:
An Alien Registration Number/USCIS Number OR Form I-94 Admission Number OR Foreign Passport Number.

1. Alien Registration Number/USCIS Number: ____________
OR
2. Form I-94 Admission Number: ____________
OR
3. Foreign Passport Number: ____________
Country of Issuance: ____________

QR Code - Section 1
Do Not Write In This Space

Signature of Employee	Today's Date *(mm/dd/yyyy)*

Preparer and/or Translator Certification (check one):

☐ I did not use a preparer or translator. ☐ A preparer(s) and/or translator(s) assisted the employee in completing Section 1.

(Fields below must be completed and signed when preparers and/or translators assist an employee in completing Section 1.)

I attest, under penalty of perjury, that I have assisted in the completion of Section 1 of this form and that to the best of my knowledge the information is true and correct.

Signature of Preparer or Translator	Today's Date *(mm/dd/yyyy)*

Last Name *(Family Name)*	First Name *(Given Name)*

Address *(Street Number and Name)*	City or Town	State	ZIP Code

STOP *Employer Completes Next Page* STOP

Employment Eligibility Verification
Department of Homeland Security
U.S. Citizenship and Immigration Services

USCIS
Form I-9
OMB No. 1615-0047
Expires 08/31/2019

Section 2. Employer or Authorized Representative Review and Verification

(Employers or their authorized representative must complete and sign Section 2 within 3 business days of the employee's first day of employment. You must physically examine one document from List A OR a combination of one document from List B and one document from List C as listed on the "Lists of Acceptable Documents.")

Employee Info from Section 1	Last Name *(Family Name)*	First Name *(Given Name)*	M.I.	Citizenship/Immigration Status

List A Identity and Employment Authorization	OR	List B Identity	AND	List C Employment Authorization
Document Title		Document Title		Document Title
Issuing Authority		Issuing Authority		Issuing Authority
Document Number		Document Number		Document Number
Expiration Date *(if any)(mm/dd/yyyy)*		Expiration Date *(if any)(mm/dd/yyyy)*		Expiration Date *(if any)(mm/dd/yyyy)*
Document Title		Additional Information		QR Code - Sections 2 & 3 Do Not Write In This Space
Issuing Authority				
Document Number				
Expiration Date *(if any)(mm/dd/yyyy)*				
Document Title				
Issuing Authority				
Document Number				
Expiration Date *(if any)(mm/dd/yyyy)*				

Certification: I attest, under penalty of perjury, that (1) I have examined the document(s) presented by the above-named employee, (2) the above-listed document(s) appear to be genuine and to relate to the employee named, and (3) to the best of my knowledge the employee is authorized to work in the United States.

The employee's first day of employment *(mm/dd/yyyy)*: ____________ ***(See instructions for exemptions)***

Signature of Employer or Authorized Representative	Today's Date *(mm/dd/yyyy)*	Title of Employer or Authorized Representative

Last Name of Employer or Authorized Representative	First Name of Employer or Authorized Representative	Employer's Business or Organization Name

Employer's Business or Organization Address (Street Number and Name)	City or Town	State	ZIP Code

Section 3. Reverification and Rehires *(To be completed and signed by employer or authorized representative.)*

A. New Name *(if applicable)*			**B.** Date of Rehire *(if applicable)*
Last Name *(Family Name)*	First Name *(Given Name)*	Middle Initial	Date *(mm/dd/yyyy)*

C. If the employee's previous grant of employment authorization has expired, provide the information for the document or receipt that establishes continuing employment authorization in the space provided below.

Document Title	Document Number	Expiration Date *(if any) (mm/dd/yyyy)*

I attest, under penalty of perjury, that to the best of my knowledge, this employee is authorized to work in the United States, and if the employee presented document(s), the document(s) I have examined appear to be genuine and to relate to the individual.

Signature of Employer or Authorized Representative	Today's Date *(mm/dd/yyyy)*	Name of Employer or Authorized Representative

LISTS OF ACCEPTABLE DOCUMENTS
All documents must be UNEXPIRED

Employees may present one selection from List A or a combination of one selection from List B and one selection from List C.

LIST A **Documents that Establish Both Identity and Employment Authorization**	**OR**	**LIST B** **Documents that Establish Identity**	**AND**	**LIST C** **Documents that Establish Employment Authorization**
1. U.S. Passport or U.S. Passport Card		**1.** Driver's license or ID card issued by a State or outlying possession of the United States provided it contains a photograph or information such as name, date of birth, gender, height, eye color, and address		**1.** A Social Security Account Number card, unless the card includes one of the following restrictions: (1) NOT VALID FOR EMPLOYMENT (2) VALID FOR WORK ONLY WITH INS AUTHORIZATION (3) VALID FOR WORK ONLY WITH DHS AUTHORIZATION
2. Permanent Resident Card or Alien Registration Receipt Card (Form I-551)		**2.** ID card issued by federal, state or local government agencies or entities, provided it contains a photograph or information such as name, date of birth, gender, height, eye color, and address		**2.** Certification of report of birth issued by the Department of State (Forms DS-1350, FS-545, FS-240)
3. Foreign passport that contains a temporary I-551 stamp or temporary I-551 printed notation on a machine-readable immigrant visa		**3.** School ID card with a photograph		**3.** Original or certified copy of birth certificate issued by a State, county, municipal authority, or territory of the United States bearing an official seal
4. Employment Authorization Document that contains a photograph (Form I-766)		**4.** Voter's registration card		**4.** Native American tribal document
5. For a nonimmigrant alien authorized to work for a specific employer because of his or her status: **a.** Foreign passport; and **b.** Form I-94 or Form I-94A that has the following: (1) The same name as the passport; and (2) An endorsement of the alien's nonimmigrant status as long as that period of endorsement has not yet expired and the proposed employment is not in conflict with any restrictions or limitations identified on the form.		**5.** U.S. Military card or draft record		**5.** U.S. Citizen ID Card (Form I-197)
6. Passport from the Federated States of Micronesia (FSM) or the Republic of the Marshall Islands (RMI) with Form I-94 or Form I-94A indicating nonimmigrant admission under the Compact of Free Association Between the United States and the FSM or RMI		**6.** Military dependent's ID card		**6.** Identification Card for Use of Resident Citizen in the United States (Form I-179)
		7. U.S. Coast Guard Merchant Mariner Card		**7.** Employment authorization document issued by the Department of Homeland Security
		8. Native American tribal document		
		9. Driver's license issued by a Canadian government authority		
		For persons under age 18 who are unable to present a document listed above:		
		10. School record or report card		
		11. Clinic, doctor, or hospital record		
		12. Day-care or nursery school record		

Examples of many of these documents appear in Part 13 of the Handbook for Employers (M-274).

Refer to the instructions for more information about acceptable receipts.

Chapter 12
JOBSITE SAFETY AND ENVIRONMENTAL FACTORS

Chapter Survey...

- ⇨ *Safety Standards*
- ⇨ *Safe Hiring and Training*
- ⇨ *Substance Abuse Policies*
- ⇨ *Safety Equipment*
- ⇨ *Emergency Action Plan*
- ⇨ *OSHA Recordkeeping*
- ⇨ *OSHA Injury Decision Tree*
- ⇨ *Material Safety Data Sheets (MSDS)*
- ⇨ *Underground Utility Safety*
- ⇨ *Overhead Power Line Safety*
- ⇨ *Benefits of Providing a Safe and Healthy Workplace*
- ⇨ *Employee Rights*
- ⇨ *Penalties*
- ⇨ *Environmental Considerations*
- ⇨ *U.S. Environmental Protection Agency*
- ⇨ *South Carolina Department of Health and Environmental Control*
- ⇨ *Environmental Law*
- ⇨ *Air Quality*
- ⇨ *Asbestos*
- ⇨ *Clean Water Act*
- ⇨ *Sedimentation and Erosion Control Measures*
- ⇨ *Hazardous and Non-Hazardous Waste*
- ⇨ *Hazardous Substances*
- ⇨ *Lead*
- ⇨ *Remodeling or Renovating a Home with Lead-Based Paint (Lead PRE)*
- ⇨ *Sample OSHA Forms 300, 300A, and 301*

Safety First: Creating a safe working environment is not only a good way to run your business, it is the law. Effective management and implementation of workplace safety and health programs add significant value to individuals and companies by reducing the extent, severity, and consequences of work-related injury and illness. Businesses spend approximately $171 billion a year on costs associated with occupational injuries and illness.

- ✓ Workplace injuries and illnesses are reduced by approximately 20 to 40 percent when employers establish safety and health programs.
- ✓ Workers' compensation premiums, employee retraining costs, and absenteeism are decreased by reducing workplace injuries and illnesses.
- ✓ Increased workplace safety results in increased productivity and morale and ultimately, profits.

Safety Standards

Understanding OSHA: The Occupational Safety and Health Administration (OSHA) was established by the Occupational Safety and Health Act of 1970 (OSH Act). All employers are subject to federal OSHA requirements and some states have adopted a state plan. State standards are at least as strict as the federal plan. The first step to complying with OSHA is to learn the published standards.

The OSHA standards that apply to the construction industry are

- ✓ 29 CFR 1926, Safety and Health Regulations for the Construction Industry;
- ✓ 29 CFR 1910, Occupational Safety and Health Standards; and
- ✓ 29 CFR 1904, Recording and Reporting Occupational Injuries and Illnesses.

It is the employer's responsibility to understand the OSHA standards and quickly correct any violations. Putting together a safety program with these standards in mind can help maximize employee safety and prevent violations before they occur.

OSHA Poster: All employers must post the OSHA poster (or state plan equivalent) in a prominent location in the workplace. In construction, employees are generally dispersed to different sites and the OSHA poster must be posted at the location to which employees report each day.

The OSHA poster is downloadable from the OSHA website (www.osha.gov). This website also has useful links to many safety and environmental topics including compliance assistance and laws and regulations. For more information about OSHA, contact

Occupational Safety and Health Administration (OSHA)
Office of Small Business Assistance
Directorate of Cooperative and State Programs
200 Constitution Avenue, NW
Washington, DC 20210

Phone: (800) 321-6742 (OSHA)

Website: www.osha.gov

OSHA Construction Safety Act: The Contract Work Hours and Safety Standards Act, commonly known as the Construction Safety Act, sets safety standards for construction contracts on federal projects.

South Carolina OSHA: Under the South Carolina Occupational Safety and Health Act (S.C. OSHA), employers must comply with safety and health standards adopted by the South Carolina Department of Labor, Licensing, and Regulation (LLR). Although South Carolina has its own state OSHA program, it must still adopt standards that are identical to or "at least as effective as Federal OSHA standards." To ensure compliance with the rules, LLR safety and health inspectors conduct periodic inspections. S.C. OSHA citations can carry monetary penalties of up to $70,000 per violation. For more information or to contact this department:

Department of Labor, Licensing and Regulation (LLR)
S.C. Occupational Safety and Health Administration
P.O. Box 11329
Columbia, South Carolina 29211-1329

General Information: (803) 896-7665

Website: www.scosha.llronline.com

Safe Hiring and Training

Hire Safe: The first step to improving safety in the workplace is to hire employees who have a good safety track record. The majority of accidents are caused by unsafe actions, not unsafe conditions. It is important to do thorough applicant screening and check all employment references. If you find that an applicant had safety accidents with a previous employer, chances for additional accidents while working for you are greater.

Regular Training: Training on safety practices and policies should be conducted regularly. New employees should receive a copy of your safety policies and sign off on them. Brief 10-minute training sessions can be conducted at the jobsite with your crew daily. During these training sessions, you can review policies and receive feedback from your employees on potential hazards that occur on the jobsite.

Conduct regular safety training for your employees.

Substance Abuse Policies

Your Bottom Line: Substance abuse in the workplace can have a profound effect on your business and significantly impact your bottom line. This problem costs American businesses more than $100 billion every year. This loss occurs in

- ✓ workers' compensation claims,
- ✓ medical costs,
- ✓ absenteeism,
- ✓ lost productivity, and
- ✓ employee turnover.

For this reason, you should make sure that all employees know that substance abuse is not permitted and develop a substance free workplace program.

Employee Program: Develop your program together with your employees. Talk about the benefits of having a substance free workplace and your concern for them to have a safe and healthy work environment. Eliminating substance abuse increases productivity, reduces accidents, and lowers insurance claim costs. Solicit input from your employees on how to implement the program in the workplace and any other suggestions they have.

Consider this...

Ninety percent of large businesses have drug-free workplace programs in place today, while 5 percent to 10 percent of small- and medium-sized businesses have implemented similar programs. The irony here is that 75 percent of employed Americans work for small- and medium-sized businesses.

Communicate Your Policy: Once you have developed a program, distribute it to all employees and have them sign off on it. Your policies should expressly prohibit the illegal use of drugs and/or abuse of alcohol by any employee and spell out the consequences of policy violations. All new employees should receive your policy as part of their orientation. You should also check with your workers' compensation carrier to see if you can receive a credit for having this policy in place.

Encourage employee participation in developing company safety programs.

Safety Equipment

Prevent Injuries: Using the proper safety equipment can lower the occurrences of injuries on the job. This equipment might include

- ✓ hard hats,
- ✓ safety shoes/boots,
- ✓ protective eyewear,
- ✓ gloves,
- ✓ fall protection,
- ✓ hearing protection,
- ✓ respirators,
- ✓ protective coveralls, and
- ✓ face shields.

Make sure you consult with OSHA safety standards to determine what safety equipment is required by law and assess your jobsite to determine additional equipment you want your employees to have.

Emergency Action Plan

Your Plan of Action: OSHA regulations require you to have an emergency action plan. If you have more than 10 employees, your plan must be in writing. If you have fewer than 10 employees, you may communicate the plan orally to employees. The emergency action plan must include procedures for

- ✓ reporting a fire or other emergency;
- ✓ emergency evacuation;
- ✓ employees who remain for critical operations before evacuating;
- ✓ accounting for all employees after evacuation; and
- ✓ employees performing rescue or medical duties.

The plan should also include the name or job title of the plan administrator. You must review the plan with your employees, designate and train employees to assist in a safe evacuation, and have a distinctive signal that serves as an employee alarm system.

OSHA Recordkeeping

For the Record: Every employer covered by OSHA who has more than 10 employees, except for employers in certain low-hazard industries in the retail, finance, insurance, real estate, and service sectors, must maintain three types of OSHA-specified records of job-related injuries and illnesses.

These forms are located at the end of the chapter.

- ✓ **OSHA Form 300**
- ✓ **OSHA Form 300A**
- ✓ **OSHA Form 301**

The **OSHA Form 300** is an injury/illness log, with a separate line entry for each recordable injury or illness. Such events include work-related deaths, injuries, and illnesses other than minor injuries that require only first aid treatment and that do not involve medical treatment, loss of consciousness, restriction of work, days away from work, or transfer to another job. Construction site operations that last for more than one year must keep a separate OSHA 300 log.

Each year, the employer must conspicuously post in the workplace a **Form 300A**, which includes a summary of the previous year's work-related injuries and illnesses. The data from Form 300 is used to complete this form. Form 300A must be posted by February 1 and kept in place until at least April 30 following the year covered by the form.

OSHA Form 301 is an individual incident report that provides added detail about each specific recordable injury or illness. An alternative form, such as an insurance or workers' compensation form that provides the same details may be substituted for OSHA Form 301.

Who Needs to Complete the Forms? Employers with 10 or fewer employees are exempt from maintaining these records. However, such employers must keep these records if they receive an annual illness and injury survey form either from the Bureau of Labor Statistics (BLS) or from OSHA. Employers selected for these surveys will be notified before the end of the prior year to begin keeping records during the year covered by the survey.

Timeframe to Retain Records: OSHA records must be kept by the employer for five years following the year to which they pertain.

Exposure Records and Medical Records: Exposure records (including employee exposure to toxic substances and harmful physical agents) must be maintained for 30 years and medical records for the duration of employment plus 30 years. Analysis using exposure or medical records must be kept for 30 years.

Toxic substances and harmful agents include

- ✓ any material listed in the National Institute for Occupational Safety and Health (NIOSH) Registry of Toxic Effects of Chemical Hazards (RTECHS);
- ✓ substances which have evidenced an acute chronic health hazard in testing conducted by or known to the employer; and
- ✓ substances in a material safety data sheet kept by or known to the employer, indicating that the material may pose a health hazard.

Reporting Fatalities and Hospitalizations: When a work-related fatality or incident that requires hospitalization of three or more employees occurs,

- ✓ employers must orally report the fatality or incident to the nearest OSHA Area Office; and
- ✓ if a death occurs within 30 days of the incident, employers must report it within eight hours.

Employers do not need to report a death occurring more than 30 days after a work-related incident.

Recordable Illnesses and Injuries: Cases that meet the general recording criteria involve a significant injury or illness diagnosed by a physician or other licensed health care professional, even if it does not result in death, days away from work, restricted work or job transfer, medical treatment beyond first aid, or loss of consciousness.

Medical Treatment Defined: Medical treatment means the management and care of a patient to combat a disease or disorder. It does not include

- ✓ visits to a physician or other licensed health care professional solely for observation or counseling;
- ✓ conduct of diagnostic procedures, such as x-rays and blood tests, including the administration of prescription medications used solely for diagnostic purposes (i.e., eye drops to dilate pupils); or
- ✓ first aid.

First Aid Defined: The following treatments are considered first aid according to 29 CFR 1904:

- ✓ Using a non-prescription medication at the non-prescription strength
- ✓ Administering tetanus immunizations (other immunizations, such as the Hepatitis B vaccine or rabies vaccine, are considered medical treatment)
- ✓ Cleaning, flushing or soaking wounds on the surface of the skin
- ✓ Using wound coverings such as bandages, Band-Aids™, gauze pads, etc.; or using butterfly bandages or Steri-Strips™; other wound closing devices such as sutures, staples, etc., are considered medical treatment
- ✓ Using hot or cold therapy
- ✓ Using any non-rigid means of support, such as elastic bandages, wraps, non-rigid back belts, etc.; devices with rigid stays or other systems designed to immobilize parts of the body are considered medical treatment for recordkeeping purposes
- ✓ Using temporary immobilization devices while transporting an accident victim (i.e., splints, slings, neck collars, back boards, etc.)
- ✓ Drilling of a fingernail or toenail to relieve pressure or draining fluid from a blister
- ✓ Using eye patches
- ✓ Removing foreign bodies from the eye using only irrigation or a cotton swab
- ✓ Removing splinters or foreign material from areas other than the eye by irrigation, tweezers, cotton swabs or other simple means
- ✓ Using finger guards

- ✓ Using massages; physical therapy or chiropractic treatment are considered medical treatment for recordkeeping purposes
- ✓ Drinking fluids for relief of heat stress

OSHA Injury Decision Tree

The OSHA injury decision tree below shows the steps involved in making the determination for recording work-related injuries or illnesses.

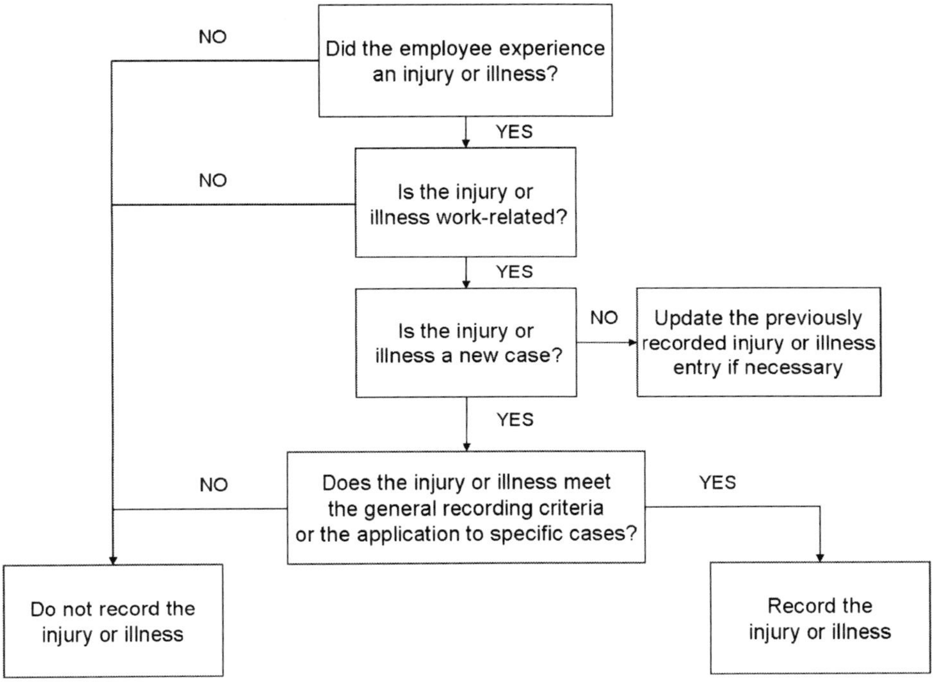

Material Safety Data Sheets (MSDS)

Chemical Safety: Material safety data sheets (MSDS) are a requirement of OSHA's Hazard Communication Standard (HCS). The purpose of the HCS is to ensure chemical safety in the workplace. Requirements of the MSDS program include:

- ✓ Manufacturers and importers of hazardous materials are required to conduct hazard evaluations of the products they manufacture or import.
- ✓ If a product is found to be hazardous under the terms of the standard, the manufacturer or importer must so indicate on containers of the material, and the first shipment of the material to a new customer must include a material safety data sheet (MSDS).
- ✓ Employers must use these MSDSs to train their employees to recognize and avoid the hazards presented by the materials.

Emergency Treatment: Employers must keep MSDSs on hand for all chemicals used in the workplace. The MSDS provides emergency information in case of contact with the chemical either internally or externally. The MSDS also explains the proper precautions to take when using a chemical. In the event of an OSHA inspection, the compliance officer will confirm that all MSDSs are at the worksite.

Inspection Guidelines: OSHA publishes inspection guidelines for enforcement of the Hazard Communication Standard. A summary of items that are reviewed during an inspection is included below:

- ✓ Is there a written hazard communication plan?
- ✓ Who is responsible for obtaining and maintaining MSDSs?
- ✓ Is there an MSDS for every chemical used?
- ✓ How are the MSDSs maintained (i.e., in notebooks in the work area(s), in a pickup truck at the jobsite, etc.) and do employees have proper access to them?
- ✓ Who is responsible for conducting training on chemicals and what are the elements of the training program?

The detailed procedure can be downloaded off the OSHA website (www.osha.gov).

Underground Utility Safety

Excavating without identifying underground utilities is a safety issue and can cost you unnecessary fines, repair costs, and utility outages. Although laws on marking underground utilities vary from state to state, contractors should identify underground utilities before digging on

- ✓ public and private property;
- ✓ public streets;
- ✓ alleys;
- ✓ utility easements; and
- ✓ all other rights-of-way.

In order to request a locater to come out to your site and locate underground utilities, the Common Ground Alliance (CGA) can be reached by calling 811. Your call is then routed to a local One Call Center. If you prefer to contact your local One Call Center directly, contact information for each state is located on the CGA website at www.call811.com

Overhead Power Line Safety

OSHA has several programs focused on safety for those who work around overhead power lines. Listed below are a few key points from OSHA to consider when formulating a health and safety program and worksite planning. Considerations include the following:

- ✓ perform a thorough site survey prior to beginning construction work;
- ✓ stay at least 10 feet away from overhead power lines;
- ✓ assume that all power lines are energized unless confirmed by proper authorities;
- ✓ call the utility company if overhead lines are present to determine voltage and if the lines can be shut off or insulated during construction work;
- ✓ use non-conductive ladders when working around overhead power lines;
- ✓ keep conductive objects at least 10 feet away from overhead power lines unless otherwise trained and qualified to use insulated tools specifically designed for high voltage lines; and
- ✓ perform thorough research on the location and voltage of overhead power lines when using cranes and heavy equipment to determine a minimum safe distance for operation.

Additional information on overhead power line safety is available on the OSHA website at www.osha.gov.

Benefits of Providing a Safe and Healthy Workplace

Ignoring safety and health regulations in the workplace is detrimental in many ways. Employees are put at risk, company reputation is at stake, and costs are high when accidents happen which affects overall company profits.

The most frequent citations that OSHA issues to the construction industry are for violations pertaining to

- ✓ scaffolding;
- ✓ fall protection (scope, application, definitions);
- ✓ excavations (general requirements and requirements for protective systems);
- ✓ ladders;
- ✓ head protection;
- ✓ hazard communication;
- ✓ fall protection (training requirements);
- ✓ construction (general safety and health provisions); and
- ✓ electrical (wiring methods, design and protection).

Ensuring workers are healthy and safe provides many direct benefits to employers.

- ✓ lower workers' compensation insurance costs;
- ✓ reduced medical expenditures;
- ✓ smaller expenditures for return-to-work programs;
- ✓ fewer faulty products;
- ✓ lower costs for job accommodations for injured workers;
- ✓ less money spent for overtime benefits.

Following safety and health regulations and proper procedures has indirect benefits as well.

- ✓ increased productivity;
- ✓ higher quality products;
- ✓ increased morale;
- ✓ better labor/management relations;
- ✓ reduced turnover;
- ✓ better use of human resources.

The impact of a safety and health program extends beyond the workplace providing employees and their families the security that their incomes are protected, family life is not hindered by injury, and overall reduced stress.

Employee Rights

The OSH Act grants employees several important rights. Among them are the rights to

- ✓ complain to OSHA about safety and health conditions in their workplaces and, to the extent permitted by law, have their identities kept confidential from employers;
- ✓ contest the amount of time OSHA allows for correcting violations of standards; and
- ✓ participate in OSHA workplace inspections.

Retaliation is Prohibited: Private sector employees who exercise their rights under OSHA can be protected against employer reprisal. Employees must notify OSHA within 30 days of the time they learned of the alleged discriminatory action. OSHA will then investigate. If it agrees that discrimination has occurred, OSHA will ask the employer to restore any lost benefits to the affected employee. If necessary, OSHA can initiate legal action against the employer. In such cases, the worker pays no legal fees. The OSHA-approved state plans have similar employee rights provisions, including protections against employer reprisal.

Penalties

OSHA Enforcement: Every establishment covered by the OSH Act is subject to inspection by OSHA compliance safety and health officers (CSHOs). These individuals are chosen for their knowledge and experience in occupational safety and health. They are thoroughly trained in OSHA standards and in the recognition of occupational safety and health hazards. In states with their own OSHA-approved state plan, state officials conduct inspections, issue citations for violations, and propose penalties in a manner that is at least as strict as the federal program.

The following table illustrates penalty types, descriptions, and amounts assessed to the employer.

Penalty Type and Description	**Penalty Amount**
Other Than Serious Violation - A violation that has a direct relationship to workplace safety and health, but probably would not cause death or serious physical harm.	Discretionary penalty up to $7,000 for each violation
Serious Violation - A violation where there is substantial probability that death or serious physical harm could result and that the employer knew, or should have known, of the hazard.	Mandatory penalty up to $7,000 for each violation

Penalty Type and Description	Penalty Amount
Willful Violation - A violation that the employer knowingly commits or commits with plain indifference to the law. The employer either knows that what he or she is doing constitutes a violation, or is aware that a hazardous condition existed and made no reasonable effort to eliminate it.	Penalties of up to $70,000 with a minimum penalty of $5,000 for each violation. If an employer is convicted of a willful violation of a standard that has resulted in the death of an employee, the offense is punishable by a court-imposed fine or by imprisonment for up to six months, or both. A fine of up to $250,000 for an individual, or $500,000 for a corporation, may be imposed for a criminal conviction.
Repeated Violation - A violation of any standard, regulation, rule, or order where, upon reinspection, a substantially similar violation is found.	Penalties of up to $70,000
Failure to Abate Prior Violation	Civil penalty of up to $7,000 for each day the violation continues beyond the prescribed abatement date
De Minimis Violation - A violation of standards which have no direct or immediate relationship to safety or health.	Violation documented but not cited

Violations may be adjusted depending on the employer's good faith (demonstrated by efforts to comply with the act), history of previous violations, and size of business.

Additional violations for which citations and proposed penalties may be issued upon conviction include the following:

- ✓ Falsifying records, reports, or applications can bring a fine of $10,000 or up to six months in jail, or both.
- ✓ Violations of posting requirements can bring a civil penalty of up to $7,000.
- ✓ Assaulting a compliance officer, or otherwise resisting, opposing, intimidating, or interfering with a compliance officer while they are engaged in the performance of their duties is a criminal offense, subject to a fine of not more than $5,000 and imprisonment for not more than three years.

Citation and penalty procedures may differ somewhat in states with their own occupational safety and health programs.

Inspections: OSHA conducts two general types of inspections: **programmed** and **unprogrammed**.

- ✓ **Programmed** inspections are performed on establishments with high injury rates.
- ✓ **Unprogrammed** inspections are used in response to fatalities, catastrophes, and complaints.

Various OSHA publications and documents detail OSHA's policies and procedures for inspections and the penalties for violations.

Citation and penalty procedures may differ somewhat in states with their own OSH programs.

Environmental Considerations

You need to be aware of the environmental considerations surrounding construction during all phases of the project.

- ✓ During the **pre-bid phase**, you must learn the regulations that pertain to the project and factor in the cost for compliance into the estimate.
- ✓ Obtaining the necessary permits occurs during the **pre-construction phase** and environmental responsibilities should be assigned to the construction crew.
- ✓ Self-audits help ensure compliance during the **construction phase.**
- ✓ For **post-construction**, you need to ensure that all the close-down procedures were done properly.

Going Green: Integrating eco-friendly practices in your business may help you control costs, tap into a new customer base, and enhance your socially responsible reputation. The demand for energy-efficient building design and construction is increasing. The Energy Star website at www.energystar.gov provides numerous resources on home improvement and commercial and residential construction. The EPA website archive at archive.epa.gov/greenbuilding/web/html/ has information on components of green building, national, state and local funding opportunities, and publications on various environmental topics.

U.S. Environmental Protection Agency

Environmental Regulation: The U.S. Environmental Protection Agency (EPA) leads the nation's environmental science, research, education, and assessment efforts. The EPA works to develop and enforce regulations that implement environmental laws enacted by Congress. The EPA is responsible for researching and setting national standards for a variety of environmental programs and delegates to states the responsibility for issuing permits and for monitoring and enforcing compliance. If national standards are not met, the EPA can issue sanctions and take other steps to assist the states in reaching the desired levels of environmental quality.

Compliance Assistance: The EPA publishes a guide called Managing Your Responsibilities: A Planning Guide for Construction and Development. This publication is available for download at: archive.epa.gov/compliance/resources/publications/assistance/sectors/web/pdf/myerguide.pdf.

This guide provides comprehensive information for all types of environmental hazards and the compliance requirements. Summarized briefly below are just some of the environmental hazards impacting construction projects.

South Carolina Department of Health and Environmental Control

The South Carolina Department of Health and Environmental Control (DHEC) is responsible for the enforcement of federal and state environmental laws and regulations and for the issuing of permits, licenses, and certifications for activities that may affect the environment. The DHEC has several outreach programs available to provide environmental assistance. The Small Business Assistance Program provides publications and technical assistance to help small businesses determine compliance requirements with applicable regulations.

The Small Business Program can be contacted at (803) 896-8940. For more information, contact:

South Carolina Department of Health and Environmental Control
2600 Bull Street
Columbia, South Carolina 29201

General Phone: (803) 898-3432

Website: www.scdhec.gov

Before beginning a project, you should assess the jobsite and determine if you need an environmental permit.

Environmental Law

There are several environmental laws that may impact your construction activities.

- ✓ The **Clean Water Act** establishes the basic structure for regulating discharges of pollutants into the waters of the United States. This act gives the EPA authority to implement pollution control programs, such as setting wastewater standards for the industry and water quality standards for all contaminants in surface waters. This act is discussed in more depth later in this chapter.
- ✓ Through the **Clean Air Act**, the EPA sets limits on how much of a pollutant is allowed in the air anywhere in the United States.
- ✓ The **Endangered Species Act (ESA)** protects threatened or endangered species from further harm. You should consider the impact of your construction activities on these species before you start your project.
- ✓ The **National Environmental Policy Act (NEPA)** applies to your construction project only if it is considered a "federal action." This act ensures that federal agencies consider environmental impacts in federal planning and decision making and covers construction and post-construction activities.
- ✓ The **National Historic Preservation Act (NHPA)** applies to your construction project if your project might have a potential impact on a property that is eligible for or included in the National Register of Historic Places (NRHP).

A thorough environmental assessment of your construction site is recommended for all projects. This assessment allows you to understand the environmental impacts of your project early, causing less delays and problems.

Air Quality

Outdoor Air Quality: Air regulations for construction activities are designed to limit the generation of particulate and ozone depleting substances.

Air quality issues that may impact your business are

- ✓ uncontrolled open burning of debris,
- ✓ dust generation,
- ✓ vehicle emissions,
- ✓ combustion gases from oil-fired equipment, and
- ✓ releases of chlorofluorocarbons (CFCs).

Indoor Air: Indoor air quality can be just as important as outdoor air quality. For the safety of those on the construction site, you should give special consideration to materials that contain harmful chemicals including

- ✓ paint/primers,
- ✓ adhesives,
- ✓ floor coatings,
- ✓ carpet, and
- ✓ plywood/particle board.

Properly installed HVAC units and drain pans are important to avoid biological contaminants that breed in stagnant water. Most air permitting requirements for construction activities are at the state and local level.

Bureau of Air Quality: The Department of Health and Environmental Control's Bureau of Air Quality is the department to contact regarding air quality permits. A construction permit may be required prior to beginning a construction project. The construction permit application may take up to 90 days for approval by the Bureau of Air Quality.

For further information on air permitting in South Carolina, contact:

South Carolina Department of Health and Environmental Control
Bureau of Air Quality
2600 Bull Street
Columbia, South Carolina 29201

Phone: (803) 898-4123

Website: www.scdhec.gov/environment/air-quality

Be aware of both indoor and outdoor pollution.

Asbestos

Before beginning any demolition or renovation activities on existing buildings, you should evaluate the potential for releasing asbestos. Exposure to asbestos can cause serious health problems and the EPA and OSHA have published rules regulating its production, use, and disposal.

Evaluation Guidelines: When evaluating whether or not asbestos may be present, you want to note possible asbestos-containing material, such as

- ✓ Insulation, including blown, rolled and wrapped
- ✓ Resilient floor coverings (tiles)
- ✓ Asbestos siding shingles
- ✓ Asbestos-cement products
- ✓ Asphalt roofing products
- ✓ Vermiculite insulation

The EPA has a comprehensive list of suspected asbestos-containing materials at: www.epa.gov/asbestos.

Inspections: If you are working with asbestos, you should have your site inspected by a certified asbestos inspector prior to construction. You must submit a written notice of intent 10 working days prior to starting construction activities. Written notices should be submitted to your delegated state/local pollution control agency and your EPA Regional Office.

South Carolina Asbestos Regulations: Contractors engaging in any asbestos project or abatement involving asbestos-containing material must be properly licensed through the South Carolina Department of Health and Environmental Control.

Before beginning a renovation or demolition project, a building inspection not more than three years old must be done to identify the presence, location, and estimated quantity of asbestos-containing material. Specific requirements exist for project notification, work practices, air sampling, cleanup, and disposal of the asbestos-containing material depending on the type of project. Project classifications include

- ✓ National Emissions Standards for Hazardous Air Pollutants (NESHAP) Projects defined as the amount of asbestos-containing material of at least 260 linear feet on pipes, 160 square feet on other facility components, or 35 cubic feet off facility components where the area or length could not be measured prior to abatement.

- ✓ Small Projects defined as the amount of asbestos-containing material of at least 25 linear feet but less than 260 linear feet on pipes, at least 25 square feet but less than 160 square feet on other facility components, or at least 10 cubic feet but less than 35 cubic feet off facility components where the area or length could not be measured prior to abatement.
- ✓ Minor Projects defined as the amount of asbestos-containing material of less than 25 linear feet on pipes, less than 25 square feet on other facility components, or less than 10 cubic feet off facility components where the area or length could not be measured prior to abatement.

For further information on asbestos regulations and standards, contact:

South Carolina Department of Health and Environmental Control
Bureau of Air Quality
2600 Bull Street
Columbia, South Carolina 29201

Phone: (803) 898-4123

Website: www.scdhec.gov/HomeAndEnvironment/Air

Clean Water Act

Water pollution can negatively affect the use of water for drinking, household needs, recreation, fishing, transportation and commerce. The EPA enforces federal clean water and safe drinking water laws, provides support for municipal wastewater treatment plants, and takes part in pollution prevention efforts aimed at protecting watersheds and sources of drinking water.

The Clean Water Act establishes the basic structure for regulating discharges of pollutants into the waters of the United States. This includes

- ✓ giving the EPA the authority to implement pollution control programs such as setting wastewater standards for industry;
- ✓ continuing requirements to set water quality standards for all contaminants in surface waters; and
- ✓ making it unlawful for any person to discharge any pollutant from a point source into navigable waters, unless a National Pollutant Discharge Elimination System (NPDES) permit was obtained under its provisions.

Stormwater Discharges and Construction Site Runoff: Before beginning any construction project, you must consider runoff and stormwater discharges that may originate from your site. These discharges often contain sediment and pollutants such as phosphorous and nitrogen (fertilizer), pesticides, oil and grease, concrete truck washout, construction chemicals, and solid wastes in quantities that could adversely affect water quality.

National Pollutant Discharge Elimination System (NPDES): The EPA has estimated that about 30 percent of known pollution to our nation's waters is attributable to stormwater runoff. In 1987, Congress directed the EPA to develop a regulatory program to address the stormwater problem. The EPA issued regulations in 1990 authorizing the creation of a NPDES permitting system for stormwater discharges from a select group, including construction activities disturbing five or more acres.

In 1999, the EPA expanded this program (called Phase II). This phase brought about two major new permittees:

- ✓ Construction sites that disturb one acre but less than five acres with possible exceptions allowing a waiver
- ✓ Small municipal separate storm sewer systems (MS4)

A "larger common plan of development or sale" is subject to stormwater permitting, even if the land is parceled off or sold, and construction occurs on plots that are less than one acre by separate, independent builders.

Assessing Stormwater Discharge: Listed below are questions that you need to consider when determining the need for a stormwater permit for your construction project:

- ✓ Will your construction project disturb one or more acres of land?
- ✓ Will your construction project disturb less than one acre of land, but is part of a larger common plan of development or sale that will disturb one or more acres?

- ✓ Will your construction project disturb less than one acre of land, but is designated by the NPDES (state agency or EPA) permitting authority as a regulated construction activity?
- ✓ Will stormwater from the construction site flow to a municipal separate storm sewer system or a water of the United States such as a lake, river, or wetland?

Municipal Technologies Agency: The EPA's Municipal Technologies Agency provides assistance in the area of municipal wastewater treatment technologies. Available assistance includes

- ✓ consultation on design, operation, and maintenance of systems;
- ✓ identification and solution of problems;
- ✓ contributions in the development of regulations; and
- ✓ technical information, guidance, assessments, evaluation, and cost estimates for the design, construction, and operation and maintenance of municipal wastewater treatment facilities.

Bureau of Water: The Department of Health and Environmental Control's Bureau of Water is the department to contact regarding water quality permits, approvals, and certifications involving a number of different activities and facilities. The Bureau of Water has a Wastewater Construction Permit Program that offers a comprehensive water pollution control program on transportation, treatment, and disposal or use of wastewater and sludge. The following programs contained in the Wastewater Construction Permit Program are

- ✓ NPDES Permit Program,
- ✓ Land Application System Permit Program,
- ✓ Pretreatment Program,
- ✓ Satellite Sewer System Program, and
- ✓ Sludge Program.

For further information on water quality permits and programs, contact:

South Carolina Department of Health and Environmental Control
Bureau of Water
2600 Bull Street
Columbia, South Carolina 29201

Phone: (803) 898-4300

Website: www.scdhec.gov/HomeAndEnvironment/Water

Sedimentation and Erosion Control Measures

During a short period of time, construction sites can contribute more sediment to streams than can be deposited naturally during several decades. Excess sediment can quickly fill rivers and lakes, requiring dredging, and destroying aquatic habitats.

Measures can be taken to minimize erosion and sedimentation on construction sites:

- ✓ Sediment control measures include a silt fence or hay bales placed at the down gradient side of the construction site.
- ✓ Erosion control measures include placing mulch and vegetation as soon as feasible to permanently stabilize the site soil.
- ✓ A water misting system can control dust generated on the jobsite and loss of soil.

Erosion and sediment control minimizes pollution and contractor costs to rework eroded areas and replace lost soil. Individual states may have required sedimentation and erosion control measures.

Hazardous and Non-Hazardous Solid Waste

In general, construction sites generate more non-hazardous waste than hazardous waste. You should be aware of the regulations surrounding both.

Non-Hazardous Waste: Common non-hazardous waste generated at construction sites includes

- ✓ scrap wood,
- ✓ drywall,
- ✓ bricks,
- ✓ concrete,
- ✓ plumbing fixtures and piping,
- ✓ roof coverings,
- ✓ metal scraps, and
- ✓ electrical wiring and components.

Non-hazardous waste is regulated at the state and local level and you should identify any requirements. For more information on state requirements, refer to the Construction Industry Compliance Assistance Center at www.cicacenter.org.

Hazardous Waste: Hazardous waste is regulated at the federal level and your state may have additional requirements.

Examples of hazardous waste are

- ✓ lead-based paint,
- ✓ used oil,
- ✓ hydraulic fluid,
- ✓ gypsum drywall (due to sulfate), and
- ✓ mercury-containing demolition wastes such as batteries and thermostats.

Proper Notification: If you discover hazardous waste on your jobsite, you must notify your state and local authorities or the National Response Center Hotline at 1-800-424-8802. Criminal charges may be filed if hazardous wastes are present at the site and proper notification does not take place. If hazardous waste is produced through construction activities, the party that generated the waste is generally responsible for cleaning it up. Hazardous waste must be treated and disposed of at a facility permitted or licensed for that purpose by the state or federal government.

Bureau of Land and Waste Management: The Department of Health and Environmental Control's Bureau of Land and Waste Management oversees the inspection and enforcement of hazardous waste treatment, transportation, and disposal within state and federal guidelines. The Bureau of Land and Waste Management also has Underground Storage Tank and Solid Waste Management Programs that provide planning, compliance, permitting, enforcement, and remediation assistance.

For further information programs offered through the Bureau of Land and Waste Management, contact:

South Carolina Department of Health and Environmental Control
Bureau of Land and Waste Management
2600 Bull Street
Columbia, South Carolina 29201

Phone: (803) 898-2000

Website: www.scdhec.gov/environment/land-management

Hazardous Substances

Site Survey: Before beginning any construction or demolition activities at your construction site, you should evaluate the site for any hazardous substances.

Hazardous substances referred to in this section are chemicals that most likely induce serious acute reactions from short-term airborne exposure.

Notification: When you do a site survey, you should review historical records to determine previous uses of the site. A review of state and local files will help you identify past environmental concerns. If during construction you uncover hazardous substances, you must stop construction activities immediately and notify the owner and contact the National Response Hotline at 1-800-424-8802.

Underground Storage Tanks (UST): An underground storage tank system (UST) is defined by the EPA as "a tank and any underground piping connected to the tank that has at least 10 percent of its combined volume underground." The federal UST regulations apply only to underground tanks and piping storing either petroleum or certain hazardous substances. Federal regulations do not apply to the following types of underground storage tanks:

- ✓ Farm and residential tanks of 1,100 gallons or less capacity holding motor fuel used for noncommercial purposes
- ✓ Tanks storing heating oil used on the premises where it is stored
- ✓ Tanks on or above the floor of underground areas, such as basements or tunnels
- ✓ Septic tanks and systems for collecting storm water and wastewater
- ✓ Flow-through process tanks
- ✓ Tanks of 110 gallons or less capacity
- ✓ Emergency spill and overfill tanks

Conduct a thorough site survey to anticipate any environmental hazards.

Lead

Exposure Hazards: Lead is considered a toxic and hazardous substance and can cause a serious risk of lead poisoning if overexposure occurs. OSHA regulates the amount of lead that workers can be exposed to (no more than 50 micrograms of lead per cubic meter of air averaged over an 8-hour day). Traditionally, the most over-exposure occurs in trades such as plumbing, welding, and painting.

Hazard Protection: The most effective way to protect workers is through good work practices and engineering controls. Respirators are not a substitute for these practices, but should be an additional measure of safety. Employers are required to supply respirators at no cost to employees who will potentially be exposed to lead and adopt a respirator program, including a written standard operating procedure, training, and regular equipment inspection.

Engineering controls to reduce worker exposure include

- ✓ exhaust ventilation, such as power tools with dust collection shrouds or other attachments exhausted through a high-efficiency particulate air (HEPA) vacuum system;
- ✓ enclosure or encapsulation of lead particles (for example, lead-based paint can be made inaccessible by encapsulating it with a material that bonds to the surface such as epoxy coating);
- ✓ substituting lead-based products or products that create lead exposure with a comparable product;
- ✓ replacing lead components with non-lead components;
- ✓ process or equipment modifications that create less lead exposure from dust; and
- ✓ isolating the lead exposure area so other areas are not contaminated.

Construction Assistance: OSHA has downloadable software on its website designed to help small business owners understand the Lead in Construction standard. Users should still refer to the OSHA standards for any specifics as the most up-to-date source.

Remodeling or Renovating a Home with Lead-Based Paint (Lead PRE)

If not conducted properly, certain types of renovations can release lead from paint and dust into the air. The Lead Pre-Renovation Education Rule (Lead PRE) is a federal regulation involving those performing renovations for compensation in residential housing that may contain lead paint.

In December 2008 (with amendments in 2010, 2011, 2015, and 2016), the EPA passed the Lead-Based Paint Renovation, Repair and Painting Program Rule that imposes additional lead-based paint regulations. Under this rule, only certified contractors can perform renovation, repair and painting projects that disturb lead-based paint in homes, child care facilities, and schools built before 1978. The EPA has authorized Alabama, Georgia, Iowa, Kansas, Massachusetts, Mississippi, North Carolina, Oregon, Rhode Island, Utah, Washington, and Wisconsin to administer their own Renovation, Repair and Painting Program. Contractors working in these states must follow the regulations put forth by the state program.

Contractors can become certified renovators by submitting an application and fee to the EPA or state-based program and taking an eight-hour training course from an EPA-accredited training provider. Certified contractors must follow specific work practices to prevent lead contamination. Three simple principles are applied when working with lead which includes:

- ✓ containing the work area to minimize lead contamination in other work areas;
- ✓ minimizing dust to prevent harmful airborne particles from being inhaled; and
- ✓ cleaning up the work area thoroughly.

Required Notification: Under Lead PRE, federal law requires that contractors provide lead information to residents before renovating pre-1978 housing. The EPA publishes a pamphlet titled Protect Your Family from Lead in Your Home which must be distributed to the owner and occupants before starting work. Confirmation of receipt of the lead pamphlet or a certificate of mailing must be kept for three years. For work in common areas of multi-family housing, renovation notices must be distributed to all tenants.

For renovations to child-occupied facilities, renovators must distribute the pamphlet titled Renovate Right: Important Lead Hazard Information for Families, Child Care Providers and Schools to owners, administrators, and parents or guardians of children under the age of six that attend these facilities.

Exemptions: This rule applies to nearly all remodeling or renovation work with the exception of the following circumstances:

- ✓ Housing for the elderly or disabled persons unless children will reside there
- ✓ Zero-bedroom dwellings
- ✓ Emergency renovations or repairs
- ✓ Minor repair and maintenance that disturb two square feet or less of paint per component
- ✓ Housing or components declared lead-free by a certified inspector or risk assessor

Lead Abatement: Work designed to permanently eliminate lead-based paint hazards is considered lead abatement and is not subject to the guidelines under Lead PRE. This does not include renovation, remodeling, landscaping, or other activities designed to repair, restore, and redesign a given building. The EPA outlines strict regulations for this type of work as discussed in the previous section on lead.

Renovation: Renovations under Lead PRE are modifications of all or part of any existing structure that disturbs a painted surface. This includes

- ✓ removal/modification of painted surfaces, components or structures;
- ✓ surface preparation activities (sanding/scraping/ other activities that may create paint dust); and
- ✓ window replacement.

Penalties: Failure to comply with regulations concerning lead is a serious violation. Non-compliance carries substantial fines of up to $37,000 per day for each violation. Criminal penalties of imprisonment for up to one year also apply to willful or intentional violation of the regulation.

Assistance: You can obtain additional information by going online to the EPA website at www.epa.gov/lead or by contacting The National Lead Information Center (NLIC) at 1-800-424-LEAD (5323).

Final Inspection...

Safety Standards: It is important to know the OSHA standards that pertain to the construction industry.

Safe Hiring and Training: Background checks can help you hire workers with good safety records. Regular training contributes to a safe working environment.

Substance Abuse Policies: Substance abuse compromises safety in the workplace. Clearly written and communicated policies are useful tools in reducing substance abuse.

Safety Equipment: Certain safety equipment may be required according to OSHA regulations, depending on the work being performed.

Emergency Action Plan: Either a written or an orally communicated emergency action plan is required by OSHA, depending on the number of employees you have.

OSHA Recordkeeping: Your company may be required to complete OSHA forms 300, 300A and 301.

OSHA Injury Decision Tree: The OSHA injury decision tree outlines the steps in making the determination for recording work-related injuries and illnesses.

Material Safety Data Sheets (MSDS): A material safety data sheet (MSDS) is required for all chemicals used.

Underground Utility Safety: Although laws on marking underground utilities vary from state to state, contractors should identify underground utilities before excavating.

Overhead Power Line Safety: Overhead power line safety should be considered when formulating a health and safety program and worksite planning. As a general rule, workers should keep a minimum distance of 10 feet from overhead power lines.

Benefits of Providing a Safe and Healthy Workplace: OSHA can assess citations for failing to provide a safe work environment. Ensuring workers are healthy and safe provides many direct and indirect benefits to employers.

Employee Rights: Employees are allowed to report OSHA violations without fear of retaliation.

Penalties: Penalties vary depending on the severity of OSHA violations. OSHA may conduct programmed or unprogrammed inspections.

Environmental Considerations: Environmental factors should be considered throughout all phases of construction. Obtaining proper permits is important for following environmental regulations.

U.S. Environmental Protection Agency (EPA): The EPA works to develop and enforce regulations that implement environmental laws enacted by Congress.

South Carolina Department of Health and Environmental Control: The South Carolina Department of Health and Environmental Control has several programs and activities that provide environmental and permitting assistance.

Environmental Law: Several laws exist to protect the environment. An assessment of environmental impacts should be done early on in the construction project.

Air Quality: Indoor and outdoor quality should be monitored throughout the construction project.

Asbestos: Before beginning remodeling or demolition of any project, assess whether you may encounter asbestos-releasing materials. Certain permitting and notification requirements may apply.

Clean Water Act: The Clean Water Act establishes the basic structure for regulating discharges of pollutants into the waters of the United States.

Sedimentation and Erosion Control Measures: Erosion and sediment control measures minimize pollution and contractor costs to rework eroded areas and replace lost soil.

Hazardous and Non-Hazardous Waste: Most construction waste is non-hazardous. Both hazardous and non-hazardous waste must be disposed of properly.

Hazardous Substances: Early identification of hazardous substances is important and proper notification is required.

Lead: Contact with lead can cause lead poisoning and you and your employees must follow specific regulations when working with it.

Remodeling or Renovating a Home with Lead-Based Paint: The Lead Pre-Renovation Education Rule (Lead PRE) is a federal regulation involving those performing renovations for compensation in residential housing that may contain lead paint.

Supplemental Forms

Supplemental forms and links are available at **NASCLAforms.org** using access code **SCR129354**. The following forms can be found in the Safety & Environmental section.

OSHA Forms for Recording Work-Related Injuries and Illnesses	OSHA forms 300, 300A and 301 with instructions
OSHA Compliance Assistance Employment Law Guide	OSHA guide summarizing employer responsibilities under the OSH Act
Managing Your Environmental Responsibilities: A Planning Guide for Construction and Development	EPA guide customized for the construction industry that outlines specific environmental responsibilities
Protect Your Family From Lead in Your Home	Mandatory brochure to distribute to the owner if you are doing renovations on pre-1978 housing

OSHA's Form 300 (Rev. 01/2004)

Log of Work-Related Injuries and Illnesses

Attention: This form contains information relating to employee health and must be used in a manner that protects the confidentiality of employees to the extent possible while the information is being used for occupational safety and health purposes.

Year 20__ __

U.S. Department of Labor

Occupational Safety and Health Administration

Form approved OMB no. 1218-0176

You must record information about every work-related death and about every work-related injury or illness that involves loss of consciousness, restricted work activity or job transfer, days away from work, or medical treatment beyond first aid. You must also record significant work-related injuries and illnesses that are diagnosed by a physician or licensed health care professional. You must also record work-related injuries and illnesses that meet any of the specific recording criteria listed in 29 CFR Part 1904.8 through 1904.12. Feel free to use two lines for a single case if you need to. You must complete an Injury and Illness Incident Report (OSHA Form 301) or equivalent form for each injury or illness recorded on this form. If you're not sure whether a case is recordable, call your local OSHA office for help.

Establishment name ________________

City ____________ State ________

Identify the person			Describe the case			Classify the case: CHECK ONLY ONE box for each case based on the most serious outcome for that case:				Enter the number of days the injured or ill worker was:		Check the "Injury" column or choose one type of illness: (M)					
(A) Case no.	(B) Employee's name	(C) Job title (*e.g., Welder*)	(D) Date of injury or onset of illness	(E) Where the event occurred (*e.g., Loading dock north end*)	(F) Describe injury or illness, parts of body affected, and object/substance that directly injured or made person ill (*e.g., Second degree burns on right forearm from acetylene torch*)	Death (G)	Remained at Work: Days away from work (H)	Remained at Work: Job transfer or restriction (I)	Remained at Work: Other record-able cases (J)	Away from work (K)	On job transfer or restriction (L)	Injury (1)	Skin disorder (2)	Respiratory condition (3)	Poisoning (4)	Hearing loss (5)	All other illnesses (6)
			/ month/day			☐	☐	☐	☐	___ days	___ days	☐	☐	☐	☐	☐	☐
			/ month/day			☐	☐	☐	☐	___ days	___ days	☐	☐	☐	☐	☐	☐
			/ month/day			☐	☐	☐	☐	___ days	___ days	☐	☐	☐	☐	☐	☐
			/ month/day			☐	☐	☐	☐	___ days	___ days	☐	☐	☐	☐	☐	☐
			/ month/day			☐	☐	☐	☐	___ days	___ days	☐	☐	☐	☐	☐	☐
			/ month/day			☐	☐	☐	☐	___ days	___ days	☐	☐	☐	☐	☐	☐
			/ month/day			☐	☐	☐	☐	___ days	___ days	☐	☐	☐	☐	☐	☐
			/ month/day			☐	☐	☐	☐	___ days	___ days	☐	☐	☐	☐	☐	☐
			/ month/day			☐	☐	☐	☐	___ days	___ days	☐	☐	☐	☐	☐	☐
			/ month/day			☐	☐	☐	☐	___ days	___ days	☐	☐	☐	☐	☐	☐
			/ month/day			☐	☐	☐	☐	___ days	___ days	☐	☐	☐	☐	☐	☐
			/ month/day			☐	☐	☐	☐	___ days	___ days	☐	☐	☐	☐	☐	☐
			/ month/day			☐	☐	☐	☐	___ days	___ days	☐	☐	☐	☐	☐	☐
					Page totals	___	___	___	___	___	___	___ Injury (1)	___ Skin disorder (2)	___ Respiratory condition (3)	___ Poisoning (4)	___ Hearing loss (5)	___ All other illnesses (6)

Be sure to transfer these totals to the Summary page (Form 300A) before you post it.

Page __ of __

Public reporting burden for this collection of information is estimated to average 14 minutes per response, including time to review the instructions, search and gather the data needed, and complete and review the collection of information. Persons are not required to respond to the collection of information unless it displays a currently valid OMB control number. If you have any comments about these estimates or any other aspects of this data collection, contact: US Department of Labor, OSHA Office of Statistical Analysis, Room N-3644, 200 Constitution Avenue, NW, Washington, DC 20210. Do not send the completed forms to this office.

OSHA's Form 300A (Rev. 01/2004)

Summary of Work-Related Injuries and Illnesses

Year 20__ __

U.S. Department of Labor
Occupational Safety and Health Administration

Form approved OMB no. 1218-0176

All establishments covered by Part 1904 must complete this Summary page, even if no work-related injuries or illnesses occurred during the year. Remember to review the Log to verify that the entries are complete and accurate before completing this summary.

Using the Log, count the individual entries you made for each category. Then write the totals below, making sure you've added the entries from every page of the Log. If you had no cases, write "0."

Employees, former employees, and their representatives have the right to review the OSHA Form 300 in its entirety. They also have limited access to the OSHA Form 301 or its equivalent. See 29 CFR Part 1904.35, in OSHA's recordkeeping rule, for further details on the access provisions for these forms.

Number of Cases

Total number of deaths	Total number of cases with days away from work	Total number of cases with job transfer or restriction	Total number of other recordable cases
______ (G)	______ (H)	______ (I)	______ (J)

Number of Days

Total number of days away from work	Total number of days of job transfer or restriction
______ (K)	______ (L)

Injury and Illness Types

Total number of . . .
(M)

(1) Injuries	______	(4) Poisonings	______
		(5) Hearing loss	______
(2) Skin disorders	______	(6) All other illnesses	______
(3) Respiratory conditions	______		

Post this Summary page from February 1 to April 30 of the year following the year covered by the form.

Public reporting burden for this collection of information is estimated to average 50 minutes per response, including time to review the instructions, search and gather the data needed, and complete and review the collection of information. Persons are not required to respond to the collection of information unless it displays a currently valid OMB control number. If you have any comments about these estimates or any other aspects of this data collection, contact: US Department of Labor, OSHA Office of Statistical Analysis, Room N-3644, 200 Constitution Avenue, NW, Washington, DC 20210. Do not send the completed forms to this office.

Establishment information

Your establishment name ____________________

Street ____________________

City ____________ State ____ ZIP ______

Industry description (*e.g., Manufacture of motor truck trailers*)

____

Standard Industrial Classification (SIC), if known (*e.g., 3715*)

__ __ __ __

OR

North American Industrial Classification (NAICS), if known (e.g., 336212)

__ __ __ __ __ __

Employment information (*If you don't have these figures, see the Worksheet on the back of this page to estimate.*)

Annual average number of employees ______

Total hours worked by all employees last year ______

Sign here

Knowingly falsifying this document may result in a fine.

I certify that I have examined this document and that to the best of my knowledge the entries are true, accurate, and complete.

____________________ ________
Company executive Title

( ) - __________ / /
Phone Date

OSHA's Form 301
Injury and Illness Incident Report

Attention: This form contains information relating to employee health and must be used in a manner that protects the confidentiality of employees to the extent possible while the information is being used for occupational safety and health purposes.

U.S. Department of Labor
Occupational Safety and Health Administration

Form approved OMB no. 1218-0176

This *Injury and Illness Incident Report* is one of the first forms you must fill out when a recordable work-related injury or illness has occurred. Together with the *Log of Work-Related Injuries and Illnesses* and the accompanying *Summary*, these forms help the employer and OSHA develop a picture of the extent and severity of work-related incidents.

Within 7 calendar days after you receive information that a recordable work-related injury or illness has occurred, you must fill out this form or an equivalent. Some state workers' compensation, insurance, or other reports may be acceptable substitutes. To be considered an equivalent form, any substitute must contain all the information asked for on this form.

According to Public Law 91-596 and 29 CFR 1904, OSHA's recordkeeping rule, you must keep this form on file for 5 years following the year to which it pertains.

If you need additional copies of this form, you may photocopy and use as many as you need.

Completed by ______________________

Title ______________________

Phone (____)______-________ Date ____/____/____

Information about the employee

1) Full name ______________________

2) Street ______________________

City ______________ State ______ ZIP ______

3) Date of birth ____/____/____

4) Date hired ____/____/____

5) ☐ Male
☐ Female

Information about the physician or other health care professional

6) Name of physician or other health care professional ______________________

7) If treatment was given away from the worksite, where was it given?

Facility ______________________

Street ______________________

City ______________ State ______ ZIP ______

8) Was employee treated in an emergency room?
☐ Yes
☐ No

9) Was employee hospitalized overnight as an in-patient?
☐ Yes
☐ No

Information about the case

10) Case number from the *Log* ____________ *(Transfer the case number from the Log after you record the case.)*

11) Date of injury or illness ____/____/____

12) Time employee began work ____________ AM / PM

13) Time of event ____________ AM / PM ☐ Check if time cannot be determined

14) ***What was the employee doing just before the incident occurred?*** Describe the activity, as well as the tools, equipment, or material the employee was using. Be specific. *Examples:* "climbing a ladder while carrying roofing materials"; "spraying chlorine from hand sprayer"; "daily computer key-entry."

15) ***What happened?*** Tell us how the injury occurred. *Examples:* "When ladder slipped on wet floor, worker fell 20 feet"; "Worker was sprayed with chlorine when gasket broke during replacement"; "Worker developed soreness in wrist over time."

16) ***What was the injury or illness?*** Tell us the part of the body that was affected and how it was affected; be more specific than "hurt," "pain," or sore." *Examples:* "strained back"; "chemical burn, hand"; "carpal tunnel syndrome."

17) ***What object or substance directly harmed the employee?*** *Examples:* "concrete floor"; "chlorine"; "radial arm saw." *If this question does not apply to the incident, leave it blank.*

18) ***If the employee died, when did death occur?*** Date of death ____/____/____

Public reporting burden for this collection of information is estimated to average 22 minutes per response, including time for reviewing instructions, searching existing data sources, gathering and maintaining the data needed, and completing and reviewing the collection of information. Persons are not required to respond to the collection of information unless it displays a current valid OMB control number. If you have any comments about this estimate or any other aspects of this data collection, including suggestions for reducing this burden, contact: US Department of Labor, OSHA Office of Statistical Analysis, Room N-3644, 200 Constitution Avenue, NW, Washington, DC 20210. Do not send the completed forms to this office.

Chapter 13
WORKING WITH SUBCONTRACTORS

Chapter Survey...

- ⇨ *Sources for Finding the Right Subcontractor*
- ⇨ *Creating a Winning Partnership*
- ⇨ *Site Rules for Contractors*
- ⇨ *Employee or Independent Contractor: IRS Guidelines*

Subcontractors contract with the general contractor or other subcontractors to complete a portion of a larger project (in South Carolina, specialty contractors are not allowed to sub-contract).

It is important to hire the right subcontractors because their work impacts your company's reputation. Just as you want employees who are easy to work with, the same applies to subcontractors.

There are basic criteria you can use to evaluate whether you want to hire a subcontractor:

- ✓ Do they sell or produce quality products?
- ✓ Are they reliable? Are they able to complete the project according to the schedule?
- ✓ Do they have good customer service skills?
- ✓ Are they able to effectively deal with problems?
- ✓ Do they give an overall impression of professionalism?
- ✓ Are they properly licensed and carry appropriate insurance coverage?
- ✓ Do they remedy situations that involve material defects or failures?
- ✓ How do they handle change orders?
- ✓ Are they competitively priced?

Now that you have established your requirements, it is time to find qualified leads.

Sources for Finding the Right Subcontractor

If you have a good reputation, the word travels fast. This also holds true for good subcontractors and suppliers. Some of your best subcontractors can come from referrals. Sources for these referrals might include

- ✓ subcontractors in a different field who have worked with other subcontractors on other jobs;
- ✓ other contractors in your field;
- ✓ members of your local trade association;
- ✓ suppliers (for example, electrical supply firms can give referrals on electricians); and
- ✓ architects or engineers.

Once you come up with credible referrals, you want to make sure that you take extra steps to organize the process.

- ✓ Keep a list of qualified subcontractors.
- ✓ Allow sufficient lead time to line up subcontractors for jobs.
- ✓ Interview subcontractors for their qualifications, even when you are not scheduling them for a job.
- ✓ Check references if you have not worked with the subcontractor before.
- ✓ Ensure all subcontractors you work with have proper insurance coverage; request copies of insurance certificates and follow up to ensure coverage is current (as discussed in Chapter 4).

Creating a Winning Partnership

Once you have done all your homework and made your subcontractor selections, you'll want to create a relationship that will set both parties up for success.

- ✓ Provide an orientation on your policies and procedures.
- ✓ Be clear on all instructions and solicit questions.
- ✓ Be open to feedback and suggestions.

- ✓ Reward good work and provide constructive comments on improvements.
- ✓ Schedule trades so the job is ready for them and there are minimal barriers for them to complete their job.
- ✓ Visit the jobsite before the start of your portion of the project to tell other subcontractors your requirements (if it applies).
- ✓ Complete an IRS W-9 form prior to starting work.

Site Rules for Contractors

As part of your orientation with your subcontractors, you may want to review your site rules. Listed below are some rules to consider:

- ✓ Keep the jobsite clean and free of debris.
- ✓ All safety policies and OSHA regulations must be followed.
- ✓ You must provide your own tools and equipment.
- ✓ Work must be compliant with all applicable codes.
- ✓ Keep radios at a moderate listening level and free of offensive content on the jobsite.
- ✓ Behave professionally and do not use foul language.
- ✓ Salvage of items is prohibited without permission.

Site rules can be posted at the jobsite so they are visible to everyone and serve as a continual reminder.

Employee or Independent Contractor: IRS Guidelines

The IRS outlines specific guidelines regarding the difference between employees and independent contractors. Make sure you are working within an independent contractor relationship and not an employer-employee basis. If you do have an employer-employee relationship, your company is liable for payroll taxes, workers' compensation and employee benefits for that subcontractor.

To determine whether an individual is an employee or an independent contractor under the common law, the relationship of the worker and your company must be examined. In any employee-independent contractor determination, all information that provides evidence of the degree of control and the degree of independence must be considered.

Evidence of the degree of control and independence fall into three categories: **behavioral control**, **financial control** and **the type of relationship of the parties**.

Behavioral Control

Facts that show whether a business has a right to direct and control how the worker does the task for which the worker is hired include the type and degree of:

- ✓ ***Instructions that the business gives to the worker:*** An employee is generally subject to the business' instructions about when, where, and how to work. In a subcontractor relationship, the business generally gives up the right to control the details of the worker's performance.
- ✓ ***Training that the business gives to the worker:*** An employee may be trained to perform services in a particular manner. Independent contractors ordinarily use their own methods.

Financial Control

Facts that show whether the business has a right to control the business aspects of the worker's job include:

- ✓ ***The extent to which the worker has un-reimbursed business expenses:*** Independent contractors are more likely to have un-reimbursed expenses than are employees. Fixed ongoing costs that are incurred regardless of whether work is currently being performed are especially important.
- ✓ ***The extent of the worker's investment:*** An independent contractor often has a significant investment in the facilities he or she uses in performing services for someone else. However, a significant investment is not necessary for independent contractor status.
- ✓ ***The extent to which the worker makes his or her services available to the relevant market:*** An employee is generally guaranteed a regular wage amount for an hourly, weekly, or other period of time. An independent contractor is usually paid by a flat fee for the job.

- ✓ ***The extent to which the worker can realize a profit or loss:*** An independent contractor can make a profit or loss.

Type of Relationship

Facts that show the parties' type of relationship include:

- ✓ **Written contracts describing the relationship the parties intended to create**
- ✓ **Whether or not the business provides the worker with employee-type benefits**, such as insurance, a pension plan, vacation pay, or sick pay
- ✓ **The permanency of the relationship:** If you engage a worker with the expectation that the relationship will continue indefinitely rather than for a specific project or period, this is generally considered an employer-employee relationship.
- ✓ **The extent to which services performed by the worker are a key aspect of the regular business of the company:** If a worker provides services that are a key aspect of your regular business activity, it is more likely that you will have a right to direct and control his or her activities, indicating an employer-employee relationship.

Now that you know the rules, let's look at a few practical examples to demonstrate how classifications are made.

Example 1: Milton Manning, an experienced tile setter, orally agreed with a corporation to perform full-time services at construction sites. He uses his own tools and performs services in the order designated by the corporation and according to its specifications. The corporation supplies all materials, makes frequent inspections of his work, pays him on a piecework basis, and carries workers' compensation insurance on him. He does not have a place of business or hold himself out to perform similar services for others. Either party can end the services at any time. Milton Manning is an employee of the corporation.

Example 2: Vera Elm, an electrician, submitted a job estimate to a housing complex for electrical work at $16 per hour for 400 hours. She is to receive $1,280 every two weeks for the next 10 weeks. This is not considered payment by the hour. Even if she works more or less than 400 hours to complete the work, Vera Elm will receive $6,400. She also performs additional electrical installations under contracts with other companies that she obtained through advertisements. Vera is an independent contractor.

Final Inspection...

Sources for Finding the Right Subcontractor: Referrals are a good way to find the right subcontractors. As you collect referrals, develop a process to organize and appropriately schedule them.

Creating a Winning Partnership: Establishing good communication and having clear policies in place set a solid foundation for positive subcontractor relationships.

Site Rules for Contractors: Subcontractors should receive an orientation on your site rules before starting work. Site rules can be posted at the jobsite so they are visible to everyone and serve as a continual reminder.

Employee or Independent Contractor: IRS Guidelines: The IRS uses behavioral control, financial control, and the type of relationship of the parties to make a determination whether someone is an employee or independent contractor.

PART 3
Office Administration

Chapter 14
FINANCIAL MANAGEMENT

Chapter Survey...

- *Bookkeeping*
- *The Accounting Cycle*
- *Methods of Accounting*
- *Contract Accounting*
- *Cash Management*
- *Equipment Records and Accounting*
- *Accounting Process for Materials*
- *Payroll Accounting*
- *Technology Solutions for Accounting*

Accounting is important to all businesses because it helps measure the financial fitness of the company. It is a process of collecting, analyzing, and reporting information to develop tools, such as financial statements, that are used to evaluate different financial aspects of the company.

Bookkeeping

The first step in the accounting process is bookkeeping. Bookkeeping involves the accurate recording of all financial transactions that occur in the business. Financial statements are derived from this information.

Here are a few tips to maintain accurate and timely bookkeeping:

- ✓ Open a separate business checking account and obtain a business credit card to keep business and personal finances separate.
- ✓ Keep track of all deductible expenses (discussed later in this chapter).
- ✓ Keep all receipts and identify the source of all receipts so you can separate business from personal receipts and taxable from non-taxable income.
- ✓ Update business records daily to have quick access to the daily financial position of your business.
- ✓ Accurately record all information in the checkbook ledger including date, who the check was written to, the amount, and the reason the check was written.
- ✓ Record expenses when they occur, so you have an accurate picture of your cash situation.
- ✓ Avoid paying with cash, so you have a "paper trail" of your expenditures.
- ✓ Balance your checking account monthly. You may want to request month-end bank statements to coordinate with other month-end records.
- ✓ Keep all financial records for the required amount of time as designated by the IRS.

Bookkeeping involves the clerical side of accounting and requires only minimal knowledge of the entire accounting cycle. You may want to consult with a professional accountant for the more complex financial decision-making of your business.

The Accounting Cycle

The accounting cycle is a series of events that is repeated each reporting period. The cycle begins with a transaction and ends with closing the books and preparing financial statements. Steps in the accounting cycle include

1. Classifying and recording transactions,
2. Posting transactions,
3. Preparing a trial balance,
4. Preparing an adjusted trial balance,
5. Preparing financial statements, and
6. Analyzing financial statements.

STEP 1 Classify and Record Transactions

The accounting cycle begins with classifying and recording daily transactions. A transaction is an event that either increases or decreases an account balance. A **source document** is the proof that a transaction took place. Examples of source documents include

- ✓ cash receipts,
- ✓ credit card receipts,
- ✓ customer invoices,
- ✓ purchase orders,
- ✓ materials invoices,
- ✓ deposit slips, and
- ✓ time cards.

Daily transactions are recorded in a set of books called **journals**. Typical journals that companies keep include:

- ✓ **Cash receipts and sales journal:** This journal is used when cash comes in or a sale is charged to a customer.
- ✓ **Purchases journal:** This journal tracks all purchases made by the company.
- ✓ **Cash disbursements journal:** This journal is used when cash is paid out. Transactions such as loan payments and payments on vendor invoices are recorded here.
- ✓ **Payroll journal:** This journal is used to record a summary of payroll details, such as salaries and wages, deductions, and employer contributions.
- ✓ **General journal:** This journal is used for non-cash transactions.

STEP 2 Post Transactions

Posting is the process of transferring the transactions recorded in the journals to the appropriate accounts. An **account** is a register of value. Each account can be totaled to determine the balance. For example, cash is an asset account having a specific balance. Most companies use five basic types of accounts:

- ✓ Asset
- ✓ Liability
- ✓ Equity
- ✓ Income
- ✓ Expense

The **chart of accounts** is a numbering system that organizes these account types. A typical chart of accounts is listed below.

1000–1999: Assets

2000–2999: Liabilities

3000–3999: Equity

4000–4999: Revenue

5000–5999: Cost of Goods Sold

6000–6999: Expenses

7000–7999: Other Revenue (i.e., interest income)

8000–8999: Other Expenses (i.e., income taxes)

The accounts are located in the **general ledger**. When you post transactions, you are transferring them from the journal to the general ledger.

STEP 3 Prepare Trial Balance

When you tally the accounts, you prepare a trial balance. The **trial balance** is a total of all the ledger accounts.

At this point in the accounting cycle, you want to make sure the debits equal the credits.

Understanding Debits and Credits: Every accounting entry in the general ledger contains both a debit and a credit which must equal each other. Depending on what type of account you are dealing with, a debit or credit will either increase or decrease the account balance. The entries that increase or decrease each type of account are listed below.

Account Type	Debit	Credit
Assets	Increases	Decreases
Liabilities	Decreases	Increases
Equity	Decreases	Increases
Income	Decreases	Increases
Expenses	Increases	Decreases

For the accounts to balance, there must be a debit in one account and a credit in another. You may hear terms such as the left side or right side of the balance sheet. Something on the left side is simply a debit and the right side is a credit.

If you have any ledger account column totals that do not balance, look for math, posting, and recording errors.

STEP 4 Prepare an Adjusted Trial Balance

There are six general types of adjusting entries:

- ✓ prepaid expense,
- ✓ accrued expense,
- ✓ accrued revenue,
- ✓ unearned revenue,
- ✓ estimated items, and
- ✓ inventory adjustment.

When you make adjusting entries, include an explanation as to why the change was made. Once adjusting entries are made, you must go back and tally the account balances where changes were made.

STEP 5 Prepare Financial Statements

Now that you have posted transactions to your accounts and made adjusting entries, you can prepare your financial statements.

Three basic types of financial statements companies use are

- ✓ **balance sheet,**
- ✓ **income statement, and**
- ✓ **statement of cash flows.**

Financial statements are tools that give insight into the financial health and activities of the company.

Balance Sheet

The balance sheet is one of the basic accounting financial statements. It gives the owner good insight into the growth and stability of the company at a particular point in time.

The balance sheet equation is comprised of assets, liabilities, and owners' equity:

Assets = Liabilities + Owners' Equity

Assets are items of value owned by the business. The cash in your bank account and other assets that can be converted into cash in less than one year are considered **current assets**. They are important because they are used to fund your daily operations and can be liquidated easily.

Property and **equipment** (sometimes referred to as **capital** or **fixed assets**) are assets needed to carry on the business of a company and are not normally consumed in the operation of the business. Land, buildings, equipment, and furniture would all be considered fixed assets.

Other current assets consist of prepaid expenses, such as security deposits, and other miscellaneous assets, such as long-term investments.

Your company may also own **intangible assets**. Examples of these include patents, franchises, and goodwill from the acquisition of another company. It is not as easy to value these assets. Generally, the value of intangible assets is a value both parties agree to when the assets are created.

Liabilities are all debt and obligations owed by the business. Liabilities that will mature and must be paid within one year are called current liabilities. Trade credit is usually considered a current liability because it is a short-term debt.

Long-term liabilities are debt obligations that extend beyond one year. Examples of this type of liability include bank loans and deferred taxes.

Owners' equity is made up of the initial investment in the business, plus accumulated net profits not paid out to the owners.

Working capital can also be determined by looking at the balance sheet. The following equation is used to determine working capital.

Current Assets - Current Liabilities = Working Capital

Working capital measures the liquidity of the company's assets. Liquid assets are those that are easily converted to cash. Licensing agencies may look at working capital to determine license limitations.

The balance sheet is usually requested by potential lenders to determine credit limits. The following sample illustrates how the balance sheet equation and accounts are used in the balance sheet.

Quality Construction Company
Balance Sheet
December 31, 20XX

ASSETS		
Current Assets:		
Cash	$ 1,200	
Accounts Receivable	25,200	
Total Current Assets		$ 26,400
Property and Equipment:		
Equipment	$ 53,200	
Building	120,000	
Land	75,000	
Total Property and Equipment		248,200
TOTAL ASSETS		$ 274,600
LIABILITIES AND OWNERS' EQUITY		
Current Liabilities:		
Accounts Payable	$ 4,900	
Payroll Taxes Payable	3,300	
Total Current Liabilities		$ 8,200
Long-term Liabilities:		
Notes Payable	$ 6,700	
Mortgage Payable	195,000	
Total Long-term Liabilities		201,700
Owners' Equity		64,700
TOTAL LIABILITIES AND OWNERS' EQUITY		$ 274,600

Income Statement

The income statement, sometimes called the **profit-and-loss statement**, is a summary of the company's revenues and expenses over a given period of time.

The profit equation provides the basis for the income statement and is comprised of the following:

Income - Cost of Goods Sold = Gross Profit

Gross Profit - Expenses = Net Income

Revenues are the income received from the daily operations of the business. Most companies have only a few revenue accounts, but if you have several lines of business, you may want to create an account for each.

Expenses are the monies paid out or owed for goods or services over a given period of time. Most companies have separate accounts for the different types of expenses incurred.

Direct costs are those directly linked with a particular project. On a construction project, your direct costs might include materials, subcontractor fees, permit fees, and labor.

Operating expenses (sometimes called indirect expenses) are the general items that contribute to the cost of operating the business. These expenses can be put into two categories, **selling expenses** and **fixed overhead**. Selling expenses are the costs incurred to market the business. Fixed overhead expenses are those that cannot be linked to a specific project but are necessary for the operation of the business. For example, if you rent warehouse space to store your equipment year round, you would include this item in your bookkeeping under fixed overhead.

Tax provision expenses are the tax liabilities your company has for federal, state, and local taxes. Depending on your business structure, this section of the income statement will vary.

Net profit is the difference between the revenues and the expenses. Net profit directly contributes to the net worth of the company.

If net profit is on the positive side, those earnings are placed in a retained earnings or equity account.

If net profit is negative, it will reduce the net worth of the company.

The income statement is used by investors or lenders to determine the profitability of the company. The following sample illustrates how the income statement equation and accounts are used in the income statement.

Quality Construction Company
Income Statement
For the Period Ended December 31, 20XX

REVENUES:		
Construction Sales	$ 545,600	
Less Direct Labor	120,500	
Less Direct Materials	257,000	
Gross Profit		$ 168,100
EXPENSES:		
Selling Expenses:		
Advertising	$ 3,400	
Salaries - Sales	49,500	
Total Selling Expense	$ 52,900	
Administrative Expenses:		
Salaries - Office	$ 34,400	
Telephone	4,800	
Insurance Expense	29,700	
Total Administrative Expenses	$ 68,900	
Total Expenses		121,800
NET INCOME		$ 46,300

Quality Construction Company
Statement of Owners' Equity
For the Period Ended December 31, 20XX

Beginning Owners' Equity	$ 92,400
Add Net Income	46,300
Less Distributions to Owners	74,000
Ending Owners' Equity	$ 64,700

Statement of Cash Flows

The statement of cash flows summarizes your current cash position, your cash sources, and use of these funds over a given period of time. This financial statement lists your changes in cash based on operating, investing, and financing activities.

The **operating activities** portion of the statement shows the performance of the company to generate a positive or negative cash flow from the operations.

The **investing activities** section lists the cash used or provided to purchase or sell revenue-producing assets.

The **financing activities** section measures the flow of cash between its owners and creditors.

If you want to finance a major project, the lender will likely want to look at your statement of cash flows. This financial statement provides good insight into the company's ability to meet its obligations. The company may appear profitable on other statements, but a lack of cash flow may indicate pending financial problems.

Notes to the Financial Statements

The notes to the financial statements contain important information that is relevant but have no specific place within the financial statement.

✓ **Accounting policies and procedures** important to the company's financial condition and results are disclosed in the notes section.

✓ Detailed information about **current and deferred income taxes** is broken down by federal, state, and local categories. The primary factors that affect the company's tax rate are described.

✓ Specific information about the assets and costs of a **pension plan and other retirement programs** are explained and indicate whether the plans are over- or underfunded.

Anything that affects the financial health of the company that cannot be reflected in the financial statements should be reported in this section.

STEP 6 Analyze Financial Statements Using Financial Ratios

By using the basic concepts of the balance sheet and income statement, you can analyze them through financial ratios. Ratios can serve as a benchmark for the company's internal performance and as a comparison against industry averages.

Liquidity Ratio

The liquidity ratio (sometimes called the **current ratio**) is calculated by dividing the current liabilities into the current assets.

Current Assets ÷ Current Liabilities = Liquidity (or Current) Ratio

The liquidity ratio determines if the company can pay its current debts. If the ratio is greater than one, the company is in a positive liquidity position. The higher the number, the better liquidity position the company has.

Quick Ratio

The quick ratio (sometimes called the **acid test ratio**) is similar to the liquidity ratio. It is calculated by dividing the current liabilities into the current assets minus inventory.

(Current Assets - Inventory) ÷ Current Liabilities = Quick Ratio

A quick ratio of one or more is generally acceptable by most creditors. A higher number indicates a stronger financial position and a lower number a weaker position.

Activity Ratio

The activity ratio measures how effectively the company manages its credit. The formula for determining the average collection period is as follows:

Revenue ÷ Days in the Business Year = Sales per Day

Current Receivables ÷ Sales per Day = Average Collection Period

The company is in a better position when the average collection period is shorter (or the number is lower). This means that the company is converting credit accounts into cash faster.

Debt Ratio

The debt ratio measures the percent of total funds provided by creditors. The formula is as follows:

Total Debt ÷ Total Assets = Debt Ratio

Companies want to keep their debt ratio relatively low to avoid overextending debt.

Profitability Ratio

The profitability ratio is used to calculate the profit margin of the company. The formula is as follows:

Net Income ÷ Revenues = Profit Margin

The higher the profit margin percentage, the more profitably the company is performing.

Return on Total Assets Ratio

The return on total assets ratio is used to determine if the company's assets are being employed in the best manner. The formula is:

Net Profit (after taxes) ÷ Total Assets = Return on Total Assets

The company is in a favorable position when the percentage return on total assets is high.

Methods of Accounting

An accounting method is a set of rules used to determine when and how income and expenses are reported. There are two basic methods of accounting that are used to keep track of the company's income and expenses. These are

✓ **Cash method**

✓ **Accrual method**

The primary difference between the methods is in when the transactions are recorded to your accounts.

Cash Method

Using the **cash method of accounting**, you report income in the year you receive it and deduct expenses in the year you paid them. This is the easier of the two accounting methods. Although it is a simpler method, it holds a significant disadvantage. The cash method does not match revenues with the expenses incurred related to that revenue. This gives an inaccurate picture of the company's overall financial situation.

Accrual Method

Using the **accrual method**, you recognize income when the services occur, not when you collect the money. The same principal is applied to expenses, which are recorded when they are incurred, not when you pay for them. Most construction businesses use the accrual method of accounting.

Changing Your Method of Accounting

Once you have set up your accounting method and file your first tax return, you must get IRS approval before you can change to another method. A change in accounting method not only includes a change in your overall system of accounting, but also a change in the treatment of any material item.

Contract Accounting

Most construction businesses use two tax accounting methods; one for their long-term contracts and one overall method for everything else. A long-term contract is defined as any contract that is not completed in the same year it was started.

The choice of your contract accounting method depends on

- ✓ the type of contracts you have;
- ✓ your contracts' completion status at the end of your tax year; and
- ✓ your average annual gross receipts.

Each method discussed assumes that you use a calendar tax year from January 1 to December 31.

Completed Contract Method

Under the completed contract method, income or loss is reported in the year the contract is completed. Direct materials, labor costs, and all indirect costs associated with the contract must be allocated or capitalized to the same account as the income or loss. If the completed contract method is used for long-term contracts (contracts spanning over two calendar years), you may not allocate costs properly and you might overstate deductions.

The advantage of the completed contract method is that it normally achieves maximum deferral of taxes.

The disadvantages of the completed contract method are

- ✓ the books and records do not show clear information on operations;
- ✓ income can be bunched into a year when a lot of jobs are completed; and
- ✓ losses on contracts are not deductible until the contracts are completed.

The completed contract method may be used only by small contractors whose average annual gross receipts do not exceed $10 million for the three tax years preceding the tax year of the contract.

Percentage of Completion Method

The percentage of completion method recognizes income as it is earned during the construction project.

The biggest advantage of using this method for long-term contracts is that it does a better job of matching revenue to the expenses incurred related to that revenue. Accurate matching of revenue to expenses gives you a better picture of your financial position.

The disadvantage of the percentage of completion method is that it relies on estimates. You are estimating the degree of completion on the project and the income and expenses. The true numbers are not realized until the project is complete.

Percentage of completion is calculated individually by project. To determine the percentage of completion, use the following formula:

Project Costs Incurred ÷ Total Estimated Costs = Percentage of Completion

Once the percentage of completion is calculated, the cumulative earnings can be figured by using the following formula:

Percentage of Completion x Contract Amount = Cumulative Earnings

Adjustments must be made on the balance sheet for billings that are over or under the cumulative earnings. To figure the amount over or under cumulative earnings, use the following formula:

Cumulative Earnings - Amount Billed to Date = Billing Overage/Deficiency

Billings in excess of the cumulative earnings are considered a current liability. Billings less than cumulative earnings are considered a current asset.

Using these formulas, a percentage of completion worksheet example is shown below:

Project Name	Contract Amount	Estimated Cost	Project Cost to Date	Percent Complete	Cumulative Earnings	Amount Billed to Date	Billing Overage/ Deficiency
Project #1	70,000	62,350	35,500	56.94%	39,858	40,150	-292
Project #2	50,000	42,150	12,140	28.80%	14,400	13,500	900
Project #3	30,000	25,110	14,050	55.95%	16,785	15,220	1,565

Cost Comparison Method

The cost comparison method is an approach that combines the completed contract and percentage of completion methods. A 10 percent deferral election is allowed under the cost comparison method. This election allows you to defer recognized revenue on a contract until the total costs incurred equal 10 percent of the estimated contract costs. The initial project costs are capitalized and deferred until costs to date exceed 10 percent of total costs. After exceeding 10 percent, all costs incurred are treated as period costs and revenue is fully recognized in that period on the level of completion as that of year-end.

Cash Management

Cash Flow

As discussed in Chapter 9, it is important to track your incoming cash and expenditures during the construction project to ensure you have enough working capital to complete the job. Balancing incoming progress payments and outgoing expenditures is important to managing the project effectively and should be a consideration when preparing your schedule.

Positive cash flow, meaning more cash is coming in than going out to pay expenses, is an important indicator to the health of your business. Without positive cash flow, your business cannot pay bills and employees. The business will eventually be unable to sustain itself and ultimately fail.

Two important aspects of maintaining a positive cash flow are collecting accounts receivable (money that is owed to your business) and billing and collecting for current projects.

Collecting Accounts Receivable: Collecting accounts receivable should be a systematic process:

- ✓ Correspondence should look professional, with the services rendered and amount due clearly displayed on the invoice.
- ✓ Follow-up invoices should be sent on a regular schedule. This will convey that you are serious about receiving prompt payment.
- ✓ If the account falls delinquent for more than three months, a stern letter outlining the consequences for non-payment should accompany your follow-up invoices.
- ✓ If you find you are having problems collecting on accounts receivable, you may want to hire a professional collection agency.

Prompt pay and lien laws may also provide additional payment and collection tools.

Billing and Collecting for Current Projects: Prompt billing for current projects is important to receiving timely payments. Once you receive the approval for partial or final payment, you should immediately send an invoice requesting payment. The payment should clearly outline payment terms. For example, if your payment terms are "Net 30," this means that full payment of the invoice is due in 30 days. If amounts due for current projects are not collected in a prompt manner, you may run into cash flow problems.

Bad Debts: When you extend credit to your customers, this debt is recorded in your accounts receivable. Bad debts are uncollectible accounts receivable. It is important to monitor accounts receivable regularly. If you notice that the amount of accounts receivable is increasing, you may need to adjust collection procedures. Bad debts affect cash flow and must be kept to a minimum.

According to IRS guidelines, a business deducts its bad debts from gross income when figuring taxable income. Bad debts may be deducted in part or in full. For more information on the specific IRS guidelines on business bad debts, refer to IRS Publication 535, Business Expenses. This publication can be downloaded from the IRS website at www.irs.gov.

Payments

Progress Payments: As discussed in Chapter 8, it is important to address the schedule of progress payments in the contract. Progress payments are partial payments made after specified phases of construction are complete.

To ensure adequate cash flow, it is important to monitor the progress payment schedule closely. You may be required to submit a partial payment estimate to the project architect or engineer prior to the payment due date. The partial payment estimate outlines the work performed and proof of materials and equipment delivery required for the next stage of construction. The architect or engineer certifies each progress payment by confirming the information in the partial payment estimate.

A retainage amount (commonly 10 percent) is usually withheld from progress payments. Retainage is released and paid out to the contractor after all final approvals are obtained at the end of a project.

Calculation of progress payments differs slightly, depending on the type of contract.

Payment for Lump Sum Contracts: Payments for lump sum contracts are calculated by the percentage of work completed. A schedule of estimated costs (sometimes called a schedule of values) is used as a basis to determine the degree of project completion.

Material and subcontractor invoices are compared against the schedule of values to support the degree of project completion.

Payment for Unit Price Contracts: Payments for unit price contracts are based on actual work units completed. The unit price payment request is more detailed and may take longer to complete, but it provides a more accurate picture of the degree of work completion.

Payment for Cost-Plus Contracts: Payments for cost-plus contracts are based on actual costs rather than a percentage of completed work. The schedule of payments should be clearly outlined in the contract. Cost-plus contracts generally include a markup in addition to costs. The payment request should include a markup proportionate to the costs. If payment estimates are required, reconciliation must be done once the actual costs occur to adjust for any amounts that fall over or under the estimate.

Final Payment: Final payment requests should include the final payment amount plus any retainages owed. Final payment is released after final inspection, acceptance by the owner, and submittal of proper documentation.

Prompt Payment Act: The Federal Prompt Payment Act ensures that federal contractors are paid in a timely manner. If late payment is made, interest penalties are charged on the amount due. Prime contractors must receive payment within 14 days after submitting a progress payment invoice. Prime contractors must pay subcontractors within seven days after receiving payment, or they must pay interest penalties.

Petty Cash Fund

Small payments may sometimes be made without writing a check. A petty cash fund is used to make these payments. When you use the petty cash fund, it is important to document your expenditure. A voucher or petty cash disbursement slip should be completed and attached to your receipt as proof of payment.

The petty cash fund should be balanced and replenished monthly.

Equipment Records and Accounting

Options for owning, renting, and leasing equipment were discussed in Chapter 7. Equipment rates were then used to construct the equipment portion of the estimate. For accounting purposes, information on equipment must be tracked. Important information to record includes

- ✓ use rate,
- ✓ use time,
- ✓ maintenance costs,
- ✓ repair costs, and
- ✓ operating costs (i.e., gas, oil, etc.).

A separate record should be prepared for each piece of equipment.

This information is also useful when analyzing the need for future equipment purchases or upgrades.

Depreciation Methods

Depreciation is the process of devaluing a fixed asset as a result of aging, wear and tear, or obsolescence. The asset is depreciated over the course of its "useful life." Depreciation is considered a non-cash expense. You can depreciate vehicles, office equipment, buildings, and machinery. Land cannot be depreciated, because it does not "wear out" like depreciable items.

To determine the annual depreciation for an item, you must know the initial cost, how many years it will provide value for your business, and the salvage cost of the item when it is fully depreciated. There are two methods to depreciate fixed assets:

- ✓ **Straight line depreciation**
- ✓ **Accelerated depreciation**

Using **straight line depreciation**, you simply take the initial cost of the item and subtract the salvage cost. Then you take that total and divide it by the number of "useful life" years.

The calculation is as follows:

Initial Asset Cost - Salvage Cost = Depreciation Cost

Depreciation Cost ÷ Useful Life Years = Yearly Depreciation Amount

Using the **accelerated depreciation** method, the asset is depreciated at a higher rate during the early part of its useful life permitting larger tax deductions. This method is typically used for an asset that will probably be replaced before the end of its useful life. Depreciation percentages are based on the type of asset.

The **modified accelerated cost recovery system (MACRS)** is a depreciation method approved by the IRS. It allows for faster depreciation over longer periods. MACRS divides property into several different classes and takes into account the date the equipment was put in service, cost of equipment, cost recovery period, convention, and depreciation method that applies to your property. Given all these factors, a percentage rate is applied.

For further information, you may refer to the IRS website (www.irs.gov) on how to depreciate property, using MACRS and MACRS's percentage tables.

Accounting Process for Materials

As discussed in Chapter 9, purchase orders are an important project management tool. Purchase orders keep your purchases organized and document exactly what you ordered. They also facilitate the receiving process and the timing of deliveries. Purchase orders help track material inventories and related expenses in the accounting system. Invoices should be matched with purchase orders to ensure that the billing is accurate.

Shipping and Delivery Expenses: In addition to the actual material costs, shipping and delivery expenses are factored into the final cost. Shipping and delivery expenses are charged in a few different ways. Two common shipping terms are:

- ✓ **FOB Freight Prepaid** requires the seller to pay for the shipping charges.
- ✓ **FOB Freight Allowed** requires the buyer to pay the shipping charges. A credit for the shipping amount is often times given by the seller on the invoice.

It is important to understand the shipping terms ahead of time and note them on the purchase order.

Payment Terms: Payment terms depend on the payment agreement between the buyer and seller. They are generally listed on the seller's invoice. Terms can vary by seller. Listed below are some common terms you may see on your invoices.

- ✓ Net 10: Payment is due 10 days after receiving the invoice.
- ✓ Net 30: Payment is due 30 days after receiving the invoice.
- ✓ Net 60: Payment is due 60 days after receiving the invoice.
- ✓ COD: Cash payment is due on delivery.
- ✓ 1/10 Net 30: A 1 percent discount is given to payments received within 10 days; otherwise, payment is due 30 days after receiving the invoice.
- ✓ EOM: Payment is due at the end of the month.
- ✓ 1/10 EOM: A 1 percent discount is given to payments received by the 10th of the month following the shipment; otherwise, payment is due at the end of the month following the shipment.

Early payment discounts are a good way to cut costs. Depending on the contract arrangements, project cost savings may be given to the contractor or credited to the overall project budget.

Payroll Accounting

If you have employees, payroll distribution is done on a regular basis. Thorough payroll records are important for several reasons, such as calculating tax liabilities and tracking labor costs. The process for preparing payroll is as follows:

- ✓ **calculate gross pay for each employee;**
- ✓ **calculate and deduct applicable taxes and other deductions;**
- ✓ **calculate net pay and issue checks; and**
- ✓ **update payroll journal.**

Calculate Gross Pay

Gross pay is determined either by a salary that you set for the employee or based on an hourly wage multiplied by the number of hours worked. Salaried employees are generally paid the same amount each pay period, no matter how many hours they work. Hourly employees generally complete timecards that track the number of hours worked.

Time cards are important documentation if an unemployment benefit dispute arises. Many states require employers to keep timecards. If projects are tracked on the timecard, this information can be used for job costing purposes. The following is a sample time card.

Project Name or Number	Hours Worked								Work Completed	Supervisor Approval
	M	Tu	W	Th	F	Sa	Su	Total		
Total										

Calculate and Deduct Applicable Taxes and Deductions

Several types of taxes must be deducted from an employee's pay.

- ✓ **Federal income tax** is based on the information the employee provided in the W-4 form. Using IRS Publication: Circular E (sample below), you can determine the appropriate deduction.
- ✓ **Social Security tax** is calculated at the current prevailing rate. The current tax rate is available online at www.ssa.gov. Employers must pay in an equal amount of Social Security tax but cannot deduct that amount from the employee's payroll.
- ✓ **Medicare tax** is calculated at the rate of 1.45 percent of gross pay. Employers must pay in an equal amount of Medicare tax but cannot deduct that amount from the employee's payroll.

Wage Bracket Method Tables for Income Tax Withholding

MARRIED Persons—**WEEKLY** Payroll Period

(For Wages Paid through December 31, 2018)

And the wages are–		And the number of withholding allowances claimed is—										
At least	But less than	0	1	2	3	4	5	6	7	8	9	10
		The amount of income tax to be withheld is—										
$ 0	$225	$0	$0	$0	$0	$0	$0	$0	$0	$0	$0	$0
225	235	1	0	0	0	0	0	0	0	0	0	0
235	245	2	0	0	0	0	0	0	0	0	0	0
245	255	3	0	0	0	0	0	0	0	0	0	0
255	265	4	0	0	0	0	0	0	0	0	0	0
265	275	5	0	0	0	0	0	0	0	0	0	0
275	285	6	0	0	0	0	0	0	0	0	0	0
285	295	7	0	0	0	0	0	0	0	0	0	0
295	305	8	0	0	0	0	0	0	0	0	0	0
305	315	9	1	0	0	0	0	0	0	0	0	0
315	325	10	2	0	0	0	0	0	0	0	0	0
325	335	11	3	0	0	0	0	0	0	0	0	0
335	345	12	4	0	0	0	0	0	0	0	0	0
345	355	13	5	0	0	0	0	0	0	0	0	0
355	365	14	6	0	0	0	0	0	0	0	0	0
365	375	15	7	0	0	0	0	0	0	0	0	0
375	385	16	8	0	0	0	0	0	0	0	0	0
385	395	17	9	1	0	0	0	0	0	0	0	0
395	405	18	10	2	0	0	0	0	0	0	0	0
405	415	19	11	3	0	0	0	0	0	0	0	0
415	425	20	12	4	0	0	0	0	0	0	0	0
425	435	21	13	5	0	0	0	0	0	0	0	0
435	445	22	14	6	0	0	0	0	0	0	0	0
445	455	23	15	7	0	0	0	0	0	0	0	0
455	465	24	16	8	0	0	0	0	0	0	0	0
465	475	25	17	9	1	0	0	0	0	0	0	0
475	485	26	18	10	2	0	0	0	0	0	0	0
485	495	27	19	11	3	0	0	0	0	0	0	0
495	505	28	20	12	4	0	0	0	0	0	0	0
505	515	29	21	13	5	0	0	0	0	0	0	0
515	525	30	22	14	6	0	0	0	0	0	0	0
525	535	31	23	15	7	0	0	0	0	0	0	0
535	545	32	24	16	8	0	0	0	0	0	0	0
545	555	33	25	17	9	1	0	0	0	0	0	0
555	565	34	26	18	10	2	0	0	0	0	0	0
565	575	35	27	19	11	3	0	0	0	0	0	0
575	585	36	28	20	12	4	0	0	0	0	0	0
585	595	37	29	21	13	5	0	0	0	0	0	0
595	605	38	30	22	14	6	0	0	0	0	0	0
605	615	39	31	23	15	7	0	0	0	0	0	0
615	625	40	32	24	16	8	0	0	0	0	0	0
625	635	42	33	25	17	9	1	0	0	0	0	0
635	645	43	34	26	18	10	2	0	0	0	0	0
645	655	44	35	27	19	11	3	0	0	0	0	0
655	665	45	36	28	20	12	4	0	0	0	0	0
665	675	46	37	29	21	13	5	0	0	0	0	0
675	685	48	38	30	22	14	6	0	0	0	0	0
685	695	49	39	31	23	15	7	0	0	0	0	0
695	705	50	40	32	24	16	8	0	0	0	0	0
705	715	51	42	33	25	17	9	1	0	0	0	0
715	725	52	43	34	26	18	10	2	0	0	0	0
725	735	54	44	35	27	19	11	3	0	0	0	0
735	745	55	45	36	28	20	12	4	0	0	0	0
745	755	56	46	37	29	21	13	5	0	0	0	0
755	765	57	48	38	30	22	14	6	0	0	0	0
765	775	58	49	39	31	23	15	7	0	0	0	0
775	785	60	50	40	32	24	16	8	0	0	0	0
785	795	61	51	42	33	25	17	9	1	0	0	0
795	805	62	52	43	34	26	18	10	2	0	0	0
805	815	63	54	44	35	27	19	11	3	0	0	0
815	825	64	55	45	36	28	20	12	4	0	0	0
825	835	66	56	46	37	29	21	13	5	0	0	0
835	845	67	57	48	38	30	22	14	6	0	0	0
845	855	68	58	49	39	31	23	15	7	0	0	0
855	865	69	60	50	40	32	24	16	8	0	0	0
865	875	70	61	51	42	33	25	17	9	1	0	0
875	885	72	62	52	43	34	26	18	10	2	0	0
885	895	73	63	54	44	35	27	19	11	3	0	0
895	905	74	64	55	45	36	28	20	12	4	0	0
905	915	75	66	56	46	37	29	21	13	5	0	0

Wage Bracket Method Tables for Income Tax Withholding

MARRIED Persons—**WEEKLY** Payroll Period

(For Wages Paid through December 31, 2018)

And the wages are–		And the number of withholding allowances claimed is—										
At least	But less than	0	1	2	3	4	5	6	7	8	9	10
		The amount of income tax to be withheld is—										
$915	**$925**	$76	$67	$57	$48	$38	$30	$22	$14	$6	$0	$0
925	**935**	78	68	58	49	39	31	23	15	7	0	0
935	**945**	79	69	60	50	41	32	24	16	8	0	0
945	**955**	80	70	61	51	42	33	25	17	9	1	0
955	**965**	81	72	62	52	43	34	26	18	10	2	0
965	**975**	82	73	63	54	44	35	27	19	11	3	0
975	**985**	84	74	64	55	45	36	28	20	12	4	0
985	**995**	85	75	66	56	47	37	29	21	13	5	0
995	**1,005**	86	76	67	57	48	38	30	22	14	6	0
1,005	**1,015**	87	78	68	58	49	39	31	23	15	7	0
1,015	**1,025**	88	79	69	60	50	41	32	24	16	8	0
1,025	**1,035**	90	80	70	61	51	42	33	25	17	9	1
1,035	**1,045**	91	81	72	62	53	43	34	26	18	10	2
1,045	**1,055**	92	82	73	63	54	44	35	27	19	11	3
1,055	**1,065**	93	84	74	64	55	45	36	28	20	12	4
1,065	**1,075**	94	85	75	66	56	47	37	29	21	13	5
1,075	**1,085**	96	86	76	67	57	48	38	30	22	14	6
1,085	**1,095**	97	87	78	68	59	49	39	31	23	15	7
1,095	**1,105**	98	88	79	69	60	50	41	32	24	16	8
1,105	**1,115**	99	90	80	70	61	51	42	33	25	17	9
1,115	**1,125**	100	91	81	72	62	53	43	34	26	18	10
1,125	**1,135**	102	92	82	73	63	54	44	35	27	19	11
1,135	**1,145**	103	93	84	74	65	55	45	36	28	20	12
1,145	**1,155**	104	94	85	75	66	56	47	37	29	21	13
1,155	**1,165**	105	96	86	76	67	57	48	38	30	22	14
1,165	**1,175**	106	97	87	78	68	59	49	39	31	23	15
1,175	**1,185**	108	98	88	79	69	60	50	41	32	24	16
1,185	**1,195**	109	99	90	80	71	61	51	42	33	25	17
1,195	**1,205**	110	100	91	81	72	62	53	43	34	26	18
1,205	**1,215**	111	102	92	82	73	63	54	44	35	27	19
1,215	**1,225**	112	103	93	84	74	65	55	45	36	28	20
1,225	**1,235**	114	104	94	85	75	66	56	47	37	29	21
1,235	**1,245**	115	105	96	86	77	67	57	48	38	30	22
1,245	**1,255**	116	106	97	87	78	68	59	49	39	31	23
1,255	**1,265**	117	108	98	88	79	69	60	50	41	32	24
1,265	**1,275**	118	109	99	90	80	71	61	51	42	33	25
1,275	**1,285**	120	110	100	91	81	72	62	53	43	34	26
1,285	**1,295**	121	111	102	92	83	73	63	54	44	35	27
1,295	**1,305**	122	112	103	93	84	74	65	55	45	36	28
1,305	**1,315**	123	114	104	94	85	75	66	56	47	37	29
1,315	**1,325**	124	115	105	96	86	77	67	57	48	38	30
1,325	**1,335**	126	116	106	97	87	78	68	59	49	39	31
1,335	**1,345**	127	117	108	98	89	79	69	60	50	41	32
1,345	**1,355**	128	118	109	99	90	80	71	61	51	42	33
1,355	**1,365**	129	120	110	100	91	81	72	62	53	43	34
1,365	**1,375**	130	121	111	102	92	83	73	63	54	44	35
1,375	**1,385**	132	122	112	103	93	84	74	65	55	45	36
1,385	**1,395**	133	123	114	104	95	85	75	66	56	47	37
1,395	**1,405**	134	124	115	105	96	86	77	67	57	48	38
1,405	**1,415**	135	126	116	106	97	87	78	68	59	49	39
1,415	**1,425**	136	127	117	108	98	89	79	69	60	50	41
1,425	**1,435**	138	128	118	109	99	90	80	71	61	51	42
1,435	**1,445**	139	129	120	110	101	91	81	72	62	53	43
1,445	**1,455**	140	130	121	111	102	92	83	73	63	54	44
1,455	**1,465**	141	132	122	112	103	93	84	74	65	55	45
1,465	**1,475**	142	133	123	114	104	95	85	75	66	56	47
1,475	**1,485**	144	134	124	115	105	96	86	77	67	57	48
1,485	**1,495**	145	135	126	116	107	97	87	78	68	59	49
1,495	**1,505**	146	136	127	117	108	98	89	79	69	60	50
1,505	**1,515**	147	138	128	118	109	99	90	80	71	61	51
1,515	**1,525**	148	139	129	120	110	101	91	81	72	62	53
1,525	**1,535**	150	140	130	121	111	102	92	83	73	63	54
1,535	**1,545**	151	141	132	122	113	103	93	84	74	65	55
1,545	**1,555**	152	142	133	123	114	104	95	85	75	66	56
1,555	**1,565**	153	144	134	124	115	105	96	86	77	67	57
1,565	**1,575**	154	145	135	126	116	107	97	87	78	68	59

$1,575 and over Use Table 1(b) for a MARRIED person on page 46. Also see the instructions on page 44.

- ✓ **State income tax** should be calculated as it applies to each individual state.
- ✓ **Other deductions** might include an employee's contribution for medical insurance, 401K, life insurance, etc.

Reporting of payroll taxes is covered in Chapter 15, Tax Basics.

Calculate Net Pay and Issue Checks

Net pay is the payroll amount the employee receives after deductions are made. Net pay is calculated as:

Gross Pay - Taxes & Deductions = Net Pay

Employees should receive a statement of earnings with their paycheck. The statement of earnings shows how the net pay was calculated. The following is a sample statement of earnings.

				Current	Year to Date
Earnings					
Description	Rate	Hours	Overtime		
			Total Earnings		
			Taxes		
Employee Name:			Federal Withholding		
Employee ID:			Social Security		
Pay Period:			Medicare		
Check Date:			State Withholding		
			Insurance Deductions		
			Total Deductions		
			Net Pay		

Update Payroll Journal

Once checks are issued, the payroll journal must be updated to reflect the new account balance. The payroll journal should contain the same information as the employee statement of earnings. This topic is discussed in the previous section. This information is important to calculating your employer tax liabilities. Instructions on how to pay in employer taxes are covered in Chapter 15, Tax Basics.

Technology Solutions for Accounting

There are many accounting software programs on the market that can help make the accounting process easier.

As with all software, you still need to know the fundamentals, but it will help streamline the process and improve accuracy.

Accounting software can automate the process of posting, creating financial statements, invoicing customers, creating purchase orders, and much more. Think of accounting software as an investment to make you more analytical and help you think strategically about your business.

When choosing the right software, consider what your needs are and how the technology can grow with your company. There are many options. You may want to look at programs that integrate job cost analysis with accounting that have been developed specifically for the construction industry.

Final Inspection...

Bookkeeping: The first step of the accounting process is bookkeeping. Bookkeeping is the accurate recording of all financial transactions that occur in the business.

The Accounting Cycle: The accounting cycle is a process that happens each reporting period, which starts with recording financial transactions and goes through analyzing financial statements.

Methods of Accounting: Cash and accrual are the two main methods of accounting. The primary difference between both methods occurs when you record the transactions to your accounts.

Contract Accounting: The methods for contract accounting include completed contract, percentage of completion, and cost comparison.

Cash Management: Positive cash flow is an important indicator to the health of your business. Collecting on accounts receivable and billing and collecting on current accounts are important to the cash management process.

Equipment Records and Accounting: Depreciation is the process of devaluing a fixed asset as a result of aging, wear and tear, or obsolescence. The two primary methods of depreciation are straight line and accelerated.

Accounting Process for Materials: Purchase orders help track material inventories and related expenses in the accounting system. Invoices should be matched with purchase orders to ensure that the billing is accurate.

Payroll Accounting: Thorough payroll records are important for such reasons as calculating tax liabilities and tracking labor costs.

Technology Solutions for Accounting: Accounting software can automate the process of posting, creating financial statements, invoicing customers, creating purchase orders, and much more.

Supplemental Forms

Supplemental forms and links are available at **NASCLAforms.org** using access code **SCR129354**. The following forms can be found in the Financial Management section.

Balance Sheet	Example featured earlier in the chapter that can be modified in Excel
Income Statement	Example featured earlier in the chapter that can be modified in Excel
Time Card	Sample featured earlier in the chapter to track employee time
Earnings Statement	Sample featured earlier in the chapter as a summary to the employee's earnings

Chapter 15
TAX BASICS

Chapter Survey...

- ⇨ *Employer Identification Number*
- ⇨ *Federal Business Taxes*
- ⇨ *Summary of Federal Tax Forms*
- ⇨ *Income Tax*
- ⇨ *Self-Employment Tax*
- ⇨ *Federal Employment Taxes*
- ⇨ *Penalties*
- ⇨ *Information Returns-1099 MISC*
- ⇨ *Tax Calendar*
- ⇨ *South Carolina State Tax Specifics*

Employer Identification Number

Before you become an employer and hire employees, you need a Federal Employer Identification Number (EIN) which is also referred to as a taxpayer identification number.

The only entities that do not need an EIN are:

- ✓ Sole proprietorships that have no employees and file no excise or pension tax returns; and
- ✓ LLCs with a single owner (where the owner will file employment tax returns).

In these instances, the owner uses his or her social security number as the taxpayer identification number.

All other types of business entities, including partnerships, are required to obtain an EIN.

The EIN is a 9-digit number that the IRS issues. The digits are arranged as follows: 00-0000000. It is used to identify the tax accounts of employers and certain others who have no employees. Use your EIN on all of the items that you send to the Internal Revenue Service (IRS) and Social Security Administration (SSA).

There are several ways to obtain an EIN through the Internal Revenue Service (IRS).

- ✓ Call the Business and Specialty Tax Line at (800) 829-4933.
- ✓ Fax the completed Form SS-4 application to the fax number designated for your state.
- ✓ Mail the completed Form SS-4 application.
- ✓ Apply online at www.irs.gov.

Federal Business Taxes

The form of business you operate determines what taxes you must pay and how you pay them. The following are three general types of business taxes that you may be responsible for.

- ✓ **Income tax**
- ✓ **Self-employment tax**
- ✓ **Employment taxes**

The following table lists the tax responsibilities by business entity type and the corresponding forms to file with the IRS.

Summary of Federal Tax Forms

IF you are a...	Then you may be liable for...	Use Form...
Sole proprietor	Income tax	1040 and Schedule C [1] or C–EZ
	Self-employment tax	1040 and Schedule SE
	Estimated tax	1040–ES
	Employment taxes:	
	• Social security and Medicare taxes and income tax withholding	941
	• Federal unemployment (FUTA) tax	940 or 940–EZ
	• Depositing employment taxes	8109 [2]
	Excise taxes	See *Excise Taxes*
Partnership	Annual return of income	1065
	Employment taxes	Same as sole proprietor
	Excise taxes	See *Excise Taxes*
Partner in a partnership (individual)	Income tax	1040 and Schedule E [3]
	Self-employment tax	1040 and Schedule SE
	Estimated tax	1040–ES
Corporation or S corporation	Income tax	1120 or 1120–A (corporation) [3] 1120S (S corporation) [3]
	Estimated tax	1120–W (corporation only) and 8109 [2]
	Employment taxes	Same as sole proprietor
	Excise taxes	See *Excise Taxes*
S corporation shareholder	Income tax	1040 and Schedule E [3]
	Estimated tax	1040–ES

[1] File a separate schedule for each business.

[2] Do not use if you deposit taxes electronically.

[3] Various other schedules may be needed.

Income Tax

All businesses except partnerships must file an annual income tax return. Partnerships file an information return. The form you use depends on how your business is organized.

Estimated Tax

The federal income tax is a "pay-as-you-go" tax. You must pay the tax as you earn or receive income during the year. If you do no pay your tax through withholding, or do not pay enough tax that way, you might owe estimated tax. If you are not required to make estimated tax payments, you pay any tax due when you file your return.

Sole proprietors, partners, and S corporation shareholders generally have to make estimated tax payments if expected owed tax is $1,000 or more when the income tax return is filed. Form 1040-ES, Estimated Tax for Individuals, is available through the IRS to figure and pay estimated tax.

Corporations generally have to make estimated tax payments if expected owed tax is $500 or more when the income tax return is filed. Form 1120-W, Estimated Tax for Corporations, is available through the IRS to figure the estimated tax. You must deposit the payments electronically, through the mail, or delivery with a payment coupon.

Self-Employment Tax

Self-employment tax (SE tax) is a social security and Medicare tax primarily for individuals who work for themselves. Your payments of SE tax contribute to your coverage under the social security system. Social security coverage provides you with retirement benefits, disability benefits, survivor benefits, and hospital insurance (Medicare) benefits.

You must pay SE tax and file Schedule SE (Form 1040) if your net earnings from self-employment were $400 or more.

You must also pay SE tax on your share of certain partnership income and your guaranteed payments.

A Word About Deductible Expenses...

As defined by the IRS, to be deductible, a business expense must be both ordinary and necessary. An ordinary expense is one that is common and accepted in your industry. A necessary expense is one that is helpful and appropriate for your trade or business.

It is important to distinguish a business expense from a personal expense. Personal expenses would include living or family expenses which would not be considered deductible business expenses. A deductible business expense would include:

- ✓ Expenses used to figure cost of goods sold, such as cost of product, storage, direct labor, and project overhead; and
- ✓ Capital expenses, such as business assets and improvements (Although you generally cannot take a current deduction for a capital expense, you may be able to recover the amount you spend through depreciation, amortization, or depletion. These recovery methods allow you to deduct part of your cost each year.)

Federal Employment Taxes

When you have employees, you have certain employment tax responsibilities and forms you must file. Most employers must withhold (except FUTA), deposit, report and pay the following taxes:

- ✓ **Social security and Medicare taxes (FICA)**
- ✓ **Federal income tax withholding**
- ✓ **Federal unemployment (FUTA) tax**

Keep all records of employment taxes for at least four years.

Circular E

The *IRS Publication Circular E: Employer's Tax Guide* is a comprehensive reference providing thorough instructions on calculating, withholding and depositing employee taxes. The Circular E is found on the IRS website at www.irs.gov and at NASCLAforms.org using access code SCR129354.

Social Security and Medicare Taxes (FICA)

Social security and Medicare taxes pay for benefits that workers and families receive under the Federal Insurance Contributions Act (FICA). Social security tax pays for benefits under the old-age, survivors, and disability insurance part of FICA. Medicare tax pays for benefits under the hospital insurance part of FICA. Medicare is a part of the Social Security Program that provides hospital and medical insurance coverage to persons age 65 and over and those who have permanent kidney failure, or end stage renal disease, and people with other disabilities.

You withhold part of these taxes from your employee's wages and your company must pay a matching amount. The withholding rate for social security is 6.2 percent of gross pay to $97,500 for 2007 and Medicare tax is 1.45 percent of gross pay.

Federal Income Tax Withholding

You generally must withhold federal income tax from your employees' wages. To figure how much to withhold from each wage payment, use the employee's form W-4, Employee's Withholding Allowance Certificate, and the methods described in the previous chapter. The W-4 deductions do not expire unless the employee gives you a new one or if the employee is claiming a tax exemption. A new W-4 form must be completed by February 15 each year from employees claiming a tax withholding exemption.

Form W-2: Copies B, C, and two of the form W-2, Wage and Tax Statement must be furnished to all employees by January 31. Form W-2 summarizes the employee's previous year's wages and withholding amounts.

If employment ends before the end of the year, the W-2 form can be given to the employee at any time but no later than January 31. If an employee asks for the W-2 form, you must furnish copies within 30 days of the request or 30 days of the final payment, whichever is later.

Employers must send Copy A of the W-2 form with the entire page of the W-3 form to the Social Security Administration (SSA) by the last day of February (or last day of March if you file electronically).

Social Security Administration
Wilkes-Barre Data Operations Center
P.O. Box 1020
Wilkes-Barre, Pennsylvania 18767-9910

Deposit Schedule

There are three deposit schedules, monthly, semiweekly and daily, for determining when you deposit social security, Medicare and withheld income taxes. Prior to the beginning of the calendar year, you must determine which schedule you are required to use.

You are a monthly schedule depositor if your total payroll tax liability for the previous four quarters (July to June) was $50,000 or less. Payments are due on the fifteenth day of the following month after the payments were made. During your first year of business, you are a monthly schedule depositor.

If your total payroll tax liability from the previous four quarters (July to June) is greater than $50,000, you are a semiweekly schedule depositor. The semiweekly deposit schedule depends on your payroll date.

If your payday is on...	Then your deposit date is...
Wednesday, Thursday and/or Friday	Wednesday
Saturday, Sunday, Monday and/or Tuesday	Friday

If your accumulated tax liability is $100,000 or more on any day during a deposit period, you must deposit it on the next banking day. If you are a monthly schedule depositor and accumulate a $100,000 tax liability on any day, you automatically become a semiweekly depositor.

Form 941: If you report less than $2,500 for the quarter, you can use the IRS Form 941, Quarterly Employer's Tax Return to make payments by the due date of the return. If your tax obligation exceeds $2,500 for the quarter, you are subject to payments according to a deposit schedule.

Federal Unemployment Tax (FUTA)

The federal unemployment tax is part of the federal and state program under the Federal Unemployment Tax Act (FUTA) that pays unemployment compensation to workers who lose their jobs.

You report and pay FUTA tax separately from social security and Medicare taxes and withheld income tax. Employers are responsible for FUTA and cannot withhold this amount from the employees' payroll.

You are generally liable for both state and federal unemployment taxes if

- ✓ you pay wages to employees totaling $1,500, or more, in any quarter of a calendar year, or
- ✓ you had at least one employee during any day of a week during 20 weeks in a calendar year, regardless of whether or not the weeks were consecutive.

Calculating FUTA: The FUTA tax rate is 6.2 percent of taxable wages. The taxable wage base is the first $7,000 paid in wages to each employee during a calendar year. Employers who pay the state unemployment tax, on a timely basis, will receive an offset credit of up to 5.4 percent regardless of the rate of tax they pay the state. Therefore, the net federal tax rate is generally 0.8 percent (6.2 percent minus 5.4 percent credit). State tax rates are based on requirements of state law.

Deposit Requirements: For deposit purposes, figure FUTA tax quarterly. If your FUTA tax liability is less than $500, you are not required to deposit the tax. Instead, carry it forward and add it to the liability figured in the next quarter to see if you must make a deposit. Use the following schedule to determine when to deposit FUTA taxes.

Quarter	Ending	Due Date
Jan-Feb-Mar	March 31	April 30
Apr-May-June	June 30	July 31
July-Aug-Sept	Sept. 30	Oct. 31
Oct-Nov-Dec	Dec. 31	Jan. 31

Form 940: Report FUTA taxes on Form 940, Employer's Annual Federal Unemployment (FUTA) Tax Return or if you qualify, you can use the simpler Form 940-EZ instead.

Penalties

Accurate and prompt deposits are required to avoid penalties which can range from 2 percent to 100 percent of your tax liability.

Penalties may apply if

- ✓ you do not make payroll tax deposits on time;
- ✓ make deposits for less than the required amount; or
- ✓ do not use the Electronic Federal Tax Payment System (EFTPS) when required.

These penalties are as follows:

2%	Deposits made 1-5 days late.
5%	Deposits made 6-15 days late.
10%	Deposits made more than 16 days late. Also applies to amounts paid within 10 days of the date of the first notice the IRS sent asking for the tax due.
10%	Deposits made at an unauthorized financial institution, paid directly to the IRS, or paid with your tax return.
10%	Amounts subject to electronic deposit requirements but not deposited using EFTPS.
15%	Amounts still unpaid more than 10 days after the date of the first notice that the IRS sent asking for the tax due or the day on which you received notice and demand for immediate payment, whichever is earlier.
100%	Failure to pay "trust fund" taxes defined as withheld income, social security and Medicare taxes. The amount of the penalty is equal to the unpaid balance of the trust fund tax.

Information Returns - 1099-MISC

You may be required to file information returns to report certain types of payments made during the year to persons not treated as employees. Form 1099-MISC, Miscellaneous Income may be used to report payments of $600 or more to independent contractors. Form 1099-MISC must be filed by January 31 for the prior year's payments. Form 1096, Annual Summary and Transmittal of U.S. Information Returns, is used to transmit 1099 forms to the IRS. Form 1096 is due by February 28 for the previous year's 1099s.

Tax Calendar

Listed below are key employment tax deadlines as outlined in the IRS Publication Circular E. IRS Publication 509-Tax Calendar is also a good resource to keep track of other various tax due dates including income and employment taxes.

By January 31	Furnish Form W-2, Wage and Tax Statement to All Employees Furnish Form 1099 to Each Other Payee (for example, independent contractors with payments of $600 or more) File Form 940 or 940-EZ, Employer's Annual Federal Unemployment Tax (FUTA) Return File Form 945, Annual Return of Withheld Federal Income Tax
By February 15	Request a New W-4 Form from Employees Claiming a Tax Withholding Exemption
On February 16	Exempt Forms W-4 Expire
By February 28	File Copy A of All Forms 1099 with Form 1096, Annual Summary and Transmittal of U.S. Information Returns with the IRS File Copy A of Forms W-2, Wage and Tax Statement with Form W-3, Transmittal of Wage and Tax Statements with the Social Security Administration
By March 31	File Electronic Forms 1099 and 8027 with IRS File Electronic W-2 Forms with the Social Security Administration
By April 30, July 31, October 31, and January 31	Deposit FUTA Taxes File Form 941, Employer's Quarterly Federal Tax Return and deposit any undeposited income, social security and Medicare taxes
Before December 1	Remind Employees to Submit New W-4 Forms if withholding allowances have changed

South Carolina State Tax Specifics

The South Carolina Department of Revenue is the regulating agency for the state tax program. It has six taxpayer service centers located throughout the state. To find a location nearest to you, visit the website at www.dor.sc.gov. The website also contains forms and helpful links on state tax topics.

For more information, contact:

South Carolina Department of Revenue
Columbia Main Office
300A Outlet Pointe Boulevard
Columbia, SC 29210

Phone: (803) 898-5000
Fax: (803) 898-1129

Website: www.dor.sc.gov

Business Income Tax

Your state business tax filings differ depending on the business structure you operate under.

Sole Proprietorships: Taxable income or loss for sole proprietorships is reported on the individual income tax return. Individual tax rates range from 2.5 percent to 7 percent.

Partnerships: South Carolina partnership taxable income is the same as federal partnership income tax provisions with certain South Carolina modifications. Multi-state partnerships determine South Carolina taxable income by applying an apportionment ratio to the various income or loss amounts of the partnership.

C Corporations: The South Carolina corporate tax rate is 5 percent. The federal taxable income amount is used to determine state corporate income tax liability.

Corporate income tax returns are due no later than the fifteenth day of the third month following the close of the taxable year.

Estimated tax payments are required for corporations whose tax liability is more than $100 annually. Payments are due by the fifteenth day of the third, sixth, ninth and twelfth months following the beginning of the taxable year.

S Corporations: S corporations are taxed differently from other corporations. For federal and South Carolina tax purposes, S corporations are treated as flow-through entities.

Federal taxable income items apportioned or allocated to South Carolina and taxable to nonresident shareholders are subject to withholding by the S corporation at a 5 percent rate.

Nonresident shareholders providing affidavits of their intention to file returns and S corporations filing a composite return on behalf of all of their nonresident shareholders are exempt from the withholding requirement. Payment of the withholding tax is due by the fifteenth day of the third month of the following year.

Limited Liability Companies (LLCs): The South Carolina tax treatment of an LLC is the same as its federal tax treatment. Therefore, if an LLC is treated as a corporation for federal tax purposes, it is classified as such for South Carolina income tax purposes. LLCs treated as partnerships for federal income tax purposes are treated as partnerships for South Carolina income tax purposes.

Sales and Use Tax

Sales and use tax is due on goods, including materials and equipment, sold, leased, or used in the State of South Carolina. **The sales tax rate is 5 percent and some counties have an additional local option tax of 1 percent to 2 percent.**

Use tax of 5 percent of the sales price is due when taxable purchases are made but South Carolina sales tax is not paid. Any individual or business purchasing taxable goods or services for use in South Carolina without paying South Carolina sales tax must pay use tax.

The sales, use, and local option (if applicable) tax must be reported and paid monthly on Form ST-3, Sales, Use and Local Option Tax Return. The Department of Revenue mandates taxpayers paying over $20,000 in one filing period to report sales tax electronically.

Corporation License Tax

Corporations and other entities taxed as a corporation are subject to an annual license tax of .001 times their capital stock and paid-in-surplus, plus $15. The initial license tax is $25 and is paid at the time of incorporation or at the time of qualification by an out-of-state corporation with the South Carolina Secretary of State.

State Unemployment Tax

The state unemployment tax rate is 1.09 percent for 2018 on the first $14,000 of earned income for new companies. After a company operates in South Carolina for 12 months, the company will be re-rated each year based on experience, with a resulting rate between 0.06 percent and 5.46 percent on the first $14,000 of earned income for 2018. These rates include Rates include the administrative assessment and unemployment tax surcharge.

The Department of Employment and Workforce administers the unemployment compensation tax for South Carolina. For more information and registration forms, contact:

South Carolina Department of Employment and Workforce
P. O. Box 995
1550 Gadsden St.
Columbia, South Carolina 29202

Phone: (803) 737-2400

Website: www.dew.sc.gov

Employers are subject to the Unemployment Compensation Act if:

- ✓ during a calendar quarter of the current or preceding calendar year, they paid wages totaling $1,500 or more; or
- ✓ during the current or preceding calendar year, they had one or more employees at any time in each of 20 calendar weeks.

Withholding Tax

South Carolina requires withholding from

- ✓ wages;
- ✓ prizes;
- ✓ royalties;
- ✓ winnings;
- ✓ nonresident contractors on contracts exceeding $10,000;
- ✓ rental payments made to nonresidents who own five or more residential units or one or more commercial properties in South Carolina; and
- ✓ net proceeds going to nonresident sellers of real estate and associated tangible personal property located in South Carolina.

To register with the South Carolina Department of Revenue to withhold South Carolina income tax, use Form SCTC-111.

South Carolina has adopted the use of the federal form W-4; therefore, it is not required that an employee file a separate form for state withholding purposes.

The withholding rate for South Carolina is between 2 percent and 7 percent. Employers need a *Withholding Booklet* to calculate the correct amount. This booklet contains tax tables similar to the Circular E used to calculate federal withholding.

Withholding tax payments can be made online at the Department of Revenue website at dor.sc.gov or by mailing payment with the Withholding Coupon Form WH-1601X. Withholding payment due dates for South Carolina follow the federal withholding calendar.

Summary of State Tax Forms

IF you are a...	THEN you may be liable for...	Forms You May Need
Sole Proprietor	State Income Tax	Form SC-1040
	Estimated Tax	Form SC-1040ES
	State Withholding Employment Tax	Form SCTC-111 (registration to withhold South Carolina income tax/business tax application) Federal Form W4 (Employee Withholding Certificate/ South Carolina uses the federal form) Form WH-1601 (Withholding Coupon) Form WH-1605 (Quarterly Tax Returns for Quarter 1, Quarter 2, and Quarter 3) Form WH-1606A (Amended Fourth Quarter/Annual Withholding Reconciliation)
	Sales and Use Tax	Form ST-3 (Sales and Use Tax Return)
	Unemployment Tax	See *Unemployment Tax*
Partnership	Annual Return of Income	Form SC-1065 (also used for LLC)
	State Withholding Employment Tax	Form SCTC-111 (registration to withhold South Carolina income tax/business tax application) Federal Form W4 (Employee Withholding Certificate/ South Carolina uses the federal form) Form WH-1601 (Withholding Coupon) Form WH-1605 (Quarterly Tax Returns for Quarter 1, Quarter 2, and Quarter 3) Form WH-1606A (Amended Fourth Quarter/Annual Withholding Reconciliation)
	Sales and Use Tax	Form ST-3 (Sales and Use Tax Return)
	Unemployment Tax	See *Unemployment Tax*
C Corporation	Income tax	Form SC-1120
	Business Tax Registration	Form SCTC-111
	State Withholding Employment Tax	Form SCTC-111 (registration to withhold South Carolina income tax/business tax application) Federal Form W4 (Employee Withholding Certificate/ South Carolina uses the federal form) Form WH-1601 (Withholding Coupon) Form WH-1605 (Quarterly Tax Returns for Quarter 1, Quarter 2, and Quarter 3) Form WH-1606A (Amended Fourth Quarter/Annual Withholding Reconciliation)

IF you are a...	THEN you may be liable for...	Forms You May Need
C Corporation, cont.	Sales and Use Tax	Form ST-3 (Sales and Use Tax Return)
	Corporation License Tax	See *Corporation License Tax*
	Unemployment Tax	See *Unemployment Tax*
S Corporation	Income tax	Form SC-1120S
	State Withholding Employment Tax	Form SCTC-111 (registration to withhold South Carolina income tax/business tax application) Federal Form W4 (Employee Withholding Certificate/ South Carolina uses the federal form) Form WH-1601 (Withholding Coupon) Form WH-1605 (Quarterly Tax Returns for Quarter 1, Quarter 2, and Quarter 3) Form WH-1606A (Amended Fourth Quarter/Annual Withholding Reconciliation)
	Sales and Use Tax	Form ST-3 (Sales and Use Tax Return)
	Corporation License Tax	See *Corporation License Tax*
	Unemployment Tax	See *Unemployment Tax*
S Corporation Shareholder	Income tax	Form SC-1120CDP
Limited Liability Company (LLC)	Income Tax	Form SC-1065
	State Withholding Employment Tax	Form SCTC-111 (registration to withhold South Carolina income tax/business tax application) Federal Form W4 (Employee Withholding Certificate/ South Carolina uses the federal form) Form WH-1601 (Withholding Coupon) Form WH-1605 (Quarterly Tax Returns for Quarter 1, Quarter 2, and Quarter 3) Form WH-1606A (Amended 4th Quarter/Annual Withholding Reconciliation)
	Sales and Use Tax	Form ST-3 (Sales and Use Tax Return)
	Unemployment Tax	See *Unemployment Tax*

Final Inspection...

Employer Identification Number: An employer identification number is used to identify the tax accounts of employers and certain others who have no employees.

Federal Business Taxes: The form of business you operate determines what taxes you must pay and how you pay them.

Summary of Federal Tax Forms: You must file the specific federal tax forms that correspond to your business entity type.

Income Tax: All businesses except partnerships must file an annual income tax return. Partnerships file an information return.

Self-Employment Tax: Self-employment tax (SE tax) is a social security and Medicare tax primarily for individuals who work for themselves.

Federal Employment Taxes: Federal employment taxes include social security and Medicare (FICA), federal income tax withholding, and federal unemployment tax (FUTA).

Penalties: Accurate and prompt deposits are required to avoid penalties which can range from 2 percent to 100 percent of your tax liability.

Information Returns-1099 MISC: Form 1099-MISC, Miscellaneous Income may be used to report payments of $600 or more to independent contractors.

Tax Calendar: IRS Publication Circular E and Publication 509 provide tax calendars for various taxes that may apply to your business.

South Carolina State Tax Specifics: Business income, sales and use, payroll, unemployment, and corporation license tax are a few state taxes that may apply to your business.

Supplemental Publications and Forms

Supplemental forms and links are available at **NASCLAforms.org** using access code **SCR129354**. The following forms can be found in the Tax Basics section.

IRS Publication 334	Tax Guide for Small Business
IRS Publication 463	Travel, Entertainment and Gift Expenses
IRS Publication 505	Tax Withholding and Estimated Tax
IRS Publication 509	General Tax Calendar
IRS Publication 535	Business Expenses
IRS Publication 538	Accounting Periods and Methods
IRS Publication 541	Tax Information on Partnerships
IRS Publication 542	Tax Information on Corporations
IRS Publication 583	Taxpayers Starting a Business
IRS Publication 587	Business Use of Your Home
IRS Publication 946	How to Begin Depreciating Your Property
IRS Publication 1544	Reporting Cash Payments of Over $10,000
IRS Form W-2	Wage and Tax Statement
IRS Form W-3	Tax Reconciliation
IRS Form W-4	Employee Withholding
IRS Form SS-4	Application for Employer Identification Number
IRS Form 940	Employer Annual Federal Unemployment Tax Return
IRS Form 941	Employer's Quarterly Federal Tax Return

IRS Form 1040	U.S. Individual Income Tax Return
IRS Schedule C	Profit or Loss from Business
IRS Schedule-EZ	Net Profit from Business
IRS Schedule SE	Self-Employment Tax
IRS Form 1040-ES	Estimated Tax for Individuals
IRS Form 1065	U.S. Partnership Return of Income Schedule K-1, Partner's Share of Income, Credits, Deductions, etc.
IRS Form 1120	U.S. Corporation Income Tax Return
IRS Form 1120S	U.S. Income Tax Return for an S Corporation Schedule K-1
IRS Form 4562	Depreciation and Amortization
IRS Form 8300	Report of Cash Payments over $10,000 Received in a Trade or Business
Employer's Tax Guide (Circular E)	Publication used to determine federal income tax withholding for employees

Department of the Treasury
Internal Revenue Service

Publication 15
Cat. No. 10000W

(Circular E), Employer's Tax Guide

For use in **2018**

Get forms and other information faster and easier at:
- *IRS.gov* (English)
- *IRS.gov/Spanish* (Español)
- *IRS.gov/Chinese* (中文)
- *IRS.gov/Korean* (한국어)
- *IRS.gov/Russian* (Русский)
- *IRS.gov/Vietnamese* (TiếngViệt)

Jan 25, 2018

Contents

Future Developments

For the latest information about developments related to Pub. 15, such as legislation enacted after it was published, go to *IRS.gov/Pub15*.

What's New

2018 federal income tax withholding. This publication includes the 2018 Percentage Method Tables and Wage Bracket Method Tables for Income Tax Withholding. The 2018 withholding tables incorporate changes to the individual tax rates based on tax legislation enacted on December 22, 2017 (P.L. 115-97). Employers should implement the 2018 withholding tables as soon as possible, but not later than February 15, 2018. Continue to use the 2017 withholding tables until you implement the 2018 withholding tables. The new withholding tables are designed to work with the Forms W-4, Employee's Withholding Allowance Certificate, that your employees previously gave you.

To help employees determine their withholding, the IRS is revising the withholding tax calculator available at *IRS.gov/W4App*. The IRS anticipates that this calculator will be available by the end of February. Encourage your employees to use the withholding calculator to determine if they should give you a new Form W-4 for 2018. The IRS is also working on revising Form W-4 for 2018. The calculator and revised Form W-4 can be used by employees who wish to update their withholding in response to the new law or changes in their personal circumstances in 2018, and by workers starting a new job. Until a new Form W-4 is issued, employees and employers should continue to use the 2017 Form W-4. For more information, go to *IRS.gov/NR1036*.

An employee who experiences a change of status that causes a reduction in the number of withholding allowances isn't required to give his or her employer a new Form W-4 until 30 days after the 2018 Form W-4 is released. An employee that has a reduction in the number of withholding allowances solely due to changes from P.L. 115-97 isn't required to give his or her employer a new Form W-4 during 2018 but may do so at any time. Employees may use the 2017 Form W-4 to report changes to withholding allowances until 30 days after the 2018 Form W-4 is released. New employees may continue to claim allowances on the 2017 Form W-4 until 30 days after the 2018 Form W-4 is released. Employees who submit new Forms W-4 for 2018 using the 2017 Form W-4 don't need to resubmit a 2018 Form W-4 when the 2018 Form W-4 is released.

Exempt Form W-4. Generally, an employee may claim exemption from federal income tax withholding because he or she had no federal income tax liability last year and expects none this year. To continue to be exempt from withholding in 2018, an employee must give you a new Form W-4 by February 28, 2018. However, the 2018 Form W-4 may not be available before February 28, 2018. Employees may claim exemption from withholding for 2018 using the 2017 Form W-4 until 30 days after the 2018 Form W-4 is released. The 2017 Form W-4 must be (1) edited by striking "2017" in the text on line 7 and entering "2018" in its place, (2) completed by entering "Exempt 2018" on line 7, or (3) not edited but signed in 2018 and submitted under procedures established by the employer for the employee to certify entitlement to exempt status for 2018 by using the 2017 Form W-4 to claim exemption from withholding for 2018. In addition to 1–3 above, the employee can use any substantially similar method to 1–3 that clearly conveys in writing the employee's intent to certify his or her exemption from withholding for 2018. Employers that have established electronic systems for furnishing withholding allowance certificates may change their electronic systems to substantially conform with the options discussed above.

If the employee doesn't give you Form W-4 by February 28, 2018, follow the withholding rules discussed in section 9 under *Exemption from federal income tax withholding*. Employees who claimed exemption from withholding for 2018 using the 2017 Form W-4, as discussed above, don't need to resubmit a 2018 Form W-4 when the 2018 Form W-4 is released.

Withholding allowance. The 2018 amount for one withholding allowance on an annual basis is $4,150.

Withholding on supplemental wages. P.L. 115-97 lowered the withholding rates on supplemental wages. See section 7 for the new rates.

Backup withholding. P.L. 115-97 lowered the backup withholding rate to 24%. For more information on backup withholding, see *Backup withholding*, later.

Moving expense reimbursement. P.L. 115-97 suspends the exclusion for qualified moving expense reimbursements from your employee's income beginning after December 31, 2017, and before January 1, 2026. However, the exclusion is still available in the case of a member of the U.S. Armed Forces on active duty who moves because of a permanent change of station. The exclusion applies only to reimbursement of moving expenses that the member could deduct if he or she had paid or incurred them without reimbursement. See *Moving Expenses* in Pub. 3, Armed Forces' Tax Guide, for the definition of what constitutes a permanent change of station and to learn which moving expenses are deductible.

Social security and Medicare tax for 2018. The social security tax rate is 6.2% each for the employee and employer, unchanged from 2017. The social security wage base limit is $128,400.

The Medicare tax rate is 1.45% each for the employee and employer, unchanged from 2017. There is no wage base limit for Medicare tax.

Social security and Medicare taxes apply to the wages of household workers you pay $2,100 or more in cash wages for 2018. Social security and Medicare taxes apply to election workers who are paid $1,800 or more in cash or an equivalent form of compensation in 2018.

Disaster tax relief. Disaster tax relief was enacted for those impacted by Hurricane Harvey, Irma, or Maria. Additionally, the IRS has provided special relief designed to support employer leave-based donation programs to aid the victims of these hurricanes and to aid the victims of the California wildfires that began October 8, 2017. For more information about disaster relief, including the treatment of amounts paid to qualified tax-exempt organizations under employer leave-based donation programs, see Pub. 976.

Reminders

Qualified small business payroll tax credit for increasing research activities. For tax years beginning after December 31, 2015, a qualified small business may elect to claim up to $250,000 of its credit for increasing research activities as a payroll tax credit against the employer's share of social security tax. The portion of the credit used against the employer's share of social security tax is allowed in the first calendar quarter beginning after the date that the qualified small business filed its income tax return. The election and determination of the credit amount that will be used against the employer's share of social security tax are made on Form 6765, Credit for Increasing Research Activities. The amount from Form 6765, line 44, must then be reported on Form 8974, Qualified Small Business Payroll Tax Credit for Increasing Research Activities. Form 8974 is used to determine the amount of the credit that can be used in the current quarter. The amount from Form 8974, line 12, is reported on Form 941 or 941-SS, line 11 (or Form 944, line 8). For more information about the payroll tax credit, see Notice 2017-23, 2017-16 I.R.B. 1100, available at *IRS.gov/irb/2017-16_IRB/ar07.html*. Also see the line 16 instructions in the Instructions for Form 941 (line 13 instructions in the Instructions for Form 944).

Certification program for professional employer organizations. The Tax Increase Prevention Act of 2014 required the IRS to establish a voluntary certification program for professional employer organizations (PEOs). PEOs handle various payroll administration and tax reporting responsibilities for their business clients and are typically paid a fee based on payroll costs. To become and remain certified under the certification program, certified professional employer organizations (CPEOs) must meet various requirements described in sections 3511 and 7705 and related published guidance. Certification as a CPEO may affect the employment tax liabilities of both the CPEO and its customers. A CPEO is generally treated as the employer of any individual who performs services for a customer of the CPEO and is covered by a contract described in section 7705(e)(2) between the CPEO and the customer (CPEO contract), but only for wages and other compensation paid to the individual by the CPEO. For more information, go to *IRS.gov/CPEO*. Also see Revenue Procedure 2017-14, 2017-3, I.R.B. 426, available at *IRS.gov/irb/2017-03_IRB/ar14.html*.

Work opportunity tax credit for qualified tax-exempt organizations hiring qualified veterans. The work opportunity tax credit is available for eligible unemployed veterans who begin work on or after November 22, 2011, and before January 1, 2020. Qualified tax-exempt organizations that hire eligible unemployed veterans can claim the work opportunity tax credit against their payroll tax liability using Form 5884-C. For more information, go to *IRS.gov/WOTC*.

COBRA premium assistance credit. Effective for tax periods beginning after December 31, 2013, the credit for COBRA premium assistance payments can't be claimed on Form 941, Employer's QUARTERLY Federal Tax Return (or Form 944, Employer's ANNUAL Federal Tax Return). Instead, after filing your Form 941 (or Form 944), file Form 941-X, Adjusted Employer's QUARTERLY Federal Tax Return or Claim for Refund (or Form 944-X, Adjusted Employer's ANNUAL Federal Tax Return or Claim for Refund), respectively, to claim the COBRA premium assistance credit. Filing a Form 941-X (or Form 944-X) before filing a Form 941 (or Form 944) for the return period may result in errors or delays in processing your Form 941-X (or Form 944-X). For more information, see the Instructions for Form 941 (or the Instructions for Form 944), or go to *IRS.gov/COBRACredit*.

Medicaid waiver payments. Notice 2014-7 provides that certain Medicaid waiver payments are excludable from income for federal income tax purposes. See Notice 2014-7, 2014-4 I.R.B. 445, available at *IRS.gov/irb/2014-4_IRB/ar06.html*. For more information, including questions and answers related to Notice 2014-7, go to *IRS.gov/MedicaidWaiverPayments*.

No federal income tax withholding on disability payments for injuries incurred as a direct result of a terrorist attack directed against the United States. Disability payments for injuries incurred as a direct result of a terrorist attack directed against the United States (or its allies) aren't included in income. Because federal income tax withholding is only required when a payment is includable in income, no federal income tax should be withheld from these payments.

Voluntary withholding on dividends and other distributions by an Alaska Native Corporation (ANC). A shareholder of an ANC may request voluntary income tax withholding on dividends and other distributions paid by an ANC. A shareholder may request voluntary withholding by giving the ANC a completed Form W-4V. For more information see Notice 2013-77, 2013-50 I.R.B. 632, available at *IRS.gov/irb/2013-50_IRB/ar10.html*.

Definition of marriage. A marriage of two individuals is recognized for federal tax purposes if the marriage is recognized by the state, possession, or territory of the United States in which the marriage is entered into, regardless of legal residence. Two individuals who enter into a relationship that is denominated as marriage under the laws of a foreign jurisdiction are recognized as married for federal tax purposes if the relationship would be recognized as marriage under the laws of at least one state, possession, or territory of the United States, regardless of legal residence. Individuals who have entered into a registered domestic partnership, civil union, or other similar relationship that isn't denominated as a marriage under the law of the state, possession, or territory of the United States where such relationship was entered into aren't lawfully married for federal tax purposes, regardless of legal residence.

Outsourcing payroll duties. Generally, you're responsible to ensure that tax returns are filed and deposits and payments are made, even if you contract with a third party to perform these acts. You remain responsible if the third party fails to perform any required action. If you choose to outsource any of your payroll and related tax duties (that is, withholding, reporting, and paying over social security, Medicare, FUTA, and income taxes) to a third-party payer, such as a payroll service provider or reporting agent, go to *IRS.gov/OutsourcingPayrollDuties* for helpful information on this topic. If a CPEO pays wages and other compensation to an individual performing services for you, and the services are covered by a contract described in section 7705(e)(2) between you and the CPEO (CPEO contract), then the CPEO is generally treated as the employer, but only for wages and other compensation paid to the individual by the CPEO. However, with respect to certain employees covered by a CPEO contract, a customer may also be treated as an employer of the employees and, consequently, may also be liable for federal employment taxes imposed on wages and other compensation paid by the CPEO to such employees. For more information on the different types of third-party payer arrangements, see section 16.

Severance payments are subject to social security and Medicare taxes, income tax withholding, and FUTA tax. Severance payments are wages subject to social security and Medicare taxes. As noted in section 15, severance payments are also subject to income tax withholding and FUTA tax.

You must receive written notice from the IRS to file Form 944. If you've been filing Forms 941 (or Forms 941-SS, Employer's QUARTERLY Federal Tax Return—American Samoa, Guam, the Commonwealth of the Northern Mariana Islands, and the U.S. Virgin Islands, or Formularios 941-PR, Planilla para la Declaración Federal TRIMESTRAL del Patrono), and believe your employment taxes for the calendar year will be $1,000 or less, and you would like to file Form 944 instead of Forms 941, you must contact the IRS during the first calendar quarter of the tax year to request to file Form 944. You must receive written notice from the IRS to file Form 944 instead of Forms 941 before you may file this form. For more information on requesting to file Form 944, including the methods and deadlines for making a request, see the Instructions for Form 944.

Employers can request to file Forms 941 instead of Form 944. If you received notice from the IRS to file Form 944 but would like to file Forms 941 instead, you must contact the IRS during the first calendar quarter of the tax year to request to file Forms 941. You must receive written notice from the IRS to file Forms 941 instead of Form 944 before you may file these forms. For more information on requesting to file Forms 941, including the methods and deadlines for making a request, see the Instructions for Form 944.

Federal tax deposits must be made by electronic funds transfer (EFT). You must use EFT to make all federal tax deposits. Generally, an EFT is made using the Electronic Federal Tax Payment System (EFTPS). If you don't want to use EFTPS, you can arrange for your tax professional, financial institution, payroll service, or other trusted third party to make electronic deposits on your behalf. Also, you may arrange for your financial institution to initiate a same-day wire payment on your behalf. EFTPS is a free service provided by the Department of Treasury. Services provided by your tax professional, financial institution, payroll service, or other third party may have a fee.

For more information on making federal tax deposits, see *How To Deposit* in section 11. To get more information about EFTPS or to enroll in EFTPS, go to *EFTPS.gov*, or call 1-800-555-4477 or 1-800-733-4829 (TDD). Additional information about EFTPS is also available in Pub. 966.

Aggregate Form 941 filers. Agents and CPEOs must complete Schedule R (Form 941), Allocation Schedule for Aggregate Form 941 Filers, when filing an aggregate Form 941. Aggregate Forms 941 are filed by agents approved by the IRS under section 3504 of the Internal Revenue Code (IRC). To request approval to act as an agent for an employer, the agent files Form 2678 with the IRS. Aggregate Forms 941 are also filed by CPEOs approved by the IRS under section 7705. CPEOs file Form 8973, Certified Professional Employer Organization/Customer Reporting Agreement, to notify the IRS that they've started or ended a service contract with a client or customer.

Aggregate Form 940 filers. Agents and CPEOs must complete Schedule R (Form 940), Allocation Schedule for Aggregate Form 940 Filers, when filing an aggregate Form 940, Employer's Annual Federal Unemployment (FUTA) Tax Return. Aggregate Forms 940 can be filed by agents acting on behalf of home care service recipients who receive home care services through a program administered by a federal, state, or local government. To request approval to act as an agent on behalf of home care service recipients, the agent files Form 2678 with the IRS. Aggregate Forms 940 are also filed by CPEOs approved by the IRS under section 7705. CPEOs file Form 8973 to notify the IRS that they've started or ended a service contract with a client or customer.

Pub. 5146 explains employment tax examinations and appeal rights. Pub. 5146 provides employers with information on how the IRS selects employment tax returns to be examined, what happens during an exam, and what options an employer has in responding to the results of an exam, including how to appeal the results. Pub. 5146 also includes information on worker classification issues and tip exams.

Electronic Filing and Payment

Now, more than ever before, businesses can enjoy the benefits of filing and paying their federal taxes electronically. Whether you rely on a tax professional or handle your own taxes, the IRS offers you convenient programs to make filing and payment easier.

Spend less time and worry on taxes and more time running your business. Use *e-file* and EFTPS to your benefit.

- For *e-file*, go to *IRS.gov/EmploymentEfile* for additional information. A fee may be charged to file electronically.
- For EFTPS, go to *EFTPS.gov* or call EFTPS Customer Service at 1-800-555-4477 or 1-800-733-4829 (TDD).
- For electronic filing of Forms W-2, Wage and Tax Statement, go to *SSA.gov/employer*.

CAUTION *If you're filing your tax return or paying your federal taxes electronically, a valid EIN is required at the time the return is filed or the payment is made. If a valid EIN isn't provided, the return or payment won't be processed. This may result in penalties.*

Electronic funds withdrawal (EFW). If you file your employment tax return electronically, you can *e-file* and use

EFW to pay the balance due in a single step using tax preparation software or through a tax professional. However, don't use EFW to make federal tax deposits. For more information on paying your taxes using EFW, go to *IRS.gov/EFW*.

Credit or debit card payments. You can pay the balance due shown on your employment tax return by credit or debit card. Don't use a credit or debit card to make federal tax deposits. For more information on paying your taxes with a credit or debit card, go to *IRS.gov/PayByCard*. Your payment will be processed by a payment processor who will charge a processing fee.

Online payment agreement. You may be eligible to apply for an installment agreement online if you can't pay the full amount of tax you owe when you file your employment tax return. For more information, see the instructions for your employment tax return or go to *IRS.gov/OPA*.

Forms in Spanish

You can provide Formulario W-4(SP), Certificado de Exención de Retenciones del Empleado, in place of Form W-4, Employee's Withholding Allowance Certificate, to your Spanish-speaking employees. For more information, see Pub. 17(SP), El Impuesto Federal sobre los Ingresos (Para Personas Físicas). For nonemployees, such as independent contractors, Formulario W-9(SP), Solicitud y Certificación del Número de Identificación del Contribuyente, may be used in place of Form W-9, Request for Taxpayer Identification Number and Certification.

Hiring New Employees

Eligibility for employment. You must verify that each new employee is legally eligible to work in the United States. This includes completing the U.S. Citizenship and Immigration Services (USCIS) Form I-9, Employment Eligibility Verification. You can get Form I-9 at *USCIS.gov/Forms*, USCIS offices, or by calling 1-800-870-3676. For more information, visit the USCIS website at *USCIS.gov/I-9-Central* or call 1-800-375-5283 or 1-800-767-1833 (TDD).

New hire reporting. You're required to report any new employee to a designated state new hire registry. A new employee is an employee who hasn't previously been employed by you or was previously employed by you but has been separated from such prior employment for at least 60 consecutive days.

Many states accept a copy of Form W-4 with employer information added. Visit the Office of Child Support Enforcement website at *acf.hhs.gov/programs/css/employers* for more information.

W-4 request. Ask each new employee to complete the 2018 Form W-4. See section 9. New employees may continue to claim allowances on the 2017 Form W-4 until 30 days after the 2018 Form W-4 is released.

Name and social security number (SSN). Record each new employee's name and SSN from his or her social security card. Any employee without a social security card should apply for one. See section 4.

Paying Wages, Pensions, or Annuities

Correcting Form 941 or Form 944. If you discover an error on a previously filed Form 941 or Form 944, make the correction using Form 941-X or Form 944-X. Forms 941-X and 944-X are stand-alone forms, meaning taxpayers can file them when an error is discovered. Forms 941-X and 944-X are used by employers to claim refunds or abatements of employment taxes, rather than Form 843. See section 13 for more information.

Income tax withholding. Withhold federal income tax from each wage payment or supplemental unemployment compensation plan benefit payment according to the employee's Form W-4 and the correct withholding table. If you have nonresident alien employees, see *Withholding income taxes on the wages of nonresident alien employees* in section 9.

In 2018, withhold from periodic pension and annuity payments as if the recipient is married claiming three withholding allowances, unless he or she has provided Form W-4P, Withholding Certificate for Pension or Annuity Payments, either electing no withholding or giving a different number of allowances, marital status, or an additional amount to be withheld. Don't withhold on direct rollovers from qualified plans or governmental section 457(b) plans. See section 9 and Pub. 15-A, Employer's Supplemental Tax Guide. Pub. 15-A includes information about withholding on pensions and annuities.

Zero wage return. If you haven't filed a "final" Form 941 or Form 944, or aren't a "seasonal" employer, you must continue to file a Form 941 or Form 944, even for periods during which you paid no wages. The IRS encourages you to file your "Zero Wage" Forms 941 or 944 electronically. Go to *IRS.gov/EmploymentEfile* for more information on electronic filing.

Information Returns

You may be required to file information returns to report certain types of payments made during the year. For example, you must file Form 1099-MISC, Miscellaneous Income, to report payments of $600 or more to persons not treated as employees (for example, independent contractors) for services performed for your trade or business. For details about filing Forms 1099 and for information about required electronic filing, see the General Instructions for Certain Information Returns for general information and the separate, specific instructions for each information return you file (for example, Instructions for Form 1099-MISC). Generally, don't use Forms 1099 to report wages and other compensation you paid to employees; report these on Form W-2. See the General Instructions for Forms W-2 and W-3 for details about filing Form W-2 and for information about required electronic filing. If you file 250 or more Forms 1099-MISC, you must file them electronically. If you file 250 or more Forms W-2, you must file them electronically. Electronic filing is the only form of magnetic media that the IRS and SSA will accept.

Information reporting customer service site. The IRS operates an information return customer service site to answer questions about reporting on Forms W-2, W-3, 1099, and other information returns. If you have questions related to reporting on information returns, call 1-866-455-7438 (toll free), 304-263-8700 (toll call), or 304-579-4827 (TDD/TTY for persons who are deaf, hard of hearing, or have a speech disability). The center can also be reached by email at *mccirp@irs.gov*. Don't include tax identification numbers (TINs) or attachments in email correspondence because electronic mail isn't secure.

Nonpayroll Income Tax Withholding

Nonpayroll federal income tax withholding (reported on Forms 1099 and Form W-2G, Certain Gambling Winnings) must be reported on Form 945, Annual Return of Withheld Federal Income Tax. Separate deposits are required for payroll (Form 941 or Form 944) and nonpayroll (Form 945) withholding. Nonpayroll items include:

- Pensions (including distributions from tax-favored retirement plans, for example, section 401(k), section 403(b), and governmental section 457(b) plans), annuities, and IRA distributions.
- Military retirement.
- Gambling winnings.
- Indian gaming profits.

Employer Responsibilities

Employer Responsibilities: The following list provides a brief summary of your basic responsibilities. Because the individual circumstances for each employer can vary greatly, responsibilities for withholding, depositing, and reporting employment taxes can differ. Each item in this list has a page reference to a more detailed discussion in this publication.

New Employees:	Page
☐ Verify work eligibility of new employees	5
☐ Record employees' names and SSNs from social security cards	5
☐ Ask employees for Form W-4	5
Each Payday:	
☐ Withhold federal income tax based on each employee's Form W-4	21
☐ Withhold employee's share of social security and Medicare taxes	24
☐ Deposit: • Withheld income tax • Withheld and employer social security taxes • Withheld and employer Medicare taxes	26
Note: *Due date of deposit generally depends on your deposit schedule (monthly or* ***semiweekly)***	
Quarterly (By April 30, July 31, October 31, and January 31):	
☐ Deposit FUTA tax if undeposited amount is over $500	37
☐ File Form 941 (pay tax with return if not required to deposit)	31

Annually (see *Calendar* for due dates):	Page
☐ File Form 944 if required (pay tax with return if not required to deposit)	31
☐ Remind employees to submit a new Form W-4 if they need to change their withholding	21
☐ Ask for a new Form W-4 from employees claiming exemption from income tax withholding	22
☐ Reconcile Forms 941 (or Form 944) with Forms W-2 and W-3	33
☐ Furnish each employee a Form W-2	9
☐ File Copy A of Forms W-2 and the transmittal Form W-3 with the SSA	9
☐ Furnish each other payee a Form 1099 (for example, Form 1099-MISC)	9
☐ File Forms 1099 and the transmittal Form 1096	9
☐ File Form 940	9
☐ File Form 945 for any nonpayroll income tax withholding	9

- Certain government payments on which the recipient elected voluntary income tax withholding.
- Dividends and other distributions by an ANC on which the recipient elected voluntary income tax withholding.
- Payments subject to backup withholding.

For details on depositing and reporting nonpayroll income tax withholding, see the Instructions for Form 945.

Distributions from nonqualified pension plans and deferred compensation plans. Because distributions to participants from some nonqualified pension plans and deferred compensation plans (including section 457(b) plans of tax-exempt organizations) are treated as wages and are reported on Form W-2, income tax withheld must be reported on Form 941 or Form 944, not on Form 945. However, distributions from such plans to a beneficiary or estate of a deceased employee aren't wages and are reported on Forms 1099-R, Distributions From Pensions, Annuities, Retirement or Profit-Sharing Plans, IRAs, Insurance Contracts, etc.; income tax withheld must be reported on Form 945.

Backup withholding. You generally must withhold 24% of certain taxable payments if the payee fails to furnish you with his or her correct taxpayer identification number (TIN). This withholding is referred to as "backup withholding."

Payments subject to backup withholding include interest, dividends, patronage dividends, rents, royalties, commissions, nonemployee compensation, payments made in settlement of payment card or third-party network transactions, and certain other payments you make in the course of your trade or business. In addition, transactions by brokers and barter exchanges and certain payments made by fishing boat operators are subject to backup withholding.

CAUTION *Backup withholding doesn't apply to wages, pensions, annuities, IRAs (including simplified employee pension (SEP) and SIMPLE retirement plans), section 404(k) distributions from an employee stock ownership plan (ESOP), medical savings accounts (MSAs), health savings accounts (HSAs), long-term-care benefits, or real estate transactions.*

You can use Form W-9 or Formulario W-9(SP) to request payees to furnish a TIN. Form W-9 or Formulario W-9 (SP) must be used when payees must certify that the number furnished is correct, or when payees must certify that they're not subject to backup withholding or are exempt from backup withholding. The Instructions for the Requester of Form W-9 or Formulario W-9(SP) includes a list of types of payees who are exempt from backup withholding. For more information, see Pub. 1281, Backup Withholding for Missing and Incorrect Name/TIN(s).

Recordkeeping

Keep all records of employment taxes for at least 4 years. These should be available for IRS review. Your records should include the following information.

- Your EIN.
- Amounts and dates of all wage, annuity, and pension payments.
- Amounts of tips reported to you by your employees.
- Records of allocated tips.
- The fair market value of in-kind wages paid.
- Names, addresses, SSNs, and occupations of employees and recipients.
- Any employee copies of Forms W-2 and W-2c returned to you as undeliverable.
- Dates of employment for each employee.
- Periods for which employees and recipients were paid while absent due to sickness or injury and the amount and weekly rate of payments you or third-party payors made to them.
- Copies of employees' and recipients' income tax withholding allowance certificates (Forms W-4, W-4P, W-4(SP), W-4S, and W-4V).
- Dates and amounts of tax deposits you made and acknowledgment numbers for deposits made by EFTPS.
- Copies of returns filed and confirmation numbers.
- Records of fringe benefits and expense reimbursements provided to your employees, including substantiation.

Change of Business Name

Notify the IRS immediately if you change your business name. Write to the IRS office where you file your returns, using the *Without a payment* address provided in the instructions for your employment tax return, to notify the IRS of any business name change. See Pub. 1635 to see if you need to apply for a new EIN.

Change of Business Address or Responsible Party

Notify the IRS immediately if you change your business address or responsible party. Complete and mail Form 8822-B to notify the IRS of a business address or responsible party change. For a definition of "responsible party," see the Form 8822-B instructions.

Private Delivery Services

You can use certain private delivery services (PDSs) designated by the IRS to meet the "timely mailing as timely filing" rule for tax returns. Go to IRS.gov/PDS for the current list of PDSs.

The PDS can tell you how to get written proof of the mailing date.

For the IRS mailing address to use if you're using a PDS, go to IRS.gov/PDSstreetAdresses.

CAUTION *PDSs can't deliver items to P.O. boxes. You must use the U.S. Postal Service to mail any item to an IRS P.O. box address.*

Telephone Help

Tax questions. You can call the IRS Business and Specialty Tax Line with your employment tax questions at 1-800-829-4933.

Help for people with disabilities. You may call 1-800-829-4059 (TDD/TTY for persons who are deaf, hard of hearing, or have a speech disability) with any employment tax questions. You may also use this number for assistance with unresolved tax problems.

Additional employment tax information. Go to IRS.gov/EmploymentTaxes for additional employment tax information.

Ordering Employer Tax Forms and Publications

You can order employer tax forms and publications and information returns online at IRS.gov/OrderForms.

Instead of ordering paper Forms W-2 and W-3, consider filing them electronically using the SSA's free *e-file* service. Visit the SSA's Employer W-2 Filing Instructions & Information website at SSA.gov/employer to register for Business Services Online. You'll be able to create Forms W-2 online and submit them to the SSA by typing your wage information into easy-to-use fill-in fields. In addition, you can print out completed copies of Forms W-2 to file with state or local governments, distribute to your employees, and keep for your records. Form W-3 will be created for you based on your Forms W-2.

Filing Addresses

Generally, your filing address for Forms 940, 941, 943, 944, 945, and CT-1 depends on the location of your residence or principal place of business and whether or not you're including a payment with your return. There are separate filing addresses for these returns if you're a tax-exempt organization or government entity. See the separate instructions for Forms 940, 941, 943, 944, 945, or CT-1 for the filing addresses.

Dishonored Payments

Any form of payment that is dishonored and returned from a financial institution is subject to a penalty. The penalty is $25 or 2% of the payment, whichever is more. However, the penalty on dishonored payments of $24.99 or less is an amount equal to the payment. For example, a dishonored payment of $18 is charged a penalty of $18.

Photographs of Missing Children

The IRS is a proud partner with the *National Center for Missing & Exploited Children® (NCMEC)*. Photographs of missing children selected by the Center may appear in this publication on pages that would otherwise be blank. You can help bring these children home by looking at the photographs and calling 1-800-THE-LOST (1-800-843-5678) if you recognize a child.

Calendar

The following is a list of important dates and responsibilities. Also see Pub. 509, Tax Calendars.

TIP *If any date shown next for filing a return, furnishing a form, or depositing taxes falls on a Saturday, Sunday, or legal holiday, the due date is the next business day. The term "legal holiday" means any legal holiday in the District of Columbia. A statewide legal holiday delays a filing due date only if the IRS office where you're required to file is located in that state. However, a statewide legal holiday doesn't delay the due date of federal tax deposits. See* Deposits Due on Business Days Only *in section 11. For any filing due date, you'll meet the "file" or "furnish" requirement if the envelope containing the return or form is properly addressed, contains sufficient postage, and is postmarked by the U.S. Postal Service on or before the due date, or sent by an IRS-designated PDS on or before the due date. See* Private Delivery Services *under* Reminders *for more information.*

By January 31

File Form 941 or Form 944. File Form 941 for the fourth quarter of the previous calendar year and deposit any undeposited income, social security, and Medicare taxes. You may pay these taxes with Form 941 if your total tax liability for the quarter is less than $2,500. File Form 944 for the previous calendar year instead of Form 941 if the IRS has notified you in writing to file Form 944 and pay any undeposited income, social security, and Medicare taxes. You may pay these taxes with Form

944 if your total tax liability for the year is less than $2,500. For additional rules on when you can pay your taxes with your return, see *Payment with return* in section 11. If you timely deposited all taxes when due, you may file by February 10.

File Form 940. File Form 940 to report any FUTA tax. However, if you deposited all of the FUTA tax when due, you may file by February 10.

Furnish Forms 1099 and W-2. Furnish each employee a completed Form W-2. Furnish Form 1099-MISC to payees for nonemployee compensation. Most Forms 1099 must be furnished to payees by January 31, but some can be furnished by February 15. For more information, see the General Instructions for Certain Information Returns.

File Form W-2. File with the SSA Copy A of all 2017 paper and electronic Forms W-2 with Form W-3, Transmittal of Wage and Tax Statements. For more information on reporting Form W-2 information to the SSA electronically, visit the SSA's Employer W-2 Filing Instructions & Information webpage at *SSA.gov/employer*. If filing electronically, via the SSA's Form W-2 Online service, the SSA will generate Form W-3 data from the electronic submission of Form(s) W-2.

File Form 1099-MISC reporting nonemployee compensation. File with the IRS Copy A of all 2017 paper and electronic Forms 1099-MISC that report nonemployee compensation, with Form 1096, Annual Summary and Transmittal of U.S. Information Returns. For information on filing information returns electronically with the IRS, see Pub. 1220, Specifications for Electronic Filing of Forms 1097, 1098, 1099, 3921, 3922, 5498, and W-2G.

File Form 945. File Form 945 to report any nonpayroll federal income tax withheld. If you deposited all taxes when due, you may file by February 10. See *Nonpayroll Income Tax Withholding* under *Reminders* for more information.

By February 28

Request a new Form W-4 from exempt employees. Ask for a new Form W-4 from each employee who claimed exemption from income tax withholding last year.

File paper 2017 Forms 1099 and 1096. File Copy A of all paper 2017 Forms 1099, except Forms 1099-MISC reporting nonemployee compensation, with Form 1096 with the IRS. For electronically filed returns, see *By March 31* below.

File paper Form 8027. File paper Form 8027, Employer's Annual Information Return of Tip Income and Allocated Tips, with the IRS. See section 6. For electronically filed returns, see *By March 31* below.

On March 1

Forms W-4 claiming exemption from withholding expire. Any Form W-4 claiming exemption from withholding for the previous year has now expired. Begin withholding for any employee who previously claimed exemption from withholding but hasn't given you a new Form W-4 for the current year. If the employee doesn't give you a new Form W-4, withhold tax based on the last valid Form W-4 you have for the employee that doesn't claim exemption from withholding or, if one doesn't exist, as if he or she is single with zero withholding allowances. See section 9 for more information. If the employee gives you a new Form W-4 claiming exemption from withholding after February 28, you may apply the exemption to future wages, but don't refund taxes withheld while the exempt status wasn't in place.

By March 31

File electronic 2017 Forms 1099 and 8027. File electronic 2017 Forms 1099, except Forms 1099-MISC reporting nonemployee compensation, and 8027 with the IRS. For information on filing information returns electronically with the IRS, see Pub. 1220 and Pub. 1239, Specifications for Electronic Filing of Form 8027, Employer's Annual Information Return of Tip Income and Allocated Tips.

By April 30, July 31, October 31, and January 31

Deposit FUTA taxes. Deposit FUTA tax for the quarter (including any amount carried over from other quarters) if over $500. If $500 or less, carry it over to the next quarter. See section 14 for more information.

File Form 941. File Form 941 and deposit any undeposited income, social security, and Medicare taxes. You may pay these taxes with Form 941 if your total tax liability for the quarter is less than $2,500. If you timely deposited all taxes when due, you may file by May 10, August 10, November 10, or February 10, respectively. Don't file Form 941 for these quarters if you have been notified to file Form 944 and you didn't request and receive written notice from the IRS to file quarterly Forms 941.

Before December 1

New Forms W-4. Remind employees to submit a new Form W-4 if their marital status or withholding allowances have changed or will change for the next year.

Introduction

This publication explains your tax responsibilities as an employer. It explains the requirements for withholding, depositing, reporting, paying, and correcting employment taxes. It explains the forms you must give to your employees, those your employees must give to you, and those you must send to the IRS and the SSA. This guide also has tax tables you need to figure the taxes to withhold from each employee for 2018. References to "income tax" in this guide apply only to "federal" income tax. Contact your state or local tax department to determine if their rules are different.

When you pay your employees, you don't pay them all the money they earned. As their employer, you have the added responsibility of withholding taxes from their paychecks. The federal income tax and employees' share of social security and Medicare taxes that you withhold from your employees' paychecks are part of their wages that you pay to the United States Treasury instead of to your employees. Your employees trust that you pay the withheld taxes to the United States Treasury by making federal tax deposits. This is the reason that these withheld taxes are called trust fund taxes. If federal income, social security, or Medicare taxes that must be withheld aren't withheld or aren't deposited or paid to the United States Treasury, the trust fund recovery penalty may apply. See section 11 for more information.

Additional employment tax information is available in Pub. 15-A. Pub. 15-A includes specialized information supplementing the basic employment tax information provided in this publication. Pub. 15-B, Employer's Tax Guide to Fringe Benefits, contains information about the employment tax treatment and valuation of various types of noncash compensation.

Most employers must withhold (except FUTA), deposit, report, and pay the following employment taxes.

- Income tax.
- Social security tax.
- Medicare tax.
- FUTA tax.

There are exceptions to these requirements. See section 15 for guidance. Railroad retirement taxes are explained in the Instructions for Form CT-1.

Comments and suggestions. We welcome your comments about this publication and your suggestions for future editions.

You can send us comments from *IRS.gov/FormComments*.

Or you can write to:

Internal Revenue Service
Tax Forms and Publications
1111 Constitution Ave. NW, IR-6526
Washington, DC 20224

Although we can't respond individually to each comment received, we do appreciate your feedback and will consider your comments as we revise our tax forms, instructions, and publications. We can't answer tax questions sent to the above address.

Federal government employers. The information in this publication, including the rules for making federal tax deposits, applies to federal agencies.

State and local government employers. Payments to employees for services in the employ of state and local government employers are generally subject to federal income tax withholding but not FUTA tax. Most elected and appointed public officials of state or local governments are employees under common law rules. See chapter 3 of Pub. 963, Federal-State Reference Guide. In addition, wages, with certain exceptions, are subject to social security and Medicare taxes. See section 15 for more information on the exceptions.

If an election worker is employed in another capacity with the same government entity, see Revenue Ruling 2000-6 on page 512 of Internal Revenue Bulletin 2000-6 at *IRS.gov/pub/irs-irbs/irb00-06.pdf*.

You can get information on reporting and social security coverage from your local IRS office. If you have any questions about coverage under a section 218 (Social Security Act) agreement, contact the appropriate state official. To find your State Social Security Administrator, visit the National Conference of State Social Security Administrators website at *NCSSSA.org*.

Disregarded entities and qualified subchapter S subsidiaries (QSubs). Eligible single-owner disregarded entities and QSubs are treated as separate entities for employment tax purposes. Eligible single-member entities must report and pay employment taxes on wages paid to their employees using the entities' own names and EINs. See Regulations sections 1.1361-4(a)(7) and 301.7701-2(c)(2)(iv).

COBRA premium assistance credit. The Consolidated Omnibus Budget Reconciliation Act of 1985 (COBRA) provides certain former employees, retirees, spouses, former spouses, and dependent children the right to temporary continuation of health coverage at group rates. COBRA generally covers multiemployer health plans and health plans maintained by private-sector employers (other than churches) with 20 or more full- and part-time employees. Parallel requirements apply to these plans under the Employee Retirement Income Security Act of 1974 (ERISA). Under the Public Health Service Act, COBRA requirements apply also to health plans covering state or local government employees. Similar requirements apply under the Federal Employees Health Benefits Program and under some state laws. For the premium assistance (or subsidy) discussed below, these requirements are all referred to as COBRA requirements.

Under the American Recovery and Reinvestment Act of 2009 (ARRA), employers are allowed a credit against "payroll taxes" (referred to in this publication as "employment taxes") for providing COBRA premium assistance to assistance-eligible individuals. For periods of COBRA continuation coverage beginning after February 16, 2009, a group health plan must treat an assistance-eligible individual as having paid the required COBRA continuation coverage premium if the individual elects COBRA coverage and pays 35% of the amount of the premium.

An assistance-eligible individual is a qualified beneficiary of an employer's group health plan who is eligible for COBRA continuation coverage during the period beginning September 1, 2008, and ending May 31, 2010, due to the involuntarily termination from employment of a covered employee during the period and elects continuation COBRA coverage. The assistance for the coverage can last up to 15 months.

The COBRA premium assistance credit was available to an employer for premiums paid on behalf of employees who were involuntarily terminated from employment between September 1, 2008, and May 31, 2010. The COBRA premium assistance credit isn't available for individuals who were involuntarily terminated after May 31, 2010. Therefore, only in rare circumstances will the credit still be available, such as instances where COBRA eligibility was delayed as a result of employer-provided health insurance coverage following termination. For more information about the credit, see Notice 2009-27, 2009-16 I.R.B. 838, available at *IRS.gov/irb/2009-16_irb/ar09.html*.

Administrators of the group health plans (or other entities) that provide or administer COBRA continuation coverage must provide notice to assistance-eligible individuals of the COBRA premium assistance.

The 65% of the premium not paid by the assistance-eligible individuals is reimbursed to the employer maintaining the group health plan. The reimbursement is made through a credit against the employer's employment tax liabilities. For information on how to claim the credit, see the Instructions for Form 941-X or the Instructions for Form 944-X. The credit is treated as a deposit made on the first day of the return period (quarter or year). In the case of a multiemployer plan, the credit is claimed by the plan, rather than the employer. In the case of an insured plan subject to state law continuation coverage requirements, the credit is claimed by the insurance company, rather than the employer.

Anyone claiming the credit for COBRA premium assistance payments must maintain the following information to support their claim, including the following.

- Information on the receipt of the assistance-eligible individuals' 35% share of the premium, including dates and amounts.
- In the case of an insurance plan, a copy of an invoice or other supporting statement from the insurance carrier and proof of timely payment of the full premium to the insurance carrier required under COBRA.
- In the case of a self-insured plan, proof of the premium amount and proof of the coverage provided to the assistance-eligible individuals.
- Attestation of involuntary termination, including the date of the involuntary termination for each covered employee whose involuntary termination is the basis for eligibility for the subsidy.
- Proof of each assistance-eligible individual's eligibility for COBRA coverage and the election of COBRA coverage.
- A record of the SSNs of all covered employees, the amount of the subsidy reimbursed with respect to each covered employee, and whether the subsidy was for one individual or two or more individuals.

For more information, go to *IRS.gov/COBRACredit*.

1. Employer Identification Number (EIN)

If you're required to report employment taxes or give tax statements to employees or annuitants, you need an EIN.

The EIN is a nine-digit number the IRS issues. The digits are arranged as follows: 00-0000000. It is used to identify the tax accounts of employers and certain others who have no employees. Use your EIN on all of the items you send to the IRS and the SSA. For more information, see Pub. 1635.

If you don't have an EIN, you may apply for one online by visiting the IRS website at *IRS.gov/EIN*. You may also apply for an EIN by faxing or mailing Form SS-4 to the IRS. Employers outside of the United States may also apply for an EIN by calling 267-941-1099 (toll call). Don't use an SSN in place of an EIN.

You should have only one EIN. If you have more than one and aren't sure which one to use, call 1-800-829-4933 or 1-800-829-4059 (TDD/TTY for persons who are deaf, hard of hearing, or have a speech disability). Give the numbers you have, the name and address to which each was assigned, and the address of your main place of business. The IRS will tell you which number to use. For more information, see Pub. 1635.

If you took over another employer's business (see *Successor employer* in section 9), don't use that employer's EIN. If you've applied for an EIN but don't have your EIN by the time a return is due, file a paper return and write "Applied For" and the date you applied for it in the space shown for the number.

2. Who Are Employees?

Generally, employees are defined either under common law or under statutes for certain situations. See Pub. 15-A for details on statutory employees and nonemployees.

Employee status under common law. Generally, a worker who performs services for you is your employee if you have the right to control what will be done and how it will be done. This is so even when you give the employee freedom of action. What matters is that you have the right to control the details of how the services are performed. See Pub. 15-A for more information on how to determine whether an individual providing services is an independent contractor or an employee.

Generally, people in business for themselves aren't employees. For example, doctors, lawyers, veterinarians, and others in an independent trade in which they offer their services to the public are usually not employees. However, if the business is incorporated, corporate officers who work in the business are employees of the corporation.

If an employer-employee relationship exists, it doesn't matter what it is called. The employee may be called an agent or independent contractor. It also doesn't matter how payments are measured or paid, what they're called, or if the employee works full or part time.

Statutory employees. If someone who works for you isn't an employee under the common law rules discussed earlier, don't withhold federal income tax from his or her pay, unless backup withholding applies. Although the following persons may not be common law employees, they're considered employees by statute for social security, Medicare, and FUTA tax purposes under certain conditions.

- An agent (or commission) driver who delivers food, beverages (other than milk), laundry, or dry cleaning for someone else.
- A full-time life insurance salesperson who sells primarily for one company.
- A homeworker who works by guidelines of the person for whom the work is done, with materials furnished by and returned to that person or to someone that person designates.
- A traveling or city salesperson (other than an agent-driver or commission-driver) who works full time (except for sideline sales activities) for one firm or person getting orders from customers. The orders must be for merchandise for resale or supplies for use in the customer's business. The customers must be retailers, wholesalers, contractors, or operators of hotels, restaurants, or other businesses dealing with food or lodging.

Statutory nonemployees. Direct sellers, qualified real estate agents, and certain companion sitters are, by law, considered nonemployees. They're generally treated as self-employed for all federal tax purposes, including income and employment taxes.

H-2A agricultural workers. On Form W-2, don't check box 13 (Statutory employee), as H-2A workers aren't statutory employees.

Treating employees as nonemployees. You'll generally be liable for social security and Medicare taxes and withheld income tax if you don't deduct and withhold these taxes because you treated an employee as a nonemployee. You may be able to calculate your liability using special IRC section 3509 rates for the employee share of social security and Medicare taxes and the federal income tax withholding. The applicable rates depend on whether you filed required Forms 1099. You can't recover the employee share of social security tax, Medicare tax, or income tax withholding from the employee if the tax is paid under IRC section 3509. You're liable for the income tax withholding regardless of whether the employee paid income tax on the wages. You continue to owe the full employer share of social security and Medicare taxes. The employee remains liable for the employee share of social security and Medicare taxes. See IRC section 3509 for details. Also see the Instructions for Form 941-X.

IRC section 3509 rates aren't available if you intentionally disregard the requirement to withhold taxes from the employee or if you withheld income taxes but not social security or Medicare taxes. IRC section 3509 isn't available for reclassifying statutory employees. See Statutory employees above.

If the employer issued required information returns, the IRC section 3509 rates are:

- For social security taxes; employer rate of 6.2% plus 20% of the employee rate of 6.2% for a total rate of 7.44% of wages.
- For Medicare taxes; employer rate of 1.45% plus 20% of the employee rate of 1.45%, for a total rate of 1.74% of wages.
- For Additional Medicare Tax; 0.18% (20% of the employee rate of 0.9%) of wages subject to Additional Medicare Tax.
- For income tax withholding, the rate is 1.5% of wages.

If the employer didn't issue required information returns, the IRC section 3509 rates are:

- For social security taxes; employer rate of 6.2% plus 40% of the employee rate of 6.2% for a total rate of 8.68% of wages.
- For Medicare taxes; employer rate of 1.45% plus 40% of the employee rate of 1.45%, for a total rate of 2.03% of wages.
- For Additional Medicare Tax; 0.36% (40% of the employee rate of 0.9%) of wages subject to Additional Medicare Tax.
- For income tax withholding, the rate is 3.0% of wages.

Relief provisions. If you have a reasonable basis for not treating a worker as an employee, you may be relieved from having to pay employment taxes for that worker. To get this relief, you must file all required federal tax returns, including information returns, on a basis consistent with your treatment of the worker. You (or your predecessor) must not have treated any worker holding a substantially similar position as an employee for any periods beginning after 1977. See Pub. 1976, Do You Qualify for Relief Under Section 530.

IRS help. If you want the IRS to determine whether a worker is an employee, file Form SS-8.

Voluntary Classification Settlement Program (VCSP). Employers who are currently treating their workers (or a class or group of workers) as independent contractors or other nonemployees and want to voluntarily reclassify their workers as employees for future tax periods may be eligible to participate in the VCSP if certain requirements are met. File Form 8952 to apply for the VCSP. For more information, go to *IRS.gov/VCSP*.

Business Owned and Operated by Spouses

If you and your spouse jointly own and operate a business and share in the profits and losses, you may be partners in a partnership, whether or not you have a formal partnership agreement. See Pub. 541 for more details. The partnership is considered the employer of any employees, and is liable for any employment taxes due on wages paid to its employees.

Exception—Qualified joint venture. For tax years beginning after December 31, 2006, the Small Business and Work Opportunity Tax Act of 2007 (Public Law 110-28) provides that a "qualified joint venture," whose only members are spouses filing a joint income tax return, can elect not to be treated as a partnership for federal tax purposes. A qualified joint venture conducts a trade or business where:

- The only members of the joint venture are spouses who file a joint income tax return,
- Both spouses materially participate (see *Material participation* in the Instructions for Schedule C (Form 1040), line G) in the trade or business (mere joint ownership of property isn't enough),
- Both spouses elect to not be treated as a partnership, and
- The business is co-owned by both spouses and isn't held in the name of a state law entity such as a partnership or limited liability company (LLC).

To make the election, all items of income, gain, loss, deduction, and credit must be divided between the spouses, in accordance with each spouse's interest in the venture, and reported on separate Schedules C or F as sole proprietors. Each spouse must also file a separate Schedule SE to pay self-employment taxes, as applicable.

Spouses using the qualified joint venture rules are treated as sole proprietors for federal tax purposes and generally don't need an EIN. If employment taxes are owed by the qualified joint venture, either spouse may report and pay the employment taxes due on the wages paid to the employees using the EIN of that spouse's sole proprietorship. Generally, filing as a qualified joint venture won't increase the spouses' total tax owed on the joint income tax return. However, it gives each spouse credit for social security earnings on which retirement benefits are based and for Medicare coverage without filing a partnership return.

Note. If your spouse is your employee, not your partner, see *One spouse employed by another* in section 3.

For more information on qualified joint ventures, go to *IRS.gov/QJV*.

Exception—Community income. If you and your spouse wholly own an unincorporated business as community property under the community property laws of a state, foreign country, or U.S. possession, you can treat the business either as a sole proprietorship (of the spouse who carried on the business) or a partnership. You may still make an election to be taxed as a qualified joint venture instead of a partnership. See *Exception—Qualified joint venture* above.

3. Family Employees

Child employed by parents. Payments for the services of a child under age 18 who works for his or her parent in a trade or business aren't subject to social security and Medicare taxes if the trade or business is a sole proprietorship or a partnership in which each partner is a parent of the child. If these payments are for work other than in a trade or business, such as domestic work in the parent's private home, they're not subject to social security and Medicare taxes until the child reaches age 21. However, see *Covered services of a child or spouse*, later. Payments for the services of a child under age 21 who works for his or her parent, whether or not in a trade or business, aren't subject to FUTA tax. Payments for the services of a child of any age who works for his or her parent are generally subject to income tax withholding unless the payments are for domestic work in the parent's home, or unless the payments are for work other than in a trade or business and are less than $50 in the quarter or the child isn't regularly employed to do such work.

One spouse employed by another. The wages for the services of an individual who works for his or her spouse in a trade or business are subject to income tax withholding and social security and Medicare taxes, but not to FUTA tax. However, the payments for services of one spouse employed by another in other than a trade or business, such as domestic service in a private home, aren't subject to social security, Medicare, and FUTA taxes.

Covered services of a child or spouse. The wages for the services of a child or spouse are subject to income tax withholding as well as social security, Medicare, and FUTA taxes if he or she works for:

- A corporation, even if it is controlled by the child's parent or the individual's spouse;
- A partnership, even if the child's parent is a partner, unless each partner is a parent of the child;
- A partnership, even if the individual's spouse is a partner; or
- An estate, even if it is the estate of a deceased parent.

Parent employed by son or daughter. When the employer is a son or daughter employing his or her parent the following rules apply.

- Payments for the services of a parent in the son's or daughter's (the employer's) trade or business are subject to income tax withholding and social security and Medicare taxes.
- Payments for the services of a parent not in the son's or daughter's (the employer's) trade or business are generally not subject to social security and Medicare taxes.

Social security and Medicare taxes do apply to payments made to a parent for domestic services if all of the following apply:

- *The parent is employed by his or her son or daughter;*
- *The son or daughter (the employer) has a child or stepchild living in the home;*
- *The son or daughter (the employer) is a widow or widower, divorced, or living with a spouse who, because of a mental or physical condition, can't care for the child or stepchild for at least 4 continuous weeks in a calendar quarter; and*
- *The child or stepchild is either under age 18 or requires the personal care of an adult for at least 4 continuous weeks in a calendar quarter due to a mental or physical condition.*

Payments made to a parent employed by his or her child aren't subject to FUTA tax, regardless of the type of services provided.

4. Employee's Social Security Number (SSN)

You're required to get each employee's name and SSN and to enter them on Form W-2. This requirement also applies to resident and nonresident alien employees. You should ask your employee to show you his or her social security card. The employee may show the card if it is available.

Don't accept a social security card that says "Not valid for employment." A social security number issued with this legend doesn't permit employment.

You may, but aren't required to, photocopy the social security card if the employee provides it. If you don't provide the correct employee name and SSN on Form W-2, you may owe a penalty unless you have reasonable cause. See Pub. 1586, Reasonable Cause Regulations & Requirements for Missing and Incorrect Name/TINs, for information on the requirement to solicit the employee's SSN.

Applying for a social security card. Any employee who is legally eligible to work in the United States and doesn't have a social security card can get one by completing Form SS-5, Application for a Social Security Card, and submitting the necessary documentation. You can get Form SS-5 from the SSA website at *SSA.gov/forms/ss-5.pdf*, at SSA offices, or by calling 1-800-772-1213 or 1-800-325-0778 (TTY). The employee must complete and sign Form SS-5; it can't be filed by the employer. You may be asked to supply a letter to accompany Form SS-5 if the employee has exceeded his or her yearly or lifetime limit for the number of replacement cards allowed.

Applying for an SSN. If you file Form W-2 on paper and your employee applied for an SSN but doesn't have one when you must file Form W-2, enter "Applied For" on the form. If you're filing electronically, enter all zeros (000-00-0000 if creating forms online or 000000000 if uploading a file) in the SSN field. When the employee receives the SSN, file Copy A of Form W-2c, Corrected Wage and Tax Statement, with the SSA to show the employee's SSN. Furnish copies B, C, and 2 of Form W-2c to the employee. Up to 25 Forms W-2c for each Form W-3c, Transmittal of Corrected Wage and Tax Statements, may now be filed per session over the Internet, with no limit on the number of sessions. For more information, visit the SSA's Employer W-2 Filing Instructions & Information webpage at *SSA.gov/employer*. Advise your employee to correct the SSN on his or her original Form W-2.

Correctly record the employee's name and SSN. Record the name and SSN of each employee as they're shown on the employee's social security card. If the employee's name isn't correct as shown on the card (for example, because of marriage or divorce), the employee should request an updated card from the SSA. Continue to report the employee's wages under the old name until the employee shows you the updated social security card with the corrected name.

If the SSA issues the employee an updated card after a name change, or a new card with a different SSN after a change in alien work status, file a Form W-2c to correct the name/SSN reported for the most recently filed Form W-2. It isn't necessary to correct other years if the previous name and number were used for years before the most recent Form W-2.

IRS individual taxpayer identification numbers (ITINs) for aliens. Don't accept an ITIN in place of an SSN for employee identification or for work. An ITIN is only available to resident and nonresident aliens who aren't eligible for U.S. employment and need identification for other tax purposes. You can identify an ITIN because it is a nine-digit number, formatted like an SSN, that starts with the number "9" and has a range of numbers from "50–65," "70–88," "90–92," and "94–99" for the fourth and fifth digits (for example, 9NN-7N-NNNN).

An individual with an ITIN who later becomes eligible to work in the United States must obtain an SSN. If the individual is currently eligible to work in the United States, instruct the individual to apply for an SSN and follow the instructions under Applying for an SSN, *earlier*. *Don't use an ITIN in place of an SSN on Form W-2.*

Verification of SSNs. Employers and authorized reporting agents can use the Social Security Number Verification Service (SSNVS) to instantly verify up to 10 names and SSNs (per screen) at a time, or submit an electronic file of up to 250,000 names and SSNs and usually receive the results the next business day. Go to *SSA.gov/employer/ssnv.htm* for more information.

Registering for SSNVS. You must register online and receive authorization from your employer to use SSNVS. To register, visit the SSA's website at *SSA.gov/bso* and click on the *Register* link under *Business Services Online*. Follow the registration instructions to obtain a user identification (ID) and password. You'll need to provide the following information about yourself and your company.

- Name.
- SSN.
- Date of birth.
- Type of employer.
- EIN.
- Company name, address, and telephone number.
- Email address.

When you have completed the online registration process, the SSA will mail a one-time activation code to your employer. You must enter the activation code online to use SSNVS.

5. Wages and Other Compensation

Wages subject to federal employment taxes generally include all pay you give to an employee for services performed. The pay may be in cash or in other forms. It includes salaries, vacation allowances, bonuses, commissions, and fringe benefits. It doesn't matter how you measure or make the payments. Amounts an employer pays as a bonus for signing or ratifying a contract in connection with the establishment of an employer-employee relationship and an amount paid to an employee for cancellation of an employment contract and relinquishment of contract rights are wages subject to social security, Medicare, and FUTA taxes and income tax withholding. Also, compensation paid to a former employee for services performed while still employed is wages subject to employment taxes.

More information. See section 6 for a discussion of tips and section 7 for a discussion of supplemental wages. Also, see section 15 for exceptions to the general rules for wages. Pub. 15-A provides additional information on wages, including nonqualified deferred compensation, and other compensation. Pub. 15-B provides information on other forms of compensation, including:

- Accident and health benefits,
- Achievement awards,
- Adoption assistance,
- Athletic facilities,
- De minimis (minimal) benefits,
- Dependent care assistance,
- Educational assistance,
- Employee discounts,
- Employee stock options,
- Employer-provided cell phones,
- Group-term life insurance coverage,
- Health savings accounts,
- Lodging on your business premises,
- Meals,
- No-additional-cost services,
- Retirement planning services,
- Transportation (commuting) benefits,
- Tuition reduction, and
- Working condition benefits.

Employee business expense reimbursements. A reimbursement or allowance arrangement is a system by which you pay the advances, reimbursements, and charges for your employees' business expenses. How you report a reimbursement or allowance amount depends on whether you have an accountable or a nonaccountable plan. If a single payment includes both wages and an expense reimbursement, you must specify the amount of the reimbursement.

These rules apply to all ordinary and necessary employee business expenses that would otherwise qualify for a deduction by the employee.

Accountable plan. To be an accountable plan, your reimbursement or allowance arrangement must require your employees to meet all three of the following rules.

1. They must have paid or incurred deductible expenses while performing services as your employees. The reimbursement or advance must be payment for the expenses and must not be an amount that would have otherwise been paid to the employee as wages.
2. They must substantiate these expenses to you within a reasonable period of time.
3. They must return any amounts in excess of substantiated expenses within a reasonable period of time.

Amounts paid under an accountable plan aren't wages and aren't subject to income, social security, Medicare, and FUTA taxes.

If the expenses covered by this arrangement aren't substantiated (or amounts in excess of substantiated expenses aren't returned within a reasonable period of time), the amount paid under the arrangement in excess of the substantiated expenses is treated as paid under a nonaccountable plan. This amount is subject to income, social security, Medicare, and FUTA taxes for the first payroll period following the end of the reasonable period of time.

A reasonable period of time depends on the facts and circumstances. Generally, it is considered reasonable if your employees receive their advance within 30 days of the time they incur the expenses, adequately account for the expenses within 60 days after the expenses were paid or incurred, and return any amounts in excess of expenses within 120 days after the expenses were paid or incurred. Also, it is considered reasonable if you give your employees a periodic statement (at least quarterly) that asks them to either return or adequately account for outstanding amounts and they do so within 120 days.

Nonaccountable plan. Payments to your employee for travel and other necessary expenses of your business under a nonaccountable plan are wages and are treated as supplemental wages and subject to income, social security, Medicare, and FUTA taxes. Your payments are treated as paid under a nonaccountable plan if:

- Your employee isn't required to or doesn't substantiate timely those expenses to you with receipts or other documentation,
- You advance an amount to your employee for business expenses and your employee isn't required to or doesn't return timely any amount he or she doesn't use for business expenses,
- You advance or pay an amount to your employee regardless of whether you reasonably expect the employee to have business expenses related to your business, or
- You pay an amount as a reimbursement you would have otherwise paid as wages.

See section 7 for more information on supplemental wages.

Per diem or other fixed allowance. You may reimburse your employees by travel days, miles, or some other fixed allowance under the applicable revenue procedure. In these cases, your employee is considered to have accounted to you if your reimbursement doesn't exceed rates established by the Federal Government. The 2017 standard mileage rate for auto expenses was 53.5 cents per mile. The rate for 2018 is 54.5 cents per mile.

The government per diem rates for meals and lodging in the continental United States can be found by visiting the U.S. General Services Administration website at GSA.gov and entering "per diem rates" in the search box. Other than the amount of these expenses, your employees' business expenses must be substantiated (for example, the business purpose of the travel or the number of business miles driven). For information on substantiation methods, see Pub. 463.

If the per diem or allowance paid exceeds the amounts substantiated, you must report the excess amount as wages. This excess amount is subject to income tax withholding and payment of social security, Medicare, and FUTA taxes. Show the amount equal to the substantiated amount (for example, the nontaxable portion) in box 12 of Form W-2 using code "L."

Wages not paid in money. If in the course of your trade or business you pay your employees in a medium that is neither cash nor a readily negotiable instrument, such as a check, you're said to pay them "in kind." Payments in kind may be in the form of goods, lodging, food, clothing, or services. Generally, the fair market value of such payments at the time they're provided is subject to federal income tax withholding and social security, Medicare, and FUTA taxes.

However, noncash payments for household work, agricultural labor, and service not in the employer's trade or business are exempt from social security, Medicare, and FUTA taxes. Withhold income tax on these payments only if you and the employee agree to do so. Nonetheless, noncash payments for agricultural labor, such as commodity wages, are treated as cash payments subject to employment taxes if the substance of the transaction is a cash payment.

Meals and lodging. The value of meals isn't taxable income and isn't subject to income tax withholding and social security, Medicare, and FUTA taxes if the meals are furnished for the employer's convenience and on the employer's premises. The value of lodging isn't subject to income tax withholding and social security, Medicare, and FUTA taxes if the lodging is furnished for the employer's convenience, on the employer's premises, and as a condition of employment.

"For the convenience of the employer" means you have a substantial business reason for providing the meals and lodging other than to provide additional compensation to the employee. For example, meals you provide at the place of work so that an employee is available for emergencies during his or her lunch period are generally considered to be for your convenience.

However, whether meals or lodging are provided for the convenience of the employer depends on all of the facts and circumstances. A written statement that the meals or lodging are for your convenience isn't sufficient.

50% test. If over 50% of the employees who are provided meals on an employer's business premises receive these meals for the convenience of the employer, all meals provided on the premises are treated as furnished for the convenience of the employer. If this 50% test is met, the value of the meals is excludable from income for all employees and isn't subject to federal income tax withholding or employment taxes. For more information, see Pub. 15-B.

Health insurance plans. If you pay the cost of an accident or health insurance plan for your employees, including an employee's spouse and dependents, your payments aren't wages and aren't subject to social security, Medicare, and FUTA taxes, or federal income tax withholding. Generally, this exclusion also applies to qualified long-term care insurance contracts. However, for income tax withholding, the value of health insurance benefits must be included in the wages of S corporation employees who own more than 2% of the S corporation (2% shareholders). For social security, Medicare, and FUTA taxes, the health insurance benefits are excluded from the wages only for employees and their dependents or for a class or classes of employees and their dependents. See Announcement 92-16 for more information. You can find Announcement 92-16 on page 53 of Internal Revenue Bulletin 1992-5.

Health savings accounts and medical savings accounts. Your contributions to an employee's health savings account (HSA) or Archer medical savings account

(MSA) aren't subject to social security, Medicare, or FUTA taxes, or federal income tax withholding if it is reasonable to believe at the time of payment of the contributions they'll be excludable from the income of the employee. To the extent it isn't reasonable to believe they'll be excludable, your contributions are subject to these taxes. Employee contributions to their HSAs or MSAs through a payroll deduction plan must be included in wages and are subject to social security, Medicare, and FUTA taxes and income tax withholding. However, HSA contributions made under a salary reduction arrangement in a section 125 cafeteria plan aren't wages and aren't subject to employment taxes or withholding. For more information, see the Instructions for Form 8889.

Medical care reimbursements. Generally, medical care reimbursements paid for an employee under an employer's self-insured medical reimbursement plan aren't wages and aren't subject to social security, Medicare, and FUTA taxes, or income tax withholding. See Pub. 15-B for an exception for highly compensated employees.

Differential wage payments. Differential wage payments are any payments made by an employer to an individual for a period during which the individual is performing service in the uniformed services while on active duty for a period of more than 30 days and represent all or a portion of the wages the individual would have received from the employer if the individual were performing services for the employer.

Differential wage payments are wages for income tax withholding, but aren't subject to social security, Medicare, or FUTA taxes. Employers should report differential wage payments in box 1 of Form W-2. For more information about the tax treatment of differential wage payments, visit IRS.gov and enter "employees in a combat zone" in the search box.

Fringe benefits. You generally must include fringe benefits in an employee's gross income (but see *Nontaxable fringe benefits* next). The benefits are subject to income tax withholding and employment taxes. Fringe benefits include cars you provide, flights on aircraft you provide, free or discounted commercial flights, vacations, discounts on property or services, memberships in country clubs or other social clubs, and tickets to entertainment or sporting events. In general, the amount you must include is the amount by which the fair market value of the benefit is more than the sum of what the employee paid for it plus any amount the law excludes. There are other special rules you and your employees may use to value certain fringe benefits. See Pub. 15-B for more information.

Nontaxable fringe benefits. Some fringe benefits aren't taxable (or are minimally taxable) if certain conditions are met. See Pub. 15-B for details. The following are some examples of nontaxable fringe benefits.

- Services provided to your employees at no additional cost to you.
- Qualified employee discounts.
- Working condition fringes that are property or services that would be allowable as a business expense or depreciation expense deduction to the employee if he or she had paid for them. Examples include a company car for business use and subscriptions to business magazines.
- Certain minimal value fringes (including an occasional cab ride when an employee must work overtime and meals you provide at eating places you run for your employees if the meals aren't furnished at below cost).
- Qualified transportation fringes subject to specified conditions and dollar limitations (including transportation in a commuter highway vehicle, any transit pass, and qualified parking).
- The use of on-premises athletic facilities operated by you, if substantially all of the use is by employees, their spouses, and their dependent children.
- Qualified tuition reduction an educational organization provides to its employees for education. For more information, see Pub. 970.
- Employer-provided cell phones provided primarily for a noncompensatory business reason.

However, don't exclude the following fringe benefits from the income of highly compensated employees unless the benefit is available to other employees on a nondiscriminatory basis.

- No-additional-cost services.
- Qualified employee discounts.
- Meals provided at an employer operated eating facility.
- Reduced tuition for education.

For more information, including the definition of a highly compensated employee, see Pub. 15-B.

When fringe benefits are treated as paid. You may choose to treat certain noncash fringe benefits as paid by the pay period, by the quarter, or on any other basis you choose as long as you treat the benefits as paid at least once a year. You don't have to make a formal choice of payment dates or notify the IRS of the dates you choose. You don't have to make this choice for all employees. You may change methods as often as you like, as long as you treat all benefits provided in a calendar year as paid by December 31 of the calendar year. See Pub. 15-B for more information, including a discussion of the special accounting rule for fringe benefits provided during November and December.

Valuation of fringe benefits. Generally, you must determine the value of fringe benefits no later than January 31 of the next year. Before January 31, you may reasonably estimate the value of the fringe benefits for purposes of withholding and depositing on time.

Withholding on fringe benefits. You may add the value of fringe benefits to regular wages for a payroll period and figure withholding taxes on the total, or you may withhold federal income tax on the value of the fringe benefits at the optional flat 22% supplemental wage rate. However, see *Withholding on supplemental wages when an employee receives more than $1 million of supplemental wages during the calendar year* in section 7.

You may choose not to withhold income tax on the value of an employee's personal use of a vehicle you provide. You must, however, withhold social security and Medicare taxes on the use of the vehicle. See Pub. 15-B for more information on this election.

Depositing taxes on fringe benefits. Once you choose when fringe benefits are paid, you must deposit taxes in the same deposit period you treat the fringe benefits as paid. To avoid a penalty, deposit the taxes following the general deposit rules for that deposit period.

If you determine by January 31 you overestimated the value of a fringe benefit at the time you withheld and deposited for it, you may claim a refund for the overpayment or have it applied to your next employment tax return. See *Valuation of fringe benefits*, earlier. If you underestimated the value and deposited too little, you may be subject to a failure-to-deposit (FTD) penalty. See section 11 for information on deposit penalties.

If you deposited the required amount of taxes but withheld a lesser amount from the employee, you can recover from the employee the social security, Medicare, or income taxes you deposited on his or her behalf, and included in the employee's Form W-2. However, you must recover the income taxes before April 1 of the following year.

Sick pay. In general, sick pay is any amount you pay under a plan to an employee who is unable to work because of sickness or injury. These amounts are sometimes paid by a third party, such as an insurance company or an employees' trust. In either case, these payments are subject to social security, Medicare, and FUTA taxes. These taxes don't apply to sick pay paid more than 6 calendar months after the last calendar month in which the employee worked for the employer. The payments are always subject to federal income tax. See Pub. 15-A for more information.

Identity protection services. The value of identity protection services provided by an employer to an employee isn't included in an employee's gross income and doesn't need to be reported on an information return (such as Form W-2) filed for employees. This includes identity protection services provided before a data breach occurs. This exception doesn't apply to cash received instead of identity protection services or to proceeds received under an identity theft insurance policy. For more information, see Announcement 2015-22, 2015-35 I.R.B. 288, available at *IRS.gov/irb/2015-35_IRB/ar12.html* and Announcement 2016-02, 2016-3 I.R.B. 283, available at *IRS.gov/irb/2016-03_IRB/ar11.html*.

6. Tips

Tips your employee receives from customers are generally subject to withholding. Your employee must report cash tips to you by the 10th of the month after the month the tips are received. The report should include tips you paid over to the employee for charge customers, tips the employee received directly from customers, and tips received from other employees under any tip-sharing arrangement. Both directly and indirectly tipped employees must report tips to you. No report is required for months when tips are less than $20. Your employee reports the tips on Form 4070 or on a similar statement. The statement must be signed by the employee and must include:

- The employee's name, address, and SSN,
- Your name and address,
- The month and year (or the beginning and ending dates, if the statement is for a period of less than 1 calendar month) the report covers, and
- The total of tips received during the month or period.

Both Forms 4070 and 4070-A, Employee's Daily Record of Tips, are included in Pub. 1244, Employee's Daily Record of Tips and Report to Employer.

TIP *You're permitted to establish a system for electronic tip reporting by employees. See Regulations section 31.6053-1(d).*

Collecting taxes on tips. You must collect income tax, employee social security tax, and employee Medicare tax on the employee's tips. The withholding rules for withholding an employee's share of Medicare tax on tips also apply to withholding the Additional Medicare Tax once wages and tips exceed $200,000 in the calendar year.

You can collect these taxes from the employee's wages or from other funds he or she makes available. See *Tips treated as supplemental wages* in section 7 for more information. Stop collecting the employee social security tax when his or her wages and tips for tax year 2018 reach $128,400; collect the income and employee Medicare taxes for the whole year on all wages and tips. You're responsible for the employer social security tax on wages and tips until the wages (including tips) reach the limit. You're responsible for the employer Medicare tax for the whole year on all wages and tips. File Form 941 or Form 944 to report withholding and employment taxes on tips.

Ordering rule. If, by the 10th of the month after the month for which you received an employee's report on tips, you don't have enough employee funds available to deduct the employee tax, you no longer have to collect it. If there aren't enough funds available, withhold taxes in the following order.

1. Withhold on regular wages and other compensation.
2. Withhold social security and Medicare taxes on tips.
3. Withhold income tax on tips.

Reporting tips. Report tips and any collected and uncollected social security and Medicare taxes on Form W-2 and on Form 941, lines 5b, 5c, and, if applicable, 5d (Form 944, lines 4b, 4c, and, if applicable, 4d). Report an adjustment on Form 941, line 9 (Form 944, line 6), for the uncollected social security and Medicare taxes. Enter the amount of uncollected social security tax and Medicare tax on Form W-2, box 12, with codes "A" and "B." Don't include any uncollected Additional Medicare Tax in box 12 of Form W-2. For additional information on reporting tips, see section 13 and the General Instructions for Forms W-2 and W-3.

Revenue Ruling 2012-18 provides guidance for employers regarding social security and Medicare taxes imposed on tips, including information on the reporting of the employer share of social security and Medicare taxes under section 3121(q), the difference between tips and service charges, and the section 45B credit. See Revenue Ruling 2012-18, 2012-26 I.R.B. 1032, available at *IRS.gov/irb/2012-26_IRB/ar07.html*.

FUTA tax on tips. If an employee reports to you in writing $20 or more of tips in a month, the tips are also subject to FUTA tax.

Allocated tips. If you operate a large food or beverage establishment, you must report allocated tips under certain circumstances. However, don't withhold income, social security, or Medicare taxes on allocated tips.

A large food or beverage establishment is one that provides food or beverages for consumption on the premises, where tipping is customary, and where there were normally more than 10 employees on a typical business day during the preceding year.

The tips may be allocated by one of three methods—hours worked, gross receipts, or good faith agreement. For information about these allocation methods, including the requirement to file Forms 8027 electronically if 250 or more forms are filed, see the Instructions for Form 8027. For information on filing Form 8027 electronically with the IRS, see Pub. 1239.

Tip Rate Determination and Education Program. Employers may participate in the Tip Rate Determination and Education Program. The program primarily consists of two voluntary agreements developed to improve tip income reporting by helping taxpayers to understand and meet their tip reporting responsibilities. The two agreements are the Tip Rate Determination Agreement (TRDA) and the Tip Reporting Alternative Commitment (TRAC). A tip agreement, the Gaming Industry Tip Compliance Agreement (GITCA), is available for the gaming (casino) industry. To get more information about TRDA and TRAC agreements, see Pub. 3144. Additionally, visit IRS.gov and enter "MSU tips" in the search box to get more information about GITCA, TRDA, or TRAC agreements.

7. Supplemental Wages

Supplemental wages are wage payments to an employee that aren't regular wages. They include, but aren't limited to, bonuses, commissions, overtime pay, payments for accumulated sick leave, severance pay, awards, prizes, back pay, retroactive pay increases, and payments for nondeductible moving expenses. Other payments subject to the supplemental wage rules include taxable fringe benefits and expense allowances paid under a nonaccountable plan. How you withhold on supplemental wages depends on whether the supplemental payment is identified as a separate payment from regular wages. See Regulations section 31.3402(g)-1 for additional guidance for wages paid after January 1, 2007. Also see Revenue Ruling 2008-29, 2008-24 I.R.B. 1149, available at *IRS.gov/irb/2008-24_IRB/ar08.html*.

Withholding on supplemental wages when an employee receives more than $1 million of supplemental wages from you during the calendar year. Special rules apply to the extent supplemental wages paid to any one employee during the calendar year exceed $1 million. If a supplemental wage payment, together with other supplemental wage payments made to the employee during the calendar year, exceeds $1 million, the excess is subject to withholding at 37% (or the highest rate of income tax for the year). Withhold using the 37% rate without regard to the employee's Form W-4. In determining supplemental wages paid to the employee during the year, include payments from all businesses under common control. For more information, see Treasury Decision 9276, 2006-37 I.R.B. 423, available at *IRS.gov/irb/2006-37_IRB/ar09.html*.

Withholding on supplemental wage payments to an employee who doesn't receive $1 million of supplemental wages during the calendar year. If the supplemental wages paid to the employee during the calendar year are less than or equal to $1 million, the following rules apply in determining the amount of income tax to be withheld.

Supplemental wages combined with regular wages. If you pay supplemental wages with regular wages but don't specify the amount of each, withhold federal income tax as if the total were a single payment for a regular payroll period.

Supplemental wages identified separately from regular wages. If you pay supplemental wages separately (or combine them in a single payment and specify the amount of each), the federal income tax withholding method depends partly on whether you withhold income tax from your employee's regular wages.

1. If you withheld income tax from an employee's regular wages in the current or immediately preceding calendar year, you can use one of the following methods for the supplemental wages.
   a. Withhold a flat 22% (no other percentage allowed).
   b. If the supplemental wages are paid concurrently with regular wages, add the supplemental wages to the concurrently paid regular wages. If there are no concurrently paid regular wages, add the supplemental wages to, alternatively, either the regular wages paid or to be paid for the current payroll period or the regular wages paid for the preceding payroll period. Figure the income tax withholding

as if the total of the regular wages and supplemental wages is a single payment. Subtract the tax already withheld or to be withheld from the regular wages. Withhold the remaining tax from the supplemental wages. If there were other payments of supplemental wages paid during the payroll period made before the current payment of supplemental wages, aggregate all the payments of supplemental wages paid during the payroll period with the regular wages paid during the payroll period, calculate the tax on the total, subtract the tax already withheld from the regular wages and the previous supplemental wage payments, and withhold the remaining tax.

2. If you didn't withhold income tax from the employee's regular wages in the current or immediately preceding calendar year, use method 1-b. This would occur, for example, when the value of the employee's withholding allowances claimed on Form W-4 is more than the wages.

Regardless of the method you use to withhold income tax on supplemental wages, they're subject to social security, Medicare, and FUTA taxes.

Example 1. You pay John Peters a base salary on the 1st of each month. He is single and claims one withholding allowance. In January he is paid $1,000. Using the wage bracket tables, you withhold $33 from this amount. In February, he receives salary of $1,000 plus a commission of $2,000, which you combine with regular wages and don't separately identify. You figure the withholding based on the total of $3,000. The correct withholding from the tables is $264.

Example 2. You pay Sharon Warren a base salary on the 1st of each month. She is single and claims one allowance. Her May 1 pay is $2,000. Using the wage bracket tables, you withhold $144. On May 15 she receives a bonus of $1,000. Electing to use supplemental wage withholding method 1-b, you:

1. Add the bonus amount to the amount of wages from the most recent base salary pay date (May 1) ($2,000 + $1,000 = $3,000).
2. Determine the amount of withholding on the combined $3,000 amount to be $264 using the wage bracket tables.
3. Subtract the amount withheld from wages on the most recent base salary pay date (May 1) from the combined withholding amount ($264 – $144 = $120).
4. Withhold $120 from the bonus payment.

Example 3. The facts are the same as in Example 2, except you elect to use the flat rate method of withholding on the bonus. You withhold 22% of $1,000, or $220, from Sharon's bonus payment.

Example 4. The facts are the same as in Example 2, except you elect to pay Sharon a second bonus of $2,000 on May 29. Using supplemental wage withholding method 1-b, you:

1. Add the first and second bonus amounts to the amount of wages from the most recent base salary pay date (May 1) ($2,000 + $1,000 + $2,000 = $5,000).
2. Determine the amount of withholding on the combined $5,000 amount to be $614 using the wage bracket tables.
3. Subtract the amounts withheld from wages on the most recent base salary pay date (May 1) and the amounts withheld from the first bonus payment from the combined withholding amount ($614 – $144 – $120 = $350).
4. Withhold $350 from the second bonus payment.

Tips treated as supplemental wages. Withhold income tax on tips from wages earned by the employee or from other funds the employee makes available. If an employee receives regular wages and reports tips, figure income tax withholding as if the tips were supplemental wages. If you haven't withheld income tax from the regular wages, add the tips to the regular wages. Then withhold income tax on the total. If you withheld income tax from the regular wages, you can withhold on the tips by method 1-a or 1-b discussed earlier in this section under Supplemental wages identified separately from regular wages.

Vacation pay. Vacation pay is subject to withholding as if it were a regular wage payment. When vacation pay is in addition to regular wages for the vacation period, treat it as a supplemental wage payment. If the vacation pay is for a time longer than your usual payroll period, spread it over the pay periods for which you pay it.

8. Payroll Period

Your payroll period is a period of service for which you usually pay wages. When you have a regular payroll period, withhold income tax for that time period even if your employee doesn't work the full period.

No regular payroll period. When you don't have a regular payroll period, withhold the tax as if you paid wages for a daily or miscellaneous payroll period. Figure the number of days (including Sundays and holidays) in the period covered by the wage payment. If the wages are unrelated to a specific length of time (for example, commissions paid on completion of a sale), count back the number of days from the payment period to the latest of:

- The last wage payment made during the same calendar year,
- The date employment began, if during the same calendar year, or
- January 1 of the same year.

Employee paid for period less than 1 week. When you pay an employee for a period of less than one week, and the employee signs a statement under penalties of perjury indicating he or she isn't working for any other employer during the same week for wages subject to withholding, figure withholding based on a weekly payroll period. If the employee later begins to work for another employer for wages subject to withholding, the employee must notify you within 10 days. You then figure withholding based on the daily or miscellaneous period.

---

9. Withholding From Employees' Wages

Income Tax Withholding

TIP *Changes made under P.L. 115-97 will affect your employees' tax liability for 2018. Encourage your employees to use the IRS withholding calculator available at IRS.gov/W4App to determine if they should give you a new Form W-4 for 2018.*

Using Form W-4 to figure withholding. To know how much federal income tax to withhold from employees' wages, you should have a Form W-4 on file for each employee. Encourage your employees to file an updated Form W-4 for 2018, especially if they owed taxes or received a large refund when filing their 2017 tax return. Advise your employees to use the IRS Withholding Calculator available at *IRS.gov/W4App* for help in determining how many withholding allowances to claim on their Forms W-4.

Ask all new employees to give you a signed Form W-4 when they start work. Make the form effective with the first wage payment. If a new employee doesn't give you a completed Form W-4, withhold income tax as if he or she is single, with no withholding allowances.

Form in Spanish. You can provide Formulario W-4(SP) in place of Form W-4, to your Spanish-speaking employees. For more information, see Pub. 17(SP). The rules discussed in this section that apply to Form W-4 also apply to Formulario W-4(SP).

Electronic system to receive Form W-4. You may establish a system to electronically receive Forms W-4 from your employees. See Regulations section 31.3402(f)(5)-1(c) for more information.

Effective date of Form W-4. A Form W-4 remains in effect until the employee gives you a new one. When you receive a new Form W-4 from an employee, don't adjust withholding for pay periods before the effective date of the new form. If an employee gives you a Form W-4 that replaces an existing Form W-4, begin withholding no later than the start of the first payroll period ending on or after the 30th day from the date when you received the replacement Form W-4. For exceptions, see *Exemption from federal income tax withholding*, *IRS review of requested Forms W-4*, and *Invalid Forms W-4*, later in this section.

CAUTION *A Form W-4 that makes a change for the next calendar year won't take effect in the current calendar year.*

Successor employer. If you're a successor employer (see *Successor employer*, later in this section), secure new Forms W-4 from the transferred employees unless the "Alternative Procedure" in section 5 of Revenue Procedure 2004-53 applies. See Revenue Procedure 2004-53, 2004-34 I.R.B. 320, available at *IRS.gov/irb/2004-34_IRB/ar13.html*.

Completing Form W-4. The amount of any federal income tax withholding must be based on marital status and withholding allowances. Your employees may not base their withholding amounts on a fixed dollar amount or percentage. However, an employee may specify a dollar amount to be withheld in addition to the amount of withholding based on filing status and withholding allowances claimed on Form W-4.

Employees may claim fewer withholding allowances than they're entitled to claim. They may wish to claim fewer allowances to ensure they have enough withholding or to offset the tax on other sources of taxable income not subject to withholding.

See Pub. 505 for more information about completing Form W-4. Along with Form W-4, you may wish to order Pub. 505 for use by your employees. Pub. 505 is being updated to incorporate changes made by P.L. 115–97. The IRS anticipates that Pub. 505 will be available by the end of February.

Don't accept any withholding or estimated tax payments from your employees in addition to withholding based on their Form W-4. If they require additional withholding, they should submit a new Form W-4 and, if necessary, pay estimated tax by filing Form 1040-ES or by using EFTPS to make estimated tax payments.

TIP *The 2018 Form W-4 may not be available before February 28, 2018. Employees may claim exemption from withholding for 2018 using the 2017 Form W-4 until 30 days after the 2018 Form W-4 is released. The 2017 Form W-4 must be (1) edited by striking "2017" in the text on line 7 and entering "2018" in its place, (2) completed by entering "Exempt 2018" on line 7, or (3) not edited but signed in 2018 and submitted under procedures established by the employer for the employee to certify entitlement to exempt status for 2018 by using the 2017 Form W-4 to claim exemption from withholding for 2018. In addition to 1–3 above, the employee can use any substantially similar method to 1–3 that clearly conveys in writing the employee's intent to certify his or her exemption from withholding for 2018. Employers that have established electronic systems for furnishing withholding allowance certificates may change their electronic systems to substantially conform with the options discussed above. The employee still must give you Form W-4 claiming exemption from federal income tax withholding by February 28, 2018. If the employee doesn't give you Form W-4 by February 28, 2018, follow the withholding rules discussed under* Exemption from federal income tax withholding.

Employees who claimed exemption from withholding for 2018 using the 2017 Form W-4, as discussed earlier, don't need to resubmit a 2018 Form W-4 when the 2018 Form W-4 is released.

Exemption from federal income tax withholding. Generally, an employee may claim exemption from federal income tax withholding because he or she had no income tax liability last year and expects none this year. See the Form W-4 instructions for more information. However, the wages are still subject to social security and Medicare taxes. See also Invalid Forms W-4, later in this section.

A Form W-4 claiming exemption from withholding is effective when it is given to the employer and only for that calendar year. To continue to be exempt from withholding for 2018, an employee must give you a new Form W-4 by February 28. If the employee doesn't give you a new Form W-4 by February 28, begin withholding based on the last Form W-4 for the employee that didn't claim an exemption from withholding or, if one wasn't furnished, then withhold tax as if he or she is single with zero withholding allowances. If the employee provides a new Form W-4 claiming exemption from withholding on March 1 or later, you may apply it to future wages but don't refund any taxes withheld while the exempt status wasn't in place.

Withholding income taxes on the wages of nonresident alien employees. In general, you must withhold federal income taxes on the wages of nonresident alien employees. However, see Pub. 515 for exceptions to this general rule. Also see section 3 of Pub. 51 for guidance on H-2A visa workers.

Withholding adjustment for nonresident alien employees. Apply the procedure discussed next to figure the amount of income tax to withhold from the wages of nonresident alien employees performing services within the United States.

TIP *Nonresident alien students from India and business apprentices from India aren't subject to this procedure.*

Instructions. To figure how much income tax to withhold from the wages paid to a nonresident alien employee performing services in the United States, use the following steps.

Step 1. Add to the wages paid to the nonresident alien employee for the payroll period the amount shown in the chart next for the applicable payroll period.

Amount to Add to Nonresident Alien Employee's Wages for Calculating Income Tax Withholding Only

Payroll Period	Add Additional
Weekly	$ 151.00
Biweekly	301.90
Semimonthly	327.10
Monthly	654.20
Quarterly	1,962.50
Semiannually	3,925.00
Annually	7,850.00
Daily or Miscellaneous (each day of the payroll period)	30.20

Step 2. Use the amount figured in *Step 1* and the number of withholding allowances claimed (generally limited to one allowance) to figure income tax withholding. Determine the value of withholding allowances by multiplying the number of withholding allowances claimed by the appropriate amount from Table 5 shown on page 45. If you're using the Percentage Method Tables for Income Tax Withholding, provided on pages 46–47, reduce the amount figured in *Step 1* by the value of withholding allowances and use that reduced amount to figure the income tax withholding. If you're using the Wage Bracket Method Tables for Income Tax Withholding, provided on pages 48–67, use the amount figured in *Step 1* and the number of withholding allowances to figure income tax withholding.

The amounts from the chart above are added to wages solely for calculating income tax withholding on the wages of the nonresident alien employee. The amounts from the chart shouldn't be included in any box on the employee's Form W-2 and don't increase the income tax liability of the employee. Also, the amounts from the chart don't increase the social security tax or Medicare tax liability of the employer or the employee, or the FUTA tax liability of the employer.

This procedure only applies to nonresident alien employees who have wages subject to income tax withholding.

Example. An employer using the percentage method of withholding pays wages of $500 for a biweekly payroll period to a married nonresident alien employee. The nonresident alien has properly completed Form W-4, entering marital status as "single" with one withholding allowance and indicating status as a nonresident alien on Form W-4, line 6 (see Nonresident alien employee's Form W-4, later in this section). The employer determines the wages to be used in the withholding tables by adding to the $500 amount of wages paid the amount of $301.90 from the chart under Step 1 ($801.90 total). The employer then applies the applicable tables to determine the income tax withholding for nonresident aliens (see Step 2).

If you use the Percentage Method Tables for Income Tax Withholding, reduce the amount figured in Step 1 by the value of withholding allowances and use that reduced amount to figure income tax withholding.

The $301.90 added to wages for calculating income tax withholding isn't reported on Form W-2, and doesn't increase the income tax liability of the employee. Also, the $301.90 added to wages doesn't affect the social security tax or Medicare tax liability of the employer or the employee, or the FUTA tax liability of the employer.

Supplemental wage payment. This procedure for determining the amount of income tax withholding doesn't apply to a supplemental wage payment (see section 7) if the 37% mandatory flat rate withholding applies or if the 22% optional flat rate withholding is being used to calculate income tax withholding on the supplemental wage payment.

Nonresident alien employee's Form W-4. When completing Forms W-4, nonresident aliens are required to:

- Not claim exemption from income tax withholding;
- Request withholding as if they're single, regardless of their actual marital status;
- Claim only one allowance (if the nonresident alien is a resident of Canada, Mexico, or South Korea, or a student or business apprentice from India, he or she may claim more than one allowance); and
- Write "Nonresident Alien" or "NRA" above the dotted line on line 6 of Form W-4.

If you maintain an electronic Form W-4 system, you should provide a field for nonresident aliens to enter nonresident alien status instead of writing "Nonresident Alien" or "NRA" above the dotted line on line 6.

A nonresident alien employee may request additional withholding at his or her option for other purposes, although such additions shouldn't be necessary for withholding to cover federal income tax liability related to employment.

Form 8233. If a nonresident alien employee claims a tax treaty exemption from withholding, the employee must submit Form 8233 with respect to the income exempt under the treaty, instead of Form W-4. For more information, see *Pay for Personal Services Performed* in the *Withholding on Specific Income* section of Pub. 515 and the Instructions for Form 8233.

IRS review of requested Forms W-4. When requested by the IRS, you must make original Forms W-4 available for inspection by an IRS employee. You may also be directed to send certain Forms W-4 to the IRS. You may receive a notice from the IRS requiring you to submit a copy of Form W-4 for one or more of your named employees. Send the requested copy or copies of Form W-4 to the IRS at the address provided and in the manner directed by the notice. The IRS may also require you to submit copies of Form W-4 to the IRS as directed by Treasury Decision 9337, 2007-35 I.R.B. 455, which is available at *IRS.gov/irb/2007-35_IRB/ar10.html*. When we refer to Form W-4, the same rules apply to Formulario W-4(SP), its Spanish translation.

After submitting a copy of a requested Form W-4 to the IRS, continue to withhold federal income tax based on that Form W-4 if it is valid (see *Invalid Forms W-4*, later in this section). However, if the IRS later notifies you in writing the employee isn't entitled to claim exemption from withholding or a claimed number of withholding allowances, withhold federal income tax based on the effective date, marital status, and maximum number of withholding allowances specified in the IRS notice (commonly referred to as a "lock-in letter").

Initial lock-in letter. The IRS uses information reported on Form W-2 to identify employees with withholding compliance problems. In some cases, if a serious underwithholding problem is found to exist for a particular employee, the IRS may issue a lock-in letter to the employer specifying the maximum number of withholding allowances and marital status permitted for a specific employee. You'll also receive a copy for the employee that identifies the maximum number of withholding allowances and marital status permitted and the process by which the employee can provide additional information to the IRS for purposes of determining the appropriate number of withholding allowances and/or modifying the specified marital status. You must furnish the employee copy to the employee within 10 business days of receipt if the employee is employed by you as of the date of the notice. Begin withholding based on the notice on the date specified in the notice.

Implementation of lock-in letter. When you receive the notice specifying the maximum number of withholding allowances and marital status permitted, you may not withhold immediately on the basis of the notice. You must begin withholding tax on the basis of the notice for any wages paid after the date specified in the notice. The delay between your receipt of the notice and the date to begin the withholding on the basis of the notice permits the employee time to contact the IRS.

Employee not performing services. If you receive a notice for an employee who isn't performing services for you, you must still furnish the employee copy to the employee and withhold based on the notice if any of the following apply.

- You're paying wages for the employee's prior services and the wages are subject to income tax withholding on or after the date specified in the notice.
- You reasonably expect the employee to resume services within 12 months of the date of the notice.
- The employee is on a leave of absence that doesn't exceed 12 months or the employee has a right to reemployment after the leave of absence.

Termination and re-hire of employees. If you must furnish and withhold based on the notice and the employment relationship is terminated after the date of the notice, you must continue to withhold based on the notice if you continue to pay any wages subject to income tax withholding. You must also withhold based on the notice or modification notice (explained next) if the employee resumes the employment relationship with you within 12 months after the termination of the employment relationship.

Modification notice. After issuing the notice specifying the maximum number of withholding allowances and marital status permitted, the IRS may issue a subsequent notice (modification notice) that modifies the original notice. The modification notice may change the marital status and/or the number of withholding allowances permitted. You must withhold federal income tax based on the effective date specified in the modification notice.

New Form W-4 after IRS notice. After the IRS issues a notice or modification notice, if the employee provides you with a new Form W-4 claiming complete exemption from withholding or claims a marital status, a number of withholding allowances, and any additional withholding that results in less withholding than would result under the IRS notice or modification notice, disregard the new Form W-4. You must withhold based on the notice or modification notice unless the IRS notifies you to withhold based on the new Form W-4. If the employee wants to put a new Form W-4 into effect that results in less withholding than required, the employee must contact the IRS.

If, after you receive an IRS notice or modification notice, your employee gives you a new Form W-4 that doesn't claim exemption from federal income tax withholding and claims a marital status, a number of withholding allowances, and any additional withholding that results in more withholding than would result under the notice or modification notice, you must withhold tax based on the new Form W-4. Otherwise, disregard any subsequent Forms W-4 provided by the employee and withhold based on the IRS notice or modification notice.

For additional information about these rules, see Treasury Decision 9337, 2007-35 I.R.B. 455, available at *IRS.gov/irb/2007-35_IRB/ar10.html*.

Substitute Forms W-4. You're encouraged to have your employees use the official version of Form W-4 to claim withholding allowances or exemption from withholding.

You may use a substitute version of Form W-4 to meet your business needs. However, your substitute Form W-4 must contain language that is identical to the official Form W-4 and your form must meet all current IRS rules for substitute forms. At the time you provide your substitute form to the employee, you must provide him or her with all tables, instructions, and worksheets from the current Form W-4.

You can't accept substitute Forms W-4 developed by employees. An employee who submits an employee-developed substitute Form W-4 after October 10, 2007, will be treated as failing to furnish a Form W-4. However, continue to honor any valid employee-developed Forms W-4 you accepted before October 11, 2007.

CAUTION *If an employee changes the 2017 Form W-4 to claim exemption from federal income tax withholding in 2018, as described earlier, it isn't considered an invalid Form W-4.*

Invalid Forms W-4. Any unauthorized change or addition to Form W-4 makes it invalid. This includes taking out any language by which the employee certifies the form is correct. A Form W-4 is also invalid if, by the date an employee gives it to you, he or she clearly indicates it is false. An employee who submits a false Form W-4 may be subject to a $500 penalty. You may treat a Form W-4 as invalid if the employee wrote "exempt" on line 7 and also entered a number on line 5 or an amount on line 6.

When you get an invalid Form W-4, don't use it to figure federal income tax withholding. Tell the employee it is invalid and ask for another one. If the employee doesn't give you a valid one, withhold tax as if the employee is single with zero withholding allowances. However, if you have an earlier Form W-4 for this worker that is valid, withhold as you did before.

Amounts exempt from levy on wages, salary, and other income. If you receive a Notice of Levy on Wages, Salary, and Other Income (Forms 668-W(ACS), 668-W(c)(DO), or 668-W(ICS)), you must withhold amounts as described in the instructions for these forms. Pub. 1494 has tables to figure the amount exempt from levy. If a levy issued in a prior year is still in effect and the taxpayer submits a new Statement of Exemptions and Filing Status, use the current year Pub. 1494 to figure the exempt amount.

Social Security and Medicare Taxes

The Federal Insurance Contributions Act (FICA) provides for a federal system of old-age, survivors, disability, and hospital insurance. The old-age, survivors, and disability insurance part is financed by the social security tax. The hospital insurance part is financed by the Medicare tax. Each of these taxes is reported separately.

Generally, you're required to withhold social security and Medicare taxes from your employees' wages and pay the employer's share of these taxes. Certain types of wages and compensation aren't subject to social security and Medicare taxes. See section 5 and section 15 for details. Generally, employee wages are subject to social security and Medicare taxes regardless of the employee's age or whether he or she is receiving social security benefits. If the employee reported tips, see section 6.

Tax rates and the social security wage base limit. Social security and Medicare taxes have different rates and only the social security tax has a wage base limit. The wage base limit is the maximum wage subject to the tax for the year. Determine the amount of withholding for social security and Medicare taxes by multiplying each payment by the employee tax rate. There are no withholding allowances for social security and Medicare taxes.

For 2018, the social security tax rate is 6.2% (amount withheld) each for the employer and employee (12.4%

total). The social security wage base limit is $128,400. The tax rate for Medicare is 1.45% (amount withheld) each for the employee and employer (2.9% total). There is no wage base limit for Medicare tax; all covered wages are subject to Medicare tax.

Additional Medicare Tax withholding. In addition to withholding Medicare tax at 1.45%, you must withhold a 0.9% Additional Medicare Tax from wages you pay to an employee in excess of $200,000 in a calendar year. You're required to begin withholding Additional Medicare Tax in the pay period in which you pay wages in excess of $200,000 to an employee and continue to withhold it each pay period until the end of the calendar year. Additional Medicare Tax is only imposed on the employee. There is no employer share of Additional Medicare Tax. All wages that are subject to Medicare tax are subject to Additional Medicare Tax withholding if paid in excess of the $200,000 withholding threshold.

For more information on what wages are subject to Medicare tax, see section 15. For more information on Additional Medicare Tax, go to *IRS.gov/ADMT*.

Successor employer. When corporate acquisitions meet certain requirements, wages paid by the predecessor are treated as if paid by the successor for purposes of applying the social security wage base and for applying the Additional Medicare Tax withholding threshold (that is, $200,000 in a calendar year). You should determine whether or not you should file Schedule D (Form 941), Report of Discrepancies Caused by Acquisitions, Statutory Mergers, or Consolidations, by reviewing the Instructions for Schedule D (Form 941). See Regulations section 31.3121(a)(1)-1(b) for more information. Also see Revenue Procedure 2004-53, 2004-34 I.R.B. 320, available at *IRS.gov/irb/2004-34_IRB/ar13.html*.

Example. Early in 2018, you bought all of the assets of a plumbing business from Mr. Martin. Mr. Brown, who had been employed by Mr. Martin and received $2,000 in wages before the date of purchase, continued to work for you. The wages you paid to Mr. Brown are subject to social security taxes on the first $126,400 ($128,400 minus $2,000). Medicare tax is due on all of the wages you pay him during the calendar year. You should include the $2,000 Mr. Brown received while employed by Mr. Martin in determining whether Mr. Brown's wages exceed the $200,000 for Additional Medicare Tax withholding threshold.

Motion picture project employers. All wages paid by a motion picture project employer to a motion picture project worker during a calendar year are subject to a single social security tax wage base ($128,400 for 2018) and a single FUTA tax wage base ($7,000 for 2018) regardless of the worker's status as a common law employee of multiple clients of the motion picture project employer. For more information, including the definition of a motion picture project employer and motion picture project worker, see Internal Revenue Code section 3512.

Withholding social security and Medicare taxes on nonresident alien employees. In general, if you pay wages to nonresident alien employees, you must withhold social security and Medicare taxes as you would for a U.S. citizen or resident alien. However, see Pub. 515 for exceptions to this general rule.

International social security agreements. The United States has social security agreements, also known as totalization agreements, with many countries that eliminate dual taxation and dual coverage. Compensation subject to social security and Medicare taxes may be exempt under one of these agreements. You can get more information and a list of agreement countries from the SSA at *SSA.gov/international* or see section 7 of Pub. 15-A.

Religious exemption. An exemption from social security and Medicare taxes is available to members of a recognized religious sect opposed to insurance. This exemption is available only if both the employee and the employer are members of the sect. For more information, see Pub. 517.

Foreign persons treated as American employers. Under IRC section 3121(z), for services performed after July 31, 2008, a foreign person who meets both of the following conditions is generally treated as an American employer for purposes of paying FICA taxes on wages paid to an employee who is a United States citizen or resident.

1. The foreign person is a member of a domestically controlled group of entities.
2. The employee of the foreign person performs services in connection with a contract between the U.S. Government (or an instrumentality of the U.S. Government) and any member of the domestically controlled group of entities. Ownership of more than 50% constitutes control.

Part-Time Workers

Part-time workers and workers hired for short periods of time are treated the same as full-time employees, for federal income tax withholding and social security, Medicare, and FUTA tax purposes.

Generally, it doesn't matter whether the part-time worker or worker hired for a short period of time has another job or has the maximum amount of social security tax withheld by another employer. See *Successor employer* above for an exception to this rule.

Income tax withholding may be figured the same way as for full-time workers or it may be figured by the part-year employment method explained in section 9 of Pub. 15-A.

10. Required Notice to Employees About the Earned Income Credit (EIC)

You must notify employees who have no federal income tax withheld that they may be able to claim a tax refund because of the EIC. Although you don't have to notify employees who claim exemption from withholding on Form W-4 about the EIC, you're encouraged to notify any employees whose wages for 2017 were less than $48,340 ($53,930 if married filing jointly) that they may be eligible to claim the credit for 2017. This is because eligible employees may get a refund of the amount of EIC that is more than the tax they owe.

You'll meet this notification requirement if you issue the employee Form W-2 with the EIC notice on the back of Copy B, or a substitute Form W-2 with the same statement. You'll also meet the requirement by providing Notice 797, Possible Federal Tax Refund Due to the Earned Income Credit (EIC), or your own statement that contains the same wording.

If a substitute for Form W-2 is given to the employee on time but doesn't have the required statement, you must notify the employee within 1 week of the date the substitute for Form W-2 is given. If Form W-2 is required but isn't given on time, you must give the employee Notice 797 or your written statement by the date Form W-2 is required to be given. If Form W-2 isn't required, you must notify the employee by February 7, 2018.

11. Depositing Taxes

Generally, you must deposit federal income tax withheld and both the employer and employee social security and Medicare taxes. You must use EFT to make all federal tax deposits. See *How To Deposit*, later in this section, for information on electronic deposit requirements.

TIP *The credit against employment taxes for COBRA assistance payments is treated as a deposit of taxes on the first day of your return period. See* COBRA premium assistance credit *under* Introduction *for more information.*

Payment with return. You may make a payment with Form 941 or Form 944 instead of depositing, without incurring a penalty, if one of the following applies.

- Your Form 941 total tax liability for either the current quarter or the prior quarter is less than $2,500, and you didn't incur a $100,000 next-day deposit obligation during the current quarter. If you aren't sure your total tax liability for the current quarter will be less than $2,500, (and your liability for the prior quarter wasn't less than $2,500), make deposits using the semiweekly or monthly rules so you won't be subject to an FTD penalty.
- You're a monthly schedule depositor (defined later) and make a payment in accordance with the *Accuracy of Deposits Rule*, discussed later in this section. This payment may be $2,500 or more.

Employers who have been notified to file Form 944 can pay their fourth quarter tax liability with Form 944 if the fourth quarter tax liability is less than $2,500. Employers must have deposited any tax liability due for the first, second, and third quarters according to the deposit rules to avoid an FTD penalty for deposits during those quarters.

Separate deposit requirements for nonpayroll (Form 945) tax liabilities. Separate deposits are required for nonpayroll and payroll income tax withholding. Don't combine deposits for Forms 941 (or Form 944) and Form 945 tax liabilities. Generally, the deposit rules for nonpayroll liabilities are the same as discussed next, except the rules apply to an annual rather than a quarterly return period. Thus, the $2,500 threshold for the deposit requirement discussed above applies to Form 945 on an annual basis. See the separate Instructions for Form 945 for more information.

When To Deposit

There are two deposit schedules—monthly and semiweekly—for determining when you deposit social security, Medicare, and withheld income taxes. These schedules tell you when a deposit is due after a tax liability arises (for example, when you have a payday). Before the beginning of each calendar year, you must determine which of the two deposit schedules you're required to use. The deposit schedule you must use is based on the total tax liability you reported on Form 941 during a lookback period, discussed next. Your deposit schedule isn't determined by how often you pay your employees or make deposits. See special rules for Forms 944 and 945, later. Also see *Application of Monthly and Semiweekly Schedules*, later in this section.

CAUTION *These rules don't apply to FUTA tax. See section 14 for information on depositing FUTA tax.*

Lookback period. If you're a Form 941 filer, your deposit schedule for a calendar year is determined from the total taxes reported on Forms 941, line 10 (line 12 for quarters beginning after December 31, 2016), in a 4-quarter lookback period. The lookback period begins July 1 and ends June 30 as shown next in Table 1. If you reported $50,000 or less of taxes for the lookback period, you're a monthly schedule depositor; if you reported more than $50,000, you're a semiweekly schedule depositor.

Table 1. Lookback Period for Calendar Year 2018

July 1, 2016 through Sep. 30, 2016	Oct. 1, 2016 through Dec. 31, 2016	Jan. 1, 2017 through Mar. 31, 2017	Apr.1, 2017 through June 30, 2017

The lookback period for a 2018 Form 941 filer who filed Form 944 in either 2016 or 2017 is calendar year 2016.

If you're a Form 944 filer for the current year or either of the preceding 2 years, your deposit schedule for a calendar year is determined from the total taxes reported during the second preceding calendar year (either on your Form 941 for all 4 quarters of that year or your Form 944 for that year). The lookback period for 2018 for a Form 944 filer is calendar year 2016. If you reported $50,000 or less of taxes for the lookback period, you're a monthly schedule depositor; if you reported more than $50,000, you're a semiweekly schedule depositor.

If you're a Form 945 filer, your deposit schedule for a calendar year is determined from the total taxes reported on line 3 of your Form 945 for the second preceding calendar year. The lookback period for 2018 for a Form 945 filer is calendar year 2016.

Adjustments and the lookback rule. Adjustments made on Form 941-X, Form 944-X, and Form 945-X don't affect the amount of tax liability for previous periods for purposes of the lookback rule.

Example. An employer originally reported a tax liability of $45,000 for the lookback period. The employer discovered, during January 2018, that the tax reported for one of the lookback period quarters was understated by $10,000 and corrected this error by filing Form 941-X. This employer is a monthly schedule depositor for 2018 because the lookback period tax liabilities are based on the amounts originally reported, and they were $50,000 or less.

Deposit period. The term deposit period refers to the period during which tax liabilities are accumulated for each required deposit due date. For monthly schedule depositors, the deposit period is a calendar month. The deposit periods for semiweekly schedule depositors are Wednesday through Friday and Saturday through Tuesday.

If you're an agent with an approved Form 2678, the deposit rules apply to you based on the total employment taxes accumulated by you for your own employees and on behalf of all employers for whom you're authorized to act. For more information on an agent with an approved Form 2678, see Revenue Procedure 2013-39, 2013-52 I.R.B. 830, available at IRS.gov/irb/2013-52_IRB/ar15.html.

Monthly Deposit Schedule

You're a monthly schedule depositor for a calendar year if the total taxes on Form 941, line 10 (line 12 for quarters beginning after December 31, 2016), for the 4 quarters in your lookback period were $50,000 or less. Under the monthly deposit schedule, deposit employment taxes on payments made during a month by the 15th day of the following month. See also Deposits Due on Business Days Only and the $100,000 Next-Day Deposit Rule, later in this section. Monthly schedule depositors shouldn't file Form 941 or Form 944 on a monthly basis.

New employers. Your tax liability for any quarter in the lookback period before you started or acquired your business is considered to be zero. Therefore, you're a monthly schedule depositor for the first calendar year of your business. However, see the $100,000 Next-Day Deposit Rule, later in this section.

Semiweekly Deposit Schedule

You're a semiweekly schedule depositor for a calendar year if the total taxes on Form 941, line 10 (line 12 for quarters beginning after December 31, 2016), during your lookback period were more than $50,000. Under the semiweekly deposit schedule, deposit employment taxes for payments made on Wednesday, Thursday, and/or Friday by the following Wednesday. Deposit taxes for payments made on Saturday, Sunday, Monday, and/or Tuesday by the following Friday. See also Deposits Due on Business Days Only, later in this section.

Semiweekly schedule depositors must complete Schedule B (Form 941), Report of Tax Liability for Semiweekly Schedule Depositors, and submit it with Form 941. If you file Form 944 and are a semiweekly schedule depositor, complete Form 945-A, Annual Record of Federal Tax Liability, and submit it with your return (instead of Schedule B).

Table 2. Semiweekly Deposit Schedule

IF the payday falls on a . . .	THEN deposit taxes by the following . . .
Wednesday, Thursday, and/or Friday	Wednesday
Saturday, Sunday, Monday, and/or Tuesday	Friday

Semiweekly deposit period spanning two quarters (Form 941 filers). If you have more than one pay date during a semiweekly period and the pay dates fall in different calendar quarters, you'll need to make **separate deposits** for the separate liabilities.

Example. If you have a pay date on Sunday, September 30, 2018 (third quarter), and another pay date on Monday, October 1, 2018 (fourth quarter), two separate deposits would be required even though the pay dates fall within the same semiweekly period. Both deposits would be due Friday, October 5, 2018.

Semiweekly deposit period spanning two return periods (Form 944 or Form 945 filers). If you have more than one pay date during a semiweekly period and the pay dates fall in different return periods, you'll need to make separate deposits for the separate liabilities. For example, if you have a pay date on Saturday, December 30, 2017, and another pay date on Tuesday, January 2, 2018, two separate deposits will be required even though the pay dates fall within the same semiweekly period. Both deposits will be due Friday, January 5, 2018 (3 business days from the end of the semiweekly deposit period).

Summary of Steps to Determine Your Deposit Schedule

1. Identify your lookback period (see *Lookback period*, earlier in this section).
2. Add the total taxes you reported on Form 941, line 10 (line 12 for quarters beginning after December 31, 2016), during the lookback period.
3. Determine if you're a monthly or semiweekly schedule depositor:

If the total taxes you reported in the lookback period were . . .	Then you're a . . .
$50,000 or less	Monthly Schedule Depositor
More than $50,000	Semiweekly Schedule Depositor

Example of Monthly and Semiweekly Schedules

Rose Co. reported Form 941 taxes as follows:

2017 Lookback Period		2018 Lookback Period	
3rd Quarter 2015	$12,000	3rd Quarter 2016	$12,000
4th Quarter 2015	12,000	4th Quarter 2016	12,000
1st Quarter 2016	12,000	1st Quarter 2017	12,000
2nd Quarter 2016	12,000	2nd Quarter 2017	15,000
	$48,000		$51,000

Rose Co. is a monthly schedule depositor for 2017 because its tax liability for the 4 quarters in its lookback period (third quarter 2015 through second quarter 2016) wasn't more than $50,000. However, for 2018, Rose Co. is a semiweekly schedule depositor because the total taxes exceeded $50,000 for the 4 quarters in its lookback period (third quarter 2016 through second quarter 2017).

Deposits Due on Business Days Only

If a deposit is required to be made on a day that isn't a business day, the deposit is considered timely if it is made by the close of the next business day. A business day is any day other than a Saturday, Sunday, or legal holiday. For example, if a deposit is required to be made on a Friday and Friday is a legal holiday, the deposit will be considered timely if it is made by the following Monday (if that Monday is a business day).

Semiweekly schedule depositors have at least 3 business days following the close of the semiweekly period to make a deposit. If any of the 3 weekdays after the end of a semiweekly period is a legal holiday, you'll have an additional day for each day that is a legal holiday to make the required deposit. For example, if a semiweekly schedule depositor accumulated taxes for payments made on Friday and the following Monday is a legal holiday, the deposit normally due on Wednesday may be made on Thursday (this allows 3 business days to make the deposit).

Legal holiday. The term "legal holiday" means any legal holiday in the District of Columbia. For purposes of the deposit rules, the term "legal holiday" doesn't include other statewide legal holidays. Legal holidays for 2018 are listed next.

- January 1— New Year's Day
- January 15— Birthday of Martin Luther King, Jr.
- February 19— Washington's Birthday
- April 16— District of Columbia Emancipation Day
- May 28— Memorial Day
- July 4— Independence Day
- September 3— Labor Day
- October 8— Columbus Day
- November 12— Veterans' Day (observed)
- November 22— Thanksgiving Day
- December 25— Christmas Day

Application of Monthly and Semiweekly Schedules

The terms "monthly schedule depositor" and "semiweekly schedule depositor" don't refer to how often your business pays its employees or even how often you're required to make deposits. The terms identify which set of deposit rules you must follow when an employment tax liability arises. The deposit rules are based on the dates when wages are paid (for example, cash basis); not on when tax liabilities are accrued for accounting purposes.

Monthly schedule example. Spruce Co. is a monthly schedule depositor with seasonal employees. It paid wages each Friday during April but didn't pay any wages during May. Under the monthly deposit schedule, Spruce Co. must deposit the combined tax liabilities for the April paydays by May 15. Spruce Co. doesn't have a deposit requirement for May (due by June 15) because no wages were paid and, therefore, it didn't have a tax liability for May.

Semiweekly schedule example. Green, Inc. is a semiweekly schedule depositor and pays wages once each month on the last Friday of the month. Although Green, Inc., has a semiweekly deposit schedule, it will deposit just once a month because it pays wages only once a month. The deposit, however, will be made under the semiweekly deposit schedule as follows: Green, Inc.'s tax liability for the April 27, 2018 (Friday), payday must be deposited by May 2, 2018 (Wednesday). Under the semiweekly deposit schedule, liabilities for wages paid on Wednesday through Friday must be deposited by the following Wednesday.

$100,000 Next-Day Deposit Rule

If you accumulate $100,000 or more in taxes on any day during a monthly or semiweekly deposit period (see Deposit period, earlier in this section), you must deposit the tax by the next business day, whether you're a monthly or semiweekly schedule depositor.

For purposes of the $100,000 rule, don't continue accumulating a tax liability after the end of a deposit period. For example, if a semiweekly schedule depositor has accumulated a liability of $95,000 on a Tuesday (of a Saturday-through-Tuesday deposit period) and accumulated a $10,000 liability on Wednesday, the $100,000 next-day deposit rule doesn't apply. Thus, $95,000 must be deposited by Friday and $10,000 must be deposited by the following Wednesday.

However, once you accumulate at least $100,000 in a deposit period, stop accumulating at the end of that day and begin to accumulate anew on the next day. For example, Fir Co. is a semiweekly schedule depositor. On Monday, Fir Co. accumulates taxes of $110,000 and must deposit this amount on Tuesday, the next business day. On Tuesday, Fir Co. accumulates additional taxes of $30,000. Because the $30,000 isn't added to the previous $110,000 and is less than $100,000, Fir Co. must deposit the $30,000 by Friday (following the semiweekly deposit schedule).

CAUTION *If you're a monthly schedule depositor and accumulate a $100,000 tax liability on any day, you become a semiweekly schedule depositor on the next day and remain so for at least the rest of the calendar year and for the following calendar year.*

Example. Elm, Inc., started its business on May 7, 2018. On Wednesday, May 9, it paid wages for the first time and accumulated a tax liability of $40,000. On Friday, May 11, Elm, Inc., paid wages and accumulated a liability of $60,000, bringing its total accumulated tax liability to $100,000. Because this was the first year of its business, the tax liability for its lookback period is considered to be zero, and it would be a monthly schedule depositor based on the lookback rules. However, since Elm, Inc., accumulated a $100,000 liability on May 11, it became a semiweekly schedule depositor on May 12. It will be a semiweekly schedule depositor for the remainder of 2018 and for 2019. Elm, Inc., is required to deposit the $100,000 by Monday, May 14, the next business day.

Accuracy of Deposits Rule

You're required to deposit 100% of your tax liability on or before the deposit due date. However, penalties won't be applied for depositing less than 100% if both of the following conditions are met.

- Any deposit shortfall doesn't exceed the greater of $100 or 2% of the amount of taxes otherwise required to be deposited.
- The deposit shortfall is paid or deposited by the shortfall makeup date as described next.

Makeup Date for Deposit Shortfall:

1. **Monthly schedule depositor.** Deposit the shortfall or pay it with your return by the due date of your return for the return period in which the shortfall occurred. You may pay the shortfall with your return even if the amount is $2,500 or more.
2. **Semiweekly schedule depositor.** Deposit by the earlier of:
   a. The first Wednesday or Friday (whichever comes first) that falls on or after the 15th day of the month following the month in which the shortfall occurred, or
   b. The due date of your return (for the return period of the tax liability).

For example, if a semiweekly schedule depositor has a deposit shortfall during June 2018, the shortfall makeup date is July 18, 2018 (Wednesday). However, if the shortfall occurred on the required April 4, 2018 (Wednesday), deposit due date for a March 30, 2018 (Friday), pay date, the return due date for the March 30, 2018, pay date (April 30, 2018) would come before the May 16, 2018 (Wednesday), shortfall makeup date. In this case, the shortfall must be deposited by April 30, 2018.

How To Deposit

You must deposit employment taxes, including Form 945 taxes, by EFT. See Payment with return, earlier in this section, for exceptions explaining when taxes may be paid with the tax return instead of being deposited.

Electronic deposit requirement. You must use EFT to make all federal tax deposits. Generally, an EFT is made using EFTPS. If you don't want to use EFTPS, you can arrange for your tax professional, financial institution, payroll service, or other trusted third party to make electronic deposits on your behalf. EFTPS is a free service provided by the Department of Treasury. To get more information about EFTPS or to enroll in EFTPS, visit EFTPS.gov, or call 1-800-555-4477 or 1-800-733-4829 (TDD). Additional information about EFTPS is also available in Pub. 966.

When you receive your EIN. If you're a new employer that indicated a federal tax obligation when requesting an EIN, you'll be pre-enrolled in EFTPS. You'll receive information about Express Enrollment in your Employer Identification Number (EIN) Package and an additional mailing containing your EFTPS personal identification number (PIN) and instructions for activating your PIN. Call the toll-free number located in your "How to Activate Your Enrollment" brochure to activate your enrollment and begin making your payroll tax deposits. If you outsource any of your payroll and related tax duties to a third party payer, such as a PSP or reporting agent, be sure to tell them about your EFTPS enrollment.

Deposit record. For your records, an EFT Trace Number will be provided with each successful payment. The number can be used as a receipt or to trace the payment.

Depositing on time. For deposits made by EFTPS to be on time, you must submit the deposit by 8 p.m. Eastern time the day before the date the deposit is due. If you use a third party to make a deposit on your behalf, they may have different cutoff times.

Same-day wire payment option. If you fail to submit a deposit transaction on EFTPS by 8 p.m. Eastern time the day before the date a deposit is due, you can still make your deposit on time by using the Federal Tax Collection Service (FTCS). To use the same-day wire payment method, you'll need to make arrangements with your financial institution ahead of time. Please check with your financial institution regarding availability, deadlines, and costs. Your financial institution may charge you a fee for payments made this way. To learn more about the information you'll need to give to your financial institution to make a same-day wire payment, go to *IRS.gov/SameDayWire*.

How to claim credit for overpayments. If you deposited more than the right amount of taxes for a quarter, you can choose on Form 941 for that quarter (or on Form 944 for that year) to have the overpayment refunded or applied as a credit to your next return. Don't ask EFTPS to request a refund from the IRS for you.

Deposit Penalties

TIP *Although the deposit penalties information provided next refers specifically to Form 941, these rules also apply to Form 945 and Form 944 (if the employer required to file Form 944 doesn't qualify for the exception to the deposit requirements discussed under* Payment with return, *earlier in this section).*

Penalties may apply if you don't make required deposits on time or if you make deposits for less than the required amount. The penalties don't apply if any failure to make a proper and timely deposit was due to reasonable cause and not to willful neglect. If you receive a penalty notice, you can provide an explanation of why you believe reasonable cause exists.

If you timely filed your employment tax return, the IRS may also waive deposit penalties if you inadvertently failed to deposit and it was the first quarter that you were required to deposit any employment tax, or if you inadvertently failed to deposit the first time after your deposit frequency changed. You must also meet the net worth and size limitations applicable to awards of administrative and litigation costs under section 7430; for individuals, this means that your net worth can't exceed $2 million, and for businesses, your net worth can't exceed $7 million and you also can't have more than 500 employees.

For amounts not properly or timely deposited, the penalty rates are as follows.

2% - Deposits made 1 to 5 days late.

5% - Deposits made 6 to 15 days late.

10% - Deposits made 16 or more days late, but before 10 days from the date of the first notice the IRS sent asking for the tax due.

10% - Amounts that should have been deposited, but instead were paid directly to the IRS, or paid with your tax return. But see *Payment with return*, earlier in this section, for an exception.

15% - Amounts still unpaid more than 10 days after the date of the first notice the IRS sent asking for the tax due or the day on which you received notice and demand for immediate payment, whichever is earlier.

Late deposit penalty amounts are determined using calendar days, starting from the due date of the liability.

Special rule for former Form 944 filers. If you filed Form 944 for the prior year and file Forms 941 for the current year, the FTD penalty won't apply to a late deposit of employment taxes for January of the current year if the taxes are deposited in full by March 15 of the current year.

Order in which deposits are applied. Deposits generally are applied to the most recent tax liability within the quarter. If you receive an FTD penalty notice, you may designate how your deposits are to be applied in order to minimize the amount of the penalty if you do so within 90 days of the date of the notice. Follow the instructions on the penalty notice you received. For more information on designating deposits, see Revenue Procedure 2001-58. You can find Revenue Procedure 2001-58 on page 579 of Internal Revenue Bulletin 2001-50 at *IRS.gov/pub/irs-irbs/irb01-50.pdf*.

Example. Cedar, Inc. is required to make a deposit of $1,000 on May 15 and $1,500 on June 15. It doesn't make the deposit on May 15. On June 15, Cedar, Inc. deposits $2,000. Under the deposits rule, which applies deposits to the most recent tax liability, $1,500 of the deposit is applied to the June 15 deposit and the remaining $500 is applied to the May deposit. Accordingly, $500 of the May 15 liability remains undeposited. The penalty on this underdeposit will apply as explained above.

Trust fund recovery penalty. If federal income, social security, or Medicare taxes that must be withheld (that is, trust fund taxes) aren't withheld or aren't deposited or paid to the United States Treasury, the trust fund recovery penalty may apply. The penalty is 100% of the unpaid trust fund tax. If these unpaid taxes can't be immediately collected from the employer or business, the trust fund recovery penalty may be imposed on all persons who are determined by the IRS to be responsible for collecting, accounting for, or paying over these taxes, and who acted willfully in not doing so.

A **responsible person** can be an officer or employee of a corporation, a partner or employee of a partnership, an accountant, a volunteer director/trustee, or an employee of a sole proprietorship, or any other person or entity that is responsible for collecting, accounting for, or paying over trust fund taxes. A responsible person also may include one who signs checks for the business or otherwise has authority to cause the spending of business funds.

Willfully means voluntarily, consciously, and intentionally. A responsible person acts willfully if the person knows the required actions of collecting, accounting for, or paying over trust fund taxes aren't taking place, or recklessly disregards obvious and known risks to the government's right to receive trust fund taxes.

Separate accounting when deposits aren't made or withheld taxes aren't paid. Separate accounting may be required if you don't pay over withheld employee social security, Medicare, or income taxes; deposit required taxes; make required payments; or file tax returns. In this case, you would receive written notice from the IRS requiring you to deposit taxes into a special trust account for the U.S. Government.

CAUTION *You may be charged with criminal penalties if you don't comply with the special bank deposit requirements for the special trust account for the U.S. Government.*

"Averaged" FTD penalty. The IRS may assess an "averaged" FTD penalty of 2% to 10% if you're a monthly schedule depositor and didn't properly complete Form 941, line 16, when your tax liability shown on Form 941, line 12, equaled or exceeded $2,500.

The IRS may also assess an "averaged" FTD penalty of 2% to 10% if you're a semiweekly schedule depositor and your tax liability shown on Form 941, line 12, equaled or exceeded $2,500 and you:

- Completed Form 941, line 16, instead of Schedule B (Form 941);
- Failed to attach a properly completed Schedule B (Form 941); or
- Improperly completed Schedule B (Form 941) by, for example, entering tax deposits instead of tax liabilities in the numbered spaces.

The FTD penalty is figured by distributing your total tax liability shown on Form 941, line 12, equally throughout the tax period. Then we apply your deposits and payments to the averaged liabilities in the date order we received your deposits. We figure the penalty on any tax not deposited, deposited late, or not deposited in the correct amounts. Your deposits and payments may not be counted as timely because the actual dates of your tax liabilities can't be accurately determined.

You can avoid an "averaged" FTD penalty by reviewing your return before you file it. Follow these steps before submitting your Form 941.

- If you're a monthly schedule depositor, report your tax liabilities (not your deposits) in the monthly entry spaces on Form 941, line 16.
- If you're a semiweekly schedule depositor, report your tax liabilities (not your deposits) on Schedule B (Form 941) in the lines that represent the dates your employees were paid.
- Verify your total liability shown on Form 941, line 16, or the bottom of Schedule B (Form 941) equals your tax liability shown on Form 941, line 12.
- Don't show negative amounts on Form 941, line 16, or Schedule B (Form 941).
- For prior period errors don't adjust your tax liabilities reported on Form 941, line 16, or on Schedule B (Form 941). Instead, file an adjusted return (Form 941-X, 944-X, or 945-X) if you're also adjusting your tax liability. If you're only adjusting your deposits in response to an FTD penalty notice, see the Instructions for Schedule B (Form 941) or the Instructions for Form 945-X (for Forms 944 and 945).

12. Filing Form 941 or Form 944

Form 941. Each quarter, if you pay wages subject to income tax withholding (including withholding on sick pay and supplemental unemployment benefits) or social security and Medicare taxes, you must file Form 941 unless you receive an IRS notification that you're eligible to file Form 944 or the following exceptions apply. Also, if you're required to file Forms 941 but believe your employment taxes for the calendar year will be $1,000 or less, and you would like to file Form 944 instead of Forms 941, you must contact the IRS during the first calendar quarter of the tax year to request to file Form 944. You must receive written notice from the IRS to file Form 944 instead of Forms 941 before you may file this form. For more information on requesting to file Form 944, including the methods and deadlines for making a request, see the Instructions for Form 944. Form 941 must be filed by the last day of the month that follows the end of the quarter. See the Calendar, earlier.

Form 944. If you receive written notification that you qualify for the Form 944 program, you must file Form 944 instead of Form 941. If you received this notification, but prefer to file Form 941, you can request to have your filing requirement changed to Form 941 during the first calendar quarter of the tax year. For more information on requesting to file Forms 941, including the methods and deadlines for making a request, see the Instructions for Form 944. Form 944 must be filed by January 31. However, if you timely deposited all taxes when due, you may file by February 10.

Exceptions. The following exceptions apply to the filing requirements for Forms 941 and 944.

- **Seasonal employers who no longer file for quarters when they regularly have no tax liability because they have paid no wages.** To alert the IRS you won't have to file a return for one or more quarters during the year, check the "Seasonal employer" box on Form 941, line 18. When you fill out Form 941, be sure to check the box on the top of the form that corresponds to the quarter reported. Generally, the IRS won't inquire about unfiled returns if at least one taxable return is filed each year. However, you must check the "Seasonal employer" box on **every** Form 941 you file. Otherwise, the IRS will expect a return to be filed for each quarter.

- **Household employers reporting social security and Medicare taxes and/or withheld income tax.** If you're a sole proprietor and file Form 941 or Form 944 for business employees, you may include taxes for household employees on your Form 941 or Form 944. Otherwise, report social security and Medicare taxes and income tax withholding for household employees on Schedule H (Form 1040). See Pub. 926 for more information.
- **Employers reporting wages for employees in American Samoa, Guam, the Commonwealth of the Northern Mariana Islands, the U.S. Virgin Islands, or Puerto Rico.** If your employees aren't subject to U.S. income tax withholding, use Forms 941-SS, 944, or Formulario 944(SP). Employers in Puerto Rico use Formularios 941-PR, 944(SP), or Form 944. If you have both employees who are subject to U.S. income tax withholding and employees who aren't subject to U.S. income tax withholding, you must file only Form 941 (or Form 944 or Formulario 944(SP)) and include all of your employees' wages on that form. For more information, see Pub. 80, Federal Tax Guide for Employers in U.S. Virgin Islands, Guam, American Samoa, and the Commonwealth of the Northern Mariana Islands, or Pub. 179, Guía Contributiva Federal para Patronos Puertorriqueños.
- **Agricultural employers reporting social security, Medicare, and withheld income taxes.** Report these taxes on Form 943. For more information, see Pub. 51.

Form 941 e-file. The Form 941 *e-file* program allows a taxpayer to electronically file Form 941 or Form 944 using a computer with an internet connection and commercial tax preparation software. For more information, go to *IRS.gov/EmploymentEfile*, or call 1-866-255-0654.

Electronic filing by reporting agents. Reporting agents filing Forms 941 or Form 944 for groups of taxpayers can file them electronically. See *Reporting Agents* in section 7 of Pub. 15-A.

Electronic filing by CPEOs. With the exception of the first quarter for which a CPEO is certified, CPEOs are required to electronically file Form 941. Under certain circumstances, the IRS may waive the electronic filing requirement. To request a waiver, the CPEO must file a written request using the IRS Online Registration System for Professional Employer Organizations at least 45 days before the due date of the return for which the CPEO is unable to electronically file. For more information on filing a waiver request electronically, go to *IRS.gov/CPEO*.

Penalties. For each whole or part month a return isn't filed when required (disregarding any extensions of the filing deadline), there is a failure-to-file (FTF) penalty of 5% of the unpaid tax due with that return. The maximum penalty is generally 25% of the tax due. Also, for each whole or part month the tax is paid late (disregarding any extensions of the payment deadline), there is a failure-to-pay (FTP) penalty of 0.5% per month of the amount of tax. For individual filers only, the FTP penalty is reduced from 0.5% per month to 0.25% per month if an installment agreement is in effect. You must have filed your return on or before the due date of the return to qualify for the reduced penalty. The maximum amount of the FTP penalty is also 25% of the tax due. If both penalties apply in any month, the FTF penalty is reduced by the amount of the FTP penalty. The penalties won't be charged if you have a reasonable cause for failing to file or pay. If you receive a penalty notice, you can provide an explanation of why you believe reasonable cause exists.

Note. In addition to any penalties, interest accrues from the due date of the tax on any unpaid balance.

If income, social security, or Medicare taxes that must be withheld aren't withheld or aren't paid, you may be personally liable for the trust fund recovery penalty. See *Trust fund recovery penalty* in section 11.

Generally, the use of a third-party payer, such as a PSP or reporting agent, doesn't relieve an employer of the responsibility to ensure tax returns are filed and all taxes are paid or deposited correctly and on time. However, see *Certified professional employer organization (CPEO)*, later, for an exception.

Don't file more than one Form 941 per quarter or more than one Form 944 per year. Employers with multiple locations or divisions must file only one Form 941 per quarter or one Form 944 per year. Filing more than one return may result in processing delays and may require correspondence between you and the IRS. For information on making adjustments to previously filed returns, see section 13.

Reminders about filing.

- Don't report more than 1 calendar quarter on a Form 941.
- If you need Form 941 or Form 944, get one from the IRS in time to file the return when due. See *Ordering Employer Tax Forms and Publications*, earlier.
- Enter your name and EIN on Form 941 or Form 944. Be sure they're exactly as they appeared on earlier returns.
- See the Instructions for Form 941 or the Instructions for Form 944 for information on preparing the form.

Final return. If you go out of business, you must file a final return for the last quarter (last year for Form 944) in which wages are paid. If you continue to pay wages or other compensation for periods following termination of your business, you must file returns for those periods. See the Instructions for Form 941 or the Instructions for Form 944 for details on how to file a final return.

If you're required to file a final return, you're also required to furnish Forms W-2 to your employees and file

Forms W-2 and W-3 with the SSA by the due date of your final return. Don't send an original or copy of your Form 941 or Form 944 to the SSA. See the General Instructions for Forms W-2 and W-3 for more information.

Filing late returns for previous years. If possible, get a copy of Form 941 or Form 944 (and separate instructions) with a revision date showing the year for which your delinquent return is being filed. See *Ordering Employer Tax Forms and Publications*, earlier. Contact the IRS at 1-800-829-4933 if you have any questions about filing late returns.

Table 3. **Social Security and Medicare Tax Rates *(for 3 prior years)***

Calendar Year	Wage Base Limit (each employee)	Tax Rate on Taxable Wages and Tips
2017–Social Security	$127,200	12.4%
2017–Medicare	All Wages	2.9%
2016–Social Security	$118,500	12.4%
2016–Medicare	All Wages	2.9%
2015–Social Security	$118,500	12.4%
2015–Medicare	All Wages	2.9%

Reconciling Forms W-2, W-3, and 941 or 944. When there are discrepancies between Forms 941 or Form 944 filed with the IRS and Forms W-2 and W-3 filed with the SSA, the IRS must contact you to resolve the discrepancies.

Take the following steps to help reduce discrepancies.

1. Report bonuses as wages and as social security and Medicare wages on Forms W-2 and on Form 941 or Form 944.
2. Report both social security and Medicare wages and taxes separately on Forms W-2, W-3, 941, and 944.
3. Report employee share of social security taxes on Form W-2 in the box for social security tax withheld (box 4), not as social security wages.
4. Report employee share of Medicare taxes on Form W-2 in the box for Medicare tax withheld (box 6), not as Medicare wages.
5. Make sure the social security wage amount for each employee doesn't exceed the annual social security wage base limit (for example, $128,400 for 2018).
6. Don't report noncash wages that aren't subject to social security or Medicare taxes as social security or Medicare wages.
7. If you used an EIN on any Form 941 or Form 944 for the year that is different from the EIN reported on Form W-3, enter the other EIN on Form W-3 in the box for "Other EIN used this year" (box h).
8. Be sure the amounts on Form W-3 are the total of amounts from Forms W-2.
9. Reconcile Form W-3 with your four quarterly Forms 941 or annual Form 944 by comparing amounts reported for the following items.
   a. Federal income tax withheld.
   b. Social security and Medicare wages.
   c. Social security and Medicare taxes. Generally, the amounts shown on Forms 941 or annual Form 944, including current year adjustments, should be approximately twice the amounts shown on Form W-3.

Don't report backup withholding or withholding on nonpayroll payments, such as pensions, annuities, and gambling winnings, on Form 941 or Form 944. Withholding on nonpayroll payments is reported on Forms 1099 or W-2G and must be reported on Form 945. Only taxes and withholding reported on Form W-2 should be reported on Form 941 or Form 944.

Amounts reported on Forms W-2, W-3, and Forms 941 or Form 944 may not match for valid reasons. For example, if you withheld any Additional Medicare Tax from your employee's wages, the amount of Medicare tax that is reported on Forms 941, line 5c, or Form 944, line 4c, won't be twice the amount of the Medicare tax withheld that is reported in box 6 of Form W-3. Make sure there are valid reasons for any mismatch. Keep your reconciliation so you'll have a record of why amounts didn't match in case there are inquiries from the IRS or the SSA. See the Instructions for Schedule D (Form 941) if you need to explain any discrepancies that were caused by an acquisition, statutory merger, or consolidation.

13. Reporting Adjustments to Form 941 or Form 944

Current Period Adjustments

In certain cases, amounts reported as social security and Medicare taxes on Form 941, lines 5a–5d, column 2 (Form 944, lines 4a–4d, column 2), must be adjusted to arrive at your correct tax liability (for example, excluding amounts withheld by a third party payor or amounts you weren't required to withhold). Current period adjustments are reported on Form 941, lines 7–9, or Form 944, line 6, and include the following types of adjustments.

Fractions-of-cents adjustment. If there is a small difference between total taxes after adjustments and credits (Form 941, line 12; Form 944, line 9) and total deposits (Form 941, line 13; Form 944, line 10), it may have been caused, all or in part, by rounding to the nearest cent each time you computed payroll. This rounding occurs when you figure the amount of social security and Medicare tax to be withheld and deposited from each employee's wages. The IRS refers to rounding differences relating to employee withholding of social security and Medicare taxes as "fractions-of-cents" adjustments. If you pay your taxes with Form 941 (or Form 944) instead of making deposits because your total taxes for the quarter (year for Form 944) are less than $2,500, you also may report a fractions-of-cents adjustment.

To determine if you have a fractions-of-cents adjustment for 2018, multiply the total wages and tips for the quarter subject to:

- Social security tax reported on Form 941 or Form 944 by 6.2% (0.062),
- Medicare tax reported on Form 941 or Form 944 by 1.45% (0.0145), and
- Additional Medicare Tax reported on Form 941 or 944 by 0.9% (0.009).

Compare these amounts (the employee share of social security and Medicare taxes) with the total social security and Medicare taxes actually withheld from employees for the quarter (from your payroll records). The difference, positive or negative, is your fractions-of-cents adjustment to be reported on Form 941, line 7, or Form 944, line 6. If the actual amount withheld is less, report a negative adjustment using a minus sign (if possible, otherwise use parentheses) in the entry space. If the actual amount is more, report a positive adjustment.

TIP *For the above adjustments, prepare and retain a brief supporting statement explaining the nature and amount of each. Don't attach the statement to Form 941 or Form 944.*

Example. Cedar, Inc., was entitled to the following current period adjustments.

- **Fractions of cents.** Cedar, Inc., determined the amounts withheld and deposited for social security and Medicare taxes during the quarter were a net $1.44 more than the employee share of the amount figured on Form 941, lines 5a–5d, column 2 (social security and Medicare taxes). This difference was caused by adding or dropping fractions of cents when figuring social security and Medicare taxes for each wage payment. Cedar, Inc., must report a positive $1.44 fractions-of-cents adjustment on Form 941, line 7.
- **Third-party sick pay.** Cedar, Inc., included taxes of $2,000 for sick pay on Form 941, lines 5a and 5c, column 2, for social security and Medicare taxes. However, the third-party payor of the sick pay withheld and paid the employee share ($1,000) of these taxes. Cedar, Inc., is entitled to a $1,000 sick pay adjustment (negative) on Form 941, line 8.
- **Life insurance premiums.** Cedar, Inc., paid group-term life insurance premiums for policies in excess of $50,000 for former employees. The former employees must pay the employee share of the social security and Medicare taxes ($200) on the policies. However, Cedar, Inc., must include the employee share of these taxes with the social security and Medicare taxes reported on Form 941, lines 5a and 5c, column 2. Therefore, Cedar, Inc., is entitled to a negative $200 adjustment on Form 941, line 9.

Adjustment of tax on third-party sick pay. Report both the employer and employee shares of social security and Medicare taxes for sick pay on Form 941, lines 5a and 5c (Form 944, lines 4a and 4c). If the aggregate wages paid for an employee by the employer and third-party payor exceed $200,000 for the calendar year, report the Additional Medicare Tax on Form 941, line 5d (Form 944, line 4d). Show as a negative adjustment on Form 941, line 8 (Form 944, line 6), the social security and Medicare taxes withheld on sick pay by a third-party payor. See section 6 of Pub. 15-A for more information.

Adjustment of tax on tips. If, by the 10th of the month after the month you received an employee's report on tips, you don't have enough employee funds available to withhold the employee's share of social security and Medicare taxes, you no longer have to collect it. However, report the entire amount of these tips on Form 941, lines 5b and 5c (Form 944, lines 4b and 4c). If the aggregate wages and tips paid for an employee exceed $200,000 for the calendar year, report the Additional Medicare Tax on Form 941, line 5d (Form 944, line 4d). Include as a negative adjustment on Form 941, line 9 (Form 944, line 6), the total uncollected employee share of the social security and Medicare taxes.

Adjustment of tax on group-term life insurance premiums paid for former employees. The employee share of social security and Medicare taxes for premiums on group-term life insurance over $50,000 for a former employee is paid by the former employee with his or her tax return and isn't collected by the employer. However, include all social security and Medicare taxes for such coverage on Form 941, lines 5a and 5c (Form 944, lines 4a and 4c). If the amount paid for an employee for premiums on group-term life insurance combined with other wages exceeds $200,000 for the calendar year, report the Additional Medicare Tax on Form 941, line 5d (Form 944, line 4d). Back out the amount of the employee share of these taxes as a negative adjustment on Form 941, line 9 (Form 944, line 6). See Pub. 15-B for more information on group-term life insurance.

No change to record of federal tax liability. Don't make any changes to your record of federal tax liability reported on Form 941, line 16, or Schedule B (Form 941) (Form 945-A for Form 944 filers) for current period adjustments. The amounts reported on the record reflect the actual amounts you withheld from employees' wages for social security and Medicare taxes. Because the current period adjustments make the amounts reported on Form 941, lines 5a–5d, column 2 (Form 944, lines 4a–4d, column 2), equal the actual amounts you withheld (the amounts reported on the record), no additional changes to the record of federal tax liability are necessary for these adjustments.

Prior Period Adjustments

Forms for prior period adjustments. Use Form 941-X or Form 944-X to make a correction after you discover an error on a previously filed Form 941 or Form 944. There are also Forms 943-X, 945-X, and CT-1 X to report corrections on the corresponding returns. Use Form 843 when requesting a refund or abatement of assessed interest or penalties.

TIP *See Revenue Ruling 2009-39, 2009-52 I.R.B. 951, for examples of how the interest-free adjustment and claim for refund rules apply in 10 different situations. You can find Revenue Ruling 2009-39, at IRS.gov/irb/2009-52_IRB/ar14.html.*

Background. Treasury Decision 9405 changed the process for making interest-free adjustments to employment taxes reported on Form 941 and Form 944 and for filing a claim for refund of employment taxes. Treasury Decision 9405, 2008-32 I.R.B. 293, is available at *IRS.gov/irb/2008-32_irb/ar13.html*. You'll use the adjustment process if you underreported employment taxes and are making a payment, or if you overreported employment taxes and will be applying the credit to the Form 941 or Form 944 period during which you file Form 941-X or Form 944-X. You'll use the claim process if you overreported employment taxes and are requesting a refund or abatement of the overreported amount. We use the terms "correct" and "corrections" to include interest-free adjustments under sections 6205 and 6413, and claims for refund and abatement under sections 6402, 6414, and 6404 of the Internal Revenue Code.

Correcting employment taxes. When you discover an error on a previously filed Form 941 or Form 944, you must:

- Correct that error using Form 941-X or Form 944-X,
- File a separate Form 941-X or Form 944-X for each Form 941 or Form 944 you're correcting, and
- File Form 941-X or Form 944-X separately. Don't file with Form 941 or Form 944.

Continue to report current quarter adjustments for fractions of cents, third-party sick pay, tips, and group-term life insurance on Form 941 using lines 7–9, and on Form 944 using line 6.

Report the correction of underreported and overreported amounts for the same tax period on a single Form 941-X or Form 944-X unless you're requesting a refund. If you're requesting a refund and are correcting both underreported and overreported amounts, file one Form 941-X or Form 944-X correcting the underreported amounts only and a second Form 941-X or Form 944-X correcting the overreported amounts.

See the chart on the back of Form 941-X or Form 944-X for help in choosing whether to use the adjustment process or the claim process. See the Instructions for Form 941-X or the Instructions for Form 944-X for details on how to make the adjustment or claim for refund or abatement.

Income tax withholding adjustments. In a current calendar year, correct prior quarter income tax withholding errors by making the correction on Form 941-X when you discover the error.

You may make an adjustment only to correct income tax withholding errors discovered during the same calendar year in which you paid the wages. This is because the employee uses the amount shown on Form W-2 or, if applicable, Form W-2C, as a credit when filing his or her income tax return (Form 1040, etc.).

You can't adjust amounts reported as income tax withheld in a prior calendar year unless it is to correct an administrative error or IRC section 3509 applies. An administrative error occurs if the amount you entered on Form 941 or Form 944 isn't the amount you actually withheld. For example, if the total income tax actually withheld was incorrectly reported on Form 941 or Form 944 due to a mathematical or transposition error, this would be an administrative error. The administrative error adjustment corrects the amount reported on Form 941 or Form 944 to agree with the amount actually withheld from employees and reported on their Forms W-2.

Additional Medicare Tax withholding adjustments. Generally, the rules discussed above under *Income tax withholding adjustments* apply to Additional Medicare Tax withholding adjustments. That is, you may make an adjustment to correct Additional Medicare Tax withholding errors discovered during the same calendar year in which you paid wages. You can't adjust amounts reported in a prior calendar year unless it is to correct an administrative error or IRC section 3509 applies. If you have overpaid Additional Medicare Tax, you can't file a claim for refund for the amount of the overpayment unless the amount wasn't actually withheld from the employee's wages (which would be an administrative error).

If a prior year error was a nonadministrative error, you may correct only the **wages and tips** subject to Additional Medicare Tax withholding.

Collecting underwithheld taxes from employees. If you withheld no income, social security, or Medicare taxes or less than the correct amount from an employee's wages, you can make it up from later pay to that employee. But you're the one who owes the underpayment. Reimbursement is a matter for settlement between you and the employee. Underwithheld income tax and Additional Medicare Tax must be recovered from the employee on or before the last day of the calendar year. There are special rules for tax on tips (see section 6) and fringe benefits (see section 5).

Refunding amounts incorrectly withheld from employees. If you withheld more than the correct amount of income, social security, or Medicare taxes from wages paid, repay or reimburse the employee the excess. Any excess income tax or Additional Medicare Tax withholding must be repaid or reimbursed to the employee before the end of the calendar year in which it was withheld. Keep in your records the employee's written receipt showing the date and amount of the repayment or record of reimbursement. If you didn't repay or reimburse the employee, you must report and pay each excess amount when you file Form 941 for the quarter (or Form 944 for the year) in which you withheld too much tax.

Correcting filed Forms W-2 and W-3. When adjustments are made to correct wages and social security and Medicare taxes because of a change in the wage totals reported for a previous year, you also need to file Form W-2c and Form W-3c with the SSA. Up to 25 Forms W-2c per Form W-3c may now be filed per session over the Internet, with no limit on the number of sessions. For more information, visit the Social Security Administration's Employer W-2 Filing Instructions & Information webpage at *SSA.gov/employer*.

Exceptions to interest-free corrections of employment taxes. A correction won't be eligible for interest-free treatment if:

- The failure to report relates to an issue raised in an IRS examination of a prior return, or
- The employer knowingly underreported its employment tax liability.

A correction won't be eligible for interest-free treatment after the earlier of the following:

- Receipt of an IRS notice and demand for payment after assessment or
- Receipt of an IRS notice of determination under Internal Revenue Code section 7436.

Wage Repayments

If an employee repays you for wages received in error, don't offset the repayments against current-year wages unless the repayments are for amounts received in error in the current year.

Repayment of current year wages. If you receive repayments for wages paid during a prior quarter in the current year, report adjustments on Form 941-X to recover income tax withholding and social security and Medicare taxes for the repaid wages.

Repayment of prior year wages. If you receive repayments for wages paid during a prior year, report an adjustment on Form 941-X or Form 944-X to recover the social security and Medicare taxes. You can't make an adjustment for income tax withholding because the wages were income to the employee for the prior year. You can't make an adjustment for Additional Medicare Tax withholding because the employee determines liability for Additional Medicare Tax on the employee's income tax return for the prior year.

You also must file Forms W-2c and W-3c with the SSA to correct social security and Medicare wages and taxes. Don't correct wages (box 1) on Form W-2c for the amount paid in error. Give a copy of Form W-2c to the employee.

Employee reporting of repayment. The wages paid in error in the prior year remain taxable to the employee for that year. This is because the employee received and had use of those funds during that year. The employee isn't entitled to file an amended return (Form 1040X) to recover the income tax on these wages. Instead, the employee may be entitled to a deduction (or credit in some cases) for the repaid wages on his or her income tax return for the year of repayment. However, the employee should file an amended return (Form 1040X) to recover any Additional Medicare Tax paid on the wages paid in error in the prior year.

14. Federal Unemployment (FUTA) Tax

The Federal Unemployment Tax Act, with state unemployment systems, provides for payments of unemployment compensation to workers who have lost their jobs. Most employers pay both a federal and a state unemployment tax. For a list of state unemployment agencies, visit the U.S. Department of Labor's website at *oui.doleta.gov/unemploy/agencies.asp*. Only the employer pays FUTA tax; it isn't withheld from the employee's wages. For more information, see the Instructions for Form 940.

TIP *Services rendered to a federally recognized Indian tribal government (or any subdivision, subsidiary, or business wholly owned by such an Indian tribe) are exempt from FUTA tax, subject to the tribe's compliance with state law. For more information, see Internal Revenue Code section 3309(d).*

Who must pay? Use the following three tests to determine whether you must pay FUTA tax. Each test applies to a different category of employee, and each is independent of the others. If a test describes your situation, you're subject to FUTA tax on the wages you pay to employees in that category during the current calendar year.

1. **General test.**
   You're subject to FUTA tax in 2018 on the wages you pay employees who aren't farmworkers or household workers if:
   a. You paid wages of $1,500 or more in any calendar quarter in 2017 or 2018, or
   b. You had one or more employees for at least some part of a day in any 20 or more different weeks in 2017 or 20 or more different weeks in 2018.
2. **Household employees test.**
   You're subject to FUTA tax if you paid total cash wages of $1,000 or more to household employees in any calendar quarter in 2017 or 2018. A household employee is an employee who performs household work in a private home, local college club, or local fraternity or sorority chapter.
3. **Farmworkers test.**
   You're subject to FUTA tax on the wages you pay to farmworkers if:
   a. You paid cash wages of $20,000 or more to farmworkers during any calendar quarter in 2017 or 2018, or
   b. You employed 10 or more farmworkers during at least some part of a day (whether or not at the

same time) during any 20 or more different weeks in 2017 or 20 or more different weeks in 2018.

Computing FUTA tax. For 2018, the FUTA tax rate is 6.0%. The tax applies to the first $7,000 you pay to each employee as wages during the year. The $7,000 is the federal wage base. Your state wage base may be different.

Generally, you can take a credit against your FUTA tax for amounts you paid into state unemployment funds. The credit may be as much as 5.4% of FUTA taxable wages. If you're entitled to the maximum 5.4% credit, the FUTA tax rate after credit is 0.6%. You're entitled to the maximum credit if you paid your state unemployment taxes in full, on time, and on all the same wages as are subject to FUTA tax, and as long as the state isn't determined to be a credit reduction state. See the Instructions for Form 940 to determine the credit.

In some states, the wages subject to state unemployment tax are the same as the wages subject to FUTA tax. However, certain states exclude some types of wages from state unemployment tax, even though they're subject to FUTA tax (for example, wages paid to corporate officers, certain payments of sick pay by unions, and certain fringe benefits). In such a case, you may be required to deposit more than 0.6% FUTA tax on those wages. See the Instructions for Form 940 for further guidance.

TIP *In years when there are credit reduction states, you must include liabilities owed for credit reduction with your fourth quarter deposit. You may deposit the anticipated extra liability throughout the year, but it isn't due until the due date for the deposit for the fourth quarter, and the associated liability should be recorded as being incurred in the fourth quarter. See the Instructions for Form 940 for more information.*

Successor employer. If you acquired a business from an employer who was liable for FUTA tax, you may be able to count the wages that employer paid to the employees who continue to work for you when you figure the $7,000 FUTA tax wage base. See the Instructions for Form 940.

Depositing FUTA tax. For deposit purposes, figure FUTA tax quarterly. Determine your FUTA tax liability by multiplying the amount of taxable wages paid during the quarter by 0.6%. Stop depositing FUTA tax on an employee's wages when he or she reaches $7,000 in taxable wages for the calendar year.

If your FUTA tax liability for any calendar quarter is $500 or less, you don't have to deposit the tax. Instead, you may carry it forward and add it to the liability figured in the next quarter to see if you must make a deposit. If your FUTA tax liability for any calendar quarter is over $500 (including any FUTA tax carried forward from an earlier quarter), you must deposit the tax by EFT. See section 11 for more information on EFT.

Household employees. You're not required to deposit FUTA taxes for household employees unless you report their wages on Form 941, 943, or 944. See Pub. 926 for more information.

When to deposit. Deposit the FUTA tax by the last day of the first month that follows the end of the quarter. If the due date for making your deposit falls on a Saturday, Sunday, or legal holiday, you may make your deposit on the next business day. See *Legal holiday*, earlier, for a list of the legal holidays for 2018.

If your liability for the fourth quarter (plus any undeposited amount from any earlier quarter) is over $500, deposit the entire amount by the due date of Form 940 (January 31). If it is $500 or less, you can make a deposit, pay the tax with a credit or debit card, or pay the tax with your 2017 Form 940 by January 31, 2018. If you file Form 940 electronically, you can e-file and use EFW to pay the balance due. For more information on paying your taxes with a credit or debit card or using EFW, go to *IRS.gov/Payments*.

Table 4. When to Deposit FUTA Taxes

Quarter	Ending	Due Date
Jan.–Feb.–Mar.	Mar. 31	Apr. 30
Apr.–May–June	June 30	July 31
July–Aug.–Sept.	Sept. 30	Oct. 31
Oct.–Nov.–Dec.	Dec. 31	Jan. 31

Reporting FUTA tax. Use Form 940 to report FUTA tax. File your 2017 Form 940 by January 31, 2018. However, if you deposited all FUTA tax when due, you may file on or before February 10, 2018.

Form 940 e-file. The Form 940 *e-file* program allows a taxpayer to electronically file Form 940 using a computer with an internet connection and commercial tax preparation software. For more information, visit the IRS website at *IRS.gov/EmploymentEfile*, or call 1-866-255-0654.

Household employees. If you didn't report employment taxes for household employees on Forms 941, 943, or 944, report FUTA tax for these employees on Schedule H (Form 1040). See Pub. 926 for more information. You must have an EIN to file Schedule H (Form 1040).

Electronic filing by reporting agents. Reporting agents filing Forms 940 for groups of taxpayers can file them electronically. See the *Reporting Agent* discussion in section 7 of Pub. 15-A.

Electronic filing by CPEOs. With the exception of the first quarter for which a CPEO is certified, CPEOs are required to electronically file Form 940. Under certain circumstances, the IRS may waive the electronic filing requirement. To request a waiver, the CPEO must file a written request using the IRS Online Registration System for Professional Employer Organizations at least 45 days before the due date of the return for which the CPEO is unable to electronically file. For more information on filing a waiver request electronically, go to *IRS.gov/CPEO*.

15. Special Rules for Various Types of Services and Payments

Section references are to the Internal Revenue Code unless otherwise noted.

Special Classes of Employment and Special Types of Payments	Treatment Under Employment Taxes		
	Income Tax Withholding	**Social Security and Medicare (including Additional Medicare Tax when wages are paid in excess of $200,000)**	**FUTA**
Aliens, nonresident.	See Pub. 515 and Pub. 519.		
Aliens, resident:			
1. Service performed in the U.S.	Same as U.S. citizen.	Same as U.S. citizen. (Exempt if any part of service as crew member of foreign vessel or aircraft is performed outside U.S.)	Same as U.S. citizen.
2. Service performed outside the U.S.	Withhold	Taxable if (1) working for an American employer or (2) an American employer by agreement covers U.S. citizens and residents employed by its foreign affiliates.	Exempt unless on or in connection with an American vessel or aircraft and either performed under contract made in U.S., or alien is employed on such vessel or aircraft when it touches U.S. port.
Cafeteria plan benefits under section 125.	If employee chooses cash, subject to all employment taxes. If employee chooses another benefit, the treatment is the same as if the benefit was provided outside the plan. See Pub. 15-B for more information.		
Deceased worker:			
1. Wages paid to beneficiary or estate in same calendar year as worker's death. See the Instructions for Forms W-2 and W-3 for details.	Exempt	Taxable	Taxable
2. Wages paid to beneficiary or estate after calendar year of worker's death.	Exempt	Exempt	Exempt
Dependent care assistance programs.	Exempt to the extent it is reasonable to believe amounts are excludable from gross income under section 129.		
Disabled worker's wages paid after year in which worker became entitled to disability insurance benefits under the Social Security Act.	Withhold	Exempt, if worker didn't perform any service for employer during the period for which payment is made.	Taxable
Employee business expense reimbursement:			
1. Accountable plan.			
a. Amounts not exceeding specified government rate for per diem or standard mileage.	Exempt	Exempt	Exempt
b. Amounts in excess of specified government rate for per diem or standard mileage.	Withhold	Taxable	Taxable
2. Nonaccountable plan. See section 5 for details.	Withhold	Taxable	Taxable
Family employees:			
1. Child employed by parent (or partnership in which each partner is a parent of the child).	Withhold	Exempt until age 18; age 21 for domestic service.	Exempt until age 21
2. Parent employed by child.	Withhold	Taxable if in course of the son's or daughter's business. For domestic services, see section 3.	Exempt
3. Spouse employed by spouse.	Withhold	Taxable if in course of spouse's business.	Exempt
See section 3 for more information.			
Fishing and related activities.	See Pub. 334.		
Foreign governments and international organizations.	Exempt	Exempt	Exempt

Special Classes of Employment and Special Types of Payments	Treatment Under Employment Taxes		
	Income Tax Withholding	**Social Security and Medicare (including Additional Medicare Tax when wages are paid in excess of $200,000)**	**FUTA**
Foreign service by U.S. citizens:			
1. As U.S. government employees.	Withhold	Same as within U.S.	Exempt
2. For foreign affiliates of American employers and other private employers.	Exempt if at time of payment (1) it is reasonable to believe employee is entitled to exclusion from income under section 911 or (2) the employer is required by law of the foreign country to withhold income tax on such payment.	Exempt unless (1) an American employer by agreement covers U.S. citizens employed by its foreign affiliates or (2) U.S. citizen works for American employer.	Exempt unless (1) on American vessel or aircraft and work is performed under contract made in U.S. or worker is employed on vessel when it touches U.S. port or (2) U.S. citizen works for American employer (except in a contiguous country with which the U.S. has an agreement for unemployment compensation) or in the U.S. Virgin Islands.
Fringe benefits.	Taxable on excess of fair market value of the benefit over the sum of an amount paid for it by the employee and any amount excludable by law. However, special valuation rules may apply. Benefits provided under cafeteria plans may qualify for exclusion from wages for social security, Medicare, and FUTA taxes. See Pub. 15-B for details.		
Government employment:			
State/local governments and political subdivisions, employees of:			
1. Salaries and wages (includes payments to most elected and appointed officials.) See chapter 3 of Pub. 963.	Withhold	Generally, taxable for (1) services performed by employees who are either (a) covered under a section 218 agreement or (b) not covered under a section 218 agreement and not a member of a public retirement system (mandatory social security and Medicare coverage), and (2) (for Medicare tax only) for services performed by employees hired or rehired after 3/31/86 who aren't covered under a section 218 agreement or the mandatory social security provisions, unless specifically excluded by law. See Pub. 963.	Exempt
2. Election workers. Election individuals are workers who are employed to perform services for state or local governments at election booths in connection with national, state, or local elections. **Note.** File Form W-2 for payments of $600 or more even if no social security, or Medicare taxes were withheld.	Exempt	Taxable if paid $1,800 or more in 2018 (lesser amount if specified by a section 218 social security agreement). See Revenue Ruling 2000-6.	Exempt
3. Emergency workers. Emergency workers who were hired on a temporary basis in response to a specific unforeseen emergency and aren't intended to become permanent employees.	Withhold	Exempt if serving on a temporary basis in case of fire, storm, snow, earthquake, flood, or similar emergency.	Exempt
U.S. federal government employees.	Withhold	Taxable for Medicare. Taxable for social security unless hired before 1984. See section 3121(b)(5).	Exempt

Special Classes of Employment and Special Types of Payments	Treatment Under Employment Taxes		
	Income Tax Withholding	**Social Security and Medicare (including Additional Medicare Tax when wages are paid in excess of $200,000)**	**FUTA**
Homeworkers (industrial, cottage industry):			
1. Common law employees.	Withhold	Taxable	Taxable
2. Statutory employees. See section 2 for details.	Exempt	Taxable if paid $100 or more in cash in a year.	Exempt
Hospital employees:			
1. Interns.	Withhold	Taxable	Exempt
2. Patients.	Withhold	Taxable (Exempt for state or local government hospitals.)	Exempt
Household employees:			
1. Domestic service in private homes. Farmers, see Pub. 51.	Exempt (withhold if both employer and employee agree).	Taxable if paid $2,100 or more in cash in 2018. Exempt if performed by an individual under age 18 during any portion of the calendar year and isn't the principal occupation of the employee.	Taxable if employer paid total cash wages of $1,000 or more in any quarter in the current or preceding calendar year.
2. Domestic service in college clubs, fraternities, and sororities.	Exempt (withhold if both employer and employee agree).	Exempt if paid to regular student; also exempt if employee is paid less than $100 in a year by an income-tax-exempt employer.	Taxable if employer paid total cash wages of $1,000 or more in any quarter in the current or preceding calendar year.
Insurance for employees:			
1. Accident and health insurance premiums under a plan or system for employees and their dependents generally or for a class or classes of employees and their dependents.	Exempt (except 2% shareholder-employees of S corporations).	Exempt	Exempt
2. Group-term life insurance costs. See Pub. 15-B for details.	Exempt	Exempt, except for the cost of group-term life insurance includible in the employee's gross income. Special rules apply for former employees.	Exempt
Insurance agents or solicitors:			
1. Full-time life insurance salesperson.	Withhold only if employee under common law. See section 2.	Taxable	Taxable if (1) employee under common law and (2) not paid solely by commissions.
2. Other salesperson of life, casualty, etc., insurance.	Withhold only if employee under common law.	Taxable only if employee under common law.	Taxable if (1) employee under common law and (2) not paid solely by commissions.
Interest on loans with below-market interest rates (foregone interest and deemed original issue discount).	See Pub. 15-A.		
Leave-sharing plans: Amounts paid to an employee under a leave-sharing plan.	Withhold	Taxable	Taxable
Newspaper carriers and vendors: Newspaper carriers under age 18; newspaper and magazine vendors buying at fixed prices and retaining receipts from sales to customers. See Pub. 15-A for information on statutory nonemployee status.	Exempt (withhold if both employer and employee voluntarily agree).	Exempt	Exempt

Special Classes of Employment and Special Types of Payments	Treatment Under Employment Taxes		
	Income Tax Withholding	**Social Security and Medicare (including Additional Medicare Tax when wages are paid in excess of $200,000)**	**FUTA**
Noncash payments:			
1. For household work, agricultural labor, and service not in the course of the employer's trade or business.	Exempt (withhold if both employer and employee voluntarily agree.)	Exempt	Exempt
2. To certain retail commission salespersons ordinarily paid solely on a cash commission basis.	Optional with employer, except to the extent employee's supplemental wages during the year exceed $1 million.	Taxable	Taxable
Nonprofit organizations.	See Pub. 15-A.		
Officers or shareholders of an S Corporation: Distributions and other payments by an S corporation to a corporate officer or shareholder must be treated as wages to the extent the amounts are reasonable compensation for services to the corporation by an employee. See the Instructions for Form 1120S.	Withhold	Taxable	Taxable
Partners: Payments to general or limited partners of a partnership. See Pub. 541 for partner reporting rules.	Exempt	Exempt	Exempt
Railroads: Payments subject to the Railroad Retirement Act. See Pub. 915 for more details.	Withhold	Exempt	Exempt
Religious exemptions.	See Pub. 15-A and Pub. 517.		
Retirement and pension plans:			
1. Employer contributions to a qualified plan.	Exempt	Exempt	Exempt
2. Elective employee contributions and deferrals to a plan containing a qualified cash or deferred compensation arrangement (for example, 401(k)).	Generally exempt, but see section 402(g) for limitation.	Taxable	Taxable
3. Employer contributions to individual retirement accounts under simplified employee pension plan (SEP).	Generally exempt, but see section 402(g) for salary reduction SEP limitation.	Exempt, except for amounts contributed under a salary reduction SEP agreement.	
4. Employer contributions to section 403(b) annuities.	Generally exempt, but see section 402(g) for limitation.	Taxable if paid through a salary reduction agreement (written or otherwise).	
5. Employee salary reduction contributions to a SIMPLE retirement account.	Exempt	Taxable	Taxable
6. Distributions from qualified retirement and pension plans and section 403(b) annuities. See Pub. 15-A for information on pensions, annuities, and employer contributions to nonqualified deferred compensation arrangements.	Withhold, but recipient may elect exemption on Form W-4P in certain cases; mandatory 20% withholding applies to an eligible rollover distribution that isn't a direct rollover; exempt for direct rollover. See Pub. 15-A.	Exempt	Exempt
7. Employer contributions to a section 457(b) plan.	Generally exempt but see section 402(g) limitation.	Taxable	Taxable
8. Employee salary reduction contributions to a section 457(b) plan.	Generally exempt but see section 402(g) salary reduction limitation.	Taxable	Taxable
Salespersons:			
1. Common law employees.	Withhold	Taxable	Taxable
2. Statutory employees.	Exempt	Taxable	Taxable, except for full-time life insurance sales agents.
3. Statutory nonemployees (qualified real estate agents, direct sellers, and certain companion sitters). See Pub. 15-A for details.	Exempt	Exempt	Exempt

Special Classes of Employment and Special Types of Payments	Treatment Under Employment Taxes		
	Income Tax Withholding	**Social Security and Medicare (including Additional Medicare Tax when wages are paid in excess of $200,000)**	**FUTA**
Scholarships and fellowship grants (includible in income under section 117(c)).	Withhold	Taxability depends on the nature of the employment and the status of the organization. See *Students, scholars, trainees, teachers, etc.* below.	
Severance or dismissal pay.	Withhold	Taxable	Taxable
Service not in the course of the employer's trade or business (other than on a farm operated for profit or for household employment in private homes).	Withhold only if employee earns $50 or more in cash in a quarter and works on 24 or more different days in that quarter or in the preceding quarter.	Taxable if employee receives $100 or more in cash in a calendar year.	Taxable only if employee earns $50 or more in cash in a quarter and works on 24 or more different days in that quarter or in the preceding quarter.
Sick pay. See Pub. 15-A for more information.	Withhold	Exempt after end of 6 calendar months after the calendar month employee last worked for employer.	
Students, scholars, trainees, teachers, etc.:			
1. Student enrolled and regularly attending classes, performing services for:			
a. Private school, college, or university.	Withhold	Exempt	Exempt
b. Auxiliary nonprofit organization operated for and controlled by school, college, or university.	Withhold	Exempt unless services are covered by a section 218 (Social Security Act) agreement.	Exempt
c. Public school, college, or university.	Withhold	Exempt unless services are covered by a section 218 (Social Security Act) agreement.	Exempt
2. Full-time student performing service for academic credit, combining instruction with work experience as an integral part of the program.	Withhold	Taxable	Exempt unless program was established for or on behalf of an employer or group of employers.
3. Student nurse performing part-time services for nominal earnings at hospital as incidental part of training.	Withhold	Exempt	Exempt
4. Student employed by organized camps.	Withhold	Taxable	Exempt
5. Student, scholar, trainee, teacher, etc., as nonimmigrant alien under section 101(a)(15)(F), (J), (M), or (Q) of Immigration and Nationality Act (that is, aliens holding F-1, J-1, M-1, or Q-1 visas).	Withhold unless excepted by regulations.	Exempt if service is performed for purpose specified in section 101(a)(15)(F), (J), (M), or (Q) of Immigration and Nationality Act. However, these taxes may apply if the employee becomes a resident alien. See the special residency tests for exempt individuals in chapter 1 of Pub. 519.	
Supplemental unemployment compensation plan benefits.	Withhold	Exempt under certain conditions. See Pub. 15-A.	
Tips:			
1. If $20 or more in a month.	Withhold	Taxable	Taxable for all tips reported in writing to employer.
2. If less than $20 in a month. See section 6 for more information.	Exempt	Exempt	Exempt
Worker's compensation.	Exempt	Exempt	Exempt

16. Third-Party Payer Arrangements

An employer may outsource some or all of its federal employment tax withholding, reporting and payment obligations. An employer who outsources payroll and related tax duties (that is, withholding, reporting, and paying over social security, Medicare, FUTA, and income taxes) to a third-party payer, generally will remain responsible for those duties, including liability for the taxes. However, see *Certified professional employer organization (CPEO)*, later, for an exception.

If an employer outsources some or all of its payroll responsibilities, the employer should consider the following information.

- The employer remains responsible for federal tax deposits and other federal tax payments even though the employer may forward the tax amounts to the third-party payer to make the deposits and payments. If the third party fails to make the deposits and payments, the IRS may assess penalties and interest on the employer's account. As the employer, you may be liable for all taxes, penalties, and interest due. The employer may also be held personally liable for certain unpaid federal taxes.
- If the employer's account has any issues, the IRS will send correspondence to the employer at the address of record. We strongly recommend that the employer maintain its address as the address of record with the IRS. Having correspondence sent to the address of the third-party payer may significantly limit the employer's ability to be informed about tax matters involving the employer's business.
- When a third party enrolls an employer in the EFTPS for federal tax deposits, the employer will receive an Inquiry PIN. Employers should activate and use this Inquiry PIN to monitor their account and ensure the third party is making the required tax deposits.

The following are common third-party payers who an employer may contract with to perform payroll and related tax duties.

- Payroll service provider (PSP).
- Reporting agent.
- Agent with approved Form 2678.
- Payer designated under section 3504.
- Certified Professional Employer Organization.

Payroll service provider (PSP). A PSP helps administer payroll and payroll-related tax duties on behalf of the employer. A PSP may prepare paychecks for employees, prepare and file employment tax returns, prepare Form W-2, and make federal tax deposits and other federal tax payments. A PSP performs these functions using the EIN of the employer. A PSP isn't liable as either an employer or an agent of the employer for the employer's employment taxes. If an employer is using a PSP to perform its tax duties, the employer remains liable for its employment tax obligations, including liability for employment taxes.

An employer who uses a PSP should ensure the PSP is using EFTPS to make federal tax deposits on behalf of the employer so the employer can confirm that the payments are being made on its behalf.

Reporting agent. A reporting agent is a type of PSP. A reporting agent helps administer payroll and payroll-related tax duties on behalf of the employer, including authorization to electronically sign and file forms set forth on Form 8655. An employer uses Form 8655 to authorize a reporting agent to perform functions on behalf of the employer. A reporting agent performs these functions using the EIN of the employer. A reporting agent isn't liable as either an employer or an agent of the employer for the employer's employment taxes. If an employer is using a reporting agent to perform its tax duties, the employer remains liable for its employment obligations, including liability for employment taxes.

A reporting agent must use EFTPS to make federal tax deposits on behalf of an employer. The employer has access to EFTPS to confirm federal tax deposits were made on its behalf.

For more information on reporting agents, see Revenue Procedure 2012-32, 2012-34 I.R.B. 267, at *IRS.gov/irb/2012-34_IRB/ar08.html* and Pub. 1474, Technical Specifications Guide for Reporting Agent Authorization and Federal Tax Depositors.

Agent with an approved Form 2678. An agent with an approved Form 2678 helps administer payroll and related tax duties on behalf of the employer. An agent authorized under section 3504 may pay wages or compensation to some or all of the employees of an employer, prepare and file employment tax returns as set forth on Form 2678, prepare Form W-2, and make federal tax deposits and other federal tax payments. An employer uses Form 2678 to request authorization to appoint an agent to perform functions on behalf of the employer. An agent with an approved Form 2678 is authorized to perform these functions using its own EIN. The agent files a Schedule R (Form 941) to allocate wages and taxes to the employers it represents as an agent.

If an employer is using an agent with an approved Form 2678 to perform its tax duties, the agent and the employer are jointly liable for the employment taxes and related tax duties for which the agent is authorized to perform.

Form 2678 doesn't apply to FUTA taxes reportable on Form 940 unless the employer is a home care service recipient receiving home care services through a program administered by a federal, state, or local government agency.

For more information on an agent with an approved Form 2678, see Revenue Procedure 2013-39, 2013-52 I.R.B. 830, at *IRS.gov/irb/2013-52_IRB/ar15.html*.

Payer designated under section 3504. In certain circumstances, the IRS may designate a third-party payer to perform the acts of an employer. The IRS will designate a third party-payer on behalf of an employer if the third-party has a service agreement with the employer. A service agreement is an agreement between the third-party payer and an employer in which the third-party payer (1) asserts it is the employer of individuals performing services for the employer; (2) pays wages to the individuals that perform services for the employer; and (3) assumes responsibility to withhold, report, and pay federal employment taxes for the wages it pays to the individuals that perform services for the employer.

A payer designated under section 3504 performs tax duties under the service agreement using its own EIN. If the IRS designates a third-party payer under section 3504, the designated payer and the employer are jointly liable for the employment taxes and related tax duties for which the third-party payer is designated.

For more information on a payer designated under section 3504, see Regulations section 31.3504-2.

Certified professional employer organization (CPEO). The Tax Increase Prevention Act of 2014 required the IRS to establish a voluntary certification program for professional employer organizations (PEOs). PEOs handle various payroll administration and tax reporting responsibilities for their business clients and are typically paid a fee based on payroll costs. To become and remain certified under the certification program, certified professional employer organizations (CPEOs) must meet various requirements described in sections 3511 and 7705 and related published guidance. Certification as a CPEO may affect the employment tax liabilities of both the CPEO and its customers. A CPEO is generally treated as the employer of any individual who performs services for a customer of the CPEO and is covered by a contract described in section 7705(e)(2) between the CPEO and the customer (CPEO contract), but only for wages and other compensation paid to the individual by the CPEO. However, with respect to certain employees covered by a CPEO contract, a customer may also be treated as an employer of the employees and, consequently, may also be liable for federal employment taxes imposed on wages and other compensation paid by the CPEO to such employees. For more information, go to *IRS.gov/CPEO*.

17. How To Use the Income Tax Withholding Tables

TIP *Changes made under P.L. 115-97 will affect your employees' tax liability for 2018. The federal income tax withholding methods described in this section are the methods that you should use for 2018. The new withholding tables are designed to work with the Forms W-4 that your employees previously gave you. See* 2018 federal income tax withholding *and* Exempt Form W-4 *under* What's New *for more information. To help employees determine their withholding, the IRS is revising the withholding tax calculator available at* IRS.gov/W4App. *The IRS anticipates that this calculator will be available by the end of February. Encourage your employees to use the withholding calculator to determine if they should give you a new Form W-4 for 2018.*

There are several ways to figure income tax withholding. The following methods of withholding are based on the information you get from your employees on Form W-4. You must first reduce the wages you pay your employees by nontaxable wages before figuring the tax to withhold on taxable wages. See section 5 and Pub. 15-B for more information about nontaxable wages. See section 9 for more information on Form W-4.

TIP *Adjustments aren't required when there will be more than the usual number of pay periods, for example, 27 biweekly pay dates instead of 26.*

Wage Bracket Method

Under the wage bracket method, find the proper table (on pages 48–67) for your payroll period and the employee's marital status as shown on his or her Form W-4. Then, based on the number of withholding allowances claimed on the Form W-4 and the amount of taxable wages, find the amount of income tax to withhold. If your employee is claiming more than 10 withholding allowances, see below.

If you can't use the wage bracket tables because taxable wages exceed the amount shown in the last bracket of the table, use the percentage method of withholding described below. Be sure to reduce taxable wages by the amount of total withholding allowances in *Table 5* before using the percentage method tables (pages 46–47).

Adjusting wage bracket withholding for employees claiming more than 10 withholding allowances. The wage bracket tables can be used if an employee claims up to 10 allowances. More than 10 allowances may be claimed because of the special withholding allowance, additional allowances for deductions and credits, and the system itself.

Adapt the tables to more than 10 allowances as follows:

1. Multiply the number of withholding allowances over 10 by the allowance value for the payroll period. The allowance values are in *Table 5*, later.
2. Subtract the result from the employee's taxable wages.
3. On this amount, find and withhold the tax in the column for 10 allowances.

This is a voluntary method. If you use the wage bracket tables, you may continue to withhold the amount in the "10" column when your employee has more than 10 allowances, using the method above. You can also use any other method described next.

Percentage Method

If you don't want to use the wage bracket tables on pages 48–67 to figure how much income tax to withhold, you can use a percentage computation based on *Table 5*, later, and the appropriate rate table. This method works for any number of withholding allowances the employee claims and any amount of wages.

Use these steps to figure the income tax to withhold under the percentage method.

1. Multiply one withholding allowance for your payroll period (see *Table 5*, later) by the number of allowances the employee claims.
2. Subtract that amount from the employee's taxable wages.
3. Determine the amount to withhold from the appropriate table on pages 46–47.

Table 5. **Percentage Method—2018 Amount for One Withholding Allowance**

Payroll Period	One Withholding Allowance
Weekly	$ 79.80
Biweekly	159.60
Semimonthly	172.90
Monthly	345.80
Quarterly	1,037.50
Semiannually	2,075.00
Annually	4,150.00
Daily or miscellaneous (each day of the payroll period)	16.00

Example. An unmarried employee is paid $800 weekly. This employee has in effect a Form W-4 claiming two withholding allowances. Using the percentage method, figure the income tax to withhold as follows:

1.	Total wage payment		$800.00
2.	One allowance	$79.80	
3.	Allowances claimed on Form W-4	2	
4.	Multiply line 2 by line 3		$159.60
5.	Amount subject to withholding (subtract line 4 from line 1)		$640.40
6.	Tax to be withheld on $640.40 from Table 1—single person, page 46		$64.67

To figure the income tax to withhold, you may reduce the last digit of the wages to zero, or figure the wages to the nearest dollar. You may also round the tax for the pay period to the nearest dollar. If rounding is used, it must be used consistently. Withheld tax amounts should be rounded to the nearest whole dollar by dropping amounts under 50 cents and increasing amounts from 50 to 99 cents to the next dollar. For example, $2.30 becomes $2 and $2.50 becomes $3. This rounding meets the tolerances under section 3402(h)(4).

Annual income tax withholding. Figure the income tax to withhold on annual wages under the *Percentage Method* for an annual payroll period. Then prorate the tax back to the payroll period.

Example. A married person claims four withholding allowances. She is paid $1,000 a week. Multiply the weekly wages by 52 weeks to figure the annual wage of $52,000. Subtract $16,600 (the value of four withholding allowances for 2018) for a balance of $35,400. Using Table 7(b) on page 47, $2,481 is withheld. Divide the annual tax by 52. The weekly income tax to withhold is $47.71.

Alternative Methods of Income Tax Withholding

Rather than the *Wage Bracket Method* or *Percentage Method* described in this section, you can use an alternative method to withhold income tax. Pub. 15-A describes these alternative methods and contains:

- Formula tables for percentage method withholding (for automated payroll systems),
- Wage bracket percentage method tables (for automated payroll systems), and
- Combined income, social security, and Medicare tax withholding tables.

Some of the alternative methods explained in Pub. 15-A are annualized wages, average estimated wages, cumulative wages, and part-year employment.

Percentage Method Tables for Income Tax Withholding

(For Wages Paid in 2018)

TABLE 1—WEEKLY Payroll Period

(a) SINGLE person (including head of household)—				(b) MARRIED person—			
If the amount of wages (after subtracting withholding allowances) is:		The amount of income tax to withhold is:		If the amount of wages (after subtracting withholding allowances) is:		The amount of income tax to withhold is:	
Not over $71		$0		Not over $222		$0	
Over—	**But not over—**		**of excess over—**	**Over—**	**But not over—**		**of excess over—**
$71	—$254	$0.00 plus 10%	—$71	$222	—$588	$0.00 plus 10%	—$222
$254	—$815	$18.30 plus 12%	—$254	$588	—$1,711	$36.60 plus 12%	—$588
$815	—$1,658	$85.62 plus 22%	—$815	$1,711	—$3,395	$171.36 plus 22%	—$1,711
$1,658	—$3,100	$271.08 plus 24%	—$1,658	$3,395	—$6,280	$541.84 plus 24%	—$3,395
$3,100	—$3,917	$617.16 plus 32%	—$3,100	$6,280	—$7,914	$1,234.24 plus 32%	—$6,280
$3,917	—$9,687	$878.60 plus 35%	—$3,917	$7,914	—$11,761	$1,757.12 plus 35%	—$7,914
$9,687		$2,898.10 plus 37%	—$9,687	$11,761		$3,103.57 plus 37%	—$11,761

TABLE 2—BIWEEKLY Payroll Period

(a) SINGLE person (including head of household)—				(b) MARRIED person—			
If the amount of wages (after subtracting withholding allowances) is:		The amount of income tax to withhold is:		If the amount of wages (after subtracting withholding allowances) is:		The amount of income tax to withhold is:	
Not over $142		$0		Not over $444		$0	
Over—	**But not over—**		**of excess over—**	**Over—**	**But not over—**		**of excess over—**
$142	—$509	$0.00 plus 10%	—$142	$444	—$1,177	$0.00 plus 10%	—$444
$509	—$1,631	$36.70 plus 12%	—$509	$1,177	—$3,421	$73.30 plus 12%	—$1,177
$1,631	—$3,315	$171.34 plus 22%	—$1,631	$3,421	—$6,790	$342.58 plus 22%	—$3,421
$3,315	—$6,200	$541.82 plus 24%	—$3,315	$6,790	—$12,560	$1,083.76 plus 24%	—$6,790
$6,200	—$7,835	$1,234.22 plus 32%	—$6,200	$12,560	—$15,829	$2,468.56 plus 32%	—$12,560
$7,835	—$19,373	$1,757.42 plus 35%	—$7,835	$15,829	—$23,521	$3,514.64 plus 35%	—$15,829
$19,373		$5,795.72 plus 37%	—$19,373	$23,521		$6,206.84 plus 37%	—$23,521

TABLE 3—SEMIMONTHLY Payroll Period

(a) SINGLE person (including head of household)—				(b) MARRIED person—			
If the amount of wages (after subtracting withholding allowances) is:		The amount of income tax to withhold is:		If the amount of wages (after subtracting withholding allowances) is:		The amount of income tax to withhold is:	
Not over $154		$0		Not over $481		$0	
Over—	**But not over—**		**of excess over—**	**Over—**	**But not over—**		**of excess over—**
$154	—$551	$0.00 plus 10%	—$154	$481	—$1,275	$0.00 plus 10%	—$481
$551	—$1,767	$39.70 plus 12%	—$551	$1,275	—$3,706	$79.40 plus 12%	—$1,275
$1,767	—$3,592	$185.62 plus 22%	—$1,767	$3,706	—$7,356	$371.12 plus 22%	—$3,706
$3,592	—$6,717	$587.12 plus 24%	—$3,592	$7,356	—$13,606	$1,174.12 plus 24%	—$7,356
$6,717	—$8,488	$1,337.12 plus 32%	—$6,717	$13,606	—$17,148	$2,674.12 plus 32%	—$13,606
$8,488	—$20,988	$1,903.84 plus 35%	—$8,488	$17,148	—$25,481	$3,807.56 plus 35%	—$17,148
$20,988		$6,278.84 plus 37%	—$20,988	$25,481		$6,724.11 plus 37%	—$25,481

TABLE 4—MONTHLY Payroll Period

(a) SINGLE person (including head of household)—				(b) MARRIED person—			
If the amount of wages (after subtracting withholding allowances) is:		The amount of income tax to withhold is:		If the amount of wages (after subtracting withholding allowances) is:		The amount of income tax to withhold is:	
Not over $308		$0		Not over $963		$0	
Over—	**But not over—**		**of excess over—**	**Over—**	**But not over—**		**of excess over—**
$308	—$1,102	$0.00 plus 10%	—$308	$963	—$2,550	$0.00 plus 10%	—$963
$1,102	—$3,533	$79.40 plus 12%	—$1,102	$2,550	—$7,413	$158.70 plus 12%	—$2,550
$3,533	—$7,183	$371.12 plus 22%	—$3,533	$7,413	—$14,713	$742.26 plus 22%	—$7,413
$7,183	—$13,433	$1,174.12 plus 24%	—$7,183	$14,713	—$27,213	$2,348.26 plus 24%	—$14,713
$13,433	—$16,975	$2,674.12 plus 32%	—$13,433	$27,213	—$34,296	$5,348.26 plus 32%	—$27,213
$16,975	—$41,975	$3,807.56 plus 35%	—$16,975	$34,296	—$50,963	$7,614.82 plus 35%	—$34,296
$41,975		$12,557.56 plus 37%	—$41,975	$50,963		$13,448.27 plus 37%	—$50,963

Percentage Method Tables for Income Tax Withholding (continued)

(For Wages Paid in 2018)

TABLE 5—QUARTERLY Payroll Period

(a) SINGLE person (including head of household)—

If the amount of wages (after subtracting withholding allowances) is: Not over $925 — The amount of income tax to withhold is: $0

Over—	But not over—	The amount of income tax to withhold is:	of excess over—
$925	—$3,306	$0.00 plus 10%	—$925
$3,306	—$10,600	$238.10 plus 12%	—$3,306
$10,600	—$21,550	$1,113.38 plus 22%	—$10,600
$21,550	—$40,300	$3,522.38 plus 24%	—$21,550
$40,300	—$50,925	$8,022.38 plus 32%	—$40,300
$50,925	—$125,925	$11,422.38 plus 35%	—$50,925
$125,925		$37,672.38 plus 37%	—$125,925

(b) MARRIED person—

If the amount of wages (after subtracting withholding allowances) is: Not over $2,888 — The amount of income tax to withhold is: $0

Over—	But not over—	The amount of income tax to withhold is:	of excess over—
$2,888	—$7,650	$0.00 plus 10%	—$2,888
$7,650	—$22,238	$476.20 plus 12%	—$7,650
$22,238	—$44,138	$2,226.76 plus 22%	—$22,238
$44,138	—$81,638	$7,044.76 plus 24%	—$44,138
$81,638	—$102,888	$16,044.76 plus 32%	—$81,638
$102,888	—$152,888	$22,844.76 plus 35%	—$102,888
$152,888		$40,344.76 plus 37%	—$152,888

TABLE 6—SEMIANNUAL Payroll Period

(a) SINGLE person (including head of household)—

If the amount of wages (after subtracting withholding allowances) is: Not over $1,850 — The amount of income tax to withhold is: $0

Over—	But not over—	The amount of income tax to withhold is:	of excess over—
$1,850	—$6,613	$0.00 plus 10%	—$1,850
$6,613	—$21,200	$476.30 plus 12%	—$6,613
$21,200	—$43,100	$2,226.74 plus 22%	—$21,200
$43,100	—$80,600	$7,044.74 plus 24%	—$43,100
$80,600	—$101,850	$16,044.74 plus 32%	—$80,600
$101,850	—$251,850	$22,844.74 plus 35%	—$101,850
$251,850		$75,344.74 plus 37%	—$251,850

(b) MARRIED person—

If the amount of wages (after subtracting withholding allowances) is: Not over $5,775 — The amount of income tax to withhold is: $0

Over—	But not over—	The amount of income tax to withhold is:	of excess over—
$5,775	—$15,300	$0.00 plus 10%	—$5,775
$15,300	—$44,475	$952.50 plus 12%	—$15,300
$44,475	—$88,275	$4,453.50 plus 22%	—$44,475
$88,275	—$163,275	$14,089.50 plus 24%	—$88,275
$163,275	—$205,775	$32,089.50 plus 32%	—$163,275
$205,775	—$305,775	$45,689.50 plus 35%	—$205,775
$305,775		$80,689.50 plus 37%	—$305,775

TABLE 7—ANNUAL Payroll Period

(a) SINGLE person (including head of household)—

If the amount of wages (after subtracting withholding allowances) is: Not over $3,700 — The amount of income tax to withhold is: $0

Over—	But not over—	The amount of income tax to withhold is:	of excess over—
$3,700	—$13,225	$0.00 plus 10%	—$3,700
$13,225	—$42,400	$952.50 plus 12%	—$13,225
$42,400	—$86,200	$4,453.50 plus 22%	—$42,400
$86,200	—$161,200	$14,089.50 plus 24%	—$86,200
$161,200	—$203,700	$32,089.50 plus 32%	—$161,200
$203,700	—$503,700	$45,689.50 plus 35%	—$203,700
$503,700		$150,689.50 plus 37%	—$503,700

(b) MARRIED person—

If the amount of wages (after subtracting withholding allowances) is: Not over $11,550 — The amount of income tax to withhold is: $0

Over—	But not over—	The amount of income tax to withhold is:	of excess over—
$11,550	—$30,600	$0.00 plus 10%	—$11,550
$30,600	—$88,950	$1,905.00 plus 12%	—$30,600
$88,950	—$176,550	$8,907.00 plus 22%	—$88,950
$176,550	—$326,550	$28,179.00 plus 24%	—$176,550
$326,550	—$411,550	$64,179.00 plus 32%	—$326,550
$411,550	—$611,550	$91,379.00 plus 35%	—$411,550
$611,550		$161,379.00 plus 37%	—$611,550

TABLE 8—DAILY or MISCELLANEOUS Payroll Period

(a) SINGLE person (including head of household)—

If the amount of wages (after subtracting withholding allowances) divided by the number of days in the payroll period is: Not over $14.20 — The amount of income tax to withhold per day is: $0

Over—	But not over—	The amount of income tax to withhold per day is:	of excess over—
$14.20	—$50.90	$0.00 plus 10%	—$14.20
$50.90	—$163.10	$3.67 plus 12%	—$50.90
$163.10	—$331.50	$17.13 plus 22%	—$163.10
$331.50	—$620.00	$54.18 plus 24%	—$331.50
$620.00	—$783.50	$123.42 plus 32%	—$620.00
$783.50	—$1,937.30	$175.74 plus 35%	—$783.50
$1,937.30		$579.57 plus 37%	—$1,937.30

(b) MARRIED person—

If the amount of wages (after subtracting withholding allowances) divided by the number of days in the payroll period is: Not over $44.40 — The amount of income tax to withhold per day is: $0

Over—	But not over—	The amount of income tax to withhold per day is:	of excess over—
$44.40	—$117.70	$0.00 plus 10%	—$44.40
$117.70	—$342.10	$7.33 plus 12%	—$117.70
$342.10	—$679.00	$34.26 plus 22%	—$342.10
$679.00	—$1,256.00	$108.38 plus 24%	—$679.00
$1,256.00	—$1,582.90	$246.86 plus 32%	—$1,256.00
$1,582.90	—$2,352.10	$351.47 plus 35%	—$1,582.90
$2,352.10		$620.69 plus 37%	—$2,352.10

Wage Bracket Method Tables for Income Tax Withholding

SINGLE Persons—**WEEKLY** Payroll Period

(For Wages Paid through December 31, 2018)

And the wages are–		And the number of withholding allowances claimed is—										
At least	But less than	0	1	2	3	4	5	6	7	8	9	10
		The amount of income tax to be withheld is—										
$ 0	**$75**	$0	$0	$0	$0	$0	$0	$0	$0	$0	$0	$0
75	**80**	1	0	0	0	0	0	0	0	0	0	0
80	**85**	1	0	0	0	0	0	0	0	0	0	0
85	**90**	2	0	0	0	0	0	0	0	0	0	0
90	**95**	2	0	0	0	0	0	0	0	0	0	0
95	**100**	3	0	0	0	0	0	0	0	0	0	0
100	**105**	3	0	0	0	0	0	0	0	0	0	0
105	**110**	4	0	0	0	0	0	0	0	0	0	0
110	**115**	4	0	0	0	0	0	0	0	0	0	0
115	**120**	5	0	0	0	0	0	0	0	0	0	0
120	**125**	5	0	0	0	0	0	0	0	0	0	0
125	**130**	6	0	0	0	0	0	0	0	0	0	0
130	**135**	6	0	0	0	0	0	0	0	0	0	0
135	**140**	7	0	0	0	0	0	0	0	0	0	0
140	**145**	7	0	0	0	0	0	0	0	0	0	0
145	**150**	8	0	0	0	0	0	0	0	0	0	0
150	**155**	8	0	0	0	0	0	0	0	0	0	0
155	**160**	9	1	0	0	0	0	0	0	0	0	0
160	**165**	9	1	0	0	0	0	0	0	0	0	0
165	**170**	10	2	0	0	0	0	0	0	0	0	0
170	**175**	10	2	0	0	0	0	0	0	0	0	0
175	**180**	11	3	0	0	0	0	0	0	0	0	0
180	**185**	11	3	0	0	0	0	0	0	0	0	0
185	**190**	12	4	0	0	0	0	0	0	0	0	0
190	**195**	12	4	0	0	0	0	0	0	0	0	0
195	**200**	13	5	0	0	0	0	0	0	0	0	0
200	**210**	13	5	0	0	0	0	0	0	0	0	0
210	**220**	14	6	0	0	0	0	0	0	0	0	0
220	**230**	15	7	0	0	0	0	0	0	0	0	0
230	**240**	16	8	0	0	0	0	0	0	0	0	0
240	**250**	17	9	1	0	0	0	0	0	0	0	0
250	**260**	18	10	2	0	0	0	0	0	0	0	0
260	**270**	20	11	3	0	0	0	0	0	0	0	0
270	**280**	21	12	4	0	0	0	0	0	0	0	0
280	**290**	22	13	5	0	0	0	0	0	0	0	0
290	**300**	23	14	6	0	0	0	0	0	0	0	0
300	**310**	24	15	7	0	0	0	0	0	0	0	0
310	**320**	26	16	8	0	0	0	0	0	0	0	0
320	**330**	27	17	9	1	0	0	0	0	0	0	0
330	**340**	28	18	10	2	0	0	0	0	0	0	0
340	**350**	29	20	11	3	0	0	0	0	0	0	0
350	**360**	30	21	12	4	0	0	0	0	0	0	0
360	**370**	32	22	13	5	0	0	0	0	0	0	0
370	**380**	33	23	14	6	0	0	0	0	0	0	0
380	**390**	34	24	15	7	0	0	0	0	0	0	0
390	**400**	35	26	16	8	0	0	0	0	0	0	0
400	**410**	36	27	17	9	1	0	0	0	0	0	0
410	**420**	38	28	18	10	2	0	0	0	0	0	0
420	**430**	39	29	20	11	3	0	0	0	0	0	0
430	**440**	40	30	21	12	4	0	0	0	0	0	0
440	**450**	41	32	22	13	5	0	0	0	0	0	0
450	**460**	42	33	23	14	6	0	0	0	0	0	0
460	**470**	44	34	24	15	7	0	0	0	0	0	0
470	**480**	45	35	26	16	8	0	0	0	0	0	0
480	**490**	46	36	27	17	9	1	0	0	0	0	0
490	**500**	47	38	28	18	10	2	0	0	0	0	0
500	**510**	48	39	29	20	11	3	0	0	0	0	0
510	**520**	50	40	30	21	12	4	0	0	0	0	0
520	**530**	51	41	32	22	13	5	0	0	0	0	0
530	**540**	52	42	33	23	14	6	0	0	0	0	0
540	**550**	53	44	34	24	15	7	0	0	0	0	0
550	**560**	54	45	35	26	16	8	1	0	0	0	0
560	**570**	56	46	36	27	17	9	2	0	0	0	0
570	**580**	57	47	38	28	18	10	3	0	0	0	0
580	**590**	58	48	39	29	20	11	4	0	0	0	0
590	**600**	59	50	40	30	21	12	5	0	0	0	0
600	**610**	60	51	41	32	22	13	6	0	0	0	0
610	**620**	62	52	42	33	23	14	7	0	0	0	0
620	**630**	63	53	44	34	24	15	8	0	0	0	0
630	**640**	64	54	45	35	26	16	9	1	0	0	0

Wage Bracket Method Tables for Income Tax Withholding

SINGLE Persons—**WEEKLY** Payroll Period

(For Wages Paid through December 31, 2018)

And the wages are–		And the number of withholding allowances claimed is—										
At least	But less than	0	1	2	3	4	5	6	7	8	9	10
		The amount of income tax to be withheld is—										
$640	**$650**	$65	$56	$46	$36	$27	$17	$10	$2	$0	$0	$0
650	**660**	66	57	47	38	28	19	11	3	0	0	0
660	**670**	68	58	48	39	29	20	12	4	0	0	0
670	**680**	69	59	50	40	30	21	13	5	0	0	0
680	**690**	70	60	51	41	32	22	14	6	0	0	0
690	**700**	71	62	52	42	33	23	15	7	0	0	0
700	**710**	72	63	53	44	34	25	16	8	0	0	0
710	**720**	74	64	54	45	35	26	17	9	1	0	0
720	**730**	75	65	56	46	36	27	18	10	2	0	0
730	**740**	76	66	57	47	38	28	19	11	3	0	0
740	**750**	77	68	58	48	39	29	20	12	4	0	0
750	**760**	78	69	59	50	40	31	21	13	5	0	0
760	**770**	80	70	60	51	41	32	22	14	6	0	0
770	**780**	81	71	62	52	42	33	23	15	7	0	0
780	**790**	82	72	63	53	44	34	25	16	8	0	0
790	**800**	83	74	64	54	45	35	26	17	9	1	0
800	**810**	84	75	65	56	46	37	27	18	10	2	0
810	**820**	86	76	66	57	47	38	28	19	11	3	0
820	**830**	88	77	68	58	48	39	29	20	12	4	0
830	**840**	90	78	69	59	50	40	31	21	13	5	0
840	**850**	92	80	70	60	51	41	32	22	14	6	0
850	**860**	94	81	71	62	52	43	33	23	15	7	0
860	**870**	97	82	72	63	53	44	34	25	16	8	0
870	**880**	99	83	74	64	54	45	35	26	17	9	1
880	**890**	101	84	75	65	56	46	37	27	18	10	2
890	**900**	103	86	76	66	57	47	38	28	19	11	3
900	**910**	105	88	77	68	58	49	39	29	20	12	4
910	**920**	108	90	78	69	59	50	40	31	21	13	5
920	**930**	110	92	80	70	60	51	41	32	22	14	6
930	**940**	112	94	81	71	62	52	43	33	23	15	7
940	**950**	114	97	82	72	63	53	44	34	25	16	8
950	**960**	116	99	83	74	64	55	45	35	26	17	9
960	**970**	119	101	84	75	65	56	46	37	27	18	10
970	**980**	121	103	86	76	66	57	47	38	28	19	11
980	**990**	123	105	88	77	68	58	49	39	29	20	12
990	**1,000**	125	108	90	78	69	59	50	40	31	21	13
1,000	**1,010**	127	110	92	80	70	61	51	41	32	22	14
1,010	**1,020**	130	112	94	81	71	62	52	43	33	23	15
1,020	**1,030**	132	114	97	82	72	63	53	44	34	25	16
1,030	**1,040**	134	116	99	83	74	64	55	45	35	26	17
1,040	**1,050**	136	119	101	84	75	65	56	46	37	27	18
1,050	**1,060**	138	121	103	86	76	67	57	47	38	28	19
1,060	**1,070**	141	123	105	88	77	68	58	49	39	29	20
1,070	**1,080**	143	125	108	90	78	69	59	50	40	31	21
1,080	**1,090**	145	127	110	92	80	70	61	51	41	32	22
1,090	**1,100**	147	130	112	94	81	71	62	52	43	33	23
1,100	**1,110**	149	132	114	97	82	73	63	53	44	34	25
1,110	**1,120**	152	134	116	99	83	74	64	55	45	35	26
1,120	**1,130**	154	136	119	101	84	75	65	56	46	37	27
1,130	**1,140**	156	138	121	103	86	76	67	57	47	38	28
1,140	**1,150**	158	141	123	105	88	77	68	58	49	39	29
1,150	**1,160**	160	143	125	108	90	79	69	59	50	40	31
1,160	**1,170**	163	145	127	110	92	80	70	61	51	41	32
1,170	**1,180**	165	147	130	112	95	81	71	62	52	43	33
1,180	**1,190**	167	149	132	114	97	82	73	63	53	44	34
1,190	**1,200**	169	152	134	116	99	83	74	64	55	45	35
1,200	**1,210**	171	154	136	119	101	85	75	65	56	46	37
1,210	**1,220**	174	156	138	121	103	86	76	67	57	47	38
1,220	**1,230**	176	158	141	123	106	88	77	68	58	49	39
1,230	**1,240**	178	160	143	125	108	90	79	69	59	50	40
1,240	**1,250**	180	163	145	127	110	92	80	70	61	51	41
1,250	**1,260**	182	165	147	130	112	95	81	71	62	52	43
1,260	**1,270**	185	167	149	132	114	97	82	73	63	53	44
1,270	**1,280**	187	169	152	134	117	99	83	74	64	55	45
1,280	**1,290**	189	171	154	136	119	101	85	75	65	56	46

$1,290 and over — Use Table 1(a) for a SINGLE person on page 46. Also see the instructions on page 44.

Wage Bracket Method Tables for Income Tax Withholding

MARRIED Persons—**WEEKLY** Payroll Period

(For Wages Paid through December 31, 2018)

And the wages are–		And the number of withholding allowances claimed is—										
At least	But less than	0	1	2	3	4	5	6	7	8	9	10
		The amount of income tax to be withheld is—										
$ 0	**$225**	$0	$0	$0	$0	$0	$0	$0	$0	$0	$0	$0
225	**235**	1	0	0	0	0	0	0	0	0	0	0
235	**245**	2	0	0	0	0	0	0	0	0	0	0
245	**255**	3	0	0	0	0	0	0	0	0	0	0
255	**265**	4	0	0	0	0	0	0	0	0	0	0
265	**275**	5	0	0	0	0	0	0	0	0	0	0
275	**285**	6	0	0	0	0	0	0	0	0	0	0
285	**295**	7	0	0	0	0	0	0	0	0	0	0
295	**305**	8	0	0	0	0	0	0	0	0	0	0
305	**315**	9	1	0	0	0	0	0	0	0	0	0
315	**325**	10	2	0	0	0	0	0	0	0	0	0
325	**335**	11	3	0	0	0	0	0	0	0	0	0
335	**345**	12	4	0	0	0	0	0	0	0	0	0
345	**355**	13	5	0	0	0	0	0	0	0	0	0
355	**365**	14	6	0	0	0	0	0	0	0	0	0
365	**375**	15	7	0	0	0	0	0	0	0	0	0
375	**385**	16	8	0	0	0	0	0	0	0	0	0
385	**395**	17	9	1	0	0	0	0	0	0	0	0
395	**405**	18	10	2	0	0	0	0	0	0	0	0
405	**415**	19	11	3	0	0	0	0	0	0	0	0
415	**425**	20	12	4	0	0	0	0	0	0	0	0
425	**435**	21	13	5	0	0	0	0	0	0	0	0
435	**445**	22	14	6	0	0	0	0	0	0	0	0
445	**455**	23	15	7	0	0	0	0	0	0	0	0
455	**465**	24	16	8	0	0	0	0	0	0	0	0
465	**475**	25	17	9	1	0	0	0	0	0	0	0
475	**485**	26	18	10	2	0	0	0	0	0	0	0
485	**495**	27	19	11	3	0	0	0	0	0	0	0
495	**505**	28	20	12	4	0	0	0	0	0	0	0
505	**515**	29	21	13	5	0	0	0	0	0	0	0
515	**525**	30	22	14	6	0	0	0	0	0	0	0
525	**535**	31	23	15	7	0	0	0	0	0	0	0
535	**545**	32	24	16	8	0	0	0	0	0	0	0
545	**555**	33	25	17	9	1	0	0	0	0	0	0
555	**565**	34	26	18	10	2	0	0	0	0	0	0
565	**575**	35	27	19	11	3	0	0	0	0	0	0
575	**585**	36	28	20	12	4	0	0	0	0	0	0
585	**595**	37	29	21	13	5	0	0	0	0	0	0
595	**605**	38	30	22	14	6	0	0	0	0	0	0
605	**615**	39	31	23	15	7	0	0	0	0	0	0
615	**625**	40	32	24	16	8	0	0	0	0	0	0
625	**635**	42	33	25	17	9	1	0	0	0	0	0
635	**645**	43	34	26	18	10	2	0	0	0	0	0
645	**655**	44	35	27	19	11	3	0	0	0	0	0
655	**665**	45	36	28	20	12	4	0	0	0	0	0
665	**675**	46	37	29	21	13	5	0	0	0	0	0
675	**685**	48	38	30	22	14	6	0	0	0	0	0
685	**695**	49	39	31	23	15	7	0	0	0	0	0
695	**705**	50	40	32	24	16	8	0	0	0	0	0
705	**715**	51	42	33	25	17	9	1	0	0	0	0
715	**725**	52	43	34	26	18	10	2	0	0	0	0
725	**735**	54	44	35	27	19	11	3	0	0	0	0
735	**745**	55	45	36	28	20	12	4	0	0	0	0
745	**755**	56	46	37	29	21	13	5	0	0	0	0
755	**765**	57	48	38	30	22	14	6	0	0	0	0
765	**775**	58	49	39	31	23	15	7	0	0	0	0
775	**785**	60	50	40	32	24	16	8	0	0	0	0
785	**795**	61	51	42	33	25	17	9	1	0	0	0
795	**805**	62	52	43	34	26	18	10	2	0	0	0
805	**815**	63	54	44	35	27	19	11	3	0	0	0
815	**825**	64	55	45	36	28	20	12	4	0	0	0
825	**835**	66	56	46	37	29	21	13	5	0	0	0
835	**845**	67	57	48	38	30	22	14	6	0	0	0
845	**855**	68	58	49	39	31	23	15	7	0	0	0
855	**865**	69	60	50	40	32	24	16	8	0	0	0
865	**875**	70	61	51	42	33	25	17	9	1	0	0
875	**885**	72	62	52	43	34	26	18	10	2	0	0
885	**895**	73	63	54	44	35	27	19	11	3	0	0
895	**905**	74	64	55	45	36	28	20	12	4	0	0
905	**915**	75	66	56	46	37	29	21	13	5	0	0

Wage Bracket Method Tables for Income Tax Withholding

MARRIED Persons—**WEEKLY** Payroll Period

(For Wages Paid through December 31, 2018)

And the wages are–		And the number of withholding allowances claimed is—										
At least	But less than	0	1	2	3	4	5	6	7	8	9	10
		The amount of income tax to be withheld is—										
$915	**$925**	$76	$67	$57	$48	$38	$30	$22	$14	$6	$0	$0
925	**935**	78	68	58	49	39	31	23	15	7	0	0
935	**945**	79	69	60	50	41	32	24	16	8	0	0
945	**955**	80	70	61	51	42	33	25	17	9	1	0
955	**965**	81	72	62	52	43	34	26	18	10	2	0
965	**975**	82	73	63	54	44	35	27	19	11	3	0
975	**985**	84	74	64	55	45	36	28	20	12	4	0
985	**995**	85	75	66	56	47	37	29	21	13	5	0
995	**1,005**	86	76	67	57	48	38	30	22	14	6	0
1,005	**1,015**	87	78	68	58	49	39	31	23	15	7	0
1,015	**1,025**	88	79	69	60	50	41	32	24	16	8	0
1,025	**1,035**	90	80	70	61	51	42	33	25	17	9	1
1,035	**1,045**	91	81	72	62	53	43	34	26	18	10	2
1,045	**1,055**	92	82	73	63	54	44	35	27	19	11	3
1,055	**1,065**	93	84	74	64	55	45	36	28	20	12	4
1,065	**1,075**	94	85	75	66	56	47	37	29	21	13	5
1,075	**1,085**	96	86	76	67	57	48	38	30	22	14	6
1,085	**1,095**	97	87	78	68	59	49	39	31	23	15	7
1,095	**1,105**	98	88	79	69	60	50	41	32	24	16	8
1,105	**1,115**	99	90	80	70	61	51	42	33	25	17	9
1,115	**1,125**	100	91	81	72	62	53	43	34	26	18	10
1,125	**1,135**	102	92	82	73	63	54	44	35	27	19	11
1,135	**1,145**	103	93	84	74	65	55	45	36	28	20	12
1,145	**1,155**	104	94	85	75	66	56	47	37	29	21	13
1,155	**1,165**	105	96	86	76	67	57	48	38	30	22	14
1,165	**1,175**	106	97	87	78	68	59	49	39	31	23	15
1,175	**1,185**	108	98	88	79	69	60	50	41	32	24	16
1,185	**1,195**	109	99	90	80	71	61	51	42	33	25	17
1,195	**1,205**	110	100	91	81	72	62	53	43	34	26	18
1,205	**1,215**	111	102	92	82	73	63	54	44	35	27	19
1,215	**1,225**	112	103	93	84	74	65	55	45	36	28	20
1,225	**1,235**	114	104	94	85	75	66	56	47	37	29	21
1,235	**1,245**	115	105	96	86	77	67	57	48	38	30	22
1,245	**1,255**	116	106	97	87	78	68	59	49	39	31	23
1,255	**1,265**	117	108	98	88	79	69	60	50	41	32	24
1,265	**1,275**	118	109	99	90	80	71	61	51	42	33	25
1,275	**1,285**	120	110	100	91	81	72	62	53	43	34	26
1,285	**1,295**	121	111	102	92	83	73	63	54	44	35	27
1,295	**1,305**	122	112	103	93	84	74	65	55	45	36	28
1,305	**1,315**	123	114	104	94	85	75	66	56	47	37	29
1,315	**1,325**	124	115	105	96	86	77	67	57	48	38	30
1,325	**1,335**	126	116	106	97	87	78	68	59	49	39	31
1,335	**1,345**	127	117	108	98	89	79	69	60	50	41	32
1,345	**1,355**	128	118	109	99	90	80	71	61	51	42	33
1,355	**1,365**	129	120	110	100	91	81	72	62	53	43	34
1,365	**1,375**	130	121	111	102	92	83	73	63	54	44	35
1,375	**1,385**	132	122	112	103	93	84	74	65	55	45	36
1,385	**1,395**	133	123	114	104	95	85	75	66	56	47	37
1,395	**1,405**	134	124	115	105	96	86	77	67	57	48	38
1,405	**1,415**	135	126	116	106	97	87	78	68	59	49	39
1,415	**1,425**	136	127	117	108	98	89	79	69	60	50	41
1,425	**1,435**	138	128	118	109	99	90	80	71	61	51	42
1,435	**1,445**	139	129	120	110	101	91	81	72	62	53	43
1,445	**1,455**	140	130	121	111	102	92	83	73	63	54	44
1,455	**1,465**	141	132	122	112	103	93	84	74	65	55	45
1,465	**1,475**	142	133	123	114	104	95	85	75	66	56	47
1,475	**1,485**	144	134	124	115	105	96	86	77	67	57	48
1,485	**1,495**	145	135	126	116	107	97	87	78	68	59	49
1,495	**1,505**	146	136	127	117	108	98	89	79	69	60	50
1,505	**1,515**	147	138	128	118	109	99	90	80	71	61	51
1,515	**1,525**	148	139	129	120	110	101	91	81	72	62	53
1,525	**1,535**	150	140	130	121	111	102	92	83	73	63	54
1,535	**1,545**	151	141	132	122	113	103	93	84	74	65	55
1,545	**1,555**	152	142	133	123	114	104	95	85	75	66	56
1,555	**1,565**	153	144	134	124	115	105	96	86	77	67	57
1,565	**1,575**	154	145	135	126	116	107	97	87	78	68	59
$1,575 and over		Use Table 1(b) for a MARRIED person on page 46. Also see the instructions on page 44.										

Wage Bracket Method Tables for Income Tax Withholding

SINGLE Persons—BIWEEKLY Payroll Period

(For Wages Paid through December 31, 2018)

And the wages are–		And the number of withholding allowances claimed is—										
At least	But less than	0	1	2	3	4	5	6	7	8	9	10
		The amount of income tax to be withheld is—										
$ 0	**$145**	$0	$0	$0	$0	$0	$0	$0	$0	$0	$0	$0
145	**150**	1	0	0	0	0	0	0	0	0	0	0
150	**155**	1	0	0	0	0	0	0	0	0	0	0
155	**160**	2	0	0	0	0	0	0	0	0	0	0
160	**165**	2	0	0	0	0	0	0	0	0	0	0
165	**170**	3	0	0	0	0	0	0	0	0	0	0
170	**175**	3	0	0	0	0	0	0	0	0	0	0
175	**180**	4	0	0	0	0	0	0	0	0	0	0
180	**185**	4	0	0	0	0	0	0	0	0	0	0
185	**190**	5	0	0	0	0	0	0	0	0	0	0
190	**195**	5	0	0	0	0	0	0	0	0	0	0
195	**200**	6	0	0	0	0	0	0	0	0	0	0
200	**205**	6	0	0	0	0	0	0	0	0	0	0
205	**210**	7	0	0	0	0	0	0	0	0	0	0
210	**215**	7	0	0	0	0	0	0	0	0	0	0
215	**220**	8	0	0	0	0	0	0	0	0	0	0
220	**225**	8	0	0	0	0	0	0	0	0	0	0
225	**230**	9	0	0	0	0	0	0	0	0	0	0
230	**235**	9	0	0	0	0	0	0	0	0	0	0
235	**240**	10	0	0	0	0	0	0	0	0	0	0
240	**245**	10	0	0	0	0	0	0	0	0	0	0
245	**250**	11	0	0	0	0	0	0	0	0	0	0
250	**260**	11	0	0	0	0	0	0	0	0	0	0
260	**270**	12	0	0	0	0	0	0	0	0	0	0
270	**280**	13	0	0	0	0	0	0	0	0	0	0
280	**290**	14	0	0	0	0	0	0	0	0	0	0
290	**300**	15	0	0	0	0	0	0	0	0	0	0
300	**310**	16	0	0	0	0	0	0	0	0	0	0
310	**320**	17	1	0	0	0	0	0	0	0	0	0
320	**330**	18	2	0	0	0	0	0	0	0	0	0
330	**340**	19	3	0	0	0	0	0	0	0	0	0
340	**350**	20	4	0	0	0	0	0	0	0	0	0
350	**360**	21	5	0	0	0	0	0	0	0	0	0
360	**370**	22	6	0	0	0	0	0	0	0	0	0
370	**380**	23	7	0	0	0	0	0	0	0	0	0
380	**390**	24	8	0	0	0	0	0	0	0	0	0
390	**400**	25	9	0	0	0	0	0	0	0	0	0
400	**410**	26	10	0	0	0	0	0	0	0	0	0
410	**420**	27	11	0	0	0	0	0	0	0	0	0
420	**430**	28	12	0	0	0	0	0	0	0	0	0
430	**440**	29	13	0	0	0	0	0	0	0	0	0
440	**450**	30	14	0	0	0	0	0	0	0	0	0
450	**460**	31	15	0	0	0	0	0	0	0	0	0
460	**470**	32	16	0	0	0	0	0	0	0	0	0
470	**480**	33	17	1	0	0	0	0	0	0	0	0
480	**490**	34	18	2	0	0	0	0	0	0	0	0
490	**500**	35	19	3	0	0	0	0	0	0	0	0
500	**520**	37	21	5	0	0	0	0	0	0	0	0
520	**540**	39	23	7	0	0	0	0	0	0	0	0
540	**560**	42	25	9	0	0	0	0	0	0	0	0
560	**580**	44	27	11	0	0	0	0	0	0	0	0
580	**600**	46	29	13	0	0	0	0	0	0	0	0
600	**620**	49	31	15	0	0	0	0	0	0	0	0
620	**640**	51	33	17	1	0	0	0	0	0	0	0
640	**660**	54	35	19	3	0	0	0	0	0	0	0
660	**680**	56	37	21	5	0	0	0	0	0	0	0
680	**700**	58	39	23	7	0	0	0	0	0	0	0
700	**720**	61	42	25	9	0	0	0	0	0	0	0
720	**740**	63	44	27	11	0	0	0	0	0	0	0
740	**760**	66	46	29	13	0	0	0	0	0	0	0
760	**780**	68	49	31	15	0	0	0	0	0	0	0
780	**800**	70	51	33	17	1	0	0	0	0	0	0
800	**820**	73	54	35	19	3	0	0	0	0	0	0
820	**840**	75	56	37	21	5	0	0	0	0	0	0
840	**860**	78	58	39	23	7	0	0	0	0	0	0
860	**880**	80	61	42	25	9	0	0	0	0	0	0
880	**900**	82	63	44	27	11	0	0	0	0	0	0
900	**920**	85	66	46	29	13	0	0	0	0	0	0
920	**940**	87	68	49	31	15	0	0	0	0	0	0
940	**960**	90	70	51	33	17	1	0	0	0	0	0

Wage Bracket Method Tables for Income Tax Withholding

SINGLE Persons—**BIWEEKLY** Payroll Period

(For Wages Paid through December 31, 2018)

And the wages are–		And the number of withholding allowances claimed is—										
At least	But less than	0	1	2	3	4	5	6	7	8	9	10
		The amount of income tax to be withheld is—										
$960	**$980**	$92	$73	$54	$35	$19	$3	$0	$0	$0	$0	$0
980	**1,000**	94	75	56	37	21	5	0	0	0	0	0
1,000	**1,020**	97	78	58	39	23	7	0	0	0	0	0
1,020	**1,040**	99	80	61	42	25	9	0	0	0	0	0
1,040	**1,060**	102	82	63	44	27	11	0	0	0	0	0
1,060	**1,080**	104	85	66	47	29	13	0	0	0	0	0
1,080	**1,100**	106	87	68	49	31	15	0	0	0	0	0
1,100	**1,120**	109	90	70	51	33	17	1	0	0	0	0
1,120	**1,140**	111	92	73	54	35	19	3	0	0	0	0
1,140	**1,160**	114	94	75	56	37	21	5	0	0	0	0
1,160	**1,180**	116	97	78	59	39	23	7	0	0	0	0
1,180	**1,200**	118	99	80	61	42	25	9	0	0	0	0
1,200	**1,220**	121	102	82	63	44	27	11	0	0	0	0
1,220	**1,240**	123	104	85	66	47	29	13	0	0	0	0
1,240	**1,260**	126	106	87	68	49	31	15	0	0	0	0
1,260	**1,280**	128	109	90	71	51	33	17	1	0	0	0
1,280	**1,300**	130	111	92	73	54	35	19	3	0	0	0
1,300	**1,320**	133	114	94	75	56	37	21	5	0	0	0
1,320	**1,340**	135	116	97	78	59	39	23	7	0	0	0
1,340	**1,360**	138	118	99	80	61	42	25	9	0	0	0
1,360	**1,380**	140	121	102	83	63	44	27	11	0	0	0
1,380	**1,400**	142	123	104	85	66	47	29	13	0	0	0
1,400	**1,420**	145	126	106	87	68	49	31	15	0	0	0
1,420	**1,440**	147	128	109	90	71	51	33	17	1	0	0
1,440	**1,460**	150	130	111	92	73	54	35	19	3	0	0
1,460	**1,480**	152	133	114	95	75	56	37	21	5	0	0
1,480	**1,500**	154	135	116	97	78	59	39	23	7	0	0
1,500	**1,520**	157	138	118	99	80	61	42	25	9	0	0
1,520	**1,540**	159	140	121	102	83	63	44	27	11	0	0
1,540	**1,560**	162	142	123	104	85	66	47	29	13	0	0
1,560	**1,580**	164	145	126	107	87	68	49	31	15	0	0
1,580	**1,600**	166	147	128	109	90	71	51	33	17	1	0
1,600	**1,620**	169	150	130	111	92	73	54	35	19	3	0
1,620	**1,640**	171	152	133	114	95	75	56	37	21	5	0
1,640	**1,660**	176	154	135	116	97	78	59	40	23	7	0
1,660	**1,680**	180	157	138	119	99	80	61	42	25	9	0
1,680	**1,700**	184	159	140	121	102	83	63	44	27	11	0
1,700	**1,720**	189	162	142	123	104	85	66	47	29	13	0
1,720	**1,740**	193	164	145	126	107	87	68	49	31	15	0
1,740	**1,760**	198	166	147	128	109	90	71	52	33	17	1
1,760	**1,780**	202	169	150	131	111	92	73	54	35	19	3
1,780	**1,800**	206	171	152	133	114	95	75	56	37	21	5
1,800	**1,820**	211	176	154	135	116	97	78	59	40	23	7
1,820	**1,840**	215	180	157	138	119	99	80	61	42	25	9
1,840	**1,860**	220	184	159	140	121	102	83	64	44	27	11
1,860	**1,880**	224	189	162	143	123	104	85	66	47	29	13
1,880	**1,900**	228	193	164	145	126	107	87	68	49	31	15
1,900	**1,920**	233	198	166	147	128	109	90	71	52	33	17
1,920	**1,940**	237	202	169	150	131	111	92	73	54	35	19
1,940	**1,960**	242	206	171	152	133	114	95	76	56	37	21
1,960	**1,980**	246	211	176	155	135	116	97	78	59	40	23
1,980	**2,000**	250	215	180	157	138	119	99	80	61	42	25
2,000	**2,020**	255	220	184	159	140	121	102	83	64	44	27
2,020	**2,040**	259	224	189	162	143	123	104	85	66	47	29
2,040	**2,060**	264	228	193	164	145	126	107	88	68	49	31
2,060	**2,080**	268	233	198	167	147	128	109	90	71	52	33
2,080	**2,100**	272	237	202	169	150	131	111	92	73	54	35
2,100	**2,120**	277	242	206	171	152	133	114	95	76	56	37
2,120	**2,140**	281	246	211	176	155	135	116	97	78	59	40
2,140	**2,160**	286	250	215	180	157	138	119	100	80	61	42
2,160	**2,180**	290	255	220	185	159	140	121	102	83	64	44
2,180	**2,200**	294	259	224	189	162	143	123	104	85	66	47
2,200	**2,220**	299	264	228	193	164	145	126	107	88	68	49
2,220	**2,240**	303	268	233	198	167	147	128	109	90	71	52
2,240	**2,260**	308	272	237	202	169	150	131	112	92	73	54

$2,260 and over — Use Table 2(a) for a SINGLE person on page 46. Also see the instructions on page 44.

Wage Bracket Method Tables for Income Tax Withholding

MARRIED Persons—**BIWEEKLY** Payroll Period

(For Wages Paid through December 31, 2018)

And the wages are–		And the number of withholding allowances claimed is—										
At least	But less than	0	1	2	3	4	5	6	7	8	9	10
		The amount of income tax to be withheld is—										
$ 0	$445	$0	$0	$0	$0	$0	$0	$0	$0	$0	$0	$0
445	455	1	0	0	0	0	0	0	0	0	0	0
455	465	2	0	0	0	0	0	0	0	0	0	0
465	475	3	0	0	0	0	0	0	0	0	0	0
475	485	4	0	0	0	0	0	0	0	0	0	0
485	495	5	0	0	0	0	0	0	0	0	0	0
495	505	6	0	0	0	0	0	0	0	0	0	0
505	525	7	0	0	0	0	0	0	0	0	0	0
525	545	9	0	0	0	0	0	0	0	0	0	0
545	565	11	0	0	0	0	0	0	0	0	0	0
565	585	13	0	0	0	0	0	0	0	0	0	0
585	605	15	0	0	0	0	0	0	0	0	0	0
605	625	17	1	0	0	0	0	0	0	0	0	0
625	645	19	3	0	0	0	0	0	0	0	0	0
645	665	21	5	0	0	0	0	0	0	0	0	0
665	685	23	7	0	0	0	0	0	0	0	0	0
685	705	25	9	0	0	0	0	0	0	0	0	0
705	725	27	11	0	0	0	0	0	0	0	0	0
725	745	29	13	0	0	0	0	0	0	0	0	0
745	765	31	15	0	0	0	0	0	0	0	0	0
765	785	33	17	1	0	0	0	0	0	0	0	0
785	805	35	19	3	0	0	0	0	0	0	0	0
805	825	37	21	5	0	0	0	0	0	0	0	0
825	845	39	23	7	0	0	0	0	0	0	0	0
845	865	41	25	9	0	0	0	0	0	0	0	0
865	885	43	27	11	0	0	0	0	0	0	0	0
885	905	45	29	13	0	0	0	0	0	0	0	0
905	925	47	31	15	0	0	0	0	0	0	0	0
925	945	49	33	17	1	0	0	0	0	0	0	0
945	965	51	35	19	3	0	0	0	0	0	0	0
965	985	53	37	21	5	0	0	0	0	0	0	0
985	1,005	55	39	23	7	0	0	0	0	0	0	0
1,005	1,025	57	41	25	9	0	0	0	0	0	0	0
1,025	1,045	59	43	27	11	0	0	0	0	0	0	0
1,045	1,065	61	45	29	13	0	0	0	0	0	0	0
1,065	1,085	63	47	31	15	0	0	0	0	0	0	0
1,085	1,105	65	49	33	17	1	0	0	0	0	0	0
1,105	1,125	67	51	35	19	3	0	0	0	0	0	0
1,125	1,145	69	53	37	21	5	0	0	0	0	0	0
1,145	1,165	71	55	39	23	7	0	0	0	0	0	0
1,165	1,185	73	57	41	25	9	0	0	0	0	0	0
1,185	1,205	75	59	43	27	11	0	0	0	0	0	0
1,205	1,225	78	61	45	29	13	0	0	0	0	0	0
1,225	1,245	80	63	47	31	15	0	0	0	0	0	0
1,245	1,265	83	65	49	33	17	1	0	0	0	0	0
1,265	1,285	85	67	51	35	19	3	0	0	0	0	0
1,285	1,305	87	69	53	37	21	5	0	0	0	0	0
1,305	1,325	90	71	55	39	23	7	0	0	0	0	0
1,325	1,345	92	73	57	41	25	9	0	0	0	0	0
1,345	1,365	95	75	59	43	27	11	0	0	0	0	0
1,365	1,385	97	78	61	45	29	13	0	0	0	0	0
1,385	1,405	99	80	63	47	31	15	0	0	0	0	0
1,405	1,425	102	83	65	49	33	17	1	0	0	0	0
1,425	1,445	104	85	67	51	35	19	3	0	0	0	0
1,445	1,465	107	87	69	53	37	21	5	0	0	0	0
1,465	1,485	109	90	71	55	39	23	7	0	0	0	0
1,485	1,505	111	92	73	57	41	25	9	0	0	0	0
1,505	1,525	114	95	76	59	43	27	11	0	0	0	0
1,525	1,545	116	97	78	61	45	29	13	0	0	0	0
1,545	1,565	119	99	80	63	47	31	15	0	0	0	0
1,565	1,585	121	102	83	65	49	33	17	1	0	0	0
1,585	1,605	123	104	85	67	51	35	19	3	0	0	0
1,605	1,625	126	107	88	69	53	37	21	5	0	0	0
1,625	1,645	128	109	90	71	55	39	23	7	0	0	0
1,645	1,665	131	111	92	73	57	41	25	9	0	0	0
1,665	1,685	133	114	95	76	59	43	27	11	0	0	0
1,685	1,705	135	116	97	78	61	45	29	13	0	0	0
1,705	1,725	138	119	100	80	63	47	31	15	0	0	0
1,725	1,745	140	121	102	83	65	49	33	17	1	0	0
1,745	1,765	143	123	104	85	67	51	35	19	3	0	0

Wage Bracket Method Tables for Income Tax Withholding

MARRIED Persons—**BIWEEKLY** Payroll Period

(For Wages Paid through December 31, 2018)

And the wages are–		And the number of withholding allowances claimed is—										
At least	But less than	0	1	2	3	4	5	6	7	8	9	10
		The amount of income tax to be withheld is—										
$1,765	**$1,785**	$145	$126	$107	$88	$69	$53	$37	$21	$5	$0	$0
1,785	**1,805**	147	128	109	90	71	55	39	23	7	0	0
1,805	**1,825**	150	131	112	92	73	57	41	25	9	0	0
1,825	**1,845**	152	133	114	95	76	59	43	27	11	0	0
1,845	**1,865**	155	135	116	97	78	61	45	29	13	0	0
1,865	**1,885**	157	138	119	100	80	63	47	31	15	0	0
1,885	**1,905**	159	140	121	102	83	65	49	33	17	1	0
1,905	**1,925**	162	143	124	104	85	67	51	35	19	3	0
1,925	**1,945**	164	145	126	107	88	69	53	37	21	5	0
1,945	**1,965**	167	147	128	109	90	71	55	39	23	7	0
1,965	**1,985**	169	150	131	112	92	73	57	41	25	9	0
1,985	**2,005**	171	152	133	114	95	76	59	43	27	11	0
2,005	**2,025**	174	155	136	116	97	78	61	45	29	13	0
2,025	**2,045**	176	157	138	119	100	80	63	47	31	15	0
2,045	**2,065**	179	159	140	121	102	83	65	49	33	17	1
2,065	**2,085**	181	162	143	124	104	85	67	51	35	19	3
2,085	**2,105**	183	164	145	126	107	88	69	53	37	21	5
2,105	**2,125**	186	167	148	128	109	90	71	55	39	23	7
2,125	**2,145**	188	169	150	131	112	92	73	57	41	25	9
2,145	**2,165**	191	171	152	133	114	95	76	59	43	27	11
2,165	**2,185**	193	174	155	136	116	97	78	61	45	29	13
2,185	**2,205**	195	176	157	138	119	100	81	63	47	31	15
2,205	**2,225**	198	179	160	140	121	102	83	65	49	33	17
2,225	**2,245**	200	181	162	143	124	104	85	67	51	35	19
2,245	**2,265**	203	183	164	145	126	107	88	69	53	37	21
2,265	**2,285**	205	186	167	148	128	109	90	71	55	39	23
2,285	**2,305**	207	188	169	150	131	112	93	73	57	41	25
2,305	**2,325**	210	191	172	152	133	114	95	76	59	43	27
2,325	**2,345**	212	193	174	155	136	116	97	78	61	45	29
2,345	**2,365**	215	195	176	157	138	119	100	81	63	47	31
2,365	**2,385**	217	198	179	160	140	121	102	83	65	49	33
2,385	**2,405**	219	200	181	162	143	124	105	85	67	51	35
2,405	**2,425**	222	203	184	164	145	126	107	88	69	53	37
2,425	**2,445**	224	205	186	167	148	128	109	90	71	55	39
2,445	**2,465**	227	207	188	169	150	131	112	93	73	57	41
2,465	**2,485**	229	210	191	172	152	133	114	95	76	59	43
2,485	**2,505**	231	212	193	174	155	136	117	97	78	61	45
2,505	**2,525**	234	215	196	176	157	138	119	100	81	63	47
2,525	**2,545**	236	217	198	179	160	140	121	102	83	65	49
2,545	**2,565**	239	219	200	181	162	143	124	105	85	67	51
2,565	**2,585**	241	222	203	184	164	145	126	107	88	69	53
2,585	**2,605**	243	224	205	186	167	148	129	109	90	71	55
2,605	**2,625**	246	227	208	188	169	150	131	112	93	73	57
2,625	**2,645**	248	229	210	191	172	152	133	114	95	76	59
2,645	**2,665**	251	231	212	193	174	155	136	117	97	78	61
2,665	**2,685**	253	234	215	196	176	157	138	119	100	81	63
2,685	**2,705**	255	236	217	198	179	160	141	121	102	83	65
2,705	**2,725**	258	239	220	200	181	162	143	124	105	85	67
2,725	**2,745**	260	241	222	203	184	164	145	126	107	88	69
2,745	**2,765**	263	243	224	205	186	167	148	129	109	90	71
2,765	**2,785**	265	246	227	208	188	169	150	131	112	93	74
2,785	**2,805**	267	248	229	210	191	172	153	133	114	95	76
2,805	**2,825**	270	251	232	212	193	174	155	136	117	97	78
2,825	**2,845**	272	253	234	215	196	176	157	138	119	100	81
2,845	**2,865**	275	255	236	217	198	179	160	141	121	102	83
2,865	**2,885**	277	258	239	220	200	181	162	143	124	105	86
2,885	**2,905**	279	260	241	222	203	184	165	145	126	107	88
2,905	**2,925**	282	263	244	224	205	186	167	148	129	109	90
2,925	**2,945**	284	265	246	227	208	188	169	150	131	112	93
2,945	**2,965**	287	267	248	229	210	191	172	153	133	114	95
2,965	**2,985**	289	270	251	232	212	193	174	155	136	117	98
2,985	**3,005**	291	272	253	234	215	196	177	157	138	119	100
3,005	**3,025**	294	275	256	236	217	198	179	160	141	121	102
3,025	**3,045**	296	277	258	239	220	200	181	162	143	124	105
3,045	**3,065**	299	279	260	241	222	203	184	165	145	126	107
3,065	**3,085**	301	282	263	244	224	205	186	167	148	129	110
$3,085 and over		Use Table 2(b) for a MARRIED person on page 46. Also see the instructions on page 44.										

Wage Bracket Method Tables for Income Tax Withholding

SINGLE Persons—**SEMIMONTHLY** Payroll Period

(For Wages Paid through December 31, 2018)

And the wages are–		And the number of withholding allowances claimed is—										
At least	But less than	0	1	2	3	4	5	6	7	8	9	10
		The amount of income tax to be withheld is—										
$ 0	$160	$0	$0	$0	$0	$0	$0	$0	$0	$0	$0	$0
160	165	1	0	0	0	0	0	0	0	0	0	0
165	170	1	0	0	0	0	0	0	0	0	0	0
170	175	2	0	0	0	0	0	0	0	0	0	0
175	180	2	0	0	0	0	0	0	0	0	0	0
180	185	3	0	0	0	0	0	0	0	0	0	0
185	190	3	0	0	0	0	0	0	0	0	0	0
190	195	4	0	0	0	0	0	0	0	0	0	0
195	200	4	0	0	0	0	0	0	0	0	0	0
200	205	5	0	0	0	0	0	0	0	0	0	0
205	210	5	0	0	0	0	0	0	0	0	0	0
210	215	6	0	0	0	0	0	0	0	0	0	0
215	220	6	0	0	0	0	0	0	0	0	0	0
220	225	7	0	0	0	0	0	0	0	0	0	0
225	230	7	0	0	0	0	0	0	0	0	0	0
230	235	8	0	0	0	0	0	0	0	0	0	0
235	240	8	0	0	0	0	0	0	0	0	0	0
240	245	9	0	0	0	0	0	0	0	0	0	0
245	250	9	0	0	0	0	0	0	0	0	0	0
250	260	10	0	0	0	0	0	0	0	0	0	0
260	270	11	0	0	0	0	0	0	0	0	0	0
270	280	12	0	0	0	0	0	0	0	0	0	0
280	290	13	0	0	0	0	0	0	0	0	0	0
290	300	14	0	0	0	0	0	0	0	0	0	0
300	310	15	0	0	0	0	0	0	0	0	0	0
310	320	16	0	0	0	0	0	0	0	0	0	0
320	330	17	0	0	0	0	0	0	0	0	0	0
330	340	18	1	0	0	0	0	0	0	0	0	0
340	350	19	2	0	0	0	0	0	0	0	0	0
350	360	20	3	0	0	0	0	0	0	0	0	0
360	370	21	4	0	0	0	0	0	0	0	0	0
370	380	22	5	0	0	0	0	0	0	0	0	0
380	390	23	6	0	0	0	0	0	0	0	0	0
390	400	24	7	0	0	0	0	0	0	0	0	0
400	410	25	8	0	0	0	0	0	0	0	0	0
410	420	26	9	0	0	0	0	0	0	0	0	0
420	430	27	10	0	0	0	0	0	0	0	0	0
430	440	28	11	0	0	0	0	0	0	0	0	0
440	450	29	12	0	0	0	0	0	0	0	0	0
450	460	30	13	0	0	0	0	0	0	0	0	0
460	470	31	14	0	0	0	0	0	0	0	0	0
470	480	32	15	0	0	0	0	0	0	0	0	0
480	490	33	16	0	0	0	0	0	0	0	0	0
490	500	34	17	0	0	0	0	0	0	0	0	0
500	520	36	18	1	0	0	0	0	0	0	0	0
520	540	38	20	3	0	0	0	0	0	0	0	0
540	560	40	22	5	0	0	0	0	0	0	0	0
560	580	42	24	7	0	0	0	0	0	0	0	0
580	600	44	26	9	0	0	0	0	0	0	0	0
600	620	47	28	11	0	0	0	0	0	0	0	0
620	640	49	30	13	0	0	0	0	0	0	0	0
640	660	52	32	15	0	0	0	0	0	0	0	0
660	680	54	34	17	0	0	0	0	0	0	0	0
680	700	56	36	19	2	0	0	0	0	0	0	0
700	720	59	38	21	4	0	0	0	0	0	0	0
720	740	61	40	23	6	0	0	0	0	0	0	0
740	760	64	43	25	8	0	0	0	0	0	0	0
760	780	66	45	27	10	0	0	0	0	0	0	0
780	800	68	48	29	12	0	0	0	0	0	0	0
800	820	71	50	31	14	0	0	0	0	0	0	0
820	840	73	52	33	16	0	0	0	0	0	0	0
840	860	76	55	35	18	0	0	0	0	0	0	0
860	880	78	57	37	20	2	0	0	0	0	0	0
880	900	80	60	39	22	4	0	0	0	0	0	0
900	920	83	62	41	24	6	0	0	0	0	0	0
920	940	85	64	44	26	8	0	0	0	0	0	0
940	960	88	67	46	28	10	0	0	0	0	0	0
960	980	90	69	48	30	12	0	0	0	0	0	0
980	1,000	92	72	51	32	14	0	0	0	0	0	0
1,000	1,020	95	74	53	34	16	0	0	0	0	0	0

Wage Bracket Method Tables for Income Tax Withholding

SINGLE Persons—SEMIMONTHLY Payroll Period

(For Wages Paid through December 31, 2018)

And the wages are–		And the number of withholding allowances claimed is—										
At least	But less than	0	1	2	3	4	5	6	7	8	9	10
		The amount of income tax to be withheld is—										
$1,020	**$1,040**	$97	$76	$56	$36	$18	$1	$0	$0	$0	$0	$0
1,040	**1,060**	100	79	58	38	20	3	0	0	0	0	0
1,060	**1,080**	102	81	60	40	22	5	0	0	0	0	0
1,080	**1,100**	104	84	63	42	24	7	0	0	0	0	0
1,100	**1,120**	107	86	65	45	26	9	0	0	0	0	0
1,120	**1,140**	109	88	68	47	28	11	0	0	0	0	0
1,140	**1,160**	112	91	70	49	30	13	0	0	0	0	0
1,160	**1,180**	114	93	72	52	32	15	0	0	0	0	0
1,180	**1,200**	116	96	75	54	34	17	0	0	0	0	0
1,200	**1,220**	119	98	77	57	36	19	2	0	0	0	0
1,220	**1,240**	121	100	80	59	38	21	4	0	0	0	0
1,240	**1,260**	124	103	82	61	41	23	6	0	0	0	0
1,260	**1,280**	126	105	84	64	43	25	8	0	0	0	0
1,280	**1,300**	128	108	87	66	45	27	10	0	0	0	0
1,300	**1,320**	131	110	89	69	48	29	12	0	0	0	0
1,320	**1,340**	133	112	92	71	50	31	14	0	0	0	0
1,340	**1,360**	136	115	94	73	53	33	16	0	0	0	0
1,360	**1,380**	138	117	96	76	55	35	18	1	0	0	0
1,380	**1,400**	140	120	99	78	57	37	20	3	0	0	0
1,400	**1,420**	143	122	101	81	60	39	22	5	0	0	0
1,420	**1,440**	145	124	104	83	62	41	24	7	0	0	0
1,440	**1,460**	148	127	106	85	65	44	26	9	0	0	0
1,460	**1,480**	150	129	108	88	67	46	28	11	0	0	0
1,480	**1,500**	152	132	111	90	69	49	30	13	0	0	0
1,500	**1,520**	155	134	113	93	72	51	32	15	0	0	0
1,520	**1,540**	157	136	116	95	74	53	34	17	0	0	0
1,540	**1,560**	160	139	118	97	77	56	36	19	1	0	0
1,560	**1,580**	162	141	120	100	79	58	38	21	3	0	0
1,580	**1,600**	164	144	123	102	81	61	40	23	5	0	0
1,600	**1,620**	167	146	125	105	84	63	42	25	7	0	0
1,620	**1,640**	169	148	128	107	86	65	45	27	9	0	0
1,640	**1,660**	172	151	130	109	89	68	47	29	11	0	0
1,660	**1,680**	174	153	132	112	91	70	49	31	13	0	0
1,680	**1,700**	176	156	135	114	93	73	52	33	15	0	0
1,700	**1,720**	179	158	137	117	96	75	54	35	17	0	0
1,720	**1,740**	181	160	140	119	98	77	57	37	19	2	0
1,740	**1,760**	184	163	142	121	101	80	59	39	21	4	0
1,760	**1,780**	186	165	144	124	103	82	61	41	23	6	0
1,780	**1,800**	191	168	147	126	105	85	64	43	25	8	0
1,800	**1,820**	195	170	149	129	108	87	66	46	27	10	0
1,820	**1,840**	199	172	152	131	110	89	69	48	29	12	0
1,840	**1,860**	204	175	154	133	113	92	71	50	31	14	0
1,860	**1,880**	208	177	156	136	115	94	73	53	33	16	0
1,880	**1,900**	213	180	159	138	117	97	76	55	35	18	1
1,900	**1,920**	217	182	161	141	120	99	78	58	37	20	3
1,920	**1,940**	221	184	164	143	122	101	81	60	39	22	5
1,940	**1,960**	226	188	166	145	125	104	83	62	42	24	7
1,960	**1,980**	230	192	168	148	127	106	85	65	44	26	9
1,980	**2,000**	235	197	171	150	129	109	88	67	46	28	11
2,000	**2,020**	239	201	173	153	132	111	90	70	49	30	13
2,020	**2,040**	243	205	176	155	134	113	93	72	51	32	15
2,040	**2,060**	248	210	178	157	137	116	95	74	54	34	17
2,060	**2,080**	252	214	180	160	139	118	97	77	56	36	19
2,080	**2,100**	257	219	183	162	141	121	100	79	58	38	21
2,100	**2,120**	261	223	185	165	144	123	102	82	61	40	23
2,120	**2,140**	265	227	189	167	146	125	105	84	63	42	25
2,140	**2,160**	270	232	194	169	149	128	107	86	66	45	27
2,160	**2,180**	274	236	198	172	151	130	109	89	68	47	29
2,180	**2,200**	279	241	203	174	153	133	112	91	70	50	31
2,200	**2,220**	283	245	207	177	156	135	114	94	73	52	33
2,220	**2,240**	287	249	211	179	158	137	117	96	75	54	35
2,240	**2,260**	292	254	216	181	161	140	119	98	78	57	37
2,260	**2,280**	296	258	220	184	163	142	121	101	80	59	39
2,280	**2,300**	301	263	225	187	165	145	124	103	82	62	41
2,300	**2,320**	305	267	229	191	168	147	126	106	85	64	43
$2,320 and over		Use Table 3(a) for a SINGLE person on page 46. Also see the instructions on page 44.										

Wage Bracket Method Tables for Income Tax Withholding

MARRIED Persons—**SEMIMONTHLY** Payroll Period

(For Wages Paid through December 31, 2018)

And the wages are–		And the number of withholding allowances claimed is—										
At least	But less than	0	1	2	3	4	5	6	7	8	9	10
		The amount of income tax to be withheld is—										
$ 0	$485	$0	$0	$0	$0	$0	$0	$0	$0	$0	$0	$0
485	495	1	0	0	0	0	0	0	0	0	0	0
495	505	2	0	0	0	0	0	0	0	0	0	0
505	525	3	0	0	0	0	0	0	0	0	0	0
525	545	5	0	0	0	0	0	0	0	0	0	0
545	565	7	0	0	0	0	0	0	0	0	0	0
565	585	9	0	0	0	0	0	0	0	0	0	0
585	605	11	0	0	0	0	0	0	0	0	0	0
605	625	13	0	0	0	0	0	0	0	0	0	0
625	645	15	0	0	0	0	0	0	0	0	0	0
645	665	17	0	0	0	0	0	0	0	0	0	0
665	685	19	2	0	0	0	0	0	0	0	0	0
685	705	21	4	0	0	0	0	0	0	0	0	0
705	725	23	6	0	0	0	0	0	0	0	0	0
725	745	25	8	0	0	0	0	0	0	0	0	0
745	765	27	10	0	0	0	0	0	0	0	0	0
765	785	29	12	0	0	0	0	0	0	0	0	0
785	805	31	14	0	0	0	0	0	0	0	0	0
805	825	33	16	0	0	0	0	0	0	0	0	0
825	845	35	18	1	0	0	0	0	0	0	0	0
845	865	37	20	3	0	0	0	0	0	0	0	0
865	885	39	22	5	0	0	0	0	0	0	0	0
885	905	41	24	7	0	0	0	0	0	0	0	0
905	925	43	26	9	0	0	0	0	0	0	0	0
925	945	45	28	11	0	0	0	0	0	0	0	0
945	965	47	30	13	0	0	0	0	0	0	0	0
965	985	49	32	15	0	0	0	0	0	0	0	0
985	1,005	51	34	17	0	0	0	0	0	0	0	0
1,005	1,025	53	36	19	2	0	0	0	0	0	0	0
1,025	1,045	55	38	21	4	0	0	0	0	0	0	0
1,045	1,065	57	40	23	6	0	0	0	0	0	0	0
1,065	1,085	59	42	25	8	0	0	0	0	0	0	0
1,085	1,105	61	44	27	10	0	0	0	0	0	0	0
1,105	1,125	63	46	29	12	0	0	0	0	0	0	0
1,125	1,145	65	48	31	14	0	0	0	0	0	0	0
1,145	1,165	67	50	33	16	0	0	0	0	0	0	0
1,165	1,185	69	52	35	18	0	0	0	0	0	0	0
1,185	1,205	71	54	37	20	2	0	0	0	0	0	0
1,205	1,225	73	56	39	22	4	0	0	0	0	0	0
1,225	1,245	75	58	41	24	6	0	0	0	0	0	0
1,245	1,265	77	60	43	26	8	0	0	0	0	0	0
1,265	1,285	79	62	45	28	10	0	0	0	0	0	0
1,285	1,305	82	64	47	30	12	0	0	0	0	0	0
1,305	1,325	84	66	49	32	14	0	0	0	0	0	0
1,325	1,345	87	68	51	34	16	0	0	0	0	0	0
1,345	1,365	89	70	53	36	18	1	0	0	0	0	0
1,365	1,385	91	72	55	38	20	3	0	0	0	0	0
1,385	1,405	94	74	57	40	22	5	0	0	0	0	0
1,405	1,425	96	76	59	42	24	7	0	0	0	0	0
1,425	1,445	99	78	61	44	26	9	0	0	0	0	0
1,445	1,465	101	80	63	46	28	11	0	0	0	0	0
1,465	1,485	103	83	65	48	30	13	0	0	0	0	0
1,485	1,505	106	85	67	50	32	15	0	0	0	0	0
1,505	1,525	108	87	69	52	34	17	0	0	0	0	0
1,525	1,545	111	90	71	54	36	19	2	0	0	0	0
1,545	1,565	113	92	73	56	38	21	4	0	0	0	0
1,565	1,585	115	95	75	58	40	23	6	0	0	0	0
1,585	1,605	118	97	77	60	42	25	8	0	0	0	0
1,605	1,625	120	99	79	62	44	27	10	0	0	0	0
1,625	1,645	123	102	81	64	46	29	12	0	0	0	0
1,645	1,665	125	104	83	66	48	31	14	0	0	0	0
1,665	1,685	127	107	86	68	50	33	16	0	0	0	0
1,685	1,705	130	109	88	70	52	35	18	0	0	0	0
1,705	1,725	132	111	91	72	54	37	20	2	0	0	0
1,725	1,745	135	114	93	74	56	39	22	4	0	0	0
1,745	1,765	137	116	95	76	58	41	24	6	0	0	0
1,765	1,785	139	119	98	78	60	43	26	8	0	0	0
1,785	1,805	142	121	100	80	62	45	28	10	0	0	0
1,805	1,825	144	123	103	82	64	47	30	12	0	0	0
1,825	1,845	147	126	105	84	66	49	32	14	0	0	0

Wage Bracket Method Tables for Income Tax Withholding

MARRIED Persons—**SEMIMONTHLY** Payroll Period

(For Wages Paid through December 31, 2018)

And the wages are–		And the number of withholding allowances claimed is—										
At least	But less than	0	1	2	3	4	5	6	7	8	9	10
		The amount of income tax to be withheld is—										
$1,845	**$1,865**	$149	$128	$107	$87	$68	$51	$34	$16	$0	$0	$0
1,865	**1,885**	151	131	110	89	70	53	36	18	1	0	0
1,885	**1,905**	154	133	112	92	72	55	38	20	3	0	0
1,905	**1,925**	156	135	115	94	74	57	40	22	5	0	0
1,925	**1,945**	159	138	117	96	76	59	42	24	7	0	0
1,945	**1,965**	161	140	119	99	78	61	44	26	9	0	0
1,965	**1,985**	163	143	122	101	80	63	46	28	11	0	0
1,985	**2,005**	166	145	124	104	83	65	48	30	13	0	0
2,005	**2,025**	168	147	127	106	85	67	50	32	15	0	0
2,025	**2,045**	171	150	129	108	88	69	52	34	17	0	0
2,045	**2,065**	173	152	131	111	90	71	54	36	19	2	0
2,065	**2,085**	175	155	134	113	92	73	56	38	21	4	0
2,085	**2,105**	178	157	136	116	95	75	58	40	23	6	0
2,105	**2,125**	180	159	139	118	97	77	60	42	25	8	0
2,125	**2,145**	183	162	141	120	100	79	62	44	27	10	0
2,145	**2,165**	185	164	143	123	102	81	64	46	29	12	0
2,165	**2,185**	187	167	146	125	104	84	66	48	31	14	0
2,185	**2,205**	190	169	148	128	107	86	68	50	33	16	0
2,205	**2,225**	192	171	151	130	109	88	70	52	35	18	0
2,225	**2,245**	195	174	153	132	112	91	72	54	37	20	2
2,245	**2,265**	197	176	155	135	114	93	74	56	39	22	4
2,265	**2,285**	199	179	158	137	116	96	76	58	41	24	6
2,285	**2,305**	202	181	160	140	119	98	78	60	43	26	8
2,305	**2,325**	204	183	163	142	121	100	80	62	45	28	10
2,325	**2,345**	207	186	165	144	124	103	82	64	47	30	12
2,345	**2,365**	209	188	167	147	126	105	84	66	49	32	14
2,365	**2,385**	211	191	170	149	128	108	87	68	51	34	16
2,385	**2,405**	214	193	172	152	131	110	89	70	53	36	18
2,405	**2,425**	216	195	175	154	133	112	92	72	55	38	20
2,425	**2,445**	219	198	177	156	136	115	94	74	57	40	22
2,445	**2,465**	221	200	179	159	138	117	96	76	59	42	24
2,465	**2,485**	223	203	182	161	140	120	99	78	61	44	26
2,485	**2,505**	226	205	184	164	143	122	101	81	63	46	28
2,505	**2,525**	228	207	187	166	145	124	104	83	65	48	30
2,525	**2,545**	231	210	189	168	148	127	106	85	67	50	32
2,545	**2,565**	233	212	191	171	150	129	108	88	69	52	34
2,565	**2,585**	235	215	194	173	152	132	111	90	71	54	36
2,585	**2,605**	238	217	196	176	155	134	113	93	73	56	38
2,605	**2,625**	240	219	199	178	157	136	116	95	75	58	40
2,625	**2,645**	243	222	201	180	160	139	118	97	77	60	42
2,645	**2,665**	245	224	203	183	162	141	120	100	79	62	44
2,665	**2,685**	247	227	206	185	164	144	123	102	81	64	46
2,685	**2,705**	250	229	208	188	167	146	125	105	84	66	48
2,705	**2,725**	252	231	211	190	169	148	128	107	86	68	50
2,725	**2,745**	255	234	213	192	172	151	130	109	89	70	52
2,745	**2,765**	257	236	215	195	174	153	132	112	91	72	54
2,765	**2,785**	259	239	218	197	176	156	135	114	93	74	56
2,785	**2,805**	262	241	220	200	179	158	137	117	96	76	58
2,805	**2,825**	264	243	223	202	181	160	140	119	98	78	60
2,825	**2,845**	267	246	225	204	184	163	142	121	101	80	62
2,845	**2,865**	269	248	227	207	186	165	144	124	103	82	64
2,865	**2,885**	271	251	230	209	188	168	147	126	105	85	66
2,885	**2,905**	274	253	232	212	191	170	149	129	108	87	68
2,905	**2,925**	276	255	235	214	193	172	152	131	110	89	70
2,925	**2,945**	279	258	237	216	196	175	154	133	113	92	72
2,945	**2,965**	281	260	239	219	198	177	156	136	115	94	74
2,965	**2,985**	283	263	242	221	200	180	159	138	117	97	76
2,985	**3,005**	286	265	244	224	203	182	161	141	120	99	78
3,005	**3,025**	288	267	247	226	205	184	164	143	122	101	81
3,025	**3,045**	291	270	249	228	208	187	166	145	125	104	83
3,045	**3,065**	293	272	251	231	210	189	168	148	127	106	85
3,065	**3,085**	295	275	254	233	212	192	171	150	129	109	88
3,085	**3,105**	298	277	256	236	215	194	173	153	132	111	90
3,105	**3,125**	300	279	259	238	217	196	176	155	134	113	93
3,125	**3,145**	303	282	261	240	220	199	178	157	137	116	95
3,145	**3,165**	305	284	263	243	222	201	180	160	139	118	97
$3,165 and over		Use Table 3(b) for a MARRIED person on page 46. Also see the instructions on page 44.										

Wage Bracket Method Tables for Income Tax Withholding

SINGLE Persons—**MONTHLY** Payroll Period

(For Wages Paid through December 31, 2018)

And the wages are–		And the number of withholding allowances claimed is—										
At least	But less than	0	1	2	3	4	5	6	7	8	9	10
		The amount of income tax to be withheld is—										
$ 0	**$305**	$0	$0	$0	$0	$0	$0	$0	$0	$0	$0	$0
305	**325**	1	0	0	0	0	0	0	0	0	0	0
325	**345**	3	0	0	0	0	0	0	0	0	0	0
345	**365**	5	0	0	0	0	0	0	0	0	0	0
365	**385**	7	0	0	0	0	0	0	0	0	0	0
385	**405**	9	0	0	0	0	0	0	0	0	0	0
405	**425**	11	0	0	0	0	0	0	0	0	0	0
425	**445**	13	0	0	0	0	0	0	0	0	0	0
445	**465**	15	0	0	0	0	0	0	0	0	0	0
465	**485**	17	0	0	0	0	0	0	0	0	0	0
485	**505**	19	0	0	0	0	0	0	0	0	0	0
505	**525**	21	0	0	0	0	0	0	0	0	0	0
525	**545**	23	0	0	0	0	0	0	0	0	0	0
545	**565**	25	0	0	0	0	0	0	0	0	0	0
565	**585**	27	0	0	0	0	0	0	0	0	0	0
585	**605**	29	0	0	0	0	0	0	0	0	0	0
605	**645**	32	0	0	0	0	0	0	0	0	0	0
645	**685**	36	1	0	0	0	0	0	0	0	0	0
685	**725**	40	5	0	0	0	0	0	0	0	0	0
725	**765**	44	9	0	0	0	0	0	0	0	0	0
765	**805**	48	13	0	0	0	0	0	0	0	0	0
805	**845**	52	17	0	0	0	0	0	0	0	0	0
845	**885**	56	21	0	0	0	0	0	0	0	0	0
885	**925**	60	25	0	0	0	0	0	0	0	0	0
925	**965**	64	29	0	0	0	0	0	0	0	0	0
965	**1,005**	68	33	0	0	0	0	0	0	0	0	0
1,005	**1,045**	72	37	3	0	0	0	0	0	0	0	0
1,045	**1,085**	76	41	7	0	0	0	0	0	0	0	0
1,085	**1,125**	80	45	11	0	0	0	0	0	0	0	0
1,125	**1,165**	85	49	15	0	0	0	0	0	0	0	0
1,165	**1,205**	89	53	19	0	0	0	0	0	0	0	0
1,205	**1,245**	94	57	23	0	0	0	0	0	0	0	0
1,245	**1,285**	99	61	27	0	0	0	0	0	0	0	0
1,285	**1,325**	104	65	31	0	0	0	0	0	0	0	0
1,325	**1,365**	109	69	35	0	0	0	0	0	0	0	0
1,365	**1,405**	113	73	39	4	0	0	0	0	0	0	0
1,405	**1,445**	118	77	43	8	0	0	0	0	0	0	0
1,445	**1,485**	123	81	47	12	0	0	0	0	0	0	0
1,485	**1,525**	128	86	51	16	0	0	0	0	0	0	0
1,525	**1,565**	133	91	55	20	0	0	0	0	0	0	0
1,565	**1,605**	137	96	59	24	0	0	0	0	0	0	0
1,605	**1,645**	142	101	63	28	0	0	0	0	0	0	0
1,645	**1,685**	147	105	67	32	0	0	0	0	0	0	0
1,685	**1,725**	152	110	71	36	1	0	0	0	0	0	0
1,725	**1,765**	157	115	75	40	5	0	0	0	0	0	0
1,765	**1,805**	161	120	79	44	9	0	0	0	0	0	0
1,805	**1,845**	166	125	83	48	13	0	0	0	0	0	0
1,845	**1,885**	171	129	88	52	17	0	0	0	0	0	0
1,885	**1,925**	176	134	93	56	21	0	0	0	0	0	0
1,925	**1,965**	181	139	98	60	25	0	0	0	0	0	0
1,965	**2,005**	185	144	102	64	29	0	0	0	0	0	0
2,005	**2,045**	190	149	107	68	33	0	0	0	0	0	0
2,045	**2,085**	195	153	112	72	37	3	0	0	0	0	0
2,085	**2,125**	200	158	117	76	41	7	0	0	0	0	0
2,125	**2,165**	205	163	122	80	45	11	0	0	0	0	0
2,165	**2,205**	209	168	126	85	49	15	0	0	0	0	0
2,205	**2,245**	214	173	131	90	53	19	0	0	0	0	0
2,245	**2,285**	219	177	136	94	57	23	0	0	0	0	0
2,285	**2,325**	224	182	141	99	61	27	0	0	0	0	0
2,325	**2,365**	229	187	146	104	65	31	0	0	0	0	0
2,365	**2,405**	233	192	150	109	69	35	0	0	0	0	0
2,405	**2,445**	238	197	155	114	73	39	4	0	0	0	0
2,445	**2,485**	243	201	160	118	77	43	8	0	0	0	0
2,485	**2,525**	248	206	165	123	82	47	12	0	0	0	0
2,525	**2,565**	253	211	170	128	87	51	16	0	0	0	0
2,565	**2,605**	257	216	174	133	91	55	20	0	0	0	0
2,605	**2,645**	262	221	179	138	96	59	24	0	0	0	0
2,645	**2,685**	267	225	184	142	101	63	28	0	0	0	0
2,685	**2,725**	272	230	189	147	106	67	32	0	0	0	0
2,725	**2,765**	277	235	194	152	111	71	36	2	0	0	0

Wage Bracket Method Tables for Income Tax Withholding

SINGLE Persons—MONTHLY Payroll Period

(For Wages Paid through December 31, 2018)

And the wages are–		And the number of withholding allowances claimed is—										
At least	But less than	0	1	2	3	4	5	6	7	8	9	10
		The amount of income tax to be withheld is—										
$2,765	**$2,805**	$281	$240	$198	$157	$115	$75	$40	$6	$0	$0	$0
2,805	**2,845**	286	245	203	162	120	79	44	10	0	0	0
2,845	**2,885**	291	249	208	166	125	83	48	14	0	0	0
2,885	**2,925**	296	254	213	171	130	88	52	18	0	0	0
2,925	**2,965**	301	259	218	176	135	93	56	22	0	0	0
2,965	**3,005**	305	264	222	181	139	98	60	26	0	0	0
3,005	**3,045**	310	269	227	186	144	103	64	30	0	0	0
3,045	**3,085**	315	273	232	190	149	107	68	34	0	0	0
3,085	**3,125**	320	278	237	195	154	112	72	38	3	0	0
3,125	**3,165**	325	283	242	200	159	117	76	42	7	0	0
3,165	**3,205**	329	288	246	205	163	122	80	46	11	0	0
3,205	**3,245**	334	293	251	210	168	127	85	50	15	0	0
3,245	**3,285**	339	297	256	214	173	131	90	54	19	0	0
3,285	**3,325**	344	302	261	219	178	136	95	58	23	0	0
3,325	**3,365**	349	307	266	224	183	141	100	62	27	0	0
3,365	**3,405**	353	312	270	229	187	146	104	66	31	0	0
3,405	**3,445**	358	317	275	234	192	151	109	70	35	0	0
3,445	**3,485**	363	321	280	238	197	155	114	74	39	4	0
3,485	**3,525**	368	326	285	243	202	160	119	78	43	8	0
3,525	**3,565**	374	331	290	248	207	165	124	82	47	12	0
3,565	**3,605**	382	336	294	253	211	170	128	87	51	16	0
3,605	**3,645**	391	341	299	258	216	175	133	92	55	20	0
3,645	**3,685**	400	345	304	262	221	179	138	96	59	24	0
3,685	**3,725**	409	350	309	267	226	184	143	101	63	28	0
3,725	**3,765**	418	355	314	272	231	189	148	106	67	32	0
3,765	**3,805**	426	360	318	277	235	194	152	111	71	36	2
3,805	**3,845**	435	365	323	282	240	199	157	116	75	40	6
3,845	**3,885**	444	369	328	286	245	203	162	120	79	44	10
3,885	**3,925**	453	377	333	291	250	208	167	125	84	48	14
3,925	**3,965**	462	386	338	296	255	213	172	130	89	52	18
3,965	**4,005**	470	394	342	301	259	218	176	135	93	56	22
4,005	**4,045**	479	403	347	306	264	223	181	140	98	60	26
4,045	**4,085**	488	412	352	310	269	227	186	144	103	64	30
4,085	**4,125**	497	421	357	315	274	232	191	149	108	68	34
4,125	**4,165**	506	430	362	320	279	237	196	154	113	72	38
4,165	**4,205**	514	438	366	325	283	242	200	159	117	76	42
4,205	**4,245**	523	447	371	330	288	247	205	164	122	81	46
4,245	**4,285**	532	456	380	334	293	251	210	168	127	85	50
4,285	**4,325**	541	465	389	339	298	256	215	173	132	90	54
4,325	**4,365**	550	474	398	344	303	261	220	178	137	95	58
4,365	**4,405**	558	482	406	349	307	266	224	183	141	100	62
4,405	**4,445**	567	491	415	354	312	271	229	188	146	105	66
4,445	**4,485**	576	500	424	358	317	275	234	192	151	109	70
4,485	**4,525**	585	509	433	363	322	280	239	197	156	114	74
4,525	**4,565**	594	518	442	368	327	285	244	202	161	119	78
4,565	**4,605**	602	526	450	374	331	290	248	207	165	124	82
4,605	**4,645**	611	535	459	383	336	295	253	212	170	129	87
4,645	**4,685**	620	544	468	392	341	299	258	216	175	133	92
4,685	**4,725**	629	553	477	401	346	304	263	221	180	138	97
4,725	**4,765**	638	562	486	409	351	309	268	226	185	143	102
4,765	**4,805**	646	570	494	418	355	314	272	231	189	148	106
4,805	**4,845**	655	579	503	427	360	319	277	236	194	153	111
4,845	**4,885**	664	588	512	436	365	323	282	240	199	157	116
4,885	**4,925**	673	597	521	445	370	328	287	245	204	162	121
4,925	**4,965**	682	606	530	453	377	333	292	250	209	167	126
4,965	**5,005**	690	614	538	462	386	338	296	255	213	172	130
5,005	**5,045**	699	623	547	471	395	343	301	260	218	177	135
5,045	**5,085**	708	632	556	480	404	347	306	264	223	181	140
5,085	**5,125**	717	641	565	489	413	352	311	269	228	186	145
5,125	**5,165**	726	650	574	497	421	357	316	274	233	191	150
5,165	**5,205**	734	658	582	506	430	362	320	279	237	196	154
5,205	**5,245**	743	667	591	515	439	367	325	284	242	201	159
5,245	**5,285**	752	676	600	524	448	372	330	288	247	205	164
5,285	**5,325**	761	685	609	533	457	380	335	293	252	210	169
5,325	**5,365**	770	694	618	541	465	389	340	298	257	215	174
5,365	**5,405**	778	702	626	550	474	398	344	303	261	220	178
$5,405 and over		Use Table 4(a) for a SINGLE person on page 46. Also see the instructions on page 44.										

Wage Bracket Method Tables for Income Tax Withholding

MARRIED Persons—**MONTHLY** Payroll Period

(For Wages Paid through December 31, 2018)

And the wages are—		And the number of withholding allowances claimed is—										
At least	But less than	0	1	2	3	4	5	6	7	8	9	10
		The amount of income tax to be withheld is—										
$ 0	$950	$0	$0	$0	$0	$0	$0	$0	$0	$0	$0	$0
950	990	1	0	0	0	0	0	0	0	0	0	0
990	1,030	5	0	0	0	0	0	0	0	0	0	0
1,030	1,070	9	0	0	0	0	0	0	0	0	0	0
1,070	1,110	13	0	0	0	0	0	0	0	0	0	0
1,110	1,150	17	0	0	0	0	0	0	0	0	0	0
1,150	1,190	21	0	0	0	0	0	0	0	0	0	0
1,190	1,230	25	0	0	0	0	0	0	0	0	0	0
1,230	1,270	29	0	0	0	0	0	0	0	0	0	0
1,270	1,310	33	0	0	0	0	0	0	0	0	0	0
1,310	1,350	37	2	0	0	0	0	0	0	0	0	0
1,350	1,390	41	6	0	0	0	0	0	0	0	0	0
1,390	1,430	45	10	0	0	0	0	0	0	0	0	0
1,430	1,470	49	14	0	0	0	0	0	0	0	0	0
1,470	1,510	53	18	0	0	0	0	0	0	0	0	0
1,510	1,550	57	22	0	0	0	0	0	0	0	0	0
1,550	1,590	61	26	0	0	0	0	0	0	0	0	0
1,590	1,630	65	30	0	0	0	0	0	0	0	0	0
1,630	1,670	69	34	0	0	0	0	0	0	0	0	0
1,670	1,710	73	38	4	0	0	0	0	0	0	0	0
1,710	1,750	77	42	8	0	0	0	0	0	0	0	0
1,750	1,790	81	46	12	0	0	0	0	0	0	0	0
1,790	1,830	85	50	16	0	0	0	0	0	0	0	0
1,830	1,870	89	54	20	0	0	0	0	0	0	0	0
1,870	1,910	93	58	24	0	0	0	0	0	0	0	0
1,910	1,950	97	62	28	0	0	0	0	0	0	0	0
1,950	1,990	101	66	32	0	0	0	0	0	0	0	0
1,990	2,030	105	70	36	1	0	0	0	0	0	0	0
2,030	2,070	109	74	40	5	0	0	0	0	0	0	0
2,070	2,110	113	78	44	9	0	0	0	0	0	0	0
2,110	2,150	117	82	48	13	0	0	0	0	0	0	0
2,150	2,190	121	86	52	17	0	0	0	0	0	0	0
2,190	2,230	125	90	56	21	0	0	0	0	0	0	0
2,230	2,270	129	94	60	25	0	0	0	0	0	0	0
2,270	2,310	133	98	64	29	0	0	0	0	0	0	0
2,310	2,350	137	102	68	33	0	0	0	0	0	0	0
2,350	2,390	141	106	72	37	2	0	0	0	0	0	0
2,390	2,430	145	110	76	41	6	0	0	0	0	0	0
2,430	2,470	149	114	80	45	10	0	0	0	0	0	0
2,470	2,510	153	118	84	49	14	0	0	0	0	0	0
2,510	2,550	157	122	88	53	18	0	0	0	0	0	0
2,550	2,590	161	126	92	57	22	0	0	0	0	0	0
2,590	2,630	166	130	96	61	26	0	0	0	0	0	0
2,630	2,670	171	134	100	65	30	0	0	0	0	0	0
2,670	2,710	176	138	104	69	34	0	0	0	0	0	0
2,710	2,750	180	142	108	73	38	4	0	0	0	0	0
2,750	2,790	185	146	112	77	42	8	0	0	0	0	0
2,790	2,830	190	150	116	81	46	12	0	0	0	0	0
2,830	2,870	195	154	120	85	50	16	0	0	0	0	0
2,870	2,910	200	158	124	89	54	20	0	0	0	0	0
2,910	2,950	204	163	128	93	58	24	0	0	0	0	0
2,950	2,990	209	168	132	97	62	28	0	0	0	0	0
2,990	3,030	214	172	136	101	66	32	0	0	0	0	0
3,030	3,070	219	177	140	105	70	36	1	0	0	0	0
3,070	3,110	224	182	144	109	74	40	5	0	0	0	0
3,110	3,150	228	187	148	113	78	44	9	0	0	0	0
3,150	3,190	233	192	152	117	82	48	13	0	0	0	0
3,190	3,230	238	196	156	121	86	52	17	0	0	0	0
3,230	3,270	243	201	160	125	90	56	21	0	0	0	0
3,270	3,310	248	206	165	129	94	60	25	0	0	0	0
3,310	3,350	252	211	169	133	98	64	29	0	0	0	0
3,350	3,390	257	216	174	137	102	68	33	0	0	0	0
3,390	3,430	262	220	179	141	106	72	37	3	0	0	0
3,430	3,470	267	225	184	145	110	76	41	7	0	0	0
3,470	3,510	272	230	189	149	114	80	45	11	0	0	0
3,510	3,550	276	235	193	153	118	84	49	15	0	0	0
3,550	3,590	281	240	198	157	122	88	53	19	0	0	0
3,590	3,630	286	244	203	161	126	92	57	23	0	0	0
3,630	3,670	291	249	208	166	130	96	61	27	0	0	0
3,670	3,710	296	254	213	171	134	100	65	31	0	0	0

Wage Bracket Method Tables for Income Tax Withholding

MARRIED Persons—**MONTHLY** Payroll Period

(For Wages Paid through December 31, 2018)

And the wages are–		And the number of withholding allowances claimed is—										
At least	But less than	0	1	2	3	4	5	6	7	8	9	10
		The amount of income tax to be withheld is—										
$3,710	**$3,750**	$300	$259	$217	$176	$138	$104	$69	$35	$0	$0	$0
3,750	**3,790**	305	264	222	181	142	108	73	39	4	0	0
3,790	**3,830**	310	268	227	185	146	112	77	43	8	0	0
3,830	**3,870**	315	273	232	190	150	116	81	47	12	0	0
3,870	**3,910**	320	278	237	195	154	120	85	51	16	0	0
3,910	**3,950**	324	283	241	200	158	124	89	55	20	0	0
3,950	**3,990**	329	288	246	205	163	128	93	59	24	0	0
3,990	**4,030**	334	292	251	209	168	132	97	63	28	0	0
4,030	**4,070**	339	297	256	214	173	136	101	67	32	0	0
4,070	**4,110**	344	302	261	219	178	140	105	71	36	2	0
4,110	**4,150**	348	307	265	224	182	144	109	75	40	6	0
4,150	**4,190**	353	312	270	229	187	148	113	79	44	10	0
4,190	**4,230**	358	316	275	233	192	152	117	83	48	14	0
4,230	**4,270**	363	321	280	238	197	156	121	87	52	18	0
4,270	**4,310**	368	326	285	243	202	160	125	91	56	22	0
4,310	**4,350**	372	331	289	248	206	165	129	95	60	26	0
4,350	**4,390**	377	336	294	253	211	170	133	99	64	30	0
4,390	**4,430**	382	340	299	257	216	174	137	103	68	34	0
4,430	**4,470**	387	345	304	262	221	179	141	107	72	38	3
4,470	**4,510**	392	350	309	267	226	184	145	111	76	42	7
4,510	**4,550**	396	355	313	272	230	189	149	115	80	46	11
4,550	**4,590**	401	360	318	277	235	194	153	119	84	50	15
4,590	**4,630**	406	364	323	281	240	198	157	123	88	54	19
4,630	**4,670**	411	369	328	286	245	203	162	127	92	58	23
4,670	**4,710**	416	374	333	291	250	208	167	131	96	62	27
4,710	**4,750**	420	379	337	296	254	213	171	135	100	66	31
4,750	**4,790**	425	384	342	301	259	218	176	139	104	70	35
4,790	**4,830**	430	388	347	305	264	222	181	143	108	74	39
4,830	**4,870**	435	393	352	310	269	227	186	147	112	78	43
4,870	**4,910**	440	398	357	315	274	232	191	151	116	82	47
4,910	**4,950**	444	403	361	320	278	237	195	155	120	86	51
4,950	**4,990**	449	408	366	325	283	242	200	159	124	90	55
4,990	**5,030**	454	412	371	329	288	246	205	163	128	94	59
5,030	**5,070**	459	417	376	334	293	251	210	168	132	98	63
5,070	**5,110**	464	422	381	339	298	256	215	173	136	102	67
5,110	**5,150**	468	427	385	344	302	261	219	178	140	106	71
5,150	**5,190**	473	432	390	349	307	266	224	183	144	110	75
5,190	**5,230**	478	436	395	353	312	270	229	187	148	114	79
5,230	**5,270**	483	441	400	358	317	275	234	192	152	118	83
5,270	**5,310**	488	446	405	363	322	280	239	197	156	122	87
5,310	**5,350**	492	451	409	368	326	285	243	202	160	126	91
5,350	**5,390**	497	456	414	373	331	290	248	207	165	130	95
5,390	**5,430**	502	460	419	377	336	294	253	211	170	134	99
5,430	**5,470**	507	465	424	382	341	299	258	216	175	138	103
5,470	**5,510**	512	470	429	387	346	304	263	221	180	142	107
5,510	**5,550**	516	475	433	392	350	309	267	226	184	146	111
5,550	**5,590**	521	480	438	397	355	314	272	231	189	150	115
5,590	**5,630**	526	484	443	401	360	318	277	235	194	154	119
5,630	**5,670**	531	489	448	406	365	323	282	240	199	158	123
5,670	**5,710**	536	494	453	411	370	328	287	245	204	162	127
5,710	**5,750**	540	499	457	416	374	333	291	250	208	167	131
5,750	**5,790**	545	504	462	421	379	338	296	255	213	172	135
5,790	**5,830**	550	508	467	425	384	342	301	259	218	176	139
5,830	**5,870**	555	513	472	430	389	347	306	264	223	181	143
5,870	**5,910**	560	518	477	435	394	352	311	269	228	186	147
5,910	**5,950**	564	523	481	440	398	357	315	274	232	191	151
5,950	**5,990**	569	528	486	445	403	362	320	279	237	196	155
5,990	**6,030**	574	532	491	449	408	366	325	283	242	200	159
6,030	**6,070**	579	537	496	454	413	371	330	288	247	205	164
6,070	**6,110**	584	542	501	459	418	376	335	293	252	210	169
6,110	**6,150**	588	547	505	464	422	381	339	298	256	215	173
6,150	**6,190**	593	552	510	469	427	386	344	303	261	220	178
6,190	**6,230**	598	556	515	473	432	390	349	307	266	224	183
6,230	**6,270**	603	561	520	478	437	395	354	312	271	229	188
6,270	**6,310**	608	566	525	483	442	400	359	317	276	234	193
6,310	**6,350**	612	571	529	488	446	405	363	322	280	239	197

$6,350 and over — Use Table 4(b) for a MARRIED person on page 46. Also see the instructions on page 44.

Wage Bracket Method Tables for Income Tax Withholding

SINGLE Persons—**DAILY** Payroll Period

(For Wages Paid through December 31, 2018)

And the wages are–		And the number of withholding allowances claimed is—										
At least	But less than	0	1	2	3	4	5	6	7	8	9	10
		The amount of income tax to be withheld is—										
$ 0	**$18**	$0	$0	$0	$0	$0	$0	$0	$0	$0	$0	$0
18	**21**	1	0	0	0	0	0	0	0	0	0	0
21	**24**	1	0	0	0	0	0	0	0	0	0	0
24	**27**	1	0	0	0	0	0	0	0	0	0	0
27	**30**	1	0	0	0	0	0	0	0	0	0	0
30	**33**	2	0	0	0	0	0	0	0	0	0	0
33	**36**	2	0	0	0	0	0	0	0	0	0	0
36	**39**	2	1	0	0	0	0	0	0	0	0	0
39	**42**	3	1	0	0	0	0	0	0	0	0	0
42	**45**	3	1	0	0	0	0	0	0	0	0	0
45	**48**	3	2	0	0	0	0	0	0	0	0	0
48	**51**	4	2	0	0	0	0	0	0	0	0	0
51	**54**	4	2	1	0	0	0	0	0	0	0	0
54	**57**	4	3	1	0	0	0	0	0	0	0	0
57	**60**	5	3	1	0	0	0	0	0	0	0	0
60	**63**	5	3	2	0	0	0	0	0	0	0	0
63	**66**	5	3	2	0	0	0	0	0	0	0	0
66	**69**	6	4	2	1	0	0	0	0	0	0	0
69	**72**	6	4	2	1	0	0	0	0	0	0	0
72	**75**	6	4	3	1	0	0	0	0	0	0	0
75	**78**	7	5	3	1	0	0	0	0	0	0	0
78	**81**	7	5	3	2	0	0	0	0	0	0	0
81	**84**	7	6	4	2	0	0	0	0	0	0	0
84	**87**	8	6	4	2	1	0	0	0	0	0	0
87	**90**	8	6	4	3	1	0	0	0	0	0	0
90	**93**	9	7	5	3	1	0	0	0	0	0	0
93	**96**	9	7	5	3	2	0	0	0	0	0	0
96	**99**	9	7	5	4	2	0	0	0	0	0	0
99	**102**	10	8	6	4	2	1	0	0	0	0	0
102	**105**	10	8	6	4	3	1	0	0	0	0	0
105	**108**	10	8	7	5	3	1	0	0	0	0	0
108	**111**	11	9	7	5	3	2	0	0	0	0	0
111	**114**	11	9	7	5	3	2	0	0	0	0	0
114	**117**	11	10	8	6	4	2	1	0	0	0	0
117	**120**	12	10	8	6	4	2	1	0	0	0	0
120	**123**	12	10	8	6	4	3	1	0	0	0	0
123	**126**	12	11	9	7	5	3	1	0	0	0	0
126	**129**	13	11	9	7	5	3	2	0	0	0	0
129	**132**	13	11	9	7	6	4	2	0	0	0	0
132	**135**	14	12	10	8	6	4	2	1	0	0	0
135	**138**	14	12	10	8	6	4	3	1	0	0	0
138	**141**	14	12	10	9	7	5	3	1	0	0	0
141	**144**	15	13	11	9	7	5	3	2	0	0	0
144	**147**	15	13	11	9	7	5	4	2	0	0	0
147	**150**	15	13	12	10	8	6	4	2	1	0	0
150	**153**	16	14	12	10	8	6	4	3	1	0	0
153	**156**	16	14	12	10	8	7	5	3	1	0	0
156	**159**	16	15	13	11	9	7	5	3	2	0	0
159	**162**	17	15	13	11	9	7	5	3	2	0	0
162	**165**	17	15	13	11	10	8	6	4	2	1	0
165	**168**	18	16	14	12	10	8	6	4	2	1	0
168	**171**	19	16	14	12	10	8	6	4	3	1	0
171	**174**	19	16	14	13	11	9	7	5	3	1	0
174	**177**	20	17	15	13	11	9	7	5	3	2	0
177	**180**	21	17	15	13	11	9	7	6	4	2	0
180	**183**	21	18	16	14	12	10	8	6	4	2	1
183	**186**	22	18	16	14	12	10	8	6	4	3	1
186	**189**	23	19	16	14	12	10	9	7	5	3	1
189	**192**	23	20	17	15	13	11	9	7	5	3	2
192	**195**	24	20	17	15	13	11	9	7	5	4	2
195	**198**	24	21	17	15	13	12	10	8	6	4	2
198	**201**	25	22	18	16	14	12	10	8	6	4	3
201	**204**	26	22	19	16	14	12	10	8	7	5	3
204	**207**	26	23	19	16	15	13	11	9	7	5	3
207	**210**	27	24	20	17	15	13	11	9	7	5	3
210	**213**	28	24	21	17	15	13	11	10	8	6	4
213	**216**	28	25	21	18	16	14	12	10	8	6	4
216	**219**	29	26	22	19	16	14	12	10	8	6	5
219	**222**	30	26	23	19	16	14	13	11	9	7	5
222	**225**	30	27	23	20	17	15	13	11	9	7	5

Wage Bracket Method Tables for Income Tax Withholding

SINGLE Persons—**DAILY** Payroll Period

(For Wages Paid through December 31, 2018)

And the wages are–		And the number of withholding allowances claimed is—										
At least	But less than	0	1	2	3	4	5	6	7	8	9	10
		The amount of income tax to be withheld is—										
$225	**$228**	$31	$28	$24	$21	$17	$15	$13	$11	$9	$8	$6
228	**231**	32	28	25	21	18	16	14	12	10	8	6
231	**234**	32	29	25	22	18	16	14	12	10	8	6
234	**237**	33	30	26	23	19	16	14	12	10	9	7
237	**240**	34	30	27	23	20	17	15	13	11	9	7
240	**243**	34	31	27	24	20	17	15	13	11	9	7
243	**246**	35	32	28	25	21	17	15	13	12	10	8
246	**249**	36	32	29	25	22	18	16	14	12	10	8
249	**252**	36	33	29	26	22	19	16	14	12	10	8
252	**255**	37	34	30	26	23	19	16	15	13	11	9
255	**258**	38	34	31	27	24	20	17	15	13	11	9
258	**261**	38	35	31	28	24	21	17	15	13	11	10
261	**264**	39	35	32	28	25	21	18	16	14	12	10
264	**267**	40	36	33	29	26	22	19	16	14	12	10
267	**270**	40	37	33	30	26	23	19	16	14	13	11
270	**273**	41	37	34	30	27	23	20	17	15	13	11
273	**276**	42	38	35	31	28	24	21	17	15	13	11
276	**279**	42	39	35	32	28	25	21	18	16	14	12
279	**282**	43	39	36	32	29	25	22	18	16	14	12
282	**285**	44	40	37	33	30	26	23	19	16	14	12
285	**288**	44	41	37	34	30	27	23	20	17	15	13
288	**291**	45	41	38	34	31	27	24	20	17	15	13
291	**294**	46	42	39	35	32	28	25	21	18	15	14
294	**297**	46	43	39	36	32	29	25	22	18	16	14
297	**300**	47	43	40	36	33	29	26	22	19	16	14
300	**303**	48	44	41	37	34	30	27	23	19	17	15
303	**306**	48	45	41	38	34	31	27	24	20	17	15
306	**309**	49	45	42	38	35	31	28	24	21	17	15
309	**312**	50	46	43	39	36	32	28	25	21	18	16
312	**315**	50	47	43	40	36	33	29	26	22	19	16
315	**318**	51	47	44	40	37	33	30	26	23	19	16
318	**321**	52	48	45	41	37	34	30	27	23	20	17
321	**324**	52	49	45	42	38	35	31	28	24	21	17
324	**327**	53	49	46	42	39	35	32	28	25	21	18
327	**330**	54	50	46	43	39	36	32	29	25	22	18
330	**333**	54	51	47	44	40	37	33	30	26	23	19
333	**336**	55	51	48	44	41	37	34	30	27	23	20
336	**339**	56	52	48	45	41	38	34	31	27	24	20
339	**341**	56	53	49	46	42	38	35	31	28	24	21
341	**343**	57	53	49	46	42	39	35	32	28	25	21
343	**345**	57	53	50	46	43	39	36	32	29	25	22
345	**347**	58	54	50	47	43	40	36	33	29	26	22
347	**349**	58	54	51	47	44	40	37	33	30	26	23
349	**351**	59	55	51	48	44	41	37	34	30	27	23
351	**353**	59	55	52	48	45	41	38	34	31	27	24
353	**355**	60	56	52	49	45	42	38	35	31	28	24
355	**357**	60	56	53	49	46	42	39	35	31	28	24
357	**359**	61	57	53	49	46	42	39	35	32	28	25
359	**361**	61	57	53	50	46	43	39	36	32	29	25
361	**363**	62	58	54	50	47	43	40	36	33	29	26
363	**365**	62	58	54	51	47	44	40	37	33	30	26
365	**367**	62	59	55	51	48	44	41	37	34	30	27
367	**369**	63	59	55	52	48	45	41	38	34	31	27
369	**371**	63	60	56	52	49	45	42	38	35	31	28
371	**373**	64	60	56	53	49	46	42	39	35	31	28
373	**375**	64	61	57	53	49	46	42	39	35	32	28
375	**377**	65	61	57	53	50	46	43	39	36	32	29
377	**379**	65	62	58	54	50	47	43	40	36	33	29
379	**381**	66	62	58	54	51	47	44	40	37	33	30
381	**383**	66	62	59	55	51	48	44	41	37	34	30
383	**385**	67	63	59	55	52	48	45	41	38	34	31
385	**387**	67	63	60	56	52	49	45	42	38	35	31
387	**389**	68	64	60	56	53	49	46	42	39	35	31
389	**391**	68	64	61	57	53	49	46	42	39	35	32
391	**393**	69	65	61	57	53	50	46	43	39	36	32
393	**395**	69	65	62	58	54	50	47	43	40	36	33
$ 395 and over		Use Table 8(a) for a SINGLE person on page 47. Also see the instructions on page 44.										

Wage Bracket Method Tables for Income Tax Withholding

MARRIED Persons—**DAILY** Payroll Period

(For Wages Paid through December 31, 2018)

And the wages are–		And the number of withholding allowances claimed is—										
At least	But less than	0	1	2	3	4	5	6	7	8	9	10
		The amount of income tax to be withheld is—										
$ 0	$50	$0	$0	$0	$0	$0	$0	$0	$0	$0	$0	$0
50	53	1	0	0	0	0	0	0	0	0	0	0
53	56	1	0	0	0	0	0	0	0	0	0	0
56	59	1	0	0	0	0	0	0	0	0	0	0
59	62	2	0	0	0	0	0	0	0	0	0	0
62	65	2	0	0	0	0	0	0	0	0	0	0
65	68	2	1	0	0	0	0	0	0	0	0	0
68	71	3	1	0	0	0	0	0	0	0	0	0
71	74	3	1	0	0	0	0	0	0	0	0	0
74	77	3	2	0	0	0	0	0	0	0	0	0
77	80	3	2	0	0	0	0	0	0	0	0	0
80	83	4	2	1	0	0	0	0	0	0	0	0
83	86	4	2	1	0	0	0	0	0	0	0	0
86	89	4	3	1	0	0	0	0	0	0	0	0
89	92	5	3	1	0	0	0	0	0	0	0	0
92	95	5	3	2	0	0	0	0	0	0	0	0
95	98	5	4	2	0	0	0	0	0	0	0	0
98	101	6	4	2	1	0	0	0	0	0	0	0
101	104	6	4	3	1	0	0	0	0	0	0	0
104	107	6	5	3	1	0	0	0	0	0	0	0
107	110	6	5	3	2	0	0	0	0	0	0	0
110	113	7	5	4	2	0	0	0	0	0	0	0
113	116	7	5	4	2	1	0	0	0	0	0	0
116	119	7	6	4	3	1	0	0	0	0	0	0
119	122	8	6	4	3	1	0	0	0	0	0	0
122	125	8	6	5	3	2	0	0	0	0	0	0
125	128	8	7	5	3	2	0	0	0	0	0	0
128	131	9	7	5	4	2	1	0	0	0	0	0
131	134	9	7	6	4	2	1	0	0	0	0	0
134	137	9	8	6	4	3	1	0	0	0	0	0
137	140	10	8	6	5	3	1	0	0	0	0	0
140	143	10	8	7	5	3	2	0	0	0	0	0
143	146	11	9	7	5	4	2	0	0	0	0	0
146	149	11	9	7	6	4	2	1	0	0	0	0
149	152	11	9	7	6	4	3	1	0	0	0	0
152	155	12	10	8	6	5	3	1	0	0	0	0
155	158	12	10	8	6	5	3	2	0	0	0	0
158	161	12	10	9	7	5	4	2	0	0	0	0
161	164	13	11	9	7	5	4	2	1	0	0	0
164	167	13	11	9	7	6	4	3	1	0	0	0
167	170	13	12	10	8	6	4	3	1	0	0	0
170	173	14	12	10	8	6	5	3	2	0	0	0
173	176	14	12	10	8	7	5	3	2	0	0	0
176	179	15	13	11	9	7	5	4	2	1	0	0
179	182	15	13	11	9	7	6	4	2	1	0	0
182	185	15	13	11	9	8	6	4	3	1	0	0
185	188	16	14	12	10	8	6	5	3	1	0	0
188	191	16	14	12	10	8	7	5	3	2	0	0
191	194	16	14	12	11	9	7	5	4	2	0	0
194	197	17	15	13	11	9	7	6	4	2	1	0
197	200	17	15	13	11	9	7	6	4	3	1	0
200	203	17	15	14	12	10	8	6	5	3	1	0
203	206	18	16	14	12	10	8	6	5	3	2	0
206	209	18	16	14	12	10	9	7	5	4	2	0
209	212	18	17	15	13	11	9	7	5	4	2	1
212	215	19	17	15	13	11	9	7	6	4	3	1
215	218	19	17	15	13	12	10	8	6	4	3	1
218	221	20	18	16	14	12	10	8	6	5	3	2
221	224	20	18	16	14	12	10	8	7	5	3	2
224	227	20	18	16	15	13	11	9	7	5	4	2
227	230	21	19	17	15	13	11	9	7	6	4	2
230	233	21	19	17	15	13	11	9	8	6	4	3
233	236	21	19	18	16	14	12	10	8	6	5	3
236	239	22	20	18	16	14	12	10	8	7	5	3
239	242	22	20	18	16	14	12	11	9	7	5	4
242	245	22	21	19	17	15	13	11	9	7	6	4
245	248	23	21	19	17	15	13	11	9	7	6	4
248	251	23	21	19	17	15	14	12	10	8	6	5
251	254	24	22	20	18	16	14	12	10	8	6	5
254	257	24	22	20	18	16	14	12	10	9	7	5

Wage Bracket Method Tables for Income Tax Withholding

MARRIED Persons—**DAILY** Payroll Period

(For Wages Paid through December 31, 2018)

And the wages are–		And the number of withholding allowances claimed is—										
At least	But less than	0	1	2	3	4	5	6	7	8	9	10
		The amount of income tax to be withheld is—										
$257	**$260**	$24	$22	$20	$18	$17	$15	$13	$11	$9	$7	$5
260	**263**	25	23	21	19	17	15	13	11	9	7	6
263	**266**	25	23	21	19	17	15	13	12	10	8	6
266	**269**	25	23	21	20	18	16	14	12	10	8	6
269	**272**	26	24	22	20	18	16	14	12	10	8	7
272	**275**	26	24	22	20	18	16	15	13	11	9	7
275	**278**	26	24	23	21	19	17	15	13	11	9	7
278	**281**	27	25	23	21	19	17	15	13	11	10	8
281	**284**	27	25	23	21	19	18	16	14	12	10	8
284	**287**	27	26	24	22	20	18	16	14	12	10	8
287	**290**	28	26	24	22	20	18	16	14	13	11	9
290	**293**	28	26	24	22	21	19	17	15	13	11	9
293	**296**	29	27	25	23	21	19	17	15	13	11	9
296	**299**	29	27	25	23	21	19	17	15	14	12	10
299	**302**	29	27	25	24	22	20	18	16	14	12	10
302	**305**	30	28	26	24	22	20	18	16	14	12	10
305	**308**	30	28	26	24	22	20	18	17	15	13	11
308	**311**	30	28	27	25	23	21	19	17	15	13	11
311	**314**	31	29	27	25	23	21	19	17	15	13	12
314	**317**	31	29	27	25	23	21	20	18	16	14	12
317	**320**	31	30	28	26	24	22	20	18	16	14	12
320	**323**	32	30	28	26	24	22	20	18	16	15	13
323	**326**	32	30	28	26	24	23	21	19	17	15	13
326	**329**	33	31	29	27	25	23	21	19	17	15	13
329	**332**	33	31	29	27	25	23	21	19	18	16	14
332	**335**	33	31	29	27	26	24	22	20	18	16	14
335	**338**	34	32	30	28	26	24	22	20	18	16	14
338	**341**	34	32	30	28	26	24	22	21	19	17	15
341	**343**	34	32	30	28	27	25	23	21	19	17	15
343	**345**	35	33	31	29	27	25	23	21	19	17	15
345	**347**	35	33	31	29	27	25	23	21	19	17	16
347	**349**	36	33	31	29	27	25	23	22	20	18	16
349	**351**	36	33	31	29	28	26	24	22	20	18	16
351	**353**	36	34	32	30	28	26	24	22	20	18	16
353	**355**	37	34	32	30	28	26	24	22	20	18	17
355	**357**	37	34	32	30	28	26	24	23	21	19	17
357	**359**	38	34	32	30	29	27	25	23	21	19	17
359	**361**	38	35	33	31	29	27	25	23	21	19	17
361	**363**	39	35	33	31	29	27	25	23	21	19	17
363	**365**	39	36	33	31	29	27	25	23	22	20	18
365	**367**	40	36	33	31	29	28	26	24	22	20	18
367	**369**	40	36	34	32	30	28	26	24	22	20	18
369	**371**	40	37	34	32	30	28	26	24	22	20	18
371	**373**	41	37	34	32	30	28	26	24	23	21	19
373	**375**	41	38	34	32	30	29	27	25	23	21	19
375	**377**	42	38	35	33	31	29	27	25	23	21	19
377	**379**	42	39	35	33	31	29	27	25	23	21	19
379	**381**	43	39	36	33	31	29	27	25	23	22	20
381	**383**	43	40	36	33	31	29	28	26	24	22	20
383	**385**	43	40	36	34	32	30	28	26	24	22	20
385	**387**	44	40	37	34	32	30	28	26	24	22	20
387	**389**	44	41	37	34	32	30	28	26	24	23	21
389	**391**	45	41	38	34	32	30	29	27	25	23	21
391	**393**	45	42	38	35	33	31	29	27	25	23	21
393	**395**	46	42	39	35	33	31	29	27	25	23	21
395	**397**	46	43	39	36	33	31	29	27	25	23	22
397	**399**	47	43	40	36	33	31	29	28	26	24	22
399	**401**	47	43	40	36	34	32	30	28	26	24	22
401	**403**	47	44	40	37	34	32	30	28	26	24	22
403	**405**	48	44	41	37	34	32	30	28	26	24	23
405	**407**	48	45	41	38	34	32	30	29	27	25	23
407	**409**	49	45	42	38	35	33	31	29	27	25	23
409	**411**	49	46	42	39	35	33	31	29	27	25	23
411	**413**	50	46	43	39	36	33	31	29	27	25	23
413	**415**	50	47	43	40	36	33	31	29	28	26	24
415	**417**	51	47	43	40	36	34	32	30	28	26	24
$ 417 and over		Use Table 8(b) for a MARRIED person on page 47. Also see the instructions on page 44.										

How To Get Tax Help

If you have questions about a tax issue, need help preparing your tax return, or want to download free publications, forms, or instructions, go to IRS.gov and find resources that can help you right away.

Preparing and filing your tax return. Go to *IRS.gov/EmploymentEfile* for more information on filing your employment tax returns electronically.

Getting answers to your tax questions. On IRS.gov get answers to your tax questions anytime, anywhere.

- Go to *IRS.gov/Help* or *IRS.gov/LetUsHelp* pages for a variety of tools that will help you get answers to some of the most common tax questions.
- You may also be able to access tax law information in your electronic filing software.

Getting tax forms and publications. Go to *IRS.gov/Forms* to view, download, or print most of the forms and publications you may need. You can also download and view popular tax publications and instructions (including Pub. 15) on mobile devices as an eBook at no charge. Or, you can go to *IRS.gov/OrderForms* to place an order and have forms mailed to you within 10 business days.

Getting a transcript or copy of a return. You can get a copy of your tax transcript or a copy of your return by calling 800-829-4933 or by mailing Form 4506-T (transcript request) or Form 4506 (copy of return) to the IRS.

Resolving tax-related identity theft issues.

- The IRS doesn't initiate contact with taxpayers by email or telephone to request personal or financial information. This includes any type of electronic communication, such as text messages and social media channels.
- Go to *IRS.gov/IDProtection* for information and videos.
- If your EIN has been lost or stolen or you suspect you're a victim of tax-related identity theft, visit *IRS.gov/ID* to learn what steps you should take.

Making a tax payment. The IRS uses the latest encryption technology to ensure your electronic payments are safe and secure. You can make electronic payments online, by phone, and from a mobile device using the IRS2Go app. Paying electronically is quick, easy, and faster than mailing in a check or money order. Go to *IRS.gov/Payments* to make a payment using any of the following options.

- **Debit or credit card:** Choose an approved payment processor to pay online, by phone, and by mobile device.
- **Electronic Funds Withdrawal:** Offered only when filing your federal taxes using tax preparation software or through a tax professional.
- **Electronic Federal Tax Payment System:** Best option for businesses. Enrollment is required.
- **Check or money order:** Mail your payment to the address listed on the notice or instructions.
- **Cash:** You may be able to pay your taxes with cash at a participating retail store.

What if I can't pay now? Go to *IRS.gov/Payments* for more information about your options.

- Apply for an *online payment agreement* (*IRS.gov/OPA*) to meet your tax obligation in monthly installments if you can't pay your taxes in full today. Once you complete the online process, you will receive immediate notification of whether your agreement has been approved.
- Use the *Offer in Compromise Pre-Qualifier* (*IRS.gov/OIC*) to see if you can settle your tax debt for less than the full amount you owe.

Understanding an IRS notice or letter. Go to *IRS.gov/Notices* to find additional information about responding to an IRS notice or letter.

Contacting your local IRS office. Keep in mind, many questions can be answered on IRS.gov without visiting an IRS Tax Assistance Center (TAC). Go to *IRS.gov/LetUsHelp* for the topics people ask about most. If you still need help, IRS TACs provide tax help when a tax issue can't be handled online or by phone. All TACs now provide service by appointment so you'll know in advance that you can get the service you need without long wait times. Before you visit, go to *IRS.gov/TACLocator* to find the nearest TAC, check hours, available services, and appointment options. Or, on the IRS2Go app, under the Stay Connected tab, choose the Contact Us option and click on "Local Offices."

Watching IRS videos. The IRS Video portal (*IRSvideos.gov*) contains video and audio presentations for individuals, small businesses, and tax professionals.

Getting tax information in other languages. For taxpayers whose native language isn't English, we have the following resources available. Taxpayers can find information on IRS.gov in the following languages.

- *Spanish* (*IRS.gov/Spanish*).
- *Chinese* (*IRS.gov/Chinese*).
- *Vietnamese* (*IRS.gov/Vietnamese*).
- *Korean* (*IRS.gov/Korean*).
- *Russian* (*IRS.gov/Russian*).

The IRS TACs provide over-the-phone interpreter service in over 170 languages, and the service is available free to taxpayers.

The Taxpayer Advocate Service Is Here To Help You

What is the Taxpayer Advocate Service?

The Taxpayer Advocate Service (TAS) is an ***independent*** organization within the IRS that helps taxpayers and protects taxpayer rights. Our job is to ensure that every taxpayer is treated fairly and that you know and understand your rights under the *Taxpayer Bill of Rights*.

What Can the Taxpayer Advocate Service Do For You?

We can help you resolve problems that you can't resolve with the IRS. And our service is free. If you qualify for our assistance, you will be assigned to one advocate who will work with you throughout the process and will do everything possible to resolve your issue. TAS can help you if:

- Your problem is causing financial difficulty for you, your family, or your business,
- You face (or your business is facing) an immediate threat of adverse action, or
- You've tried repeatedly to contact the IRS but no one has responded, or the IRS hasn't responded by the date promised.

How Can You Reach Us?

We have offices *in every state, the District of Columbia, and Puerto Rico*. Your local advocate's number is in your local directory and at *TaxpayerAdvocate.IRS.gov/Contact-Us*. You can also call us at 877-777-4778.

How Can You Learn About Your Taxpayer Rights?

The Taxpayer Bill of Rights describes 10 basic rights that all taxpayers have when dealing with the IRS. Our Tax Toolkit at *TaxpayerAdvocate.IRS.gov* can help you understand *what these rights mean to you* and how they apply. These are ***your*** rights. Know them. Use them.

How Else Does the Taxpayer Advocate Service Help Taxpayers?

TAS works to resolve large-scale problems that affect many taxpayers. If you know of one of these broad issues, please report it to us at *IRS.gov/SAMS*.

Index

To help us develop a more useful index, please let us know if you have ideas for index entries. See "Comments and Suggestions" in the "Introduction" for the ways you can reach us.

Chapter 16
SOUTH CAROLINA MECHANICS' LIEN LAW

Chapter Survey...

- *What is a Lien?*
- *Who is Entitled to a Mechanics' Lien?*
- *Notice of Project Commencement*
- *Notice to Owner by Laborer, Subcontractor, or Supplier*
- *Dissolution of Lien for Failure to Serve Statement*
- *Time in Which to File a Lien Foreclosure Petition*
- *Collecting on a Lien*
- *Monetary Awards*
- *Notice of Non-Responsibility*
- *Offer of Settlement*
- *Sale of Land to Satisfy Lien*

What is a Lien?

Mechanic's and materialmen's liens "cloud" the title to real property but can be an effective method (and sometimes the only method) for securing payment for labor or materials used in the improvement of real property. The lien stops the owner from selling the property with a clear title. The lien may be foreclosed in a lawsuit. The court can order that property be sold and the proceeds used to pay the contractor, subcontractor, laborer, or material supplier. This may be true even if the owner has already paid a general contractor, meaning that the owner may have to pay twice. This is one of the reasons that a lien can be such a powerful collection tool.

The law governing mechanics' liens is found in the South Carolina Code of Laws, Title 29, Chapter 5 (Appendix H). The state statutes and court opinions establish a strict procedure to perfect and foreclose a lien. It is strongly recommended that a professional be routinely used to record and foreclose on construction liens.

Who is Entitled to a Mechanics' Lien?

State statutes designate lien rights for those "to whom a debt is due for labor performed or furnished or for materials furnished and actually used in the erection, alteration, or repair of a building or structure upon real estate or the boring and equipping of wells." This includes general contractors, subcontractors, suppliers, site work contractors, architects, engineers, laborers, and even a private security company used at the construction site. Keep in mind statute 40-59-30(B): Notwithstanding Section 29-5-10, or another provision of law, a person or firm who first has not procured a license or registered with the commission and is required to do so by law may not file a mechanics' lien or bring an action at law or in equity to enforce the provisions of a contract for residential building or residential specialty contracting which the person or firm entered into in violation of this chapter.

Contract with the Property Owner: Generally speaking, the general contractor has a direct contract with the owner. Subcontractors and suppliers then contract with the general contractor and subcontractors may contract with additional subcontractors and suppliers. The state statutes allow all of these parties to file a lien.

Notice of Project Commencement

Within 15 days after beginning work, a contractor with a direct contractual relationship with the property owner may file a Notice of Project Commencement with the county clerk's office where the property is located.

Required Information: The Notice of Project Commencement should include the following information:

- ✓ Name and address of the person filing the Notice of Commencement
- ✓ Name and address of the owner or developer
- ✓ General description of the improvement
- ✓ Location of the project

Posting Requirements: After filing a Notice of Project Commencement, the name and address of the contractor must be posted at the jobsite. A location notice must also be posted at the job site. The location notice must contain the following statement: "The contractor on the project has filed a notice of project commencement at the county courthouse. Sub-subcontractors and suppliers to subcontractors shall comply with Section 29-5-20 when filing liens in connection with this project." This statement requires them to provide by certified or registered mail to the contractor the following information:

- ✓ Name of the subcontractor or supplier who claims payment
- ✓ Name of the person with whom the claimant contracted or by whom he was employed
- ✓ Description of the labor, service, or materials furnished and the contract price or value thereof (Note: Materials specially fabricated by a person other than the one giving notice and the contract price or value thereof shall be separately stated in the notice.)
- ✓ Description of the project for identification
- ✓ Date when the first and the last item of labor or service or materials was actually furnished or scheduled to be furnished
- ✓ Amount claimed to be due

After sending this notice, no payment by the contractor to the subcontractor will lessen the amount recoverable by the person giving the notice. This notice should also be sent to the property owner.

Time in Which to File: The Notice of Project Commencement must be filed within 15 days from the commencement of work.

Cost to File: The cost to file a Notice of Project Commencement is $15.

Not a "Cloud" on the Title of the Property: The filing of a Notice of Project Commencement shall not constitute a cloud, lien, or encumbrance on the title of the real property involved.

Notice to Owner by Laborer, Subcontractor, or Supplier

Persons supplying labor or materials without a contract directly with the owner must give written notice to the owner of what was furnished and its value. This notice is a prerequisite to having lien rights.

Dissolution of Lien for Failure to Serve Statement

A lien dissolves unless, within 90 days after the lienor last provided materials and/or labor for the construction project, a notice is given to the owner containing the following information:

- ✓ Name of the person who claims payment
- ✓ Description of labor, services, or materials furnished
- ✓ Contracted amount or value of labor, services, or materials furnished
- ✓ Description of the liened property
- ✓ Amount claimed to be due

This notice must be sworn to and also recorded at the county clerk's office.

Note: There are two notices that a person who does not have a contract directly with the owner should give to preserve the right to lien. The first notice is given at the start of the work or supplying materials. The second written notice is given within 90 days after the work is done or the materials supplied.

Time in Which to File a Lien Foreclosure Petition

A lawsuit to foreclose on the lien must be filed within six months after the lienor last provided materials and/or labor for the construction project.

Collecting on a Lien

Enforcement of a lien is done by filing a lawsuit in the county in which the property is located.

Lawsuit Contents: The lien lawsuit must contain:

- ✓ Brief statement of the contract
- ✓ Amount due (Note: The lienor must calculate the lien accurately and honestly. If the court decides that the amount due is intentionally overstated, the lien is in jeopardy of being invalidated.)
- ✓ Description of the property
- ✓ Any material facts or circumstances
- ✓ Statement that the property may be sold and the proceeds used to release the lien

Multiple Lien Claimants: Multiple parties may join together to file one lien petition to foreclose the liens.

Monetary Awards

Aggregate Amount: When multiple liens exist "in no event shall the aggregate amount of liens set up exceed the amount due by the owner on the contract price of the improvement made."

Prorating Liens: If the amount due to the contractor is not sufficient to pay all the lienors, the owner will prorate the amount due to all of those claiming a lien.

If the amount due to the sub-subcontractors or suppliers is not sufficient, the contractor will prorate the amount due to all of those claiming a lien.

Impact on Monetary Awards: The aggregate amount of any liens filed by a sub-subcontractor or supplier should not exceed the amount due by the contractor to the subcontractor to whom the sub-subcontractor or supplier has supplied labor, material, or services unless the sub-subcontractor or supplier has provided notice of furnishing labor or materials by certified or registered mail to the contractor.

Notice of Non-Responsibility

A Notice of Non-Responsibility can be filed by the owner who does not have a contract with the person supplying labor or materials that he will not be responsible for their fees. This prevents a lien from attaching to the property owner. This notice must be given to the person supplying the labor or materials.

Offer of Settlement

Either party may serve an Offer of Settlement after the lawsuit is filed to foreclose on the lien. The process for completing an Offer of Settlement is as follows:

- ✓ Initial offer must be made no less than 15 days before the first term of court at which the trial is set.
- ✓ Party being served may respond within 10 days.
- ✓ If agreement is not reached, a subsequent offer may be made 15 days prior to the next term of court.
- ✓ Response to the subsequent offer may be made within 10 days.

If acceptance of the Offer of Settlement is not made in writing, a trial will take place. The party whose offer is closer to the verdict reached is considered the prevailing party in the action. If the difference between both offers and the verdict is equal, neither party is considered to be the prevailing party for purposes of determining the award of costs and attorney's fees (South Carolina Code of Laws Section 29-5-10).

Sale of Land to Satisfy Lien

The judge can order the sale of the land to pay the lien or can remove the lien if it is not valid. An owner can also bond around the lien in the amount of one and one-third times the lien. The owner's bond allows the sale of the land with clear title, but also has the bond available to pay the lien holder if the lawsuit is successful.

Lien Process for Those in a Direct Contractual Relationship with Property Owner

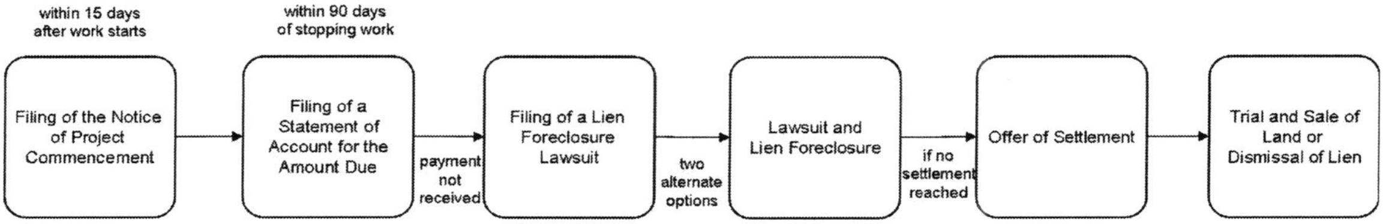

Lien Process for Subcontractors and Suppliers

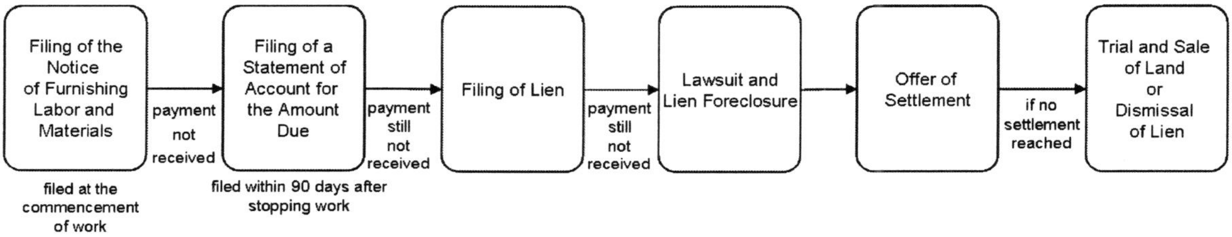

Final Inspection...

What is a Lien? A lien can be a useful tool in securing payment for labor or materials for improvement on real property.

Who is Entitled to a Mechanics' Lien? General contractors, subcontractors, suppliers, site work contractors, architects, engineers, laborers, and even a private security company used at the construction site have lien rights.

Notice of Project Commencement: Contractors with a direct contractual relationship to the owner may file a Notice of Project Commencement within 15 days after beginning work.

Notice to Owner by Laborer, Subcontractor, or Supplier: To preserve lien rights, those without a direct contractual relationship to the owner must provide a written notice of the labor and/or materials furnished and their value.

Dissolution of Lien for Failure to Serve Statement: Lien rights are forfeited if a written notice of labor and/or materials is not supplied within 90 days after last providing the materials and/or labor.

Time in Which to File a Lien Foreclosure Petition: A lien foreclosure petition must be filed within six months of last providing labor and/or materials.

Collecting on a Lien: A lien lawsuit must be filed in the county where the property is located and contain the required information.

Monetary Awards: If multiple liens exist, the total amount cannot exceed the contracted amount.

Notice of Non-Responsibility: To prevent a lien from attaching to the property, the owner who is not contracting to have the work done can file a Notice of Non-Responsibility.

Offer of Settlement: An Offer of Settlement may be served as a way of reaching an agreement without a trial.

Sale of Land to Satisfy Lien: To pay a lien, a judge may order the sale of the land that was improved. To release the lien, the owner may post a bond in the amount of one and one-third times the amount of the lien.

Appendix A: Glossary

A

Accelerated Depreciation: A method of depreciation where an asset is depreciated at a higher rate during the early part of its useful life permitting larger tax deductions.

Acceptance (Legal): An agreement to an offer made and generally is done by signing the offer. In some cases, a counteroffer is made. A counteroffer is not considered acceptance. It is only when both parties agree to the contract terms that you obtain acceptance.

Accounting Cycle: A process that happens each financial reporting period which starts with recording financial transactions and goes through analysis of financial statements.

Accounts Receivable: Monies that are owed to a business for products and/or services provided.

Accrual Method of Accounting: A method of accounting where income is recognized when the services occur, not when the money is collected. Expenses are recorded when they are incurred, not when they are paid.

Acid Test Ratio: See Quick Ratio.

Activity Ratio: A formula that measures how effectively a company manages its credit. It is calculated by dividing sales per day into current receivables.

Addenda or Addendum: Changes made to bid documents after they are issued but before they are due. Addenda ultimately become part of the contract after the bid is accepted.

ADA: The abbreviation for the Americans with Disabilities Act. See Americans with Disabilities Act.

AGC: The abbreviation for the Associated General Contractors of America.

Age Discrimination in Employment Act (ADEA): A federal law that prohibits discrimination against individuals who are age 40 or older.

AIA: The abbreviation for the American Institute of Architects.

All-Risk Builders' Risk Insurance: A form of property insurance that covers property owners and builders for buildings under construction typically covering machinery, equipment, materials, supplies, and fixtures that are part of the structure or will become part of the structure. Additional coverage can be added for items, such as temporary structures and scaffolding, used during construction. In general, major construction defects such as poor workmanship and faulty design are not covered.

Allowance: A specified amount designated in an estimate for items that are not specified in the project plans, such as finish materials (carpeting, fixtures, lighting, etc.).

Americans with Disabilities Act (ADA): The Americans with Disabilities Act (ADA) makes it unlawful to discriminate in employment against a qualified individual with a disability.

Arbitration: Arbitration uses a third-party arbitrator or arbitrators to act as a judge or judges to render a decision by which all parties are legally bound. Arbitration is held in a format less formal than a trial.

Asbestos: These naturally occurring, fibrous materials are woven together to create a product with high tensile strength. This material is commonly found in thermal insulation and fireproofing, roofing, and flooring materials.

When these fibers become airborne, they cause a hazard due to their ability to enter the lungs. Diseases associated with asbestos include asbestosis, lung cancer, and mesothelioma.

Asset: Items of value owned by a business.

At-Will Employment: An employment agreement where either the employer or the employee may terminate employment at any time without notice or cause.

Automobile Insurance: A type of insurance providing coverage for liability and physical damage associated with a company vehicle or a fleet of vehicles. All states require vehicle owners to carry some level of liability insurance covering bodily injury and property damage incurred in a vehicle accident.

B

Bad Debt: Uncollectible accounts receivable which is deducted from gross income when figuring taxable income.

Balance Sheet: One of the basic accounting financial statements that shows a company's assets, liabilities, and owners' equity.

Bank Letter of Credit: A cash guarantee that can be converted to a payment to the owner by a bank or lending institution.

Bid: A formal offer to complete a project according to the terms and conditions of the contract for a specified price.

Bid Bond: A type of bond that guarantees the contractor, if awarded the job, will do work at the submitted bid price, enter into a contract with the owner, and furnish the required performance and payment bonds.

Bid Documents: A bid package put together in a competitive bid situation. It may include an invitation to bid, bid instructions, bid sheet, bid schedule, bidder's questionnaire on experience, financial responsibility and capability, copy of the contract, and supplements.

Bid Peddling: An unethical situation where the subcontractor approaches the general contractor after the project is awarded with the intent of lowering the original price submitted on bid day.

Bid Rigging: A form of collusion where contractors coordinate their bids to fix the award outcome of a project.

Bid Shopping: An unethical situation where the general contractor approaches subcontractors other than those who have submitted bids to seek a lower offer than what was quoted in the original bids.

Boilerplate Provisions: Standard language or clauses used in a legal contract that generally appear at the end of the contract. Their purpose is to protect the business in the event of a lawsuit.

Bond: A risk transfer mechanism between a surety bonding company, the contractor, and the project owner. The agreement binds the contractor to comply with the terms and conditions of a contract. If the contractor cannot perform the contract, the surety bonding company assumes the contractor's responsibilities and ensures that the project is completed.

Breach of Contract: When one of the parties involved fails to perform in accordance with any of the terms and conditions of a contract.

Burglary and Theft Insurance: A type of insurance covering loss or damage caused by burglary, theft, larceny, robbery, forgery, fraud, and vandalism.

Business Owner's Policies (BOPs): A type of insurance that bundles property and liability coverage together to eliminate policy gaps or overlaps.

Business Plan: A planning document that outlines business strategies and goals. It is particularly useful for newly-formed or early-stage businesses and companies making major strategic changes. Typical contents are an executive and company summary, products and services description, market analysis, marketing plan, and financial plan.

C

Capital Assets: See Fixed Assets.

Cash Method of Accounting: A method of accounting where income is reported in the year it is received and expenses are deducted in the year they are paid.

Certificate of Occupancy: A certificate issued by a building inspector that deems a structure meets all applicable codes and is safe for occupancy.

Certificate of Substantial Completion: A certificate issued by the architect that deems a structure can be used for its intended purpose.

CFR: The abbreviation for Code of Federal Regulations.

Change Order: A written agreement between the owner and contractor to change the contract. Change orders add to, delete from, or otherwise alter the work set forth in the construction documents.

Circular E: An IRS Publication that provides instructions on calculating, withholding and depositing employee taxes and tax tables.

Clean Air Act: A federal law that allows the EPA to set limits on how much of a pollutant is allowed in the air anywhere in the United States.

Clean Water Act: A federal law that establishes the basic structure for regulating discharges of pollutants into the waters of the United States. This act gives the EPA authority to implement pollution control programs, such as setting wastewater standards for the industry and water quality standards for all contaminants in surface waters.

Collaborative Law: A facilitative process wherein all parties agree at the onset to work to identify a solution that is beneficial to all parties involved. In collaborative law, the parties use their advocates, most often their lawyers, to facilitate a mutually beneficial result through the process of negotiation.

Commercial General Liability Insurance (CGL): A basic liability insurance covering bodily injury that results in actual physical damage or loss for individuals who are not employees, damage or loss to property not belonging to the business, personal injury, including slander or damage to reputation, and advertising injury, including charges of negligence that result from promotion of goods or services.

Company Overhead: The expenses that are necessary to keep business operations running but not directly associated with a project (e.g. taxes, legal fees, etc.).

Completed Contract Method: A method of contract accounting where income or loss is reported in the year the contract is completed.

Completed Operations Liability Insurance: A type of liability insurance that provides coverage for loss arising out of completed projects.

Completion Bond: A type of bond that provides assurance to the financial backers of a construction project that it will be completed on time.

Conceptual Estimate: An estimate prepared by the architect using cost models from previous projects.

Consideration (Legal): When both parties give up something of value, typically, services and products in exchange for monetary compensation.

Consolidated Omnibus Budget Act of 1985 (COBRA): A federal law that gives "qualified beneficiaries" (a covered employee's spouse and dependent children) the right to maintain, at their own expense, coverage under their health plan that would be lost due to a "qualifying event," such as termination of employment, at a cost comparable to what it would be if they were still members of the employer's group.

Construction Management (Contracting): A type of contracting where the project owner contracts with a professional construction manager to coordinate and manage a construction project.

Construction Safety Act: See Contract Work Hours and Safety Standards Act.

Construction Wrap-Up Liability Insurance: A type of insurance that bundles liability and workers' compensation insurance for general contractors and subcontractors on large construction projects to eliminate gaps in coverage. To qualify for this type of insurance, certain contract cost requirements must be met. These requirements vary by state.

Contingency: A specified amount added to an estimate to protect the contractor if an unanticipated problem or condition arises during the course of the project.

Contract: Legally binding agreement between two or more parties with the main purpose of preventing disputes between parties entering into the agreement. A legally binding contract must have offer and acceptance, consideration, competent parties, and legal purpose.

Contract Work Hours and Safety Standards Act: A federal law that sets overtime standards for service and construction contracts on federal projects. Commonly referred to as the Construction Safety Act.

Contractor's Protective Public and Property Damage Liability Insurance: A type of liability insurance that protects contractors who supervise and subsequently are held liable for actions of subcontractors from claims for personal injury and property damage.

Contractual Liability Insurance: A type of liability insurance that provides contractors with protection for damages that result from their negligence while under written contract.

Corporation (sometimes referred to as C Corporation): A legal business entity that has independent ownership of assets and liabilities from its shareholders. Its existence continues even if one or more shareholders leave.

Cost Comparison Method: A method of contract accounting that combines the completed contract and percentage of completion methods.

Cost-Plus Contract: A type of contract where the contractor is reimbursed for the actual cost of labor and materials and is paid a markup fee for overhead and profit.

Critical Path: The sequence of tasks that determines the duration of the project. Subsequent project tasks cannot begin until a critical path item is complete.

Current Assets: Cash and other assets that can be converted into cash in less than one year.

Current Liabilities: Liabilities that will mature and must be paid within one year.

Current Ratio: See Liquidity Ratio.

D

Davis-Bacon Act: The federal law that requires payment of prevailing wage rates and fringe benefits on federally-financed or assisted construction.

Debt Ratio: A formula that measures the percent of total funds provided by creditors. It is calculated by dividing total assets into total debt.

De Minimis Violation: A violation of standards which have no direct or immediate relationship to safety or health.

Depreciation: The process of devaluing a fixed asset as a result of aging, wear and tear, or obsolescence.

Design/Build: A type of contracting where the owner contracts with one company to complete a construction project from start to finish. The company awarded the design/build contract puts together a team of construction professionals, which may include designers, architects, engineers, and contractors.

Direct Costs: Costs directly linked with a particular project.

E

EEOC: Abbreviation for the Equal Employment Opportunity Commission.

Employee Polygraph Protection Act: A federal law that prohibits most private employers from using any type of lie detector test, either for pre-employment screening of job applicants or for testing current employees during the course of employment.

Endangered Species Act (ESA): A federal law that protects threatened or endangered species from further harm.

Entrepreneur: A person engaged in strategic activities that involve the initiation and development of a new business, created to build long-term value and steady cash flow streams.

Equal Pay Act of 1963: A federal law that prohibits employers from paying different wages to men and women who perform essentially the same work under similar working conditions.

Equipment Floater Policy: A type of inland marine insurance covering direct physical loss to equipment and mobile equipment while it is stored on premises, in transit, or at temporary locations or jobsites.

Errors and Omissions Insurance: See Professional Liability Insurance.

Expenses: Monies paid out or owed for goods or services.

F

Failure to Abate Prior Violation: A safety violation given when a previous violation has not been corrected.

Fair Labor Standards Act (FLSA): The federal law which prescribes standards for the basic minimum wage and overtime pay and affects most private and public employment. It applies to employers who have one or more employees. FLSA is administered by the Employment Standards Administration's Wage and Hour Division within the U.S. Department of Labor.

Family and Medical Leave Act (FMLA): A federal law that entitles eligible employees of covered employers to take up to 12 weeks of unpaid job-protected leave each year, with the maintenance of group health insurance, for the birth and care of a child, for the placement of a child for adoption or foster care, for the care of a child, spouse, or parent with a serious health condition, or for the employee's serious health condition.

Fast Track Construction: A phased approach where the construction process begins before completion of the contract documents. Generally, the cost is not fixed until after construction documents are complete and some construction commitments have already been made.

Federal Employer Identification Number (EIN): A 9-digit number issued by the IRS, which is used to identify the tax accounts of employers and certain others who have no employees (also referred to as a taxpayer identification number).

Federal Unemployment Tax Act (FUTA): The federal unemployment tax that is part of the federal and state program under which unemployment compensation is paid to workers who lose their jobs.

Fidelity Bond: A type of bond that covers business owners for losses due to dishonest acts by their employees.

Fixed Assets: Assets needed to carry on the business of a company, which are not normally consumed in the operation of the business (sometimes referred to as capital assets).

Foreign Entity: A business originally established in another state or another country.

Foreman: An individual who assists the superintendent with daily project operations and usually supervises specific areas by trade.

For Profit Corporation: A corporation in existence to make a profit for its owners or shareholders. Corporate tax status is determined by the Internal Revenue Service.

FUTA: An abbreviation for Federal Unemployment Tax Act.

H

Health Insurance Portability and Accountability Act of 1996 (HIPAA): A federal law that provides for improved portability and continuity of health insurance coverage connected with employment.

I

I-9 Form: The form required for employers to complete to verify employment eligibility under the Immigration and Nationality Act. I-9 forms must be kept on file for at least three years after the date of hire or for one year after the date employment ends, whichever is later.

Immaterial Breach (Partial Breach): A less serious violation of a contract that usually does not result in termination of the contract. The injured party may only sue for the value of the damages.

Immigration and Nationality Act (INA): A federal law that outlines the conditions for the temporary and permanent employment of aliens in the United States. It includes provisions for all employers that address employment eligibility and employment verification.

Income Statement: A financial statement that provides a summary of the company's revenues and expenses over a given period of time (sometimes called the profit-and-loss statement).

Indemnification: A way to transfer risk and exemption from loss that absolves the indemnified party from any payment for losses and damages incurred by a third party.

Indemnity: A way to transfer risk and exemption from loss incurred by any course of action. Sometimes an insurance payout is called an indemnity.

Indirect Expenses: See Operating Expenses.

Inland Marine Insurance (Equipment Theft Insurance): A type of property insurance for your tools and equipment that provides coverage for goods in transit and projects under construction.

Insurance: A protective measure in which coverage is obtained for a specific risk (or set of risks) through a contract. In this contract or policy, one party indemnifies another against specified loss in return for premiums paid.

K

Key Man Insurance: A type of insurance coverage for a specific individual necessary for the continuing success of a business. Key man insurance is available as life insurance, disability insurance, or both.

L

Lead-Based Paint Renovation, Repair and Painting Program: This federal regulation involves those who perform renovations for compensation in residential housing that may contain lead paint. It requires for additional provisions to the Lead PRE regulations. Under the Lead-Based Paint Renovation, Repair and Painting Program, contractors must be certified to perform renovation work that disturbs lead-based paint in homes, child care facilities, and schools built before 1978.

Lead PRE: This federal regulation involves those who perform renovations for compensation in residential housing built before 1978 that may contain lead paint. It requires mandatory notification for owners and occupants of the building being renovated.

Liabilities: All debt and obligations owed by a business.

Liability Insurance: A type of insurance designed to protect against third-party claims that arise from alleged negligence resulting in bodily injury or property damage.

Lien Bond: A type of bond that guarantees liens cannot be placed against the owner's property by contractors for payment of services.

Liquid Assets: Assets that are easily converted to cash.

Limited Liability Company (LLC): A legal business entity that has characteristics of both sole proprietorships and corporations. Federal income taxes are paid only on income distributed to members as ordinary income. Members have protection from liability for actions taken by the company or by other members of your company but are not protected from liability for personal actions.

Liquidity Ratio: A calculation used to determine if a company can pay its current debts. Calculated by dividing current liabilities into the current assets (sometimes called current ratio).

Little Miller Acts: Laws enacted by individual states and local governments regarding required bonds to bid and perform public works projects.

Long-Term Liabilities: Debt obligations that extend beyond one year.

Lump Sum Contract: A contract where the contractor agrees to complete the project for a predetermined, specified price. The contractor essentially assumes all of the risk under this contract agreement because the contractor is responsible for additional costs associated with unforeseen circumstances.

M

Maintenance Bond: A type of bond that guarantees for a stated period, typically for one year, no defective workmanship or material will appear in the completed project.

Marketing: Strategies and techniques used to bring in new customers and retain current customers to ensure a steady flow of leads and customers. This process includes advertising and promotion, pricing strategies, timely distribution, and product design and attributes to meet customer needs.

Marketing Plan: A formal document focusing on a company's marketing strategy by outlining the company's vision, customer base, methods of promotion (e.g. advertising, public relations, online marketing, direct sales, etc.), marketing budget, individual responsible for executing the plan, and industry opportunities and challenges.

MasterFormat: A classification system published by the Construction Specifications Institute that includes numbers and job tasks grouped by major construction activities.

Material Breach: A serious violation of a contract that may void the contract and will most likely end up in litigation.

Material Safety Data Sheet (MSDS): A form that accompanies chemicals and is important to workplace safety. The MSDS contains information such as first aid when contact occurs, disposal, storage, protective equipment required, and spill handling procedures.

Materials Expediter: An individual who supervises the materials procurement process to ensure accurate and timely delivery of materials.

Mechanics' Lien: A legal action that "clouds" the title to real property and serves as an effective method (and sometimes the only method) for securing payment for labor or materials used in the improvement of real property. The lien stops the owner from selling the property with a clear title.

Medicare: Social Security and Medicare taxes pay for benefits that workers and families receive under the Federal Insurance Contributions Act (FICA). Medicare tax pays for benefits under the hospital insurance part of FICA.

Miller Act: The Miller Act requires performance and payment bonds on all federal construction projects valued at greater than $100,000.

Minimum Wage: The minimum amount an employer can pay employees. FLSA and individual state laws designate the minimum pay rate.

Minor: An individual under 18 years of age.

Modified Accelerated Cost Recovery System (MACRS): A depreciation method approved by the IRS that allows for faster depreciation over longer periods.

Motor Truck Cargo Insurance: A type of inland marine insurance protecting the transporter in the event of damaged or lost freight.

N

Named Peril Builders' Risk Insurance: An insurance policy with narrower coverage than all-risk insurance that specifies which perils are covered.

National Environmental Policy Act (NEPA): A federal law that ensures that federal agencies consider environmental impacts in federal planning and decision making and covers construction and post-construction activities.

National Historic Preservation Act (NHPA): A federal law that protects property that is eligible for or included on the National Register of Historic Places (NRHP).

Negotiation (Alternative Dispute Resolution): A dialogue entered into for the purpose of resolving disputes or producing an agreed upon course or courses of action.

Negotiation (Contract): The process where the owner and contractor come to an agreement on the price and terms of the contract.

Net Pay: The payroll amount an employee receives after taxes and deductions are taken out.

Net Profit: The difference between revenues and expenses. Net profit directly contributes to the net worth of the company.

NPDES: The abbreviation for the National Pollutant Discharge Elimination System.

O

Occupational Safety and Health Act (OSHA): Federal law governing safe and healthy working conditions by developing standards, providing assistance, information and training, and conducting research.

Offer: An offer specifically outlines the obligations of the contract, including the work to be done and compensation for this work (e.g. estimate or bid).

Operating Expenses: General items that contribute to the cost of operating the business. These expenses can be put into two categories, selling expenses and fixed overhead (sometimes called indirect expenses).

OSHA: An abbreviation for Occupational Safety and Health Administration; Occupational Safety and Health Act.

OSHA Form 300: An OSHA form that serves as an injury/illness log, with a separate line entry for each recordable injury or illness.

OSHA Form 300A: An OSHA form that includes a summary of the previous year's work-related injuries and illnesses.

OSHA Form 301: An OSHA form that serves as an individual incident report providing details about each specific recordable injury or illness.

Other Than Serious Violation: A safety violation that has a direct relationship to workplace safety and health, but probably would not cause death or serious physical harm.

Overhead: See company overhead; project overhead.

Overtime: The hours an employee works when it exceeds more than 40 hours in a workweek. FLSA designates that eligible employees are paid one-and-one-half-times the regular rate for overtime hours.

Owners' Equity: Consists of the initial investment in a business, plus accumulated net profits not paid out to the owners.

Owner's Representative (Owner's Agent): An appointed representative designated to oversee a project and serve as a liaison to the owner. The owner's representative (agent) may have legal authority to make certain legal decisions on behalf of the owner.

P

Partnership: A business relationship between two or more persons who join to carry on a trade or business. Each person contributes money, property, labor, or skill, and each partner expects to share in the profits and losses of the business.

Payment Bond: A type of bond that guarantees subcontractors and suppliers will be paid for work if they perform properly under the contract.

Percentage of Completion Method: A method of contract accounting that recognizes income as it is earned during the construction project.

Performance Bond: A type of bond that guarantees the contractor will complete a contract within its time frame and conditions.

Petty Cash Fund: A cash fund used to make small payments instead of writing a check.

Positive Cash Flow: A term used to describe when more cash is received than is going out to pay expenses.

Professional Liability Insurance (sometimes called Errors and Omissions Insurance): A type of liability insurance that protects contractors from negligence resulting from errors or omissions of designers and architects.

Profitability Ratio: A formula used to calculate the profit margin of a company. It is calculated by dividing revenues into net income.

Profit-and-Loss Statement: See Income Statement.

Progressive Discipline: A method of corrective action where the consequences of the improper behavior become more significant if it continues.

Progress Payments: Partial payments made after completion of specified phases of construction. Payments are generally calculated by taking the difference between the completed work and materials delivered and a predetermined schedule of unit costs.

Project Manager: An individual who plans and coordinates a construction project to meet the overall goals of the project and serves as the main contact with the owner.

Project Overhead: Items necessary to complete the project but not directly associated with labor and materials (e.g. temporary storage, dumpsters, etc.).

Property Insurance: An insurance policy covering property when damage, theft, or loss occurs. Specific risk provisions are often available for occurrences such as fire or theft. Broad-based policies cover a variety of risks (including fire, theft, vandalism, and "acts of God" such as lightning strikes).

Q

Quick Ratio: Similar to the liquidity ratio, it is calculated by dividing the current liabilities into the current assets minus inventory (sometimes called the acid test ratio).

R

Recitals (Legal): Language at the beginning of a contract that provides background to the contract.

Repeated Violation: A safety violation of any standard, regulation, rule, or order where, upon reinspection, a substantially similar violation is found.

Retainage: A specified amount withheld from each progress payment as protection for the owner to ensure completion of the construction project and provide protection against liens, claims, and defaults.

Return on Total Assets Ratio: A formula used to determine if the company's assets are being employed in the best manner. It is calculated by dividing total assets into net profit (after taxes).

Revenues: The income received from the daily operations of the business.

Right-to-Work Laws: Laws passed at the state-level that secure the right of employees to decide for themselves whether or not to join or financially support a union.

Risk Management: An assessment of all areas of a business from operations to administrative functions for the risk of financial loss, lower profit margins, and unnecessary liabilities.

S

S Corporation: A legal business entity formed under the rules of Subchapter S of the Internal Revenue Code. It is taxed like a partnership by passing items of income, loss, deduction, and credits through to its shareholders to be included on their separate returns.

Self-Employment Tax: A social security and Medicare tax primarily for individuals who work for themselves.

Serious Violation: A violation where there is substantial probability that death or serious physical harm could result and that the employer knew, or should have known, of the hazard.

Service Contract Act: The federal act that requires payment of prevailing wage rates and fringe benefits on contracts to provide services to the federal government.

Single Prime Contracting: Traditional form of contracting where the project owner typically hires an architectural firm to design the project and the contractor then performs the work according to the specifications of the project and is responsible for the costs of all materials and labor to obtain project completion.

Social Security Tax: Social Security and Medicare taxes pay for benefits that workers and families receive under the Federal Insurance Contributions Act (FICA). Social Security tax pays for benefits under the old-age, survivors, and disability insurance part of FICA.

Sole Proprietorship: A business that has one individual as the owner (proprietor) who is responsible for 100% of the decisions made on behalf of the business and owns all of the business assets. It can employ others but may just be the owner who works for the business.

Square-Foot Method Estimate: An estimate based on a calculation of the square footage of the project multiplied by a unit cost.

Statement of Cash Flows: A financial statement that summarizes current cash position, cash sources, and use of these funds over a given period of time.

Statute of Limitations: Laws that set a maximum period of time within which a lawsuit or claim may be filed.

Straight Line Depreciation: A method of depreciation where the salvage cost is subtracted from the initial cost of the item.

Subcontractor: An individual or business that contracts with the general contractor or other subcontractors to complete a portion of a larger project.

Subcontractor's Bond: A type of bond that protects the general contractor in the event that the subcontractor does not fully perform the contract and/or pay for labor and materials.

Superintendent: An onsite supervisor responsible for the daily operations.

SUTA Dumping: The transfer of employees between businesses for the purpose of obtaining a lower unemployment compensation tax rate. SUTA dumping is illegal and subject to criminal and/or civil penalties.

T

Taxpayer Identification Number: See Federal Employer Identification Number.

Tax Provision Expenses: Tax liabilities owed for federal, state, and local taxes.

Title III of the Consumer Credit Protection Act (CCPA): A federal law that protects employees from being discharged by their employers because their wages have been garnished for any one debt and limits the amount of employees' earnings that may be garnished in any one week.

Title VII of the Civil Rights Act of 1964: A federal law that prohibits discrimination on the basis of race, color, religion, national origin, and sex.

Transportation Floater Insurance: A type of inland marine insurance protecting the transporter against damage that occurs to freight during transport.

Turnkey Construction: Similar to the design/build model, the contractor puts together and manages the construction and design team but also obtains financing and land.

U

Unemployment Insurance: A type of insurance that provides unemployment benefits to eligible workers who become unemployed through no fault of their own and meet certain other eligibility requirements. This program is jointly financed through federal and state employer payroll taxes.

Uniformed Services Employment and Reemployment Rights Act (USERRA): A federal law that protects service members' reemployment rights when returning from a period of service in the uniformed services, including those called up from the reserves or National Guard, and prohibits employer discrimination based on military service or obligation.

Unit-Price Contract: A type of contract where a price per unit is calculated for each item and the contractor is paid according to the actual quantities used.

Unit Price Estimating Method: A method of estimating that bundles all of the cost factors such as labor, materials, equipment, and subcontractors to come up with a unit price for the entire task.

V

Value Engineering: A project management approach with the primary objective of understanding the owner's cost, quality, and time priorities to deliver a product of the highest value.

W

Wage Garnishment Law: A federal law that limits the amount an individual's income may be legally garnished and prohibits firing an employee whose pay is garnished for payment of a single debt.

Walsh-Healey Public Contracts Act: A federal law that requires payment of minimum wage rates and overtime pay on contracts that provide goods to the federal government.

Willful Violation: A safety violation that the employer knowingly commits or commits with plain indifference to the law.

Work Hours: As defined under FLSA, hours that ordinarily include all time during which an employee is required to be on the employer's premises, on duty, or at a prescribed work place.

Worker Adjustment and Retraining Notification Act (WARN): A federal law that offers protection to workers, their families, and communities by requiring employers to provide notice 60 days in advance of covered plant closings and covered mass layoffs.

Workers' Compensation Insurance: A type of insurance providing monetary compensation to employees who are injured or disabled on the job and benefits for dependents of those workers who are killed because of work-related accidents or illnesses. The insurance is purchased by the employer; no part of it should be paid for by employees or deducted from their pay.

Working Capital: The amount of cash available after liabilities or debts are paid. Working capital measures the liquidity of the company's assets.

Workweek: As defined under FLSA, it is a period of 168 hours during seven consecutive 24-hour periods. It may begin on any day of the week and at any hour of the day established by the employer.

Appendix B: Business Plan Template

The following business plan template can be customized for your company. These forms are also located at **NASCLAforms.org** using access code **SCR129354** in case you need to modify them on your computer. You may want to work through this plan as you review each chapter, as some of the business plan section topics are covered in more depth.

Business Plan Outline	
Section 1: Cover Sheet 1a. Name of Business 1b. Contact Information **Section 2: Executive Summary** 2a. Plan Highlights 2b. Keys to Success **Section 3: Company Summary** 3a. Vision 3b. Mission 3c. Legal Structure 3d. Management and Personnel Plan 3e. Proposed Location 3f. Facilities Requirements 3g. Operational Hours **Section 4: Products and/or Service** 4a. Product and/or Service Description 4b. Vendors 4c. Technology 4d. Expansion Opportunities	**Section 5: Market Analysis** 5a. Target Market Definition 5b. Market Needs 5c. Market Trends 5d. Market Growth 5e. Competitive Comparison **Section 6: Marketing Strategy** 6a. Value Proposition 6b. Competitive Edge 6c. Pricing Strategy 6d. Promotion Strategy 6e. Marketing Programs **Section 7: Financial Plan** 7a. Sales Forecast and Assumptions 7b. Profit and Loss Pro Forma 7c. Source of Financing

Note: You may also refer to the Financial Management chapter for additional financial documents such as a balance sheet, income statement, and statement of cash flows. The profit and loss pro forma is a good tool for newly-established businesses to determine how much revenue is needed to break even.

Section 1: Cover Sheet

The cover sheet should contain the name of the business, address, phone number, fax number, email address, and contact name. Some cover sheets also contain a confidentiality statement.

Section 2: Executive Summary

A business plan normally starts with an executive summary, which should be concise and interesting. This summary includes the highlights of your plan and serves as an introduction to the rest of your plan. Topics in your executive summary should include, but not be limited to, the following:

- ✓ Business name
- ✓ Business location
- ✓ Product or service offered
- ✓ Purpose of the plan
- ✓ Projected sales
- ✓ Profitability
- ✓ Keys to success

The executive summary should only be a page or two long. Although the executive summary appears first in the printed document, most business plan developers do not write it until after the plan is complete.

Section 3: Company Summary

1. **Vision and Mission:** Include a vision and mission statement for your company. The vision should be a short statement about the company's aspirations for the future. The mission describes the company's primary business purpose or goal. These statements outline the business concept and provide a concise definition of where your company fits in the market.
2. **Legal Structure:** Define the legal structure of your company (i.e., sole proprietorship, partnership, corporation, or limited liability company). Explain why you chose this structure and the benefits it will provide to you and your company. Legal structure is covered in Chapter 2.
3. **Management:** Outline the key management personnel needed to run your business. Can you run the business yourself or do you need to hire managers to help run the operations? What are the job responsibilities of these managers?
4. **Employees:** How many employees do you require? What are the job responsibilities of the employees?
5. **Location:** Describe the location of your business. You do not need to provide a specific address if you do not have one, but identify the area (e.g., downtown location, at home, in a rural area). Explain why this location will provide you with the best opportunity for success.
6. **Facility Requirements:** Identify your facility requirements. Do you need office space, a production area, storage space, or mobile storage? You may want to draw a diagram of the space.
7. **Hours of Operation:** What are your hours of operation? Explain how these hours will provide the maximum benefit to your customer. How will you handle emergency situations that arise outside of normal working hours?

Section 4: Product or Service Description

Defining your product or service (or both) may seem simple. You must describe not only your product or service but how you will provide it to your customers. For example, you may be a general contractor, but without reliable subcontractors and suppliers, you may not be able to complete your projects in the time frame promised to the customer.

1. **Product or Service Description:** Write a summary explaining your specialty. For example, are you a general contractor, plumbing contractor, etc.?
2. **Legal Requirements:** Do you have any licensing or registration requirements? Are there any legal requirements for practicing your trade or running your business?
3. **Subcontractors and Suppliers:** Who will be your primary subcontractors and suppliers? What process will you use to evaluate subcontractors and suppliers?
4. **Technology Trends:** Summarize how technology will affect your business. Are there efficiencies that can be gained through technology? For example, can you integrate scheduling or estimating systems into your business processes?
5. **Growth Opportunities:** What expansion opportunities exist in the future after your company is established? Can you offer additional products or services, or expand your customer base to other locations?

Section 5: Market Analysis

A market analysis is often performed as one of the first tasks in researching and formulating a business plan. Understanding your customers, the demand for your work, and your competition is important to the future success of your business.

1. **Target Market:** Define the target market for your product or service. Describe the key characteristics of your customers. For example, do your primary customers include families, retired adults, or businesses?
2. **Product or Service Description:** Describe the need your product or service will be filling for your customers. If you will provide both products and services, describe how these will benefit your customers.
3. **Trends:** Describe how your product or service aligns with the consumer trends of your customers. What are the construction trends for your trade and how do these fit your customer's needs?
4. **Growth Opportunities:** Outline growth opportunities that exist within your target market. For example, if you are a pool builder and your target market is young families, you may want to concentrate on single-family homes rather than commercial projects.
5. **Competition:** List your major competitors. Are they local, regional, or national?

Section 6: Marketing Strategy

A marketing strategy is easily formulated by using the "4 P's:" Product, Price, Promotion, and Place. Product is not just your product or service, but how it will benefit your customer. Price refers to your pricing strategy, which can vary based on the market, your goals, and your competition. Promotion deals with marketing in a traditional sense. Your customers will find out about your business through your promotional efforts. Place defines your distribution strategy. In the construction industry, distribution defines the type of customers you want to target. For example, you may decide to differentiate yourself by specializing in certain types of construction.

1. **Value Proposition:** Describe the value that your company will provide your customers. What benefits of using your company will you promote to your customers? For example, you may promote your level of quality or service.
2. **Competitive Edge:** Describe what makes your product or service unique and how you have differentiated yourself from your competitors.
3. **Pricing Strategy:** What pricing strategy will you use? Some options include:
   - ✓ Cost-plus pricing, where you determine a markup percentage and add it to the cost of the job.
   - ✓ Consistency with competition, where your pricing reflects what the competition is charging.
   - ✓ Value pricing, where you try to undercut your competition with lower prices.

4. **Promotion:** How will you familiarize potential customers with your business? Will you promote your product in special venues (i.e., trade shows or special events)? Are there any businesses you can build a co-op relationship with so you can cross-promote each other? For example, you might partner with another trade or supplier to promote each other.
5. **Advertising:** How will you advertise? Will you use media such as radio, TV, newspapers, and the Internet? How often will you advertise?
6. **Sales:** Will you hire sales representatives to promote your company? If so, how many? How will the sales force be divided up? By area or region?

Section 7: Financial Plan

A financial plan can include several aspects of the potential financial health of the company. At a minimum, it should include projected profits over a specific period. This template, for example, shows the first three years of operation. The financial plan should also explain projected cash flow and identify any additional capital required from outside investors or loans.

The profit-and-loss statement is a tabulation of the gross sales income for the company from which all attributed costs must be deducted. A *pro forma* is a "best guess" at these sales numbers and the associated costs. From this pro forma, you can see your profit or loss based on the numbers you projected and adjust your budget accordingly. A blank profit-and-loss form is located at the end of this section, if you are unable to use the form on the **NASCLAforms.org** website. If you use the spreadsheet located on the website, it will automatically calculate gross profit and net income.These calculations were derived from the following formulas:

Income - Cost of Goods Sold = Gross Profit
Gross Profit - Expenses = Net Income

You learn about financial calculations in the financial management chapter (Chapter 14).

Sales/Income

Use the following points to help you make your sales and expense projections.

You need to determine the average price of the jobs you perform and the number of customers you are projecting for the year. This is your "best guess," but if you have any historical sales data, you may want to use this information in your calculations to determine how your business sales will grow over time.

However you determine your sales, you must list your assumptions so the person reviewing your business plan will understand the numbers presented in your plan.

Projected sales numbers

	Sales (in dollars)
Year 1	
Year 2	
Year 3	

Transfer sales numbers into the profit-and-loss worksheet.

Cost of Goods Sold (COGS)

Cost of goods sold shows the cost of materials and production of the goods a business sells. For each year, enter your inventory cost and the cost to produce the final product for the customer and add together to show the totals. This total represents the cost of goods sold.

	Year 1	Year 2	Year 3
Inventory			
Production Payroll			
Total			

Transfer COGS numbers into the profit-and-loss worksheet.

Management Salaries

Determine how many managers or supervisors you will need to operate your business. A published salary survey will help you estimate what they earn in your type of business and in your region. Determine if you will need to add managers or supervisors in years two and three if you have an increase in business.

	Number of Managers	Manager Annual Salary	Total Management Salaries
Year 1			
Year 2			
Year 3			

Enter the total management salaries in the respective boxes on your spreadsheet.

Payroll Taxes

Payroll taxes are calculated at approximately 13% of the salaries listed on your spreadsheet. A formula has been entered to calculate that amount automatically.

Payroll taxes include the following items:

- ✓ Social Security, also known as FICA (a set percentage deducted from an employee's check and EMPLOYER MATCHED)
- ✓ Medicare, also called FICA Medicare (a set percentage deducted from an employee's check and EMPLOYER MATCHED)
- ✓ FUTA - Federal Unemployment Tax Act, authorizes the IRS to use monies for job service and training funded through the federal employment agency; EMPLOYER PAID ONLY
- ✓ SUTA - State Unemployment Tax Act, authorizes the state to use monies for job service/training and retraining of displaced workers; EMPLOYER-PAID ONLY
- ✓ FUI - Federal Unemployment Insurance; EMPLOYER-PAID ONLY
- ✓ SUI - State Unemployment Insurance; EMPLOYER-PAID ONLY

More details on payroll taxes are provided in Chapter 15.

Outside Services

These services apply to people or businesses who provide services to your company not directly related to the sales or income of the company. They would not appear on your payroll. Estimate your annual expenses for the following outside services. Keep in mind that the cost may be higher in the first year due to start-up needs. The cost may drop in the second year and then level off in the third year.

	Year 1	Year 2	Year 3
Lawyer			
Accountant			
Technology Consultant			
Total			

Enter the year totals into the spreadsheet.

Advertising and Promotion

Consider the type of marketing you will need. If you are creating a radio, print media, online, social media, or TV ad, get an estimate on what that would cost. Don't forget to calculate the frequency of advertising you will do. For example, let's say a magazine ad costs $1,000 for a quarter-page ad and the magazine comes out monthly. Your advertising cost would be $12,000 a year. You may want to advertise by printing flyers and mailing them out. Calculate the printing costs as well as the postage to send out the flyers.

	Year 1	Year 2	Year 3
Radio			
TV			
Newspaper			
Magazine			
Flyers			
Direct Mail			
Special Events			
Online Ads			
Other (i.e., social media) Please Specify:			
Total			

Enter the year totals into the spreadsheet.

Rent

If you rent a facility, determine the rental costs per year. If you have not decided on a location, you may want to look at a few locations and calculate an average rent cost to determine a figure for this category. Keep in mind the square footage requirements that you have set out.

	Annual Rent
Location #1	
Location #2	
Location #3	
Average of all three locations	

If you are going to stay in one location, your rent should remain fixed over three years. If you plan on expanding in years two and three, you may want to increase rent accordingly.

Enter the average of all three locations in the rent column on your spreadsheet.

Office Supplies

Office supplies include items such as paper, pens, printer cartridges, tape, and other materials as well as cleaning supplies. As your business increases, the consumption of these supplies may increase accordingly.

	Year 1	Year 2	Year 3
Office Supplies			
Cleaning Supplies			
Total			

Enter the year totals into the spreadsheet.

Dues, Subscriptions, and Licenses

You may want to join a Chamber of Commerce or trade group or subscribe to trade publications. Your business may also need a license to operate. For example, if you are starting a plumbing company, you may be required to get a contractor's license.

	Year 1	Year 2	Year 3
Chamber of Commerce Membership			
Business Organization Membership (i.e., National Homebuilders Association)			
Magazine/Newspaper Subscriptions			
Business License Fees			
Total			

Enter the year totals into the spreadsheet.

Travel

Does your business require you to travel to meet with customers? Will you travel locally, regionally, or nationally? What are the air travel, rental car, and hotel costs for this travel requirement? Note that the spreadsheet has a separate section for automobile expenses, where you enter costs such as gasoline or repairs. Use the automobile expense section for trips that will be taken in a company or personal vehicle.

	Year 1	Year 2	Year 3
Air Travel			
Rental Cars			
Hotel			
Other Please Specify:			
Total			

Enter the year totals into the spreadsheet.

Meals and Entertainment

Determine if you will be providing meals or taking your clients and vendors out for entertainment.

Keep in mind that the IRS allows you to take only a 50 percent deduction on meals and entertainment. It is not considered a 100 percent business expense. Although you enter the full amount on your profit-and-loss statement, your tax accountant will make the proper adjustments on your tax return at the end of the year.

	Year 1	Year 2	Year 3
Meals			
Entertainment			
Total			

Enter the year totals into the spreadsheet.

Automobile Expense

Determine if you will need one or more automobiles or trucks to operate your business. The cost to purchase each vehicle appears under "Assets" on your balance sheet, and the cost to operate the vehicles appears under automobile expense on the profit-and-loss statement.

	Year 1	Year 2	Year 3
Gasoline			
Oil Changes			
Car Washes			
Other (Repairs) Please Specify:			
Total			

Enter the annual totals into the spreadsheet.

Utilities and Telephone

Determine what your utilities and telephone costs will be for the first three years your business is operational. To arrive at this estimate, you will need to determine how many telephone lines and cell phones you need. You should also itemize Internet service and record these totals under this line item.

	Year 1	Year 2	Year 3
Electric			
Water			
Garbage			
Telephone			
Internet Service			
Other Please Specify:			
Total			

Enter the annual totals into the spreadsheet.

Auto Insurance

If you have business vehicles, you will need to carry insurance on them. If you increase the number of vehicles in years two and three, insurance expenses will increase as well. Certain vehicles may also cost more to insure than others. For example, if you have delivery trucks, the insurance will probably be more expensive than a mid-size car.

	Year 1	Year 2	Year 3
Vehicle #1			
Vehicle #2			
Vehicle #3			
Total			

Enter the annual totals into the spreadsheet.

Group Medical Insurance

You may want to carry medical, dental, or life insurance for your employees as a benefit and to increase employee retention.

	Year 1	Year 2	Year 3
Medical			
Dental			
Life			
Total			

Enter the annual totals into the spreadsheet.

Business Insurance

By law, businesses are required to carry workers' compensation insurance. Business liability insurance protects your business against accidents such as fire, flooding, burglary, etc. Business liability insurance is not required by law but by contract. For example, most landlords require you to carry business liability insurance, as do banks and governmental agencies with which you have a contract. Insurance and risk management are covered in more detail in the managing risk chapter (Chapter 4).

	Year 1	Year 2	Year 3
Workers' Compensation			
Business Liability			
Total			

Enter the annual totals into the spreadsheet.

Worksheet

This is a scratch sheet for entering estimates and data that can then be entered in the spreadsheet.

	Year 1	Year 2	Year 3
Income			
Sales			
Total Income	0.00	0.00	0.00
Cost of Goods Sold			
Inventory Cost			
Production Payroll Cost			
Total COGS	0.00	0.00	0.00
Gross Profit	0.00	0.00	0.00
Expense			
Management Salaries			
Payroll Taxes	0.00	0.00	0.00
Outside Services			
Advertising and Promotion			
Rent			
Office Supplies			
Dues, Subscriptions, and Licenses			
Travel			
Meals and Entertainment			
Automobile Expense			
Utilities/Telephone			
Insurance Auto			
Insurance Group Medical			
Business Insurance			
Total Expense	0.00	0.00	0.00
Net Income	**0.00**	**0.00**	**0.00**

Appendix C: Useful Links

Listed below are website links that relate to each of the chapters. These websites are provided for your reference for more in-depth searches of the topic areas contained in this book. Internet links to these websites are provided at **NASCLAforms.org** using access code **SCR129354**.

Chapter 1 - The Plan

American Express Small Business	American Express offers business planning links and an area where you can post questions for a small business advisor.	www.americanexpress.com/us/small-business/openforum/explore
Business Plan Pro	This site offers tools on how to write a business plan, including samples.	www.bplans.com
Sample Business Plans	These sites provide sample business plans and other valuable business management materials.	www.allbusiness.com www.inc.com www.bizmove.com/small-business/business-plan.htm www.bizmove.com/starting/m1e2.htm
SBA Business Planning	The SBA has several different links on writing and using your business plan.	www.sba.gov/business-guide/plan-your-business/write-your-business-plan

Chapter 2 - Choosing Your Business Structure

IRS Business Structures	The IRS provides a summary of tax considerations by business structure.	www.irs.gov/businesses/small-businesses-self-employed
SBA Legal Aspects	The SBA has several different links on forms of ownership and licenses.	www.sba.gov/business-guide/launch-your-business/apply-licenses-and-permits
South Carolina Secretary of the State	The South Carolina Secretary of the State, Corporations Division has information on business filings and forms.	www.scsos.com

Chapter 3 - Becoming a Licensed Contractor

PSI Exams Online	Licensing candidates can register online for exams and download the Candidate Information Bulletin.	candidate.psiexams.com
South Carolina Department of Labor, Licensing and Regulation	The South Carolina Department of Labor, Licensing and Regulation regulates contractor licensing. Their website has useful information on the licensing process and licensing forms.	www.llr.sc.gov/POL/Contractors

Chapter 4 - Managing Risk

Entrepreneur.com	Entrepreneur.com has links to insurance resources.	www.entrepreneur.com/topic/insurance
South Carolina Department of Labor, Licensing and Regulation	This site provides information on unemployment tax and compensation facts that South Carolina employers and workers need to know.	www.llr.sc.gov
South Carolina Workers' Compensation Commission	This site has information on the rules, practice, and procedures involved with workers' compensation.	wcc.sc.gov
Surety Information Office	This site has resources related to bonding, bank letters of credit and publishes the "Construction Project Owners Guide to Surety Bond Claims."	www.sio.org

Chapter 5 - Your Business Toolbox

SBA Special Interests	The SBA has several different links for women and minority entrepreneurs.	www.sba.gov/business-guide/grow-your-business/women-owned-businesses
Service Corps of Retired Executives (SCORE)	The SCORE website has useful links for small business and a listing of local SCORE centers.	www.score.org
Small Business Administration (SBA)	The SBA website has resources for small businesses and a link to the South Carolina District Office website.	www.sba.gov/offices/district/sc/columbia
Small Business Administration (SBA) Small Disadvantaged Business Certification	The SBA website has resources for small disadvantaged business certifications.	https://www.sba.gov/federal-contracting/contracting-assistance-programs/8a-business-development-program
South Carolina Department of Commerce	The South Carolina Department of Commerce has information on starting and growing your business.	www.sccommerce.com
U.S. Department of Commerce, Economic Development Administration	The U.S. Department of Commerce, EDA division has information on funding opportunities and additional resources.	www.eda.gov
U.S. Minority Business Development Agency (MBDA)	The U.S. MBDA website has links on starting, managing, and financing your business.	www.mbda.gov
USA.gov Website	The USA.gov website provides several online resources to federal, state, and local information for business owners.	www.usa.gov/business

Chapter 6 - Marketing and Sales

Entrepreneur.com Marketing	Entrepreneur.com has several articles on small business marketing.	www.entrepreneur.com/topic/marketing
KnowThis.com Sample Marketing Plans	KnowThis.com has information on writing marketing plans and sample plans.	www.knowthis.com/how-to-write-a-marketing-plan/marketing-plan-intro/
SBA Marketing Basics	The SBA has several different links on marketing research and writing your marketing plan.	www.sba.gov/business-guide/manage-your-business/marketing-sales

Chapter 7 - Bidding and Estimating

DMOZ.com Estimating Software	This site gives a comprehensive list of estimating software.	dmoztools.net/Business/Construction_and_Maintenance/Estimating/
U.S. Department of Labor, Bureau of Labor Statistics	The Bureau of Labor Statistics site has helpful information on wages, earnings, and business costs.	www.bls.gov

Chapter 8 - Contract Law

B4UBuild.com	B4UBuild.com has articles on contract law for residential builders.	www.b4ubuild.com/site/articles/residential-construction-contract
Free Advice.com	Free Advice.com has links to different contract topics.	law.freeadvice.com/general_practice/contract_law
Nolo.com	Nolo.com has articles about contract law.	www.nolo.com

Chapter 9 - Scheduling and Project Management

Construction place.com	Constructionplace.com has an informative glossary of terms focused on construction management.	www.constructionplace.com/glossary.asp
Free Download Center.com	Free Download Center.com has project management software downloads.	http://freedownloadscenter.com/windows/business/

Chapter 10 - Customer Relations

Microsoft for Enterprise	The Microsoft site offers helpful customer relations links.	enterprise.microsoft.com/en-us/

Chapter 11 - Employee Management

DOL Employment Law Guide	The Department of Labor has several links on employment law compliance, a compliance guide, and compliance advisor.	webapps.dol.gov/elaws/elg/index.htm webapps.dol.gov/elaws/
IRS Forms	This site contains IRS forms, such as the W-4 that you can download.	www.irs.gov/forms-instructions
SBA Employment Law	The SBA has several different links on employment law.	www.sba.gov/business-guide/manage-your-business/hire-manage-employees
South Carolina Workers' Compensation Commission	This site has information on the rules, practice, and procedures involved with workers' compensation.	wcc.sc.gov
South Carolina Department of Labor, Licensing and Regulation (LLR)	The South Carolina LLR site gives information on employment laws and resources for employers	www.llr.sc.gov
South Carolina New Hire Reporting	The South Carolina new hire link has information on reporting requirements for new hires.	newhire.sc.gov
U.S. Citizenship and Immigration Services	The I-9 form can be downloaded from this site.	www.uscis.gov
U.S. Equal Employment Opportunity Commission (EEOC)	The EEOC provides compliance assistance resources for ADA.	www.eeoc.gov

Chapter 12 - Jobsite Safety and Environmental Considerations

Common Ground Alliance (CGA)	The Common Ground Alliance is available by calling 811. CGA can connect contractors to One Call Centers to locate underground utilities.	www.call811.com
Construction Industry Compliance Center	The Construction Industry Compliance Center website has information available on environmental regulations including hazardous and nonhazardous waste.	www.cicacenter.org
Energy Star	The Energy Star website has eco-friendly resources for home improvement and residential and commercial construction.	www.energystar.gov
Environmental Protection Agency—Asbestos-Containing Materials List	The Environmental Protection Agency website provides a list of asbestos-containing materials.	www.epa.gov/asbestos

Environmental Protection Agency—Green Building	The Environmental Protection Agency archive website provides information on components of green building, national, state and local funding opportunities, and publications on various environmental topics.	archive.epa.gov/greenbuilding/web/html
Environmental Protection Agency—Lead in Paint, Dust, and Soil	The EPA's website provides information on lead hazards.	www.epa.gov/lead
OSHA	The OSHA website has links regarding safety on the job and safety laws and programs.	www.osha.gov
OSHA Compliance Assistance for Construction	The OSHA website has a page with numerous construction compliance assistance links.	www.osha.gov/doc
South Carolina Department of Labor, Licensing and Regulation, OSHA Division	The South Carolina LLR OSHA division site provides environmental compliance assistance and permitting information.	www.scosha.llronline.com
South Carolina Safe Digging	South Carolina's digging safety website and hotline. This site provides information on underground safety and procedures.	www.sc811.com
U.S. Green Building Council	The USGBC is committed to transforming the way buildings are designed, constructed, and operated through LEED—the top third-party verification system for sustainable structures around the world.	new.usgbc.org

Chapter 13 - Working with Subcontractors

IRS Publication 1779	This IRS publication provides criteria to determine employee versus independent contractor status.	www.irs.gov/pub/irs-pdf/p1779.pdf

Chapter 14 - Financial Management

IRS Publication 15: Circular E	The Circular E, used for federal income tax withholding, is available on the IRS website.	www.irs.gov/publications/p15
SBA Balance Sheet Template	The SBA has a balance sheet template that you can customize.	www.sba.gov/sites/default/files/balance_sheet.xlt
SBA Financing Basics	The SBA has several different links on financing and financial statements.	www.sba.gov/business-guide/plan-your-business/calculate-your-startup-costs

SBA Income Statement Template	The SBA has an income statement template that you can customize.	www.sba.gov/sites/default/files/income_statement.xlt
Social Security Administration	The Social Security Administration website has information on the current social security tax rate.	www.ssa.gov

Chapter 15 - Tax Basics

How to Apply for an EIN	There are several ways to apply for an EIN. The IRS outlines the procedures on their website.	www.irs.gov/businesses/small-businesses-selfemployed/how-to-apply-for-an-ein
IRS Service	The IRS site has tax forms, publications and useful information for small businesses.	www.irs.gov
SBA Tax Basics	The SBA has several different links on federal, state, and local taxes.	www.sba.gov/business-guide/manage-your-business/pay-taxes
South Carolina Department of Revenue	The South Carolina Department of Revenue site provides helpful information on state taxes.	dor.sc.gov
South Carolina Secretary of State	The South Carolina Secretary of State site has information on general business and franchise tax.	http://www.sos.sc.gov/BusinessFilings

Chapter 16 - Mechanics' and Materialmen's Lien Law

Find Law.com	Find Law.com has useful articles on lien law.	www.findlaw.com
South Carolina General Assembly	You can search for legislation including mechanics' lien law on the South Carolina Legislature site.	www.scstatehouse.gov

Trade Links

American Institute of Architects (AIA)	This site has information about the organization and contract documents for purchase.	www.aia.org
American National Standards Institute (ANSI)	The ANSI website has information on membership, accreditation services, and educational resources.	www.ansi.org
American Society of Civil Engineers (ASCE)	The ASCE website has information on membership, conferences, publications, and continuing education.	www.asce.org
American Society of Plumbing Engineers (ASPE)	The ASPE website has information on membership, certifications, and useful resources.	www.aspe.org

American Water Works Association (AWWA)	The AWWA website has information on membership, accreditation services, and educational resources.	www.awwa.org
Associated Builders and Contractors (ABC)	The ABC website has information on membership, training, a list of contractors, and links to business development, safety, insurance, and legal resources.	www.abc.org
Associated General Contractors (AGC)	This site has information for construction contractors and industry related companies.	www.agc.org
International Association of Plumbing and Mechanical Officials (IAPMO)	The IAPMO website has information on membership, certification, and educational resources.	www.iapmo.org
National Association of Home Builders (NAHB)	This site is for those interested in homebuilding and the industry.	www.nahb.org
National Association of the Remodeling Industry (NARI)	This site is for those interested in the remodeling industry.	www.nari.org
National Association of State Contractor Licensing Agencies (NASCLA)	This site contains useful information about the state licensing agencies and information about the organization.	www.nascla.org
National Association of Women in Construction (NAWIC)	This site has information for women in the construction industry.	www.nawic.org
National Electrical Contractors Association (NECA)	The NECA website has information on membership, codes and standards, industry news, and educational resources.	www.necanet.org
American Subcontractors Association (ASA)	This site has information for subcontractors and suppliers in the construction industry.	www.asaonline.com
Plumbing, Heating and Cooling Contractors Association (PHCC)	The PHCC website has information on membership, educational resources, and a list of contractors.	www.phccweb.org
Water Quality Association (WQA)	The WQA website has information on membership, certifications, educational resources, and a list of contractors.	www.wqa.org

Appendix D: New Business Checklist

The following is a checklist of steps to starting your business. These steps provide a general overview, but you should check with a professional to determine the legal, financial, and tax obligations specific to your business.

Complete Your Business Plan (covered in Chapter 1 and Appendix B)

- ✓ Establish your business vision and mission.
- ✓ Determine your management structure.
- ✓ Identify your facility requirements and location.
- ✓ Research your market and identify your competitors.
- ✓ Establish a marketing plan and expansion goals.
- ✓ Determine your break-even point and your financial goals.

Choose Your Form of Organization (covered in Chapter 2)

- ✓ Hire a lawyer to prepare organization documents and give legal advice on business issues.
- ✓ Choose a form of organization (i.e., sole proprietorship, partnership, or corporation).
- ✓ Prepare and file business organization documents (i.e., Partnership Agreement, Articles of Organization, Articles of Incorporation, etc.).
- ✓ Register any fictitious names with the proper state and local municipalities.
- ✓ Obtain the required business licenses from state and local municipalities.

Set Up Business Finances

- ✓ Select an accountant to prepare financial documents and give business financial advice.
- ✓ Select a banker and open a business checking account.
- ✓ Apply for business loans (if applicable).
- ✓ Apply for business credit cards and establish a line of credit.

Obtain the Proper Contractor's Licensure (covered in Chapter 3)

- ✓ Obtain the proper application materials and review the process for obtaining licensure.
- ✓ Complete application materials with required documentation.
- ✓ Understand the requirements for maintaining proper licensure.

Assess Your Areas of Risk and Obtain the Proper Insurance Coverage (covered in Chapter 4)

- ✓ Select an insurance company and agent to help assess your risk and coverage requirements.
- ✓ Obtain business insurance (liability, workers' compensation, automobile, etc.).
- ✓ Obtain required bonds.
- ✓ Obtain unemployment insurance registration materials from the proper state agency.

Obtain the Proper Tax Documentation (covered in Chapter 15)

- ✓ Apply for a federal employer identification number (if applicable).
- ✓ Obtain a state employer identification number (if applicable).
- ✓ Obtain the proper federal and state tax forms (i.e., sales and use tax, withholding tax, etc.).

Appendix E: South Carolina Residential Home Builders Licensing Law

ARTICLE 1.

RESIDENTIAL HOME BUILDERS GENERALLY

SECTION 40-59-5. Application of Chapter 1; conflicts.

Unless otherwise provided for in this chapter, Article 1, Chapter 1 of Title 40 applies to any entities or individuals regulated by the Department of Labor, Licensing and Regulation. If there is a conflict between this chapter and Article 1, Chapter 1 of Title 40, the provisions of this chapter control.

HISTORY: 2002 Act No. 359, Section 1.

SECTION 40-59-10. South Carolina Residential Builders Commission; membership; oath.

(A) There is created the South Carolina Residential Builders Commission which must be composed of eight persons who have been residents of the State for at least five years and two of whom must be consumers not engaged in the business of residential building, four of whom have been actively engaged in residential building for a period of at least five years before the date of their appointment, and who must be recommended to the Governor by the South Carolina Home Builders Association, and one of whom has been actively engaged in residential specialty contracting for a period of at least five years before the date of appointment. One member must be appointed from each congressional district, and one must be appointed from the State at large. Members of the commission must be appointed by the Governor with the advice and consent of the Senate for a term of four years or until their successors are appointed and qualify. A vacancy occurring by reason of death, resignation, removal for cause, or otherwise must be filled for the remainder of the unexpired term in the manner of the original appointment. The Governor may remove any member of the commission in accordance with Section 1-3-240.

(B) Before entering upon the discharge of the duties of his office, each member of the commission shall take and file with the Secretary of State, in writing, an oath to perform properly the duties of his office as a member of the commission and to uphold the Constitution of this State and the United States.

(C) Commission members from the general public may be nominated by an individual, group, or association and must be appointed by the Governor in accordance with Section 40-1- 45.

HISTORY: 2002 Act No. 359, Section 1; 2012 Act No. 279, Section 11, eff June 26, 2012.

SECTION 40-59-20. Definitions.

As used in this chapter unless the context clearly indicates otherwise:

(1) "Commission" means the South Carolina Residential Builders Commission.

(2) "Department" means the Department of Labor, Licensing and Regulation.

(3) "Director" means the Director of the Department of Labor, Licensing and Regulation.

(4) "Firm" means a business entity functioning as a sole proprietorship, partnership, limited liability partnership, professional association, professional corporation, business corporation, limited liability company, joint venture or other legally constituted organization which practices or offers to practice residential building or residential specialty contracting.

(5) "License" means a license, registration, or certification issued in accordance with this chapter.

(6) "Residential builder" means one who constructs, superintends, or offers to construct or superintend the construction, repair, improvement, or reimprovement of a residential building or structure which is not over three floors in height and which does not have more than sixteen units in any single apartment building, when the cost of the undertaking exceeds five thousand dollars. Anyone who engages or offers to engage in such undertaking in this State is considered to have engaged in the business of residential building.

(7) "Residential specialty contractor" means an independent contractor who is not a licensed residential builder, who contracts with a licensed residential builder, general contractor, or individual property owner to do construction work, repairs, improvement, or reimprovement which requires special skills and involves the use of specialized construction trades or craft, when the undertakings exceed two hundred dollars and are not regulated by the provisions of Chapter 11. Residential specialty contracting includes the following areas of contracting and other areas as the commission may recognize by regulation:

(a) plumbers;

(b) electricians;

(c) heating and air conditioning installers and repairers;

(d) vinyl and aluminum siding installers;

(e) insulation installers;

(f) roofers;

(g) floor covering installers;

(h) masons;

(i) dry wall installers;

(j) carpenters;

(k) stucco installers;

(l) painters/wall paperers.

(8) As used in this chapter, the terms defined in Section 40-1-20 have the same meaning as stated in that section.

HISTORY: 2002 Act No. 359, Section 1.

SECTION 40-59-25. Roofing contract cancellation for insurance coverage denial.

(A)(1) A person who enters into a written contract for goods or services related to a roofing system with a party who will be paid from proceeds of a property and casualty insurance policy and who subsequently receives written notice from the insurer that all or part of the claim or contract is not a covered loss under the policy may cancel the contract prior to midnight on the fifth business day after the insured has received the written notice of the denial of coverage.

(2) This section applies to the following persons performing goods or services related to a roofing system:

(a) a licensed residential builder;

(b) a registered residential specialty contractor; and

(c) a person or firm who engages or offers to engage in the business of residential building or residential specialty contracting without first having registered with the commission or procured a license from the commission.

(3) Cancellation must be evidenced by the insured giving written notice of cancellation to the builder or contractor at the address provided in the contract. Notice of cancellation, if given by mail, must be effective upon deposit into the United States mail, postage prepaid and properly addressed to the builder or contractor. Notice of cancellation need not take a particular form and shall be sufficient if it indicates, by any form of written expression, the intention of the insured not to be bound by the contract.

(4) For purposes of this subsection, "roof system" means a roof covering, roof sheathing, roof weatherproofing, roof framing, roof ventilation system, or insulation.

(B) Before entering a contract as provided in subsection (A), the builder or contractor shall:

(1) provide the insured a statement in boldface type of a minimum size of ten points, in substantially the following form:

"You may cancel this contract at any time before midnight on the fifth business day after you have received written notification from your insurer that all or any part of this claim or contract is not a covered loss under the insurance policy. This right to cancel is in addition to any other rights of cancellation which may be found in state or federal law or regulation. See attached notice of cancellation form for an explanation of this right"; and

(2) provide each insured a fully completed form, in duplicate, prominently captioned "NOTICE OF CANCELLATION", which must be attached to the contract but easily detachable, and which must contain in boldface type of a minimum size of ten points the following statement:

"NOTICE OF CANCELLATION

If you are notified by your insurer that all or any part of the claim or contract is not a covered loss under the insurance policy, you may cancel the contract by mailing or delivering a signed and dated copy of this cancellation notice or any other written notice to (insert name of contractor) at (insert address of contractor's place of business) any time prior to midnight on the fifth business day after you have received such notices from your insurer.

I HEREBY CANCEL THIS TRANSACTION

_

DATE

_

SIGNATURE OF INSURED"

(C) In circumstances in which payment may be made from the proceeds of a property and casualty insurance policy, a builder or contractor shall not require any payments from an insured until the five-day cancellation period has expired. If, however, the builder or contractor has performed any emergency services, acknowledged by the insured in writing to be necessary to prevent damage to the premises, the builder or contractor must be entitled to collect the amount due for the emergency services at the time they are rendered. A provision in a contract as provided in subsection (A) that requires payment of any fee for anything except emergency services must not be enforceable against an insured who has canceled a contract under this section.

(D)(1) A builder or contractor shall not represent or negotiate, or offer or advertise to represent or negotiate, on behalf of an owner or possessor of residential real estate on any insurance claim in connection with the repair or replacement of roof systems.

(2) Notwithstanding item (1), or any other provision of state law, an owner is not prevented from consulting with a builder, contractor, or other person of his choice to provide an evaluation of the condition of his roof system and using the evaluation he receives in the negotiation for the repair or replacement of his roof system.

(E)(1) A builder or contractor shall not advertise or promise to pay or rebate all or any portion of any insurance deductible as an inducement to the sale of goods or services.

(2) A person who violates a provision of this subsection is guilty of a misdemeanor. The violation is grounds for suspension or revocation of licenses issued pursuant to this chapter.

(3) As used in this subsection, the term "promise to pay or rebate" means:

(a) granting any allowance or offering any discount against the fees to be charged, including, but not limited to, an allowance or discount in return for displaying a sign or other advertisement at the insured's premises; or

(b) paying the insured or any person directly or indirectly associated with the property any form of compensation, gift, prize, bonus, coupon, credit, referral fee, or other item of monetary value for any reason.

HISTORY: 2013 Act No. 77, Section 1, eff July 1, 2013.

SECTION 40-59-30. License requirement; enforcement of contracts; restraining orders.

(A) A person or firm who engages or offers to engage in the business of residential building or residential specialty contracting without first having registered with the commission or procured a license from the commission, which has not expired or been revoked, suspended, or restricted or who knowingly presents to, or files with, the commission false information for the purpose of obtaining a license or registering with the commission is guilty of a misdemeanor and, upon conviction, must be fined not less than five hundred dollars or more than ten thousand dollars or imprisoned for not less than thirty days, or both.

(B) Notwithstanding Section 29-5-10, or another provision of law, a person or firm who first has not procured a license or registered with the commission and is required to do so by law may not file a mechanics' lien or bring an action at law or in equity to enforce the provisions of a contract for residential building or residential specialty contracting which the person or firm entered into in violation of this chapter.

(C) Pursuant to Article 5, Chapter 23, Title 1, the commission may petition an administrative law judge to issue a temporary restraining order enjoining a violation of this chapter, pending a full hearing to determine whether the injunction must be made permanent.

HISTORY: 2002 Act No. 359, Section 1; 2009 Act No. 40, Section 4.

SECTION 40-59-50. Compensation of members; chairman; bylaws and seal; administrator and staff; meetings; roster of licensees.

(A) The members of the commission must be compensated for their services at the regular per diem, mileage, and subsistence rates as provided by law for members of state boards, committees, and commissions and must be reimbursed for actual and necessary expenses incurred in connection with, and as a result of, their work on the commission. Compensation paid and costs and expenses incurred must be paid only from the fees received by the commission pursuant to the provisions of this chapter.

(B) The commission, at its first meeting after appointment, shall organize by electing a chairman and a vice-chairman and other officers as the commission considers appropriate who shall serve for a term of one year and until their successors are appointed and qualify. The commission shall adopt bylaws for the governance of its proceedings and shall adopt a commission seal on which shall appear the words "South Carolina Residential Builders Commission".

(C) The Director of the Department of Labor, Licensing and Regulation, pursuant to Section 40-1-50, may employ an administrator to serve at the discretion of the director of the department. The duties of the administrator must be prescribed by the director.

(D) The director may also employ clerical and stenographic assistance and other personnel as may be necessary to effectuate the provisions of this chapter. The compensation of all employees of the commission must be fixed by the director and paid from the fees received by the commission pursuant to the provisions of this chapter.

(E) The Department of Labor, Licensing and Regulation shall administer the commission as a revenue funded commission in accordance with Section 40-1-50.

(F) The commission shall meet quarterly and at other times as the chairman may designate; however, the commission shall meet within thirty days after appointment for the purpose of organizing and transacting business. Four members of the commission constitute a quorum at all meetings. The administrator shall keep records of each meeting as required by the commission.

(G) A roster including the names and places of business of the residential builders and residential specialty contractors licensed or registered by the commission during the preceding year must be prepared annually by the commission and forwarded to and filed with the clerk of court for each county.

HISTORY: 2002 Act No. 359, Section 1.

SECTION 40-59-60. Additional commission operations.

In addition to the commission operations provided in this chapter, the commission may act in accordance with those set forth in Section 40-1-60.

HISTORY: 2002 Act No. 359, Section 1.

SECTION 40-59-70. Promulgation of regulations.

The commission may promulgate regulations as may be necessary to effectuate the provisions of this chapter.

HISTORY: 2002 Act No. 359, Section 1.

SECTION 40-59-80. Investigation of complaints; initial complaints.

The Department of Labor, Licensing and Regulation shall investigate complaints and violations of this chapter as provided for in Section 40-1-80. A person, including the commission, may file an initial complaint against a licensee or registrant. The complaint must be in writing and sworn to by the person filing the complaint.

HISTORY: 2002 Act No. 359, Section 1.

SECTION 40-59-90. Hearing before commission; notice; appearance; order; appeal.

Charges, unless dismissed without hearing by the commission as unfounded or trivial, must be heard by the commission in an open hearing. A copy of the charges and a notice of the time and place of the hearing must be served on the respondent at least thirty days before the fixed date for the hearing. At the hearing the respondent may appear personally or be represented by counsel and may cross-examine witnesses against him and produce evidence and witnesses in his defense. After the commission issues its order, the respondent has thirty days to file with the commission written notice of his intention to appeal to an administrative law judge from the order of the commission. An appeal from an order of the commission is governed by the provisions of Article 3, Chapter 23 of Title 1, the Administrative Procedures Act.

HISTORY: 2002 Act No. 359, Section 1.

SECTION 40-59-100. Cease and desist order; temporary restraining order.

In addition to other remedies provided for in this chapter or Chapter 1, Title 40, the commission in accordance with Section 40-1-100 may issue a cease and desist order or may petition an administrative law judge for a temporary restraining order or other equitable relief to enjoin a violation of this chapter.

HISTORY: 2002 Act No. 359, Section 1.

SECTION 40-59-105. Administrative citations and penalties; appeal.

(A) The department may refer reports of violations of this chapter and Article 1, Chapter 1 or any reports of violations of regulations promulgated under this chapter directly to the commission or may issue administrative citations and cease and desist orders in person or by certified mail and may assess administrative penalties against an entity or individual, including unlicensed persons, for violations of this chapter as specified by the commission.

(B) Separate citations may be issued and separate administrative penalties may be assessed for each violation; however, no more than two thousand five hundred dollars in administrative penalties may be assessed against an entity or an individual per day.

(C) Administrative penalties authorized under this section are separate from and in addition to all other remedies, either civil or criminal, and these penalties may not exceed the following limits:

(1) for a first offense, not more than a five-hundred dollar penalty;

(2) for a second offense in a five-year period, the citation must be referred to the commission for action in accordance with Sections 40-59-90 and 40-59-110.

(D) An entity or individual assessed administrative penalties may appeal those penalties to the commission within ten days of receipt of the citation. If an appeal is filed, the department shall schedule a hearing before the commission, which shall make a determination in the matter. If no appeal is filed, the citation is deemed a final order and the administrative penalties must be paid within thirty days of receipt of the citation or other written demand.

HISTORY: 2002 Act No. 359, Section 1.

SECTION 40-59-110. Revocation, suspension, or restriction of license; misconduct; determination of compliance with applicable professional standards.

In addition to the grounds provided for in Section 40-1-110, the commission, upon a majority vote, may revoke, suspend, or restrict the license or registration of a licensee or registrant who the commission finds has committed fraud or deceit in obtaining a license or registration under this chapter or has engaged in misconduct in the practice of residential building or residential specialty contracting. For purposes of this section, misconduct includes a violation of Section 40-59-25, or a pattern of repeated failure by a residential builder or residential specialty contractor to pay labor or material bills. For purposes of disciplinary matters, or otherwise, compliance with the construction standards adopted by the commission is prima facie evidence of compliance with applicable professional standards.

HISTORY: 2002 Act No. 359, Section 1; 2013 Act No. 77, Section 2, eff July 1, 2013.

SECTION 40-59-115. Jurisdiction over actions of licensees and former licensees.

The commission has jurisdiction over the actions of licensees and former licensees as provided for in Section 40-1-115.

HISTORY: 2002 Act No. 359, Section 1.

SECTION 40-59-120. Fines.

Upon a determination by the commission that one or more of the grounds for discipline of a licensee exists, as provided in Section 40-59-110 or 40-1-110, the commission, in addition to the actions provided for in Section 40-1-120, may impose a fine of not more than two thousand five hundred dollars per offense.

HISTORY: 2002 Act No. 359, Section 1.

SECTION 40-59-130. Grounds for denial of license.

As provided for in Section 40-1-130, the commission may deny licensure to an applicant based on the same grounds for which the commission may take disciplinary action against a licensee.

HISTORY: 2002 Act No. 359, Section 1.

SECTION 40-59-140. Prior criminal record.

A person may be denied licensure or registration based on a person's prior criminal record only as provided for in Section 40-1-140.

HISTORY: 2002 Act No. 359, Section 1.

SECTION 40-59-150. Voluntary surrender of license.

A licensee under investigation for a violation of this chapter or a regulation promulgated under this chapter may voluntarily surrender the license in accordance with Section 40-1-150.

HISTORY: 2002 Act No. 359, Section 1.

SECTION 40-59-160. Appeal.

A person aggrieved by a final action of the commission may seek review of the decision in accordance with Section 40-1-160.

HISTORY: 2002 Act No. 359, Section 1.

SECTION 40-59-170. Costs.

A person found in violation of this chapter or regulations promulgated under this chapter may be required to pay costs associated with the investigation and prosecution of the case in accordance with Section 40-1-170.

HISTORY: 2002 Act No. 359, Section 1.

SECTION 40-59-180. Collection and enforcement.

All costs and fines imposed pursuant to this chapter must be paid in accordance with and are subject to the collection and enforcement provisions of Section 40-1-180.

HISTORY: 2002 Act No. 359, Section 1.

SECTION 40-59-190. Confidentiality.

Investigations and proceedings conducted under the provisions of this chapter are confidential and all communications are privileged as provided for in Section 40-1-190.

HISTORY: 2002 Act No. 359, Section 1.

SECTION 40-59-200. Penalties.

A person who knowingly violates the provisions of this article or regulations promulgated pursuant to this chapter is guilty of a misdemeanor and, upon conviction, must be fined not more than one thousand dollars or imprisoned for not more than two years, or both.

HISTORY: 2002 Act No. 359, Section 1.

SECTION 40-59-210. Cease and desist orders; penalties; injunction.

(A) In addition to all other remedies provided by law, when it appears to the commission, either upon complaint or otherwise, that a person or combination of persons has engaged, or is engaging, in an act of contracting, practice, or transaction which constitutes a violation of this chapter or any regulation or order of the commission, whether or not the person is properly licensed or registered with the commission, the commission may:

(1) serve upon the person not licensed or registered under the chapter, by certified mail or by personal service, a cease and desist order requiring the person to cease and desist from engaging in the act, practice, or transaction immediately upon receipt of the order. If the person fails to comply with the order, the director or a designee may file an action with an administrative law judge for enforcement of the cease and desist order or file an action pursuant to item (2) for wilful violation of the order. If the administrative law judge finds that the person wilfully failed to obey a valid cease and desist order, the court shall impose a civil penalty of not less than two hundred fifty dollars and not more than two thousand dollars for each violation. Any amount collected as a civil penalty must be remitted pursuant to subsection (B);

(2) apply, on its behalf, through the Attorney General, the Director of the Department of Consumer Affairs, the county attorney, or solicitor of the county in which the violation is alleged to have been committed, to the court of common pleas of that county for an injunction restraining the person from further violation. Upon a proper showing, a temporary restraining order, a preliminary injunction, or a permanent injunction may be granted without bond. Process in the action may be served upon the defendant in any county of this State where the defendant transacts business or is found.

(B) In actions brought under item (2) of subsection (A), each violation of this chapter or regulation or order of the commission constitutes a separate offense, and the court may impose a civil penalty not to exceed two thousand dollars for each violation which is in addition to all other penalties provided by law.

HISTORY: 2002 Act No. 359, Section 1.

SECTION 40-59-220. Licenses and certificates of registration; application; qualifications; bonds; examinations; reciprocity.

(A) All residential builders must be licensed, and all residential specialty contractors must be registered, by the commission for a period established by the commission in regulation. Licensees and registrants must pay an annual fee established by the department and based upon the department's costs in carrying out the provisions of this chapter.

(B) An applicant for a license or certificate shall file with the commission a written application on a form as may be prescribed by the commission. The application must be accompanied by the payment of all applicable fees required by the commission. A prerequisite for taking the examination for a residential builder's license is a minimum of one year of actual experience under the supervision of a licensed residential builder, or other appropriately licensed professional who is engaged in residential building construction involving the trades or crafts for which the license is desired, or other education or experience or a combination of these as may be approved by the commission. The commission, in examining an applicant, may consider the following qualifications of the applicant:

(1) experience;

(2) ability;

(3) character;

(4) financial condition;

(5) equipment;

(6) workers' compensation insurance; and

(7) other pertinent information the commission may require.

(C) The commission shall issue a residential builder's license if, as a result of examination, the commission finds that the applicant is qualified to engage in residential building in South Carolina, and the applicant submits an executed bond in the form and with a surety approved by the commission in the sum of not less than fifteen thousand dollars or proof of financial responsibility acceptable to the commission.

(D) The commission shall issue a residential specialty contractor's license for which the applicant is qualified if, as a result of examination, the commission finds that the applicant is qualified to engage in residential specialty contracting in South Carolina. When the cost of an undertaking performed by a residential specialty contractor for an individual property owner exceeds five thousand dollars, the residential specialty contractor must obtain an executed bond with a surety in an amount approved by the commission.

(E) An applicant who fails the examination must be given the opportunity to be reexamined after payment of an additional examination fee; however, if the applicant fails the examination three times, the applicant shall wait twelve months before being examined again. A record must be made and preserved by the commission of each examination of an applicant and the findings of the commission pertaining to the examination. A certified copy of the record must be furnished to an applicant requesting the record upon the payment of a fee to the commission that reasonably reflects the cost of furnishing the record to the applicant.

(F) A license may be granted by the commission without examination to those applicants who are licensed in good standing in other states which are determined by the commission to have comparable examinations.

HISTORY: 2002 Act No. 359, Section 1; 2004 Act No. 289, Section 3.

SECTION 40-59-230. Renewal; continuing education; notification of change of circumstances.

(A) Unless otherwise provided under the provisions of this chapter, the commission shall annually renew all licenses upon the applicant's submission to the commission of the completed renewal application, proof of financial responsibility or bond, acceptable to the commission and payment of all applicable fees. If a license has been in inactive status for more than three years, the person shall file a new application as in the case of the issuance of an original license and is required to take and successfully complete the examination.

(B) As a condition of license renewal, the commission may require by regulation a licensee to satisfactorily complete continuing education through a program approved by the commission.

(C) A licensee must notify the commission in writing within thirty days of any change in the information required to be on file with the commission including, but not limited to, the licensee's current mailing address.

HISTORY: 2002 Act No. 359, Section 1.

SECTION 40-59-240. Residential specialty contractors; classification; examination; county and municipal business license ordinances; bonds.

(A) The commission by regulation shall classify residential specialty contractors in a manner consistent with established usage and procedure in the construction business and may limit the field and scope of the operations of a residential specialty contractor to those in which he is to be registered or certified. Residential specialty contractor registrations and certificates issued by the commission may not be for more than three of the classifications recognized by the commission. Residential specialty contractors registered or certified or wishing to be registered or certified for more than three classifications must be examined and licensed as residential builders.

(B) Residential specialty contractors must be qualified and experienced in the particular areas of the contracting vocation in which they intend to, and do, engage. The commission, by regulation, may require examination in these areas.

(C) Residential specialty contractors are not exempt from complying with county and municipal business license ordinances or other regulatory ordinances. A county or municipality may require a residential specialty contractor to be examined and licensed in accordance with standards adopted by the county or municipality; however, if a residential specialty contractor has passed an examination in his area of contracting and approved by the commission, no additional examination may be required by a county or municipality.

(D) When the total cost of materials and labor for an undertaking performed by a residential specialty contractor for an individual property owner exceeds five thousand dollars, the residential specialty contractor shall obtain an executed bond with a surety in an amount approved by the commission and shall furnish a signed original to the commission.

HISTORY: 2002 Act No. 359, Section 1.

SECTION 40-59-250. Credit report; factors indicating reputation for timely performance; outstanding judgments.

(A) A person applying to the commission for licensure as a residential builder or registration as a residential specialty contractor must submit to a credit report. In addition to the information provided by the credit report, the commission may determine from the written application, the personal references provided by the applicant, written communications or complaints to the commission, and from any other reliable, documented sources whether an applicant for licensure as a residential builder or an applicant for registration as a residential specialty contractor has a reputation for the prompt payment of labor and material bills and for the timely completion of other contracts into which the applicant may have entered.

(B) The commission shall require the applicant to list on application and renewal forms any outstanding judgments issued against him or any entities with whom the applicant was associated for the past five years.

HISTORY: 2002 Act No. 359, Section 1.

SECTION 40-59-260. Exception for projects by property owner for personal use; exemption disclosure statement; notice filed with register of deeds.

(A) This chapter does not apply to an owner of residential property who improves the property or who builds or improves structures or appurtenances on the property if:

(1) the owner does the work himself, with his own employees, or with licensed contractors or registered entities or individuals;

(2) the structure, group of structures, or appurtenances, including the improvements, are intended for the owner's sole occupancy or occupancy by the owner's family and are not intended for sale or rent; and

(3) the general public does not have access to this structure.

(B) In an action brought under this chapter, proof of the sale or rent or the offering for sale or rent of the structure by the owner-builder within two years after completion or issuance of a certificate or occupancy is prima facie evidence that the project was undertaken for the purpose of sale or rent, unless otherwise approved by the commission, and is subject to the penalties provided in this chapter. As used in this section, "sale" or "rent" includes an arrangement by which an owner receives compensation in money, provisions, chattel, or labor from the occupancy, or the transfer of the property or the structures on the property. This section does not exempt a person who is employed by the owner and who acts in the capacity of a builder or a specialty contractor of any kind.

(C) To qualify for exemption under this section, an owner must personally appear and sign the building permit application. The local permitting agency shall provide the person with a disclosure statement, provided by the department, in substantially the following form:

"Disclosure Statement

State law requires residential construction to be done by licensed residential builders and specialty contractors. You have applied for a permit under an exemption to that law. The exemption allows you, as the owner of your property, to act as your own builder even though you do not have a license. You must supervise the construction yourself. You may build or improve a one-family or two-family residence. The building must be for your own use and occupancy. It may not be built for sale or rent. If you sell or rent a building you have built yourself within two years after the construction is complete, the law will presume that you built it for sale or rent, which is a violation of this exemption. You may not hire an unlicensed person as your residential builder or specialty contractor. It is your responsibility to make sure that people employed by you have licenses required by state law and by county or municipal licensing ordinances. Your construction must comply with all applicable laws, ordinances, building codes, and zoning regulations."

(D) At the time an owner personally appears and signs the building permit application as required by subsection (C) of this section, the local permitting agency shall provide the owner with all forms necessary to comply with subsection (E) of this section.

(E) If a residential building or structure has been constructed by an owner under the exemption provided for in this section, the owner of the residential building or structure must promptly file as a matter of public record a notice with the register of deeds, indexed under the owner's name in the grantor's index, stating that the residential building or structure was constructed by the owner as an unlicensed builder. Failure to do so revokes the statutory exemption.

(F) Nothing in this chapter may be construed to authorize an owner of a residential building or structure to hire a person or entity that is not licensed or registered in accordance with this chapter.

HISTORY: 2002 Act No. 359, Section 1.

SECTION 40-59-270. Applicability of Chapter 11; exemption of mechanical contractor.

This chapter does not apply to a person licensed under Chapter 11 for the purpose of undertaking the construction, or superintending of construction, of a building or the improvement, reimprovement, or repair of any building. A residential builder who is licensed pursuant to this chapter is not required to be licensed as a general contractor or mechanical contractor under Chapter 11 in order to engage in residential building as defined in Section 40-59-10. A mechanical contractor is exempt from this chapter relating to residential specialty contractors when engaged in contracting in the classification in which he is licensed to perform mechanical contracting. The commission is the exclusive licensing and registration entity for persons who engage solely in residential building and in residential specialty contracting.

HISTORY: 2002 Act No. 359, Section 1.

SECTION 40-59-280. Proof of licensure as condition of issuance of local building permit; reports of violations.

The building official, or other authority charged with the duty of issuing building or similar permits, of any incorporated municipality or subdivision of the municipality or county shall refuse to issue a permit for an undertaking which requires licensure or registration under this chapter unless the applicant has furnished evidence that he is either licensed or registered in accordance with this chapter or exempt from the requirements of this chapter. The building official, or other authority charged with the duty of issuing building or similar permits, also shall report to the commission the name and address of an person who, in his opinion, has violated this chapter by accepting or contracting to accomplish work requiring licensure or registration under this chapter when the person has not produced evidence of licensure or registration or exemption from this chapter.

HISTORY: 2002 Act No. 359, Section 1.

SECTION 40-59-290. Severability.

If any section, subsection, paragraph, subparagraph, sentence, clause, phrase, or word of this chapter is for any reason held to be unconstitutional or invalid, such holding shall not affect the constitutionality or validity of the remaining portions of this chapter, the General Assembly hereby declaring that it would have passed this chapter, and each and every section, subsection, paragraph, subparagraph, sentence, clause, phrase, and word thereof, irrespective of the fact that any one or more other sections, subsections, paragraphs, subparagraphs, sentences, clauses, phrases, or words hereof may be declared to be unconstitutional, invalid, or otherwise ineffective.

HISTORY: 2002 Act No. 359, Section 1.

SECTION 40-59-300. Construction of low-income housing using volunteer labor by 501(c)(3) eleemosynary organization without presence of "qualifier".

Notwithstanding any other provision of law, a 501(c)(3) eleemosynary organization may construct a residential home with volunteer labor without the presence of a qualifier if the home without consideration is to be transferred to or made available for the use of an underprivileged or low-income family or individual. "Qualifier" for purposes of this provision means a builder or specialty contractor licensed to perform the particular work being done on the site. The cost of the building permit must be borne by the 501(c)(3) organization.

HISTORY: 2003 Act No. 83, Section 2.

ARTICLE 2.

CERTIFICATES OF AUTHORIZATION

SECTION 40-59-400. Definitions.

For purposes of this article:

(1) "Branch office" means a place of business separate from the principal place of business where building services are offered or provided. A specific project or construction site office is not a branch office.

(2) "Commission" means the South Carolina Residential Builders Commission established in Article 1.

(3) "Firm" means a business entity functioning as a sole proprietorship, partnership, limited liability partnership, professional association, professional corporation, business corporation, limited liability company, joint venture, or other legally constituted organization which offers or provides building services through licensed residential builders, residential specialty contractors, or home inspectors.

(4) "Private practice firm" means a firm through which the practice of residential building, residential specialty contracting, or home inspecting requires a residential business certificate of authorization as described in this chapter.

(5) "Resident licensee" means a licensed practitioner who spends a majority of each normal workday working out of a principal or branch office and who is in responsible charge of the office and the building services provided from that office including, but not limited to, responsibility for applying for permits for the firm.

(6) "Responsible charge" means the direction of building services by a residential builder, residential specialty contractor, or home inspector to the extent that successful completion of the building services is dependent on the personal supervision, direct control, and final decisions by the qualified registrant to the extent that the qualified registrant assumes professional responsibility for the building services.

HISTORY: 2000 Act No. 324, Section 1.

SECTION 40-59-410. Residential business certificate of authorization as requirement for firm to engage in residential home building, residential specialty contracting, and home inspecting.

(A) The practice or offer to practice residential building, residential specialty contracting, or home inspecting through a firm is authorized only through entities holding a residential business certificate of authorization issued by the commission. For the purposes of this section, a residential business certificate of authorization is also required for any firm practicing in this State under a fictitious name. However, when an individual is practicing residential home building, residential specialty contracting, or home inspecting in his name as individually licensed, or if an individual has at least fifty-one percent of the ownership interest and is the sole resident licensee for the firm, that person or entity is not required to be issued a residential business certificate of authorization.

(B) The practice or offer to practice residential home building, residential specialty contracting, or home inspecting as defined in this chapter by an individual residential home builder, residential specialty contractor, or home inspector licensed or registered under this chapter through a firm offering residential building, residential specialty contracting, or home inspecting services to the public is authorized if:

(1) one or more of the corporate officers in the case of a corporation, or one or more of the principal owners in the case of a firm, or one or more employees are designated as the resident licensee in responsible charge of each principal or branch office for the building services regulated by the commission and are licensed under the provisions of this chapter;

(2) the firm has obtained an executed surety bond approved by the commission in the sum of fifteen thousand dollars initially and as subsequently provided by regulation; and

(3) the firm has been issued a residential business certificate of authorization by the commission. Nothing in this section may be construed to mean that a license or registration to practice residential home building, residential specialty contracting, or home inspecting may be held by a firm.

(C) Approval of firms seeking to incorporate or register to do business in this State under this section must be conditioned upon proper filing with the Secretary of State of the articles of incorporation and revisions to the articles, as certified by the Secretary of State. This section may not be construed to require an additional filing with the Secretary of State not otherwise required by law.

(D) A firm desiring a residential business certificate of authorization shall file with the department an application on forms provided by the department accompanied by all applicable fees. Each residential business certificate of authorization must be renewed by July first of the licensing period. A renewal form provided by the department must be completed and submitted with all applicable fees. The initial application fee and annual renewal fee are one hundred dollars and as subsequently provided by regulation. Information to be provided on the application and renewal forms shall include the names and addresses of all officers and directors of the firm or officers and partners of the partnership who are licensed or registered to practice residential home building, residential specialty contracting, or home inspecting in this State, including those in responsible charge of all principal and branch offices providing building services in the State.

(E) Disciplinary action against a firm must be administered in the same manner and on the same grounds as disciplinary action against an individual under this chapter and Section 40-1-110. No firm is relieved of responsibility for conduct or acts of its agents, officers, or employees by reason of its compliance with this section, and no individual practicing residential home building, residential specialty contracting, or home inspecting is relieved of responsibility for professional services performed by reason of his employment or relationship with the firm.

(F) Nothing in this section may be construed to prohibit firms from joining together to offer residential home building, residential specialty contracting, or home inspecting services to the public, if each separate entity providing the services in this State otherwise meets the requirements of this section. For firms practicing as a professional corporation under the laws of this State, the joint practice of residential home building, residential specialty contracting, or home inspecting with other professions is approved by the commission.

(G) If the requirements of this section are met, the commission shall issue a residential business certificate of authorization to the firm, and the firm may engage or offer to engage in the business of residential home building, residential specialty contracting, or home inspecting. The commission, however, may refuse to issue a certificate or may suspend or revoke an existing certificate for due cause. A person or organization aggrieved by an adverse determination of the commission may seek judicial review in accordance with this chapter.

(H) Residential home builders, residential specialty contractors, or home inspectors engaged in practice through firms involving the practice of residential building, residential specialty contracting, or home inspecting may maintain branch offices as well as a principal place of business.

Each principal place of business as well as each branch office must have a resident residential builder, residential specialty contractor, or home inspector in responsible charge of the field and office building work or services provided. A residential home builder must supervise the residential home building aspects of the principal or branch office and may also supervise the residential specialty contracting from that location. A residential specialty contractor may supervise residential specialty contracting services of the principal or branch office as long as the services are within the scope of residential specialty contracting in the classifications for which the individual is authorized to engage. A home inspector may supervise home inspecting services of the principal or branch office as long as the services are within the scope of home inspecting for which the individual is authorized to engage. The resident residential home builder, residential specialty contractor, or home inspector is considered in responsible charge of only one place of business at a given time.

For purposes of this subsection,"engaged in practice" means holding oneself out generally to the public as qualified and available to perform residential building, residential specialty contracting, or home inspecting services.

(I) Nothing contained in this chapter prevents an authorized residential builder or residential specialty contractor from undertaking a residential building project anywhere in the State.

HISTORY: 2000 Act No. 324, Section 1.

ARTICLE 3.

LICENSING OF HOME INSPECTORS

SECTION 40-59-500. Definitions.

As used in this article:

(1) "Administrator" means the Executive Director for the South Carolina Residential Builders Commission provided for under Section 40-59-50.

(2) "Commission" means the South Carolina Residential Builders Commission.

(3) "Director" means the Director of the Department of Labor, Licensing and Regulation.

(4) "Home inspection" means the rendering of a written or oral report in exchange for compensation of any sort, regarding the condition of the construction or improvements to a residence including, but not limited to, structural problems or conditions, damage, safety problems, deterioration, equipment, and systems that are visible and readily accessible. Home inspection does not include a contract or proposal for repair, renovation, or remodeling of the improvements to a residence. The parties to a home inspection may limit or expand the scope of the inspection by agreement.

(5) "Home inspector" means an individual who, for compensation of any sort, engages in the business of home inspection.

(6) "Residence" means a structure including, but not limited to, condominiums and townhouses intended to be used or in fact used primarily for living quarters which is not over three floors in height and which does not have more than sixteen units.

HISTORY: 2002 Act No. 359, Section 1.

SECTION 40-59-510. Administration; roster of licensed home inspectors.

The administrator is authorized to administer the provisions of this article. The administrator shall keep a register of all applicants for licensure, including the date of application and the name, qualifications, place of business, and place of residence of the applicant and the status of the license application. The administrator also shall maintain a roster including the name, place of business, residence, and business telephone number of each licensed home inspector. A copy of the roster must be available to anyone upon a written request to the commission. The commission may charge a reasonable fee for complying with a request for a roster. The amount of the fee must be established by the commission in regulation.

HISTORY: 2002 Act No. 359, Section 1.

SECTION 40-59-520. Licensing requirement; licensing of business entity.

(A) No person may engage in or transact any home inspection business or hold himself out to the public as a home inspector or offer to engage in or transact any home inspection business in this State unless the person is licensed by the commission.

(B) No license may be issued under this article to a partnership, association, corporation, firm, or group. However, nothing in this article precludes a licensed home inspector from performing home inspections for or on behalf of a partnership, association, corporation, firm, or group or from entering into contracts or enforcing contracts as a partnership, association, corporation, firm, or group.

HISTORY: 2002 Act No. 359, Section 1.

SECTION 40-59-530. Exceptions.

This article does not apply to a person:

(1) employed by the State or any political subdivision of the State as a code enforcement official when acting within the scope of that employment;

(2) inspecting a home exclusively for the use of a bank, savings and loan association, or credit union unless otherwise required by federal law or regulation;

(3) licensed, registered, or certified pursuant to Chapter 3 or a person duly licensed as a general contractor pursuant to Chapter 11 or a person duly licensed pursuant to Article 1 of Chapter 59 or a person duly licensed or registered as a professional engineer pursuant to Chapter 22. Notwithstanding the exemption from licensure under this article, the provisions of this article relating to the conduct of a person in the performance of a home inspection shall apply to that person. A violation of this article is considered a violation against the person's license and subjects the person to disciplinary action by the licensing board under which the person is licensed;

(4) who is duly licensed under the provisions of Section 46-13-55 for the purpose of issuing CL100 Wood Infestation Reports, provided such inspection is limited solely to the requirement of the CL100 report.

HISTORY: 2002 Act No. 359, Section 1.

SECTION 40-59-540. Application; examination; regulations establishing minimum standards.

(A) A person desiring to be licensed as a home inspector shall submit written application to the commission on forms as the commission prescribes. Upon the submission of a completed application form and the payment of the fee required by the commission, the applicant is entitled to take the home inspector licensing examination as prescribed by the commission. Upon successful completion of the examination, the commission shall issue the applicant a license authorizing the applicant to engage in the business of home inspection in this State. The issuance of a license is evidence that the licensee is entitled to all the rights and privileges of a licensed home inspector while the license remains active.

(B) The commission shall promulgate regulations to establish the minimum qualifications and uniform criteria for the granting of a home inspector license.

HISTORY: 2002 Act No. 359, Section 1.

SECTION 40-59-550. Display of license; address changes; renewal; inactive status.

(A) The licensee shall display the license in the manner prescribed by the commission.

(B) The licensee shall inform the commission of any change in his business or home address.

(C) A license must be renewed before July first of each year for a period of one year upon payment of the renewal fee and upon compliance with this article. If the home inspector has not complied with any provision of this article during the year, the licensee shall submit a new application as in the case of the issuance of an original license.

(D) The commission may provide for the late renewal of a license upon payment of a late fee in an amount established by the commission in regulation.

(E) A licensee who does not intend to engage in the business of home inspection for at least one year may request upon written notice to the commission that his license be placed in inactive status. While in inactive status, the person is not subject to payment of any renewal fees and may not perform home inspections in this State. When the person desires to resume the performance of home inspections, he shall file an application for license renewal, pay the renewal fee, and demonstrate continuing competence as defined by the commission in regulation. If a license has been in inactive status for more than three years, the person shall submit a new application as in the case of the issuance of an original license and shall take and successfully complete the examination.

HISTORY: 2002 Act No. 359, Section 1.

SECTION 40-59-560. Inspection reports; form; disclosure of scope and limitations.

(A) An inspection report issued by a licensed home inspector under this chapter must be on a form approved by the commission. For purposes of this section, a form that contains the same information as the commission-approved form is considered to have met the requirements of this section.

(B) Nothing in this section may require a home inspector to inspect every item contained in the commission-approved form, and nothing in this section may limit a home inspector from performing a home inspection beyond the scope of information contained in the commission-approved form. A home inspector shall indicate on the inspection report which items, if any, were not inspected.

(C) A home inspector shall disclose the scope and limitations, if any, of each inspection before performing a home inspection.

HISTORY: 2002 Act No. 359, Section 1.

SECTION 40-59-570. "Advertisement" defined.

"Advertisement" means any form of public notice, however disseminated. An advertisement by a licensed home inspector shall include the name, business name, address, and license number of the licensee. The use of any false, misleading, unfair, or deceptive practice in any advertisement is grounds for disciplinary action as provided for under this chapter.

HISTORY: 2002 Act No. 359, Section 1.

SECTION 40-59-580. Denial, suspension, or revocation; civil penalties; hearing; appeal.

(A) The commission may deny, refuse to renew, temporarily suspend, or revoke a license or issue a civil penalty under this section if the licensee or applicant for licensure:

(1) makes a false or misleading statement in that portion of a written report that deals with professional qualification or in any testimony concerning professional qualifications;

(2) engages in an act or omission involving dishonesty, fraud, or misrepresentation with the intent to substantially benefit a home inspector or other person or with the intent to substantially injure another person;

(3) engages in an act of fraud, misrepresentation, or deceit in the making of a home inspection;

(4) pays a finder's fee or a referral fee to a person in connection with an inspection of a residence;

(5) fails or refuses without good cause to exercise reasonable diligence in developing a home inspection report, preparing a report, or communicating a report;

(6) accepts a home inspection assignment when the employment itself is contingent upon the home inspector reporting a predetermined estimate, analysis, or opinion or when the fee to be paid is contingent upon the opinion, the conclusions, analysis, or report reached or upon the consequences resulting from the assignment;

(7) performs work or improvement to a residence upon which the home inspector performed a home inspection within the previous twelve months;

(8) employs fraud, deceit, or misrepresentation in obtaining or attempting to obtain a license or renewal of a license;

(9) commits an act or acts of malpractice, gross negligence, or incompetence in the performance of home inspections;

(10) practices as a licensed home inspector without a current license;

(11) engages in conduct that could result in harm or injury to the public;

(12) engages in an act or practice violative of any of the provisions of this article or a regulation promulgated by the commission under this article or aids, abets, or assists a person in such violation.

(B) The commission may impose a civil penalty for violations of any provision of this article or a regulation promulgated by the commission, as follows:

(1) for a first violation, a penalty in an amount not to exceed one hundred dollars;

(2) for a second violation, a penalty in an amount not to exceed two hundred dollars; and

(3) for a third and any subsequent violation, a penalty in an amount not to exceed one thousand dollars.

Civil penalties collected by the commission must be remitted to the State Treasurer for deposit in the state's general fund.

(C) The denial, refusal to renew, temporary suspension, or revocation of a license or the issuance of a civil penalty under this section may be ordered by a decision of a majority of the commission after a hearing held in accordance with Article 3, Chapter 23 of Title 1, the Administrative Procedures Act. A decision of the commission to deny, refuse to renew, temporarily suspend, or revoke a license or impose a civil penalty is subject to review by an administrative law judge as provided under Article 5, Chapter 23 of Title 1.

(D) An individual may apply to the commission for reinstatement of a revoked license if the revocation has been in effect for at least one year. The license may be granted upon an affirmative vote by a majority of the commission.

HISTORY: 2002 Act No. 359, Section 1.

SECTION 40-59-590. Restrictions; appraisals and real estate activities.

A home inspector is prohibited from engaging in real estate appraisal activity unless the inspector meets the requirements of Chapter 60. Further, a home inspector is prohibited from engaging in any real estate activity regulated under Chapter 57 unless the inspector meets the requirements of that chapter.

HISTORY: 2002 Act No. 359, Section 1.

SECTION 40-59-600. Penalties; actions to enforce contract; injunction.

(A) The administrator is authorized to use the powers granted to him pursuant to this chapter to enforce the provisions of this article.

(B) A home inspector who is not otherwise exempt from this article who undertakes or attempts to undertake the business of home inspection without first obtaining a license or who knowingly presents, or files with, the commission false information for the purpose of obtaining a license is guilty of a misdemeanor and:

(1) for the first offense, upon conviction, must be fined not more than one hundred dollars or imprisoned for not more than thirty days, or both;

(2) for a second offense, upon conviction, must be fined not more than two hundred dollars or imprisoned for not more than ninety days, or both.

(3) for a third and subsequent offense, upon conviction, the person must be fined not more than one thousand dollars or imprisoned not more than one hundred eighty days, or both.

(C) A home inspector who does not have a license as required by this article may not bring an action either at law or in equity to enforce the provisions of a contract for home inspection which he entered into in violation of this article.

(D) If it appears to the commission that a home inspector has violated, or is about to violate, a provision of this article, the commission may in its own name petition an administrative law judge to issue a temporary restraining order enjoining the violation of this article, pending a full hearing to determine whether or not the injunction must be made permanent.

HISTORY: 2002 Act No. 359, Section 1.

SECTION 40-59-610. Regulations.

The commission is authorized to promulgate regulations to administer the provisions of this article.

HISTORY: 2002 Act No. 359, Section 1.

SECTION 40-59-620. Applicability of building code in effect at time of construction.

When an inspection report includes a deficiency that is alleged to be a building codes violation, the inspector is responsible for determining the construction dates and building codes in effect at the time of construction and must conduct the inspection using the building codes in effect at the time of construction.

HISTORY: 2002 Act No. 359, Section 1.

ARTICLE 5.

SOUTH CAROLINA NOTICE AND OPPORTUNITY TO CURE CONSTRUCTION DWELLING DEFECTS ACT

SECTION 40-59-810. Short Title.

This article may be cited as the "South Carolina Notice and Opportunity to Cure Construction Dwelling Defects Act".

HISTORY: 2003 Act No. 82, Section 1.

SECTION 40-59-820. Definitions.

As used in this article:

(1) "Action" means any civil lawsuit or action or arbitration proceeding for damages or indemnity asserting a claim for injury or loss to a dwelling or personal property caused by an alleged defect arising out of or related to the design, construction, condition, or sale of the dwelling or a remodel of a dwelling.

(2) "Claimant" means a homeowner, including a subsequent purchaser, who asserts a claim against a contractor, subcontractor, supplier, or design professional concerning a defect in the design, construction, condition, or sale of a dwelling or in the remodel of a dwelling.

(3) "Construction defect" means a deficiency in or a deficiency arising out of the design, specifications, surveying, planning, supervision, or observation of construction or construction of residential improvements that results from any of the following:

(a) defective material, products, or components used in the construction of residential improvements;

(b) violation of the applicable codes in effect at the time of construction of residential improvements;

(c) failure of the design of residential improvements to meet the applicable professional standards of care at the time of governmental approval of the design of residential improvements; or

(d) failure to construct residential improvements in accordance with accepted trade standards for good and workmanlike construction at the time of construction. Compliance with the applicable codes in effect at the time of construction conclusively establishes construction in accordance with accepted trade standards for good and workmanlike construction, with respect to all matters specified in those codes.

(4) "Dwelling" means a single-family house or duplex or a multifamily unit not to exceed sixteen units and not to exceed three stories in height, and which is intended for residential use. A dwelling includes the systems and other components and improvements that are part of a single or multifamily unit at the time of construction.

(5) "Serve" or "service" means personal service or delivery by certified mail to the last known address of the addressee.

HISTORY: 2003 Act No. 82, Section 1.

SECTION 40-59-830. Stay of action until compliance with article.

If the claimant files an action in court before first complying with the requirements of this article, on motion of a party to the action, the court shall stay the action until the claimant has complied with the requirements of this article.

HISTORY: 2003 Act No. 82, Section 1.

SECTION 40-59-840. Notice of claim; timing; contents; request for clarification.

(A) In an action brought against a contractor or subcontractor arising out of the construction of a dwelling, the claimant must, no later than ninety days before filing the action, serve a written notice of claim on the contractor. The notice of claim must contain the following:

(1) a statement that the claimant asserts a construction defect;

(2) a description of the claim or claims in reasonable detail sufficient to determine the general nature of the construction defect; and

(3) a description of any results of the defect, if known.

The contractor or subcontractor shall advise the claimant within fifteen days of receipt of the claim if the construction defect is not sufficiently stated and shall request clarification.

HISTORY: 2003 Act No. 82, Section 1.

SECTION 40-59-850. Contractor's election to inspect, remedy, settle, or deny claim; inspection of construction defect; response to contractor's offer; admissibility.

(A) The contractor or subcontractor has thirty days from service of the notice to inspect, offer to remedy, offer to settle with the claimant, or deny the claim regarding the defects. The claimant shall receive written notice of the contractor's or subcontractor's, as applicable, election under this section. The claimant shall allow inspection of the construction defect at an agreeable time to both parties, if requested under this section. The claimant shall give the contractor and any subcontractors reasonable access to the dwelling for inspection and if repairs have been agreed to by the parties, reasonable access to affect repairs. Failure to respond within thirty days is deemed a denial of the claim.

(B) The claimant shall serve a response to the contractor's offer, if any, within ten days of receipt of the offer.

(C) If the parties cannot settle the dispute pursuant to this article, the claimant may proceed with a civil action or other remedy provided by contract or by law.

(D) Any offers of settlement, repair, or remedy pursuant to this section, are not admissible in an action.

HISTORY: 2003 Act No. 82, Section 1.

SECTION 40-59-860. Claims for personal injury or death; designation for stay on Civil Action Cover Sheet.

(A) Nothing in this article applies to actions arising out of claims for personal injury or death, or both.

(B) Court Administration must develop a designation on the Civil Action Cover Sheet which indicates whether a stay has been granted for a civil action filed pursuant to the South Carolina Notice and Opportunity to Cure Construction Defects Act.

HISTORY: 2003 Act No. 82, Section 1.

Appendix F: South Carolina Residential Builders Commission Regulations

106-1 Classification of Residential Specialty Contractors.

In furtherance of established custom and usage within the construction industry and in recognition of the historical fact that the different skills, knowledge and experience necessary to the specialized trades and crafts has customarily limited activity and participation therein, the following classifications denote those residential specialties available for registration or licensure, as determined by the Commission. Holders thereof are restricted to the scope of operations set forth as to each.

a. Plumbers: the installation, alteration and repair of water and natural gas piping systems, sewage systems and water filter and purification and conditioning systems, including all related fixtures, vents, and devices common to the residential building industry.

b. Electricians: the installation, alteration and repair of any wiring, related electrical material and equipment common to the residential building industry.

c. Heating and air conditioning installers and repairers: the installation, replacement, alteration, or repair of air conditioning equipment and systems, limited to five tons cooling and 175,000 BTU/HR heating per unit, which consist of a number of components necessary to produce conditioned air for environmental heating or cooling, or both, within a residence, including package equipment, heating and cooling systems: and the installation, alteration, and repair of ventilation systems including duct work, air filtering devices, water treatment devices, pneumatic or electrical controls, or control piping, thermal and acoustical insulation, vibration isolation materials and devices, liquid fuel piping and tanks (except those used for liquid propane gas), water and gas piping from service and heating circuits and air handling systems, including gas fired furnaces and space heaters, and factory assembled single package units and split type direct expansion equipment, including heat pumps.

d. Vinyl and aluminum siding installers: the installation, alteration and repair of vinyl and aluminum siding common to the residential building industry.

e. Insulation installers: the installation, alteration and repair of insulating materials for the purpose of temperature or sound control, excluding any exterior roofing materials such as foam and reflective coating common to the residential building industry.

f. Roofers: the installation, alteration and repair of materials common to the residential building industry that form a water tight, weather resistant surface for roofs and decks, including all accessories, flashing, valleys, gravel stops and roof insulation panels above the roof deck.

g. Floor covering installers: the installation, replacement and repair of floor covering materials and related accessories including preparation of the surface to be covered: included are materials manufactured of asphalt, vinyl, rubber, linoleum, and carpet.

h. Masons: the installation, alteration and repair of poured-in-place concrete foundations (e.g. footings or reinforced slabs), brick, concrete block, and products common to the masonry industry, including mortarless types and synthetic masonry products common to the residential building industry.

i. Dry Wall Installer: the installation, alteration and repair of plaster, gypsum wall board, pointing, accessories, taping and texturing on structures both interior and exterior common to the residential building industry.

j. Carpenters: the installation, alteration and repair of rough and general carpentry work on new and existing structures including accessories and related hardware common to the residential building industry.

k. Stucco installers: the installation, alteration and repair of stucco finishes, including Exterior Insulation and Finish Systems (EIFS), which is defined as multi-layered exterior wall systems consisting of a durable water proof finish coat, a reinforced base coat, and insulation board, all secured to plywood or other substance by means of an adhesive and/or mechanical attachment.

l. Painters/Wallpaperers: the application of materials common to the painting and decorating industry for protective or decorative purposes, includes surface preparation, caulking, sanding and cleaning preparatory to painting common to the residential building industry: and the installation, alteration and repair of surface coverings such as vinyls, wallpapers, and cloth fabrics, decorative texturing, taping and finishing of drywall in conjunction with surface painting only common to the residential building industry.

m. Solar Panel Installers: Fabricating, assembling, installing, and replacing solar panels and related components common to the residential building industry. Roof mounting of solar panels shall only be performed by a licensed Residential Builder, registered Residential Specialty Contractor with a Roofer classification or a General Contractor with General Roofing or Specialty Roofing licensed by the South Carolina Contractor's Licensing Board. Wiring and connections shall only be performed by a licensed Residential Builder, licensed Residential Electrician or a Mechanical Contractor with Electrical classification licensed by the South Carolina Contractor's Licensing Board. If a roof requires structural upgrades for the mounting and installing of solar panels, any structural upgrading of the roof must be performed by a licensed Residential Builder, or a registered Residential Specialty Contractor with a Carpenter classification or a licensed General Contractor with Building or Structural Framing classification

HISTORY: Amended by State Register Volume 17, Issue No. 5, Part III, eff May 28, 1993; State Register Volume 21, Issue No. 6, Part 2, eff June 27, 1997; State Register Volume 29, Issue No. 1, eff January 28, 2005; State Register Volume 41, Issue No. 10, eff May 25, 2018.

106-2 Residential Specialty Contractors License.

As provided by Section 40-59-220, the Commission finds that the following residential specialty classifications must be licensed after examination satisfactorily demonstrating that an applicant is qualified to engage in a residential specialty contractor classification. When the cost of an undertaking to be performed by a licensed residential specialty contractor exceeds five thousand dollars, the licensee must obtain an executed surety bond in an amount approved by the Commission not less than ten thousand dollars.

a. Heating and Air Conditioning Installer and Repairers, effective July 1, 2004, except that applicants who have lawfully engaged in this classification in good standing for not less than two years prior to July 1, 2004, shall be issued a license without examination upon surrender of the proper registration card and compliance with all other requirements for licensure. In the event that such license, issued without examination, is allowed to lapse or expire for more than three years or is suspended or revoked, examination shall be required for the license to be re-issued.

b. Plumbers, effective July 1, 2004, except that applicants who have lawfully engaged in this classification in good standing for not less than two years prior to July 1, 2004, shall be issued a license without examination upon surrender of the proper registration card and compliance with all other requirements for licensure. In the event that such license, issued without examination, is allowed to lapse or expire for more than three years or is suspended or revoked, examination shall be required for the license to be re-issued.

c. Electricians, effective July 1, 2004, except that applicants who have lawfully engaged in this classification in good standing for not less than two years prior to July 1, 2004, shall be issued a license without examination upon surrender of the proper registration card and compliance with all other requirements for licensure. In the event that such license, issued without examination, is allowed to lapse or expire for more than three years or is suspended or revoked, examination shall be required for the license to be re-issued.

HISTORY: Amended by State Register Volume 17, Issue No. 5, Part III, eff May 28, 1993; State Register Volume 29, Issue No. 1, eff January 28, 2005; State Register Volume 37, Issue No. 6, eff June 28, 2013; State Register Volume 41, Issue No. 10, eff May 25, 2018.

106-3 Initial Fees.

A. Licensed Residential Builder or Residential Specialty Contractor:

1. An application processing fee of one hundred thirty five dollars;

2. An examination fee of one hundred dollars;

3. A residential builder license fee of one hundred ten dollars:

4. An annual renewal fee of one hundred ten dollars:

5. A late fee of an additional fifty dollars for renewals received after July 1st:

6. When a renewal is received more than twelve months but not later than 3 years after expiration of the license, there will be a lapsed license reinstatement fee of two hundred sixty dollars. This includes one hundred ten dollar renewal fee, fifty dollar late fee and the lapsed fee of one hundred dollars, which will be required.

B. Registered Residential Specialty Contractor:

1. A registration fee of fifty dollars:

2. An annual renewal fee of fifty dollars:

3. A late fee of an additional twenty dollars for renewals received after July 1st:

4. A lapsed fee of ninety dollars will be required when a renewal is received more than twelve months but not later than 3 years after expiration of the registration.

C. Other Fees and Penalties:

1. A replacement fee of ten dollars for replacing any lost, destroyed, or mutilated license or registration card:

2. A fee of ten dollars for a duplicate copy of a license or registration when any change is requested to the information printed on the license or registration card.

D. Certificate of Authorization (COA):

1. A licensing fee of one hundred dollars;

2. A renewal fee of one hundred dollars.

E. Home Inspectors:

1. An application fee of eighty dollars:

2. An annual renewal fee of eighty dollars:

3. A late fee of ninety dollars for renewal received after July 1st:

4. An additional late renewal fee of one hundred ten dollars will be required when a renewal is received more than twelve months after expiration of the license:

5. A replacement fee of ten dollars for replacing any lost, destroyed or mutilated license:

6. A fee of ten dollars for a reissued license when any change is requested by the license to any information printed on the license:

7. An examination fee of eighty dollars.

HISTORY: Amended by State Register Volume 17, Issue No. 5, Part III, eff May 28, 1993; State Register Volume 29, Issue No. 1, eff January 28, 2005.

106-4 Qualifications for Home Inspectors.

A. Any person desiring to be licensed as a home inspector, without examination by the commission shall file with the commission an application on forms provided by the commission showing to the satisfaction of the commission that he is currently certified or licensed as a building or home inspector after written examination by an organization or other entity approved by the commission: and

1. Has a minimum of one year of experience as a home inspector under the direction and direct supervision of a licensed home inspector, residential builder, general contractor, engineer, or architect: or

2. Has performed a minimum of fifty residential inspections, as evidenced by the name, address, telephone number, and summary page of each inspection being submitted for review.

Upon filing a completed application and payment of the required fees, the commission shall issue the applicant a license to engage in the business of home inspection in this State.

B. Any person desiring to be licensed by examination as a home inspector shall file with the commission an application of forms provided by the commission showing to the satisfaction of the commission that he:

1. Has performed a minimum of fifty home inspections within one year prior to January 1, 1996, as evidenced by the name, address, telephone number, and summary page of each inspection being submitted for review. This provision shall apply only to persons filing an application with the commission before January 1, 1997: or

2. Has a minimum of one year of experience as a home inspector under the direction and direct supervision of a licensed home inspector, residential builder, general contractor, engineer, or architect: or

3. Has successfully completed a formal course of training or study in home inspection approved by the commission.

Upon filing of a completed application and copy of the required fees, the applicant shall be entitled to take the home inspectors licensing examination as prescribed by the commission. Upon successful completion of the examination and payment of the licensing fee, the commission shall issue the applicant a license to engage in the business of home inspection in this State. A passing score is seventy or better.

HISTORY: Amended by State Register Volume 17, Issue No. 5, Part III, eff May 28, 1993; State Register Volume 29, Issue No. 1, eff January 28, 2005.

106-5 Emergency License and Registration

A. In the instance of an event declared to be an emergency by the governor, the department, as defined by S.C. Code Ann. Section 40 59 20(2), is authorized to issue emergency licenses and registrations for out of state builders and specialty contractors.

B. To qualify for an emergency license or registration, an individual, at the time of application, must submit a verification letter issued by the state in which the applicant's principal place of business is located (home state) as proof that his or her license is in good standing. The emergency license or registration may be issued only to the individual shown on the home state license. The home state license must have been issued by examination; a "grandfathered" license or registration will not be accepted as proof of licensure.

C. In addition to proof of home state licensure, an applicant must also provide:

1. An emergency license application;

2. A national criminal background report current within fourteen (14) days of the date of application. A criminal background report showing misdemeanors listed for twenty four (24) months or felonies listed for fifteen (15) years prior to the application date will not qualify for licensure;

3. A current bond for home builders of at least Fifteen Thousand Dollars ($15,000.00) and current bond for specialty contractors of at least Five Thousand Dollars ($5,000.00); and,

4. A fee of One Hundred Dollars ($100.00).

D. An emergency license or registration will be:

1. Issued for one (1) specific event;

2. Limited to a total valuation of One Hundred Thousand Dollars ($100,000.00) for any single project for home builders, and a total valuation of Thirty five Thousand Dollars ($35,000.00) for any single project for specialty contractors;

3. Valid only for the scope of work permitted by the applicant's home state license;

4. Valid only within the area of the declared emergency; and,

5. Valid only for the duration of the emergency declaration, or as extended at the board's discretion.

HISTORY: Added by State Register Volume 36, Issue No. 6, eff June 22, 2012.

Appendix G: Board Regulation of Professions and Occupations

ARTICLE 1

SECTION 40-1-10. Extent of regulation.

(A) The right of a person to engage in a lawful profession, trade, or occupation of choice is clearly protected by both the Constitution of the United States and the Constitution of the State of South Carolina. The State cannot abridge this right except as a reasonable exercise of its police powers when it is clearly found that abridgement is necessary for the preservation of the health, safety, and welfare of the public.

(B) No statute or regulation may be imposed under this article upon a profession or occupation except for the exclusive purpose of protecting the public interest when the:

(1) unregulated practice of the profession or occupation can harm or endanger the health, safety, or welfare of the public and the potential for harm is recognizable and not remote or dependent upon tenuous argument;

(2) practice of the profession or occupation has inherent qualities peculiar to it that distinguish it from ordinary work or labor;

(3) practice of the profession or occupation requires specialized skill or training and the public needs and will benefit by assurances of initial and continuing professional and occupational ability; and

(4) public is not effectively protected by other means.

(C) If the General Assembly determines that a particular profession or occupation should be regulated or that a different degree of regulation should be imposed on the regulated profession or occupation, it shall consider the following degrees of regulation in the order provided and only shall regulate the profession or occupation to the degree necessary to fulfill the need for regulation:

(1) If existing common law and statutory causes of civil action or criminal prohibitions are not sufficient to eradicate existing harm or prevent potential harm, the General Assembly first may consider making statutory changes to provide stricter causes for civil action and criminal prosecution.

(2) If it is necessary to determine the impact of the operation of a profession or occupation on the public, the General Assembly may consider implementing a system of registration.

(3) If the public requires a substantial basis for relying on the professional services of the practitioner, the General Assembly may consider implementing a system of certification.

(4) If adequate regulation cannot be achieved by means less than licensing, the General Assembly may establish licensing procedures.

(D) In determining the proper degree of regulation, if any, the General Assembly shall determine:

(1) whether the practitioner, if unregulated, performs a service to individuals involving a hazard to the public health, safety, or welfare;

(2) what the opinion of a substantial portion of the people who do not practice the particular profession, trade, or occupation is on the need for regulation;

(3) the number of states which have regulatory provisions similar to those proposed;

(4) whether there is sufficient demand for the service for which there is no regulated substitute, and this service is required by a substantial portion of the population;

(5) whether the profession or occupation requires high standards of public responsibility, character, and performance of each individual engaged in the profession or occupation, as evidenced by established and published codes of ethics;

(6) whether the profession or occupation requires such skill that the public generally is not qualified to select a competent practitioner without some assurance that the practitioner has met minimum qualifications;

(7) whether the professional or occupational associations do not adequately protect the public from incompetent, unscrupulous, or irresponsible members of the profession or occupation;

(8) whether current laws which pertain to public health, safety, and welfare generally are ineffective or inadequate;

(9) whether the characteristics of the profession or occupation make it impractical or impossible to prohibit those practices of the profession or occupation which are detrimental to the public health, safety, and welfare;

(10) whether the practitioner performs a service for others which may have a detrimental effect on third parties relying on the expert knowledge of the practitioner.

HISTORY: 1996 Act No. 453, Section 2.

SECTION 40-1-20. Definitions.

As used in this title unless the context requires a different meaning:

(1) "Administrator" means the individual to whom the director has delegated authority to administer the programs of a specific board or of a professional or occupational group for which the department has regulatory authority or has delegated authority to administer the programs of a specific board;

(2) "Authorization to practice" or "Practice authorization" means the approval to practice the specified profession, engage in the specified occupation, or use a title protected under this article, which has been granted by the applicable board. This authorization is granted in the form of a license, permit, certification, or registration;

(3) "Board" or "Commission" means the group of individuals charged by law with the responsibility of licensing or otherwise regulating an occupation or profession within the State. Except as otherwise indicated, "board" is used in this article to refer to both boards and commissions;

(4) "Department" means the Department of Labor, Licensing and Regulation;

(5) "Director" means the Director of the Department of Labor, Licensing and Regulation or the director's official designee;

(6) "Licensee" means a person granted an authorization to practice pursuant to this article and refers to a person holding a license, permit, certification, or registration granted pursuant to this article;

(7) "Licensing act" means the individual statute or regulations, or both, of each regulated profession or occupation which include, but are not limited to, board governance, the qualifications and requirements for authorization to practice, prohibitions, and disciplinary procedures;

(8) "Person" means an individual, partnership, or corporation;

(9) "Profession" or "occupation" means a profession or occupation regulated or administered, or both, by the department pursuant to this article.

HISTORY: 1996 Act No. 453, Section 2.

SECTION 40-1-30. Authorization to practice.

It is unlawful for a person to engage in a profession or occupation regulated by a board or commission administered by the Department of Labor, Licensing and Regulation without holding a valid authorization to practice as required by statute or regulation.

An authorization to practice issued pursuant to this title is valid for up to two years and is renewable on renewal dates as established by the Director of Labor, Licensing and Regulation with the consent of each applicable regulatory board.

HISTORY: 1996 Act No. 453, Section 2.

SECTION 40-1-40. Purpose of division; domain.

(A) The purpose of the Division of Professional and Occupational Licensing, South Carolina Department of Labor, Licensing and Regulation, is to protect the public through the regulation of professional and occupational licensees and the administration of boards charged with the regulation of professional and occupational practitioners.

(B) The following boards and the professions and occupations they license or otherwise regulate must be administered by the Department of Labor, Licensing and Regulation pursuant to this article:

Board of Accountancy

Board of Architectural Examiners

Athletic Commission

Auctioneers Commission

Board of Barber Examiners

Accessibility Committee of the Building Codes Council

Building Code Council

Board of Chiropractic Examiners

Contractors' Licensing Board

Board of Cosmetology

Board of Dentistry

Engineers and Land Surveyors Board

Environmental Certification Board

Board of Registration for Foresters

Board of Funeral Service

Board of Registration for Geologists

Manufactured Housing Board

Board of Medical Examiners

Modular Buildings Board of Appeals

Board of Nursing

Long Term Health Care Administrators Board

Board of Occupational Therapy

Board of Examiners in Opticianry

Board of Examiners in Optometry

Board of Pharmacy

Board of Physical Therapy Examiners

Pilotage Commission

Board of Podiatry Examiners

Board of Examiners for Licensure of Professional Counselors and Marital and Family Therapists

Board of Examiners in Psychology

Board of Pyrotechnic Safety

Real Estate Appraisers Board

Real Estate Commission

Residential Builders Commission

Board of Social Work Examiners

Board of Examiners in Speech-Language Pathology and Audiology

Board of Veterinary Medical Examiners

(C) Each regulatory board within the department is a separate board.

(D) The Department of Labor, Licensing and Regulation is a member of the Governor's executive cabinet and must be headed by a director who must be appointed by the Governor with the advice and consent of the Senate, subject to removal from office by the Governor pursuant to Section 1-3-240(B). The director shall supervise the department under the direction and control of the Governor and shall exercise other powers and perform other duties as the Governor requires.

HISTORY: 1996 Act No. 453, Section 2.

SECTION 40-1-45. Public and consumer members of boards and panels.

The department, in consultation with currently serving board members, the Office of the Governor, members of professional and industry associations, and the general public shall encourage public and consumer membership and participation on all boards and panels associated with the department. Public and consumer membership may not include current or former, active or inactive members of the profession or occupation being regulated. Public and consumer members have the same rights and responsibilities as professionally or occupationally-related board members and shall participate fully in all discussions, deliberations, decisions, and votes of the board or panel on which they serve unless otherwise prohibited by statute or regulation.

HISTORY: 1996 Act No. 453, Section 2.

SECTION 40-1-50. Authority of department; record of board proceedings; roster of licensees; fee structures.

(A) The department is responsible for all administrative, fiscal, investigative, inspectional, clerical, secretarial, and license renewal operations and activities of the boards and commissions enumerated in Section 40-1-40.

The director shall employ and supervise personnel necessary to effectuate the provisions of this article for each board provided for in Section 40-1-40. When hiring a person charged with evaluating or administering professional qualifications or licensing standards, the director must select from a list of three candidates submitted by the appropriate licensing board. However, a candidate whose name is submitted to the director must be chosen from a list of all candidates found to be qualified by the Human Management Office of the department. The authority to remove an employee of the department is vested with the Director of the Department of Labor, Licensing and Regulation.

The director shall establish compensation for personnel assigned to the boards as the director considers necessary and appropriate for the administration of this article. Compensation and necessary expenses incurred in the performance of duties by personnel assigned to the board must be paid as an expense of the board in the administration of this article.

The director shall enter into contracts and agreements the director considers necessary or incidental to carry out the provisions of this article to provide for all services required by each board.

Board members must be compensated for their services at the usual rate for mileage, subsistence, and per diem as provided by law for members of state boards, committees, and commissions and may be reimbursed for actual and necessary expenses incurred in connection with and as a result of their work as members of the board. The director, within the limits set by the Comptroller General, shall establish reimbursement standards for travel and other expenses incurred by a board member in the performance of the board member's official duties. Compensation and reimbursements paid to board members under this subsection must be paid as an expense of the board in the administration of this article and the board's chapter and must be paid from the fees received by the board pursuant to the provisions of this article or in a manner prescribed by the Department of Labor, Licensing and Regulation.

The director shall maintain a separate account for funds collected on behalf of a board and shall indicate the expenses allotted to the board. The director shall adjust fees for revenue-funded boards in accordance with Section 40-1-50 (D).

The director annually shall prepare a report to the Governor and the General Assembly indicating those regulated trades, occupations, and professions that do not meet the spirit and intent of Section 40-1-10.

The director may perform any additional administrative functions requested by the boards.

(B) The department shall keep a record of the proceedings of each board and shall maintain a registry of all applications for licensure, permitting, certification, and registration. The registry shall include the name, age, and last known address of each applicant, the place of business of the applicant, the education, experience, and other qualifications of the applicant, type of examination required, whether or not an authorization to practice was granted, the date of the action of the department, and other information considered necessary by the board.

Except as otherwise required by law, the record of a board's proceedings and its registry of applicants must be open to public inspection, and a copy of the registry must be provided upon request and payment of a fee.

Records of a board and its registry are prima facie evidence of its proceedings, and a copy certified by the administrator or the director under seal is admissible as evidence with the same force and effect as the original.

(C) The department may prepare and publish a roster for each respective board containing the names and places of business of persons licensed under this article. A copy of the roster must be provided upon request and upon payment of a fee which may not exceed the cost of printing and distribution of the roster.

(D) Initial fees for revenue-funded boards must be established by each board and shall serve as the base for necessary administrative adjustments. Each board, on at least a biennial basis, shall provide the director with a statement of anticipated expenditures, program changes, and other information as may be used in determining fees for the next biennial period.

Fees for revenue-funded boards must be assessed, collected, and adjusted on behalf of each board by the department in accordance with this article. Fees may be adjusted biennially to ensure that they are sufficient but not excessive to cover expenses including the total of the direct and indirect costs to the State for the operations of each respective board. Fees must be deposited in accounts established for each respective board.

The following steps must be used in the development and analysis of fee structures:

> (1) Determine current financial position of the program. Each month, the department's administrative section shall prepare statements reflecting monthly revenue collection activity and related program expenses for each board program. The financial standing of a board program must be reviewed each

biennium for boards that renew biennially, annually for boards that renew on an annual basis, and more frequently if indicators evidence a significant financial fluctuation of more than ten percent variance between a program's revenue and related expenses;

(2) Project future activity and related costs of the program. By reviewing historical volume information and adjusting trends to reflect changes in the industry, changes in the program, indicators from the board members to the staff, and general economic indicators, project program activity including, but not limited to, renewals and new applicants for the upcoming two to three years. Based on these population projections, forecast program revenues using the current fee structure. With input from the board and the staff, analyze related program direct board costs for the upcoming two to three years, based on historical trends, changes in program requirements, changes to expenditure centers, and changes in staffing requirements. To these direct costs, add the program's proportionate share of other related costs of the program including, but not limited to, administration of exams, agency administration, and information systems to arrive at the total program cost;

(3) Determine the projected financial position of the program, propose changes where necessary, and compare the total projected revenue at the current fees to the total projected costs of the program over the next two to three years. If the current fees and the projected program activity do not support the projected program's expenses, develop alternative fee structures which would ensure the program's continuing financial stability as required by law;

(4) Present findings to the director and staff for discussion, revision, evaluation, and adoption. While developing fee analyses, maintain communications with staff and agency management to ensure all necessary factors are evaluated and cost savings, efficiencies, and alternative cost reduction scenarios are pursued. Present fee analyses to board staff and management for discussion and revision where necessary. Propose alternatives to the director for consideration when preparing to adopt proposed fee schedules to achieve a structure sufficient to support the program.

Fees for a board funded by general appropriations must be set by the General Assembly and deposited into the general fund. All fees are nonrefundable.

(E) Where appropriate, the director shall adopt the necessary procedures to implement the biennial renewal of authorizations to practice in a manner as to ensure that the number of renewals is reasonably evenly distributed throughout each two-year period. During any transition, fees must be proportionate to the biennial fee.

(F) A board may elect to delegate to the department the authority to issue an authorization to practice to an applicant whose proof of qualifications falls within established guidelines set by the board.

A board may elect to delegate to the department the authority to deny an authorization to practice to an applicant who has committed an act that would be grounds for disciplinary action under this article or the licensing act of the board, who has failed to comply with a final order of a board, or who has failed to demonstrate the basic qualifications or standards for practice authorization contained in the board's licensing act. The applicant may appeal the denial to the board which has final regulatory decision-making authority for reconsideration. The board may uphold the denial, order issuance of the authorization to practice, or order issuance of the authorization to practice upon conditions set by the board. If the administrative decision is upheld, the applicant may reapply at the end of a twelve-month period.

(G) The department shall suspend the practice authorization issued by a board administered by this article to a person who submits a check, money draft, or similar instrument for payment of a fee which is not honored by the financial institution named. The suspension becomes effective ten days following delivery by certified mail of written notice of the dishonor and the impending suspension to the person's address. Upon notification of suspension, the person may reinstate the authorization to practice upon payment of the fee and penalties required under statute or regulation. This suspension is exempt from the Administrative Procedures Act.

(H) The department shall revoke the authorization to practice of a person found to be in violation of the Family Independence Act as it relates to child support enforcement requirements.

(I) The department may prepare an annual report for submission to the Governor.

It is the duty of the director to notify and seek approval of the board or commission at least thirty days in advance of filing with Legislative Council as required by Section 1-23-30 of any proposed changes in any rules or regulations which may affect the practice or service of the respective licensing board or commission.

HISTORY: 1996 Act No. 453, Section 2.

SECTION 40-1-60. Officers of boards; meetings.

(A) A board annually shall elect from among its members a chairman, vice-chairman, and other officers as the board determines necessary. The board shall adopt rules and procedures reasonably necessary for the performance of its duties and the governance of its operations and proceedings.

(B) A board shall meet at least two times a year and at other times upon the call of the chairman or a majority of the board.

(C) A majority of the members of a board constitutes a quorum; however, if there is a vacancy on the board, a majority of the members serving constitutes a quorum.

(D) A board member is required to attend meetings or to provide proper notice and justification of inability to do so. Unexcused absences from meetings may result in removal from the board as provided for in Section 1-3-240.

HISTORY: 1996 Act No. 453, Section 2.

SECTION 40-1-70. Powers and duties of boards.

The powers and duties of regulatory boards include, but are not limited to:

(1) determining the eligibility of applicants for examination and licensure;

(2) examining applicants for licensure including, but not limited to:

> (a) prescribing the subjects, character, and manner of licensing examinations;
>
> (b) preparing, administering, and grading the examination or assisting in the selection of a contractor for the preparation, administration, or grading of the examination;

(3) establishing criteria for issuing, renewing, and reactivating the authorizations to practice of qualified applicants, including the issuance of active or permanent, temporary, limited, and inactive licenses, or other categories as may be created;

(4) adopting a code of professional ethics appropriate to the profession or occupation which it licenses or regulates;

(5) evaluating and approving continuing education course hours and programs;

(6) conducting hearings on alleged violations of this article and regulations promulgated under this article;

(7) resolving consumer complaints, where appropriate and possible;

(8) disciplining persons licensed under this article in a manner provided for in this article;

(9) promulgating regulations which have been submitted to the director, at least thirty days in advance of filing with Legislative Council as required by Section 1-23-30.

HISTORY: 1996 Act No. 453, Section 2.

SECTIONS 40-1-75, 40-1-77. Repealed by 2013 Act No. 45, Section 4, eff June 7, 2013.

SECTION 40-1-80. Investigations.

(A) If the director has reason to believe that a person has violated a provision of this article or a regulation promulgated under this article or the licensing act or regulation of a board or that a licensee has become unfit to practice the profession or occupation or if a person files a written complaint with the board or the director charging a person with the violation of a provision of this article or a regulation promulgated under this article, the director may initiate an investigation.

(B) In conducting the investigation, the director may subpoena witnesses, compel their attendance, take evidence, and require the production of any matter which is relevant to the investigation including, but not limited to, the existence, description, nature, custody, condition, and location of books, documents, or other tangible items and the identity and location of persons having knowledge of relevant facts or any other matter reasonably calculated to lead to the discovery of material evidence. Upon failure to obey a subpoena or to answer questions propounded by the director, the director may apply to an administrative law judge for an order requiring the person to comply.

HISTORY: 1996 Act No. 453, Section 2.

SECTION 40-1-90. Disciplinary action proceedings.

(A) The results of an investigation must be presented to the board. If from these results it appears that a violation has occurred or that a licensee has become unfit to practice the profession or occupation, the board, in accordance with the Administrative Procedures Act, may take disciplinary action authorized by Section 40-1-120. No disciplinary action may be taken unless the matter is presented to and voted upon by the board. The board may designate a hearing officer or hearing panel to conduct hearings or take other action as may be necessary under this section.

(B) For the purpose of a proceeding under this article, the department may administer oaths and issue subpoenas for the attendance and testimony of witnesses and the production and examination of books, papers, and records on behalf of the board or, upon request, on behalf of a party to the case. Upon failure to obey a subpoena or to answer questions propounded by the board or its hearing officer or panel, the board may apply to an administrative law judge for an order requiring the person to comply with the subpoena.

HISTORY: 1996 Act No. 453, Section 2.

SECTION 40-1-100. Equitable relief; immunity.

(A) When the board has reason to believe that a person is violating or intends to violate a provision of this article or a regulation promulgated under this article, in addition to all other remedies, it may order the person immediately to cease and desist from engaging in the conduct. If the person is practicing a profession or occupation without being licensed under this article, is violating a board order, a provision of this article, or a regulation promulgated under this article, the board also may apply, in accordance with the rules of the Administrative Law Court, to an administrative law judge for a temporary restraining order.

No board member or the Director of the Department of Labor, Licensing and Regulation or another employee of the department may be held liable for damages resulting from a wrongful temporary restraining order.

(B) The board may seek from an administrative law judge other equitable relief to enjoin the violation or intended violation of this article or a regulation promulgated under this article.

HISTORY: 1996 Act No. 453, Section 2.

SECTION 40-1-110. Additional grounds for disciplinary action.

In addition to other grounds contained in this article and the respective board's chapter:

(1) A board may cancel, fine, suspend, revoke, or restrict the authorization to practice of an individual who:

(a) used a false, fraudulent, or forged statement or document or committed a fraudulent, deceitful, or dishonest act or omitted a material fact in obtaining licensure under this article;

(b) has had a license to practice a regulated profession or occupation in another state or jurisdiction canceled, revoked, or suspended or who has otherwise been disciplined;

(c) has intentionally or knowingly, directly or indirectly, violated or has aided or abetted in the violation or conspiracy to violate this article or a regulation promulgated under this article;

(d) has intentionally used a fraudulent statement in a document connected with the practice of the individual's profession or occupation;

(e) has obtained fees or assisted in obtaining fees under fraudulent circumstances;

(f) has committed a dishonorable, unethical, or unprofessional act that is likely to deceive, defraud, or harm the public;

(g) lacks the professional or ethical competence to practice the profession or occupation;

(h) has been convicted of or has pled guilty to or nolo contendere to a felony or a crime involving drugs or moral turpitude;

(i) has practiced the profession or occupation while under the influence of alcohol or drugs or uses alcohol or drugs to such a degree as to render him unfit to practice his profession or occupation;

(j) has sustained a physical or mental disability which renders further practice dangerous to the public;

(k) violates a provision of this article or of a regulation promulgated under this article;

(l) violates the code of professional ethics adopted by the applicable licensing board for the regulated profession or occupation or adopted by the department with the advice of the advisory panel for the professions and occupations it directly regulates.

Each incident is considered a separate violation.

HISTORY: 1996 Act No. 453, Section 2.

SECTION 40-1-115. Term of board jurisdiction.

A board has jurisdiction over the actions committed or omitted by current and former licensees during the entire period of licensure. The board has jurisdiction to act on any matter which arises during the practice authorization period.

HISTORY: 1996 Act No. 453, Section 2.

SECTION 40-1-120. Sanctions.

(A) Upon a determination by a board that one or more of the grounds for discipline exists, in addition to the actions the board is authorized to take pursuant to its respective licensing act, the board may:

(1) issue a public reprimand;

(2) impose a fine not to exceed five hundred dollars unless otherwise specified by statute or regulation of the board;

(3) place a licensee on probation or restrict or suspend the individual's license for a definite or indefinite time and prescribe conditions to be met during probation, restriction, or suspension including, but not limited to, satisfactory completion of additional education, of a supervisory period, or of continuing education programs;

(4) permanently revoke the license.

(B) A decision by a board to discipline a licensee as authorized under this section must be by a majority vote of the total membership of the board serving at the time the vote is taken.

(C) A final order of a board disciplining a licensee under this section is public information.

(D) Upon a determination by a board that discipline is not appropriate, the board may issue a nondisciplinary letter of caution.

(E) A board may establish a procedure to allow a licensee who has been issued a public reprimand to petition the board for expungement of the reprimand from the licensee's record.

HISTORY: 1996 Act No. 453, Section 2.

SECTION 40-1-130. Board's authority to sanction.

A board may deny an authorization to practice to an applicant who has committed an act that would be grounds for disciplinary action under this article or the licensing act of the respective board. A board must deny authorization to practice to an applicant who has failed to demonstrate the qualifications or standards for licensure contained in the respective board's licensing act. The applicant shall demonstrate to the satisfaction of the board that the applicant meets all the requirements for the issuance of a license.

HISTORY: 1996 Act No. 453, Section 2.

SECTION 40-1-140. Effect of prior criminal convictions.

A person may not be refused an authorization to practice, pursue, or engage in a regulated profession or occupation solely because of a prior criminal conviction unless the criminal conviction directly relates to the profession or occupation for which the authorization to practice is sought. However, a board may refuse an authorization to practice if, based upon all information available, including the applicant's record of prior convictions, it finds that the applicant is unfit or unsuited to engage in the profession or occupation.

HISTORY: 1996 Act No. 453, Section 2.

SECTION 40-1-150. Voluntary surrender of authorization to practice.

A licensee who is under investigation for a violation provided for in Section 40-1-110 or the licensing act of the applicable board for which disciplinary action may be taken may voluntarily surrender authorization to practice to the board. The voluntary surrender invalidates the authorization to practice at the time of its relinquishment, and no person whose authorization to practice is surrendered voluntarily may practice the profession or occupation unless the board, by a majority vote, reinstates the license. A person practicing a regulated profession or occupation during the period of voluntary surrender is considered an illegal practitioner and is subject to the penalties provided by this article. The surrender of an authorization to practice may not be considered an admission of guilt in a proceeding under this article and does not preclude the board from taking disciplinary action against the licensee as provided for in this article or the board's licensing act including, but not limited to, imposing conditions that must be met before the board reinstates the license.

HISTORY: 1996 Act No. 453, Section 2.

SECTION 40-1-160. Appeal.

A person aggrieved by a final action of a board may appeal the decision to the Administrative Law Court in accordance with the Administrative Procedures Act and the rules of the Administrative Law Court. Service of a petition requesting a review does not stay the board's decision pending completion of the appellate process.

HISTORY: 1996 Act No. 453, Section 2.

SECTION 40-1-170. Costs of investigation and prosecution.

(A) In an order issued in resolution of a disciplinary proceeding before a board, a licensee found in violation of the applicable licensing act may be directed to pay a sum not to exceed the reasonable costs of the investigation and prosecution of the case in addition to other sanctions.

(B) A certified copy of the actual costs, or a good faith estimate of costs where actual costs are not available, signed by the director, or the director's designee, is prima facie evidence of reasonable costs.

(C) Failure to make timely payment in accordance with the order results in the collection of costs in accordance with Section 40-1-180.

(D) The board may conditionally renew or reinstate for a maximum of one year the license of an individual who demonstrates financial hardship and who enters into a formal agreement to reimburse the board within that one-year period for the unpaid costs.

(E) This section does not apply to a regulated profession or occupation if a specific provision in the applicable licensing act provides for recovery of costs in an administrative disciplinary proceeding.

HISTORY: 1996 Act No. 453, Section 2.

SECTION 40-1-180. Failure to pay costs or fines; remittance of funds collected.

(A) All costs and fines imposed pursuant to this article and the respective boards' licensing acts are due and payable immediately upon imposition or at the time indicated by final order of the board. Unless the costs and fines are paid within sixty days after the order becomes final, the order becomes a judgment and may be filed and executed upon in the same manner as a judgment in the court of common pleas, and the board may collect costs and attorneys' fees incurred in executing the judgment. Interest at the legal rate accrues on the amount due from the date imposed until the date paid.

(B) All fines and costs collected under this section must be remitted by the department to the State Treasurer and deposited in a special fund established for the department to defray the administrative costs associated with investigations and hearings under this article.

HISTORY: 1996 Act No. 453, Section 2.

SECTION 40-1-190. Privileged communications.

(A) A communication, whether oral or written, made by or on behalf of a person, to the director or board or a person designated by the director or board to investigate or hear matters relating to discipline of a licensee, whether by way of complaint or testimony, is privileged and no action or proceeding, civil or criminal, may be brought against the person, by or on whose behalf the communication is made, except upon proof that the communication was made with malice.

(B) Nothing in this article may be construed as prohibiting the respondent or the respondent's legal counsel from exercising the respondent's constitutional right of due process under the law or as prohibiting the respondent from normal access to the charges and evidence filed against the respondent as part of due process under the law.

(C) Notwithstanding the provisions of this section, a final order of a board disciplining a licensee is public information as provided for in Section 40-1-120.

HISTORY: 1996 Act No. 453, Section 2.

SECTION 40-1-200. Unlawful practice.

A person who practices or offers to practice a regulated profession or occupation in this State in violation of this article or who knowingly submits false information for the purpose of obtaining a license is guilty of a misdemeanor and, upon conviction, must be imprisoned not more than one year or fined not more than fifty thousand dollars.

HISTORY: 1996 Act No. 453, Section 2.

SECTION 40-1-210. Civil proceedings before Administrative Law Court.

The department, in addition to instituting a criminal proceeding, may institute a civil action through the Administrative Law Court, in the name of the State, for injunctive relief against a person violating this article, a regulation promulgated under this article, or an order of the board. For each violation the administrative law judge may impose a fine of no more than ten thousand dollars.

HISTORY: 1996 Act No. 453, Section 2.

SECTION 40-1-220. Severability.

If a provision of this article or the application of a provision of this article to a person or circumstance is held invalid, the invalidity does not affect other provisions or applications of this statute which can be given effect without the invalid provision or application, and to this end the provisions of this statute are severable.

HISTORY: 1996 Act No. 453, Section 2.

ARTICLE 3

MISCELLANEOUS LICENSURE PROVISIONS FOR MILITARY PERSONNEL

SECTION 40-1-610. Continuing education exemption.

A person whose profession or occupation is regulated by this title is exempt from completing continuing education requirements for his profession or occupation while serving on active military duty.

HISTORY: 2013 Act No. 45, Section 3, eff June 7, 2013.

SECTION 40-1-620. License fee exemption.

A person whose profession or occupation is regulated by this title may not be assessed, and is exempt from being required to pay, a license fee for his profession or occupation for a calendar year in which he serves any period of active military duty.

HISTORY: 2013 Act No. 45, Section 3, eff June 7, 2013.

SECTION 40-1-630. Temporary professional licenses; application.

(A) A board or commission that regulates the licensure of a profession or occupation under Title 40 may issue a temporary professional license for a profession or occupation it regulates to the spouse of an active duty member of the United States Armed Forces if the member is assigned to a duty station in this State pursuant to the official active duty military orders of the member.

(B)(1) A person seeking a temporary professional license under subsection (A) shall submit an application to the board or commission from which it is seeking the temporary license on forms the board or commission shall create and provide. In addition to general personal information about the applicant, the application must include proof that the:

(a) applicant is married to a member of the United States Armed Forces who is on active duty;

(b) applicant holds a valid license issued by another state, the District of Columbia, a possession or territory of the United States, or a foreign jurisdiction for the profession for which temporary licensure is sought;

(c) applicant holds the license in subitem (b) in "good standing" as evidenced by a certificate of good standing from the state, possession or territory of the United States, or foreign jurisdiction that issued the license;

(d)(i) applicant submitted at his expense to a fingerprint-based background check conducted by the State Law Enforcement Division to determine if the applicant has a criminal history in this State and a fingerprint-based background check conducted by the Federal Bureau of Investigation to determine if the person has other criminal history, and the official results of these checks must be provided to the board or commission to which application for temporary licensure is made; and

(ii) the provisions of this subitem only apply if a similar background check is required to obtain ordinary licensure in the profession or occupation for which temporary licensure is sought by the applicant; and

(e) spouse of the applicant is assigned to a duty station in this State pursuant to the official active duty military orders of the member.

(C) A temporary license issued under this section expires one year from the date of issue and may not be renewed.

HISTORY: 2013 Act No. 45, Section 3, eff June 7, 2013.

SECTION 40-1-640. Consideration of education, training, and experience completed by an individual as a member of the military.

(A) A professional or occupational board or commission governed by this title may accept the education, training, and experience completed by an individual as a member of the Armed Forces or Reserves of the United States, National Guard of any state, the Military Reserves of any state, or the Naval Militias of any state and apply this education, training, and experience in the manner most favorable toward satisfying the qualifications for issuance of the requested license or certification or approval for license examination in this State, subject to the receipt of evidence considered satisfactory by the board or commission.

(B) Nothing in this section may be construed to require the issuance of a license or certificate to an applicant who does not otherwise meet the stated eligibility standards, criteria, qualifications, or requirements for licensure, or certification, nor may the provisions be construed to automatically allow issuance of any license or certificate without testing or examination, without proper consideration by the licensing and examination board, or without proper verification that the applicant is not subject to pending criminal charges or disciplinary actions, has not been convicted of any offense prohibiting licensure or certification, and has no other impairment that would prohibit licensure or certification in this State.

HISTORY: 2013 Act No. 45, Section 3, eff June 7, 2013.

Appendix H: South Carolina Mechanics' Lien Law

SECTION 29-5-10. Lien of person furnishing labor and materials for buildings or structures; offers of settlement.

(a) A person to whom a debt is due for labor performed or furnished or for materials furnished and actually used in the erection, alteration, or repair of a building or structure upon real estate or the boring and equipping of wells, by virtue of an agreement with, or by consent of, the owner of the building or structure, or a person having authority from, or rightfully acting for, the owner in procuring or furnishing the labor or materials shall have a lien upon the building or structure and upon the interest of the owner of the building or structure in the lot of land upon which it is situated to secure the payment of the debt due to him. The costs which may arise in enforcing or defending against the lien under this chapter, including a reasonable attorney's fee, may be recovered by the prevailing party. The fee must be determined by the court in which the action is brought but the fee and the court costs may not exceed the amount of the lien. As used in this section, labor performed or furnished in the erection, alteration, or repair of any building or structure upon any real estate includes the preparation of plans, specifications, and design drawings and the work of making the real estate suitable as a site for the building or structure. The work is considered to include, but not be limited to, the grading, bulldozing, leveling, excavating, and filling of land (including the furnishing of fill soil), the grading and paving of curbs and sidewalks and all asphalt paving, the construction of ditches and other drainage facilities, and the laying of pipes and conduits for water, gas, electric, sewage, and drainage purposes, and the disposal of any construction and demolition debris, as defined in Section 44-96-40(6), including final disposal by a construction and demolition landfill. Any private security guard services provided by any person at the site of the building or structure during its erection, alteration, or repair is considered to be labor performed or furnished within the meaning of this section. As used in this section, materials furnished and actually used include tools, appliances, machinery, or equipment supplied for use on the building or structure to the extent of their reasonable rental value during their actual use. "Person" as used in this section means any individual, corporation, partnership, proprietorship, firm, enterprise, franchise, association, organization, or other entity. For purposes of this section, the term "materials" includes flooring, floor coverings, and wall coverings.

(b) Not less than fifteen days before the first term of court at which the trial is set, either party may file and serve on the other party an offer of settlement, and within ten days thereafter the party served may respond by filing and serving his offer of settlement. The offer shall state that it is made under this section and specify the amount, exclusive of interest and costs, which the party serving the offer is willing to agree constitutes a settlement of the lien. If the action is not reached for trial, then not less than fifteen days before the next term of court and subsequent terms of court at which the trial is set, either party may file and serve on the other party an offer of settlement or an amendment of a prior offer of settlement and, within ten days after that, the party served may respond by filing and serving his offer or amended offer of settlement. The offer or amended offer supersedes any offer previously made under this section by the same party.

An offer of settlement is considered rejected unless an acceptance in writing is filed and served on the party making the offer, five days before the commencement of the term.

If the offer is rejected, it may not be referred to for any purpose at the trial, but may be considered solely for the purpose of awarding costs and litigation expenses under this section.

For purposes of the award of attorney's fees, the determination of the prevailing party is based on one verdict in the action. One verdict assumes some entitlement to the mechanic's lien and the consideration of compulsory counterclaims. The party whose offer is closer to the verdict reached is considered the prevailing party in the action. If the difference between both offers and the verdict is equal, neither party is considered to be the prevailing party for purposes of determining the award of costs and attorney's fees.

If the plaintiff makes no written offer of settlement, the amount prayed for in his complaint is considered to be his final offer of settlement.

If the defendant makes no written offer of settlement, the value of his counterclaim is considered to be his negative offer of settlement. If the defendant has not asserted a counterclaim, his offer of settlement is considered to be zero.

HISTORY: 1962 Code Section 45-251; 1952 Code Section 45-251; 1942 Code Section 8727; 1932 Code Section 8727; Civ. C. '22 Section 5639; Civ. C. '12 Section 4113; Civ. C. '02 Section 3008; G.S. 2350; R. S. 2456; 1816 (6) 32; 1869 (14) 220; 1922 (32) 944; 1973 (58) 80; 1974 (58) 2183; 1976 Act No. 524, Section 1; 1986 Act No. 408, Section 1; 1990 Act No. 374, Section 2; 1999 Act No. 83, Section 1; 2003 Act No. 51, Section 22.

SECTION 29-5-15. Filing requirements; penalty for frivolous lien.

(A) To file a mechanics' lien, a contractor must provide the county clerk of court or register of deeds proof that he is licensed or registered if he is required by law to be licensed or registered. As proof of licensure or registration, the contractor must record his contractor license number or registration number on the lien document when the lien document is filed.

(B) A contractor who files a frivolous lien is subject to a fine up to five thousand dollars, the loss of his registration or contractor license, or both.

HISTORY: 2009 Act No. 40, Section 2, eff June 2, 2009.

SECTION 29-5-20. Lien of laborer, mechanic, subcontractor or materialman; limits on aggregate amount of liens filed by sub-subcontractor or supplier; limits on total aggregate amount of liens; exceptions; settlement of action to enforce lien.

(A) Every laborer, mechanic, subcontractor, or person furnishing material for the improvement of real estate when the improvement has been authorized by the owner has a lien thereon, subject to existing liens of which he has actual or constructive notice, to the value of the labor or material so furnished, including the costs of the action and a reasonable attorney's fee which must be determined by the court in which the action is brought but only if the party seeking to enforce the lien prevails. If the party defending against the lien prevails, the defending party must be awarded costs of the action and a reasonable attorney's fee as determined by the court. The fee and the court costs may not exceed the amount of the lien. The lien may be enforced as herein provided.

(B) In no event shall the aggregate amount of any liens filed by a sub-subcontractor or supplier exceed the amount due by the contractor to the subcontractor to whom the sub-subcontractor or supplier has supplied labor, material, or services unless the sub-subcontractor or supplier has provided notice of furnishing labor or materials by certified or registered mail to the contractor. Such notice of furnishing labor or materials shall include:

(1) the name of the sub-subcontractor or supplier who claims payment;

(2) the name of the person with whom the claimant contracted or by whom he was employed;

(3) a description of the labor, services, or materials furnished and the contract price or value thereof. Materials specially fabricated by a person other than the one giving notice and the contract price or value thereof shall be separately stated in the notice;

(4) a description of the project where labor, services, or materials were used sufficient for identification;

(5) the date when the first and the last item of labor or service or materials was actually furnished or scheduled to be furnished; and

(6) the amount claimed to be due, if any.

After receiving such notice, no payment by the contractor to the subcontractor will lessen the amount recoverable by the person so giving notice. However, in no event shall the total aggregate amount of liens on the improvement exceed the amount due by the owner.

(C) Not less than fifteen days before the first term of court at which the trial is set, either party may file and serve on the other party an offer of settlement, and within ten days thereafter the party served may respond by filing and serving his offer of settlement. The offer shall state that it is made under this section and specify the amount, exclusive of interest and costs, which the party serving the offer is willing to agree constitutes a settlement of the lien. If the action is not reached for trial, then not less than fifteen days before the next term of court and subsequent terms of court at which the trial is set, either party may file and serve on the other party an offer of settlement or an amendment of a prior offer of settlement and, within ten days after that, the party served may respond by filing and serving his offer or amended offer of settlement. The offer supersedes any offer previously made under this section by the same party.

An offer of settlement is considered rejected unless an acceptance in writing is filed and served on the party making the offer five days before the commencement of the term.

If the offer or amended offer is rejected, it may not be referred to for any purpose at the trial but may be considered solely for the purpose of awarding costs and litigation expenses under this section.

For purposes of the award of attorney's fees, the determination of the prevailing party is based on one verdict in the action. One verdict assumes some entitlement to the mechanic's lien and the consideration of compulsory counterclaims. The party whose offer of settlement is closer to the verdict reached is considered the prevailing party in the action. If the difference between both offers and the verdict is equal, neither party is considered to be the prevailing party for purposes of determining the award of costs and attorney's fees. If the plaintiff makes no written offer of settlement, the amount prayed for in his complaint is considered to be his final offer of settlement.

If the defendant makes no written offer of settlement, the value of his counterclaim is considered to be his negative offer of settlement. If the defendant has not asserted a counterclaim, his offer of settlement is considered to be zero.

(D) Subsection (B) does not apply to individual laborers when the amount of their lien is less than two thousand dollars.

HISTORY: 1962 Code Section 45-252; 1952 Code Section 45-252; 1942 Code Section 8728; 1932 Code Section 8728; Civ. C. '22 Section 5640; Civ. C. '12 Section 4114; Civ. C. '02 Section 3009; R. S. 2466; 1896 (22) 197; 1916 (29) 686; 1973 (58) 80; 1986 Act No. 408, Section 2; 1992 Act No. 368, Section 1; 1995 Act No. 140, Section 1; 1999 Act No. 83, Section 2.

SECTION 29-5-21. Services of surveyor and real estate licensee as improving real estate; real estate licensee's liens.

(A) A surveyor who surveys real estate by virtue of an agreement with the owner of such real estate has furnished material for the improvement of real estate within the meaning of Section 29-5-20.

(B) (1) A real estate licensee who, by virtue of a written agreement with the owner, performs professional services for which he is licensed under Title 40 incident to marketing, developing, or improving commercial real estate preparatory to or as a part of a commercial real estate lease or rental transaction involving the commercial real estate, has furnished labor or material for the improvement of commercial real estate within the meaning of Section 29-5-20.

(2) A real estate licensee shall not acquire a lien under this subsection unless:

(a) the owner of the commercial real estate or the owner's authorized agent authorizes the real estate licensee, under the terms of a written agreement, to lease an interest in the commercial real estate; and

(b) the real estate licensee or the real estate licensee's affiliated licensees provide licensed services that result, during the term of a written agreement described in item (1) of this subsection, in the procuring of a person or entity that rents or leases the commercial real estate or rents or leases an interest in the commercial real estate upon terms contained in a written agreement described in item (1) of this subsection.

(3) A real estate licensee shall not acquire a lien under this subsection upon residential real estate.

(4) Prior recorded liens shall have priority over a real estate licensee's lien. A prior recorded lien shall include, without limitation:

(i) a valid mechanic's lien claim that is recorded subsequent to the real estate licensee's lien notice of lien but which relates back to a date prior to the recording date of the real estate licensee's lien notice of lien; and

(ii) prior recorded liens securing revolving credit and future advance of construction loans as described in Section 29-3-50.

HISTORY: 1978 Act No. 465, Section 1; 2006 Act No. 263, Section 1, eff May 2, 2006.

SECTION 29-5-22. Reasonable rental value of tools, appliances, machinery, and equipment.

A person who supplies tools, appliances, machinery, or equipment used as provided in Section 29-5-10(a) is considered to have furnished material for the improvement of real estate within the meaning of Sections 29-5-20 and 29-5-40 to the extent of the reasonable rental value of the tools, appliances, machinery, or equipment for the period of actual use.

HISTORY: 1990 Act No. 374, Section 1.

SECTION 29-5-23. Notice of Project Commencement; location notice; failure to file notice.

Any person entering into a direct agreement with, or with the consent of, an owner for the improvement of real property may file with the clerk of court or register of deeds in the county or counties where the real property is situate a notice of project commencement. The notice of project commencement shall contain the following information:

(1) the name and address of the person filing the notice of commencement;

(2) the name and address of the owner or developer;

(3) a general description of the improvement; and

(4) the location of the project.

The notice must be filed within fifteen days of the commencement of work and must be accompanied by a filing fee of fifteen dollars to be deposited in that county's general fund. The name and address of the contractor must be posted at the job site. A location notice also must be posted at the job site. The location notice must contain the following statement: "The contractor on the project has filed a notice of project commencement at the county courthouse. Sub-subcontractors and suppliers to subcontractors shall comply with Section 29-5-20 when filing liens in connection with this project." The failure to file a notice of project commencement shall render the provisions of Sections 29-5-20(B) and 29-5-60(B) inapplicable. The failure to file a notice of project commencement shall also render the provisions of Sections 29-5-440, 11-35-3030(2)(c), 57-5-1660(b), and 11-1-120, relating to the requirement of a notice of providing labor, materials, or rental equipment inapplicable for a claim against a payment bond furnished by a contractor holding a direct contractual agreement with an owner. The filing of a notice of project commencement shall not constitute a cloud, lien, or encumbrance upon, or defect to, the title of the real property described in the notice, nor shall it alter the aggregate amounts of liens allowable under Section 29-5-40, nor shall it affect the priority of any mortgage filed before or after the notice, nor shall it affect any future advances under any mortgage. The clerk of court or register of deeds in each county shall maintain a separate book and index of all notices of project commencements.

HISTORY: 1992 Act No. 368, Section 3; 1997 Act No. 34, Section 1; 2000 Act No. 240, Section 5.

SECTION 29-5-25. Private security guard services at site of real estate improvement.

Any person providing private security guard services at the site of the real estate during its improvement shall be deemed to be a laborer within the meaning of Sections 29-5-20 and 29-5-40. "Person" as used in this section shall mean any individual, corporation, partnership, proprietorship, firm, enterprise, franchise, association, organization or other such entity.

HISTORY: 1976 Act No. 524, Section 2.

SECTION 29-5-26. Landscape services.

(A) A person who provides a landscape service on a parcel of real estate, which service exceeds five thousand dollars, by virtue of a written agreement with the owner of the real estate and to whom a debt is due for his performance of the landscaping service has a mechanics' lien on the real estate to secure payment of debt due to him as provided by Section 29-5-10 and Section 29-5-20. The lien attaches to the land and a building, structure, or other improvement on the land.

(B) As used in this chapter, a landscape service includes:

(1) land clearing, grading, filling, plant removal, natural obstruction removal, or other preparation of land;

(2) provision or installation, or both of them, of a landscaping item including plant material, mulch, paving, walkway, swimming pool, fountain, retaining wall, bulkhead, deck, patio, lightscaping system, irrigation system, drainage structure, drainage system, underground utility, or other feature incidental and necessary to a landscape plan or site design; or

(3) both.

(C) A landscaping service does not depend on whether the service is related to the construction, erection, alteration, or repair of a building or other structure.

HISTORY: 2009 Act No. 40, Section 1, June 2, 2009.

SECTION 29-5-27. Laborer and person defined.

Any person providing construction and demolition debris disposal services, as defined in Section 44-96-40(6), including, but not limited to, final disposal services provided by a construction and demolition landfill, is a laborer within the meaning of Sections 29-5-20 and 29-5-40. "Person" as used in this section means any individual, corporation, partnership, proprietorship, firm, enterprise, franchise, association, organization, or another entity.

HISTORY: 2003 Act No. 51, Section 23.

SECTION 29-5-30. Lien against debtor with life estate or whose estate is less than fee simple.

If the person for whom the work is done or materials are furnished has an estate for life or any other estate less than a fee simple in the land or if the property, at the time of recording the statement, is mortgaged or under any other encumbrance, the lien before provided for shall bind his whole estate and interest therein in like manner as a mortgage would have done and the creditor may cause the right of redemption or whatever other right or estate the owner had in the property to be sold and applied to the discharge of his debt, according to the provisions of this chapter.

HISTORY: 1962 Code Section 45-253; 1952 Code Section 45-253; 1942 Code Section 8762; 1932 Code Section 8762; Civ. C. '22 Section 5674; Civ. C. '12 Section 4144; Civ. C. '02 Section 3039; G. S. 2381; R. S. 2496; 1869 (14) 223.

SECTION 29-5-40. Notice to owner before lien attaches when laborer was employed by someone other than owner.

Whenever work is done or material is furnished for the improvement of real estate upon the employment of a contractor or some other person than the owner and such laborer, mechanic, contractor or materialman shall in writing notify the owner of the furnishing of such labor or material and the amount or value thereof, the lien given by Section 29-5-20 shall attach upon the real estate improved as against the true owner for the amount of the work done or material furnished. But in no event shall the aggregate amount of liens set up hereby exceed the amount due by the owner on the contract price of the improvement made.

HISTORY: 1962 Code Section 45-254; 1952 Code Section 45-254; 1942 Code Section 8729; 1932 Code Section 8729; Civ. C. '22 Section 5641; Civ. C. '12 Section 4114; Civ. C. '02 Section 3009; R. S. 2466; 1896 (22) 197; 1916 (29) 686.

SECTION 29-5-50. Lienor's preference over contractor.

Any person claiming a lien under the provisions of this chapter who shall have given the notice provided for herein shall be entitled to be paid in preference to the contractor at whose instance the labor was performed or material furnished and no payment by the owner to the contractor thereafter shall operate to lessen the amount recoverable by the person so giving the notice.

HISTORY: 1962 Code Section 45-255; 1952 Code Section 45-255; 1942 Code Section 8730; 1932 Code Section 8730; Civ. C. '22 Section 5642; 1916 (19) 686.

SECTION 29-5-60. Proration of payments among lienors.

(A) In the event the amount due the contractor by the owner is insufficient to pay all the lienors acquiring liens as herein provided it is the duty of the owner to prorate among all just claims the amount due the contractor.

(B) In the event the amount due a subcontractor by the contractor is insufficient to pay all the lienors acquiring liens under Section 29-5-20 as a result of supplying labor, materials, or services to that subcontractor, all just liens must be prorated by the contractor among sub-subcontractors and suppliers to that subcontractor.

HISTORY: 1962 Code Section 45-256; 1952 Code Section 45-256; 1942 Code Section 8731; 1932 Code Section 8731; Civ. C. '22 Section 5643; 1916 (29) 686; 1992 Act No. 368, Section 2.

SECTION 29-5-70. Force of lien against existing recorded mortgage.

Except as otherwise provided in Section 29-3-50, a lien claimed by any mechanic or materialman furnishing labor, services, or material is not enforceable against any mortgage recorded before the filing of the notice pursuant to Section 29-5-90 setting forth the statement of account upon which the lien is based.

HISTORY: 1962 Code Section 45-257; 1952 Code Section 45-257; 1942 Code Section 8733; 1932 Code Section 8733; Civ. C. '22 Section 5645; Civ. C. '12 Section 4515; Civ. C. '02 Section 3010; G. S. 2352; R. S. 2467; 1869 (14) 220; 1988 Act No. 635, Section 2.

SECTION 29-5-80. Notice of nonresponsibility by owner of building or structure.

The owner of any such building or structure in process of erection or being altered or repaired, other than the person by whom or in whose behalf a contract for labor or materials has been made, may prevent the attaching of any lien for labor thereon not at the time performed or materials not then furnished by giving notice, in writing, to the person performing or furnishing such labor or furnishing such materials that he will not be responsible therefor.

HISTORY: 1962 Code Section 45-258; 1952 Code Section 45-258; 1942 Code Section 8734; 1932 Code Section 8734; Civ. C. '22 Section 5646; Civ. C. '12 Section 4116; Civ. C. '02 Section 3011; G. S. 2356; R. S. 2468; 1869 (14) 220.

SECTION 29-5-90. Dissolution of lien for failure to serve and file statement; contents of statement.

Such a lien shall be dissolved unless the person desiring to avail himself thereof, within ninety days after he ceases to labor on or furnish labor or materials for such building or structure, serves upon the owner or, in the event the owner cannot be found, upon the person in possession and files in the office of the register of deeds or clerk of court of the county in which the building or structure is situated a statement of a just and true account of the amount due him, with all just credits given, together with a description of the property intended to be covered by the lien sufficiently accurate for identification, with the name of the owner of the property, if known, which certificate shall be subscribed and sworn to by the person claiming the lien or by someone in his behalf and shall be recorded in a book kept for the purpose by the register or clerk who shall be entitled to the same fees therefor as for recording mortgages of equal length. Provided, that in the event neither the owner nor the person in possession can be located after diligent search, and this fact is verified by affidavit of the sheriff or his deputy, the lien may be preserved by filing the statement together with the affidavit. The delivery on the register or clerk for filing, as provided in this section, shall be and constitute the delivery contemplated with regard to such liens in Title 30 of this Code.

HISTORY: 1962 Code Section 45-259; 1952 Code Section 45-259; 1942 Code Section 8735; 1932 Code Section 8735; Civ. C. '22 Section 5647; Civ. C. '12 Section 4117; Civ. C. '02 Section 3012; G. S. 2354; R. S. 2469; 1869 (14) 220; 1873 (15) 350; 1884 (18) 822; 1950 (46) 2294; 1957 (50) 180.

SECTION 29-5-100. Proceedings not invalidated by inaccuracy of statement of account.

No inaccuracy in such statement relating to the property to be covered by the lien, if the property can be reasonably recognized, or in stating the amount due for labor or materials shall invalidate the proceedings, unless it appear that the person filing the certificate has wilfully and knowingly claimed more than is his due.

HISTORY: 1962 Code Section 45-260; 1952 Code Section 45-260; 1942 Code Section 8736; 1932 Code Section 8736; Civ. C. '22 Section 5648; Civ. C. '12 Section 4118; Civ. C. '02 Section 3013; G. S. 2355; R. S. 2470; 1869 (14) 220.

SECTION 29-5-110. Release of lien upon filing written undertaking and security.

At any time after service and filing of the statement required under Section 29-5-90 the owner or any other person having an interest in or lien upon the property involved may secure the discharge of such property from such lien by filing in the office of clerk of court or register of deeds where such lien is filed his written undertaking, in an amount equal to one and one-third times the amount claimed in such statement, secured by the pledge of United States or State of South Carolina securities, by cash or by a surety bond executed by a surety company licensed to do business in this State, and upon the filing of such undertaking so secured the lien shall be discharged and the cash, securities or surety bond deposited shall take the place of the property upon which the lien existed and shall be subject to the lien. In the event of judgment for the person filing such statement in a suit brought pursuant to the provisions of this chapter, such judgment shall be paid out of the cash deposited or, in event of pledge of securities, it shall be paid from the proceeds of a sale of so much of the pledged securities as shall be necessary to satisfy such judgment or, in event of the filing of a surety bond, the surety company issuing such bond shall pay such amount found due, not to exceed the amount of the bond. Unless suit for enforcement of the lien is commenced as required by Section 29-5-120, the undertaking herein required shall be null and void and the principal therein shall have the right to have it canceled and such cash or securities deposited or pledged or surety bond filed shall be released from the lien herein provided.

HISTORY: 1962 Code Section 45-261; 1952 Code Section 45-261; 1950 (46) 2294; 1976 Act No. 635, Section 1.

SECTION 29-5-120. Time for bringing suit to enforce lien; dissolution and release of lien.

(A) Unless a suit for enforcing the lien is commenced and notice of pendency of the action is filed within six months after the person desiring to avail himself of it ceases to labor on or furnish labor or material for the building or structure, the lien must be dissolved.

(B) A mechanics' lien and associated bonds may be released by a court order, a written affidavit of the bond holder's attorney, or by a written affidavit from the defendant's attorney stating:

(1) six months has passed since the lien was attached and no suit or notice of pendency has been filed; or

(2) the failure of the filing party to take some other timely action required by this chapter. This affidavit must be in the form approved by the appropriate local office where the mechanics' lien was filed and must reference the lien's recording information.

HISTORY: 1962 Code Section 45-262; 1952 Code Section 45-262; 1942 Code Section 8737; 1932 Code Section 8737; Civ. C. '22 Section 5649; Civ. C. '12 Section 4119; Civ. C. '02 Section 3014; G. S. 2356; R. S. 2471; 1869 (14) 220; 1873 (15) 350; 1957 (50) 181; 2009 Act No. 40, Section 3, eff June 2, 2009.

SECTION 29-5-130. Enforcement of certain liens before magistrate's court.

When the amount of the claim does not exceed one hundred dollars the lien may be enforced by a petition to a magistrate. And such magistrate shall have like power and authority within his jurisdiction as herein conferred upon the court of common pleas, with like rights of appeal to the parties as exist in other civil cases.

HISTORY: 1962 Code Section 45-263; 1952 Code Section 45-263; 1942 Code Section 8739; 1932 Code Section 8739; Civ. C. '22 Section 5651; Civ. C. '12 Section 4121; Civ. C. '02 Section 3016; G. S. 2358; R. S. 2473; 1869 (14) 221.

SECTION 29-5-140. Enforcement of lien by petition to court of common pleas.

The lien may be enforced by petition to the court of common pleas for the county in which the building or structure is situated. The petition may be filed in term or in the clerk's office in vacation and the date of the filing shall be deemed the commencement of the suit.

HISTORY: 1962 Code Section 45-264; 1952 Code Section 45-264; 1942 Code Section 8738; 1932 Code Section 8738; Civ. C. '22 Section 5650; Civ. C. '12 Section 4120; Civ. C. '02 Section 3015; G. S. 2357; R. S. 2472; 1869 (14) 220.

SECTION 29-5-150. Service of petition.

The petition may be served with the summons or filed with the clerk and shall be returned and entered as other civil cases.

HISTORY: 1962 Code Section 45-265; 1952 Code Section 45-265; 1942 Code Section 8740; 1932 Code Section 8740; Civ. C. '22 Section 5652; Civ. C. '12 Section 4122; Civ. C. '02 Section 3017; G. S. 2359; R. S. 2474; 1869 (14) 221.

SECTION 29-5-160. Contents of petition.

The petition shall contain a brief statement of the contract on which it is founded and of the amount due thereon, with a description of the premises subject to the lien and all other material facts and circumstances, and shall pray that the premises may be sold and the proceeds of the sale applied to the discharge of the demand.

HISTORY: 1962 Code Section 45-266; 1952 Code Section 45-266; 1942 Code Section 8741; 1932 Code Section 8741; Civ. C. '22 Section 5653; Civ. C. '12 Section 4123; Civ. C. '02 Section 3018; G. S. 2360; R. S. 2475; 1869 (14) 220.

SECTION 29-5-170. Petition filed by multiple lienors.

Any number of persons who have actually performed labor or furnished labor or materials on one or more buildings or structures upon different lots of land, when the labor was performed for the same owner, contractor or other person, may join in the same petition for their respective liens and the same proceedings shall be had in regard to the rights of each petitioner and the respondent may defend as to each petitioner in the same manner as if he had severally petitioned for his individual lien.

HISTORY: 1962 Code Section 45-267; 1952 Code Section 45-267; 1942 Code Section 8743; 1932 Code Section 8743; Civ. C. '22 Section 5655; Civ. C. '12 Section 4125; Civ. C. '02 Section 3020; G. S. 2362; R. S. 2477; 1869 (14) 220.

SECTION 29-5-180. Amendments of pleadings.

The court may at any time allow either party to amend his pleadings as in other civil actions.

HISTORY: 1962 Code Section 45-268; 1952 Code Section 45-268; 1942 Code Section 8742; 1932 Code Section 8742; Civ. C. '22 Section 5654; Civ. C. '12 Section 4124; Civ. C. '02 Section 3019; G. S. 2361; R. S. 2476; 1869 (14) 220.

SECTION 29-5-190. Notice to owner and other creditors.

The court in which the petition is entered shall order notice to be given to the owner of the building or structure, that he may appear and answer thereto at a certain day in the same term or at the next term, by serving him with an attested copy of the petition, with the order of the court thereon, fourteen days at least before the time assigned for the hearing. And the court shall also order notice of the filing of the petition to be given to all other creditors who have a lien of the same kind upon the same estate by serving them with a copy of the last-mentioned order in like manner.

HISTORY: 1962 Code Section 45-269; 1952 Code Section 45-269; 1942 Code Section 8744; 1932 Code Section 8744; Civ. C. '22 Section 5656; Civ. C. '12 Section 4126; Civ. C. '02 Section 3021; G. S. 2363; R. S. 2478; 1869 (14) 220.

SECTION 29-5-200. Notice by publication or other than personal service.

If it appears to the court that any of the parties entitled to notice are absent or that they cannot probably be found or be served with the notice, the court may, instead of the personal notice before mentioned or in addition thereto, order notice given to all persons interested by publishing in some newspaper the substance of the petition with the order of the court thereon assigning the time and place for a hearing or may order such other notice to be given as may, under the circumstances of the case, be considered most proper and effectual.

HISTORY: 1962 Code Section 45-270; 1952 Code Section 45-270; 1942 Code Section 8745; 1932 Code Section 8745; Civ. C. '22 Section 5657; Civ. C. '12 Section 4127; Civ. C. '02 Section 3022; G. S. 2364; R. S. 2479; 1869 (14) 220.

SECTION 29-5-210. Further notice of suit.

If at the time assigned for the hearing it appears to the court that any of the persons interested had not had a sufficient notice of the suit, the court may order further notice to them in such manner as may be considered most proper and effectual.

HISTORY: 1962 Code Section 45-271; 1952 Code Section 45-271; 1942 Code Section 8746; 1932 Code Section 8746; Civ. C. '22 Section 5658; Civ. C. '12 Section 4128; Civ. C. '02 Section 3023; G. S. 2365; R. S. 2480; 1869 (14) 220.

SECTION 29-5-220. Hearing on claims of lienors.

At the time assigned for the hearing, or within such further time as the court allows for that purpose, every creditor having a lien of the kind before mentioned upon the same property may appear and prove his claim and the owner and each of the creditors may contest the several claims of every other creditor and the court shall hear and determine them in a summary manner, either with or without a jury, as the case may require.

HISTORY: 1962 Code Section 45-272; 1952 Code Section 45-272; 1942 Code Section 8747; 1932 Code Section 8747; Civ. C. '22 Section 5659; Civ. C. '12 Section 4129; Civ. C. '02 Section 3024; G. S. 2366; R. S. 2481; 1869 (14) 220.

SECTION 29-5-230. Questions for jury.

Every material question of fact arising in the case shall be submitted to a jury, if required by either party or deemed proper by the court, and the trial shall be had upon a question stated or an issue framed or otherwise, as the court may order. A jury shall be had before a magistrate only as in other civil cases.

HISTORY: 1962 Code Section 45-273; 1952 Code Section 45-273; 1942 Code Section 8748; 1932 Code Section 8748; Civ. C. '22 Section 5660; Civ. C. '12 Section 4130; Civ. C. '02 Section 3025; G. S. 2367; R. S. 2482; 1869 (14) 220.

SECTION 29-5-240. Determination of claims due but not yet payable.

The court shall ascertain and determine the amount due to each creditor who has a lien of the kind before mentioned upon the property in question and every such claim due, absolutely and without any condition, although not then payable, shall be allowed with a rebate of interest to the time when it would become payable.

HISTORY: 1962 Code Section 45-274; 1952 Code Section 45-274; 1942 Code Section 8749; 1932 Code Section 8749; Civ. C. '22 Section 5661; Civ. C. '12 Section 4131; Civ. C. '02 Section 3026; G. S. 2368; R. S. 2483; 1869 (14) 222.

SECTION 29-5-250. Recovery for part performance.

When the owner fails to perform his part of the contract and by reason thereof the other party, without his own default, is prevented from completely performing his part, he shall be entitled to a reasonable compensation for as much as he has performed in proportion to the price stipulated for the whole and the court shall adjust his claim accordingly.

HISTORY: 1962 Code Section 45-275; 1952 Code Section 45-275; 1942 Code Section 8750; 1932 Code Section 8750; Civ. C. '22 Section 5662; Civ. C. '12 Section 4132; Civ. C. '02 Section 3027; G. S. 2369; R. S. 2484; 1869 (14) 222.

SECTION 29-5-260. Sale of premises if lien established.

If the lien is established in favor of any of the creditors whose claims are presented the court shall order a sale of the property to be made by such officer as may be authorized by law to make sales of property.

HISTORY: 1962 Code Section 45-276; 1952 Code Section 45-276; 1942 Code Section 8751; 1932 Code Section 8751; Civ. C. '22 Section 5663; Civ. C. '12 Section 4133; Civ. C. '02 Section 3028; G. S. 2370; R. S. 2485; 1869 (14) 222.

SECTION 29-5-270. Sale of part of property.

If part of the property can be separated from the residue and sold without damage to the whole and if the value thereof is sufficient to satisfy all debts proved in the case, the court may order a sale of that part, if it appears to be most for the interest of all parties concerned.

HISTORY: 1962 Code Section 45-277; 1952 Code Section 45-277; 1942 Code Section 8752; 1932 Code Section 8752; Civ. C. '22 Section 5664; Civ. C. '12 Section 4134; Civ. C. '02 Section 3029; G. S. 2371; R. S. 2486; 1869 (14) 222.

SECTION 29-5-280. Notice of sale.

The officer who makes the sale shall give notice of the time and place in the manner prescribed in relation to the sale of mortgaged lands under foreclosure, unless the court orders a different notice to be given.

HISTORY: 1962 Code Section 45-278; 1952 Code Section 45-278; 1942 Code Section 8753; 1932 Code Section 8753; Civ. C. '22 Section 5665; Civ. C. '12 Section 4135; Civ. C. '02 Section 3030; G. S. 2372; R. S. 2487; 1869 (14) 222.

SECTION 29-5-290. Distribution of proceeds of sale.

If all the claims against the property covered by the lien are ascertained at the time of ordering the sale, the court may order the officer to pay over and distribute the proceeds of the sale, after deducting all lawful charges and expenses, to and among the several creditors to the amount of their respective debts, if there is sufficient therefor, and if there is not sufficient, then to divide and distribute such proceeds among the creditors in proportion to the amount due to each of them.

HISTORY: 1962 Code Section 45-279; 1952 Code Section 45-279; 1942 Code Section 8754; 1932 Code Section 8754; Civ. C. '22 Section 5666; Civ. C. '12 Section 4136; Civ. C. '02 Section 3031; G. S. 2373; R. S. 2488; 1869 (14) 222.

SECTION 29-5-300. Distribution of proceeds by court.

If all the claims are not ascertained when the sale is ordered or if for any other reason the court finds it necessary or proper to postpone the order of distribution, it may direct the officer to bring the proceeds of the sale into court, there to be disposed of according to the decree of the court, and if, by reason of the claims of attaching creditors or for any other cause, the whole cannot be conveniently distributed at once the court may make two or more successive orders of distribution, as the circumstances may require.

HISTORY: 1962 Code Section 45-280; 1952 Code Section 45-280; 1942 Code Section 8755; 1932 Code Section 8755; Civ. C. '22 Section 5667; Civ. C. '12 Section 4137; Civ. C. '02 Section 3032; G. S. 2374; R. S. 2489; 1869 (14) 222.

SECTION 29-5-310. Distribution of surplus.

If there remain any surplus of the proceeds of the sale, after making all the payments before mentioned, it shall be forthwith paid over to the owner of the property, but such surplus, before it is so paid over, shall be liable to be attached or taken on execution in like manner as if it proceeded from a sale made by the officer on an execution.

HISTORY: 1962 Code Section 45-281; 1952 Code Section 45-281; 1942 Code Section 8756; 1932 Code Section 8756; Civ. C. '22 Section 5668; Civ. C. '12 Section 4138; Civ. C. '02 Section 3033; G. S. 2375; R. S. 2490; 1869 (14) 222.

SECTION 29-5-320. Prior attaching creditor is preferred.

If the interest of the owner in the building, structure or land is under attachment at the time of filing and recording the statement of the account, the attaching creditor shall be preferred to the extent of the value of the buildings and land as they were when the statement was recorded and the court shall ascertain, by a jury or otherwise as the case may require, what proportion of the proceeds of the sale shall be held subject to the attachment as derived from the value of the property when the statement was recorded.

HISTORY: 1962 Code Section 45-282; 1952 Code Section 45-282; 1942 Code Section 8757; 1932 Code Section 8757; Civ. C. '22 Section 5669; Civ. C. '12 Section 4139; Civ. C. '02 Section 3034; G. S. 2376; R. S. 2491; 1869 (14) 223.

SECTION 29-5-330. Distribution of proceeds where there is attaching creditor.

If the attaching creditor recovers judgment he shall be entitled to receive on his execution the proportion of the proceeds held subject to his attachment, or so much thereof as may be necessary to satisfy his execution, and the residue of the proceeds shall be applied in the same manner as if there had been no such attachment.

HISTORY: 1962 Code Section 45-283; 1952 Code Section 45-283; 1942 Code Section 8758; 1932 Code Section 8758; Civ. C. '22 Section 5670; Civ. C. '12 Section 4140; Civ. C. '02 Section 3035; G. S. 2377; R. S. 2492; 1869 (14) 223.

SECTION 29-5-340. Subsequent attachments.

If the interest of the owner of the property is attached after the recording of the statement, the proceeds, after discharging all prior liens and claims, shall be applied to satisfy the execution of such attaching creditor.

HISTORY: 1962 Code Section 45-284; 1952 Code Section 45-284; 1942 Code Section 8759; 1932 Code Section 8759; Civ. C. '22 Section 5671; Civ. C. '12 Section 4141; Civ. C. '02 Section 3036; G. S. 2378; R. S. 2493; 1869 (14) 223.

SECTION 29-5-350. Attachments intervening between two liens.

If an attachment is made after the recording of such statement and if, after the attachment, another like statement is recorded, the creditor in the latter statement shall be entitled to be paid only out of the residue of the proceeds remaining after paying all that is due on the demand a statement of which was recorded before the attachment and satisfying the attaching creditor.

HISTORY: 1962 Code Section 45-285; 1952 Code Section 45-285; 1942 Code Section 8760; 1932 Code Section 8760; Civ. C. '22 Section 5672; Civ. C. '12 Section 4142; Civ. C. '02 Section 3037; G. S. 2379; R. S. 2494; 1869 (14) 223.

SECTION 29-5-360. Rights of creditors among themselves.

When there are several attaching creditors, they shall, as between themselves, be entitled to be paid according to the order of their attachments. But when several creditors who are entitled to the lien provided for in this chapter have equal rights as between themselves and the fund is insufficient to pay the whole, they shall share it equally in proportion to their respective debts.

HISTORY: 1962 Code Section 45-286; 1952 Code Section 45-286; 1942 Code Section 8761; 1932 Code Section 8761; Civ. C. '22 Section 5673; Civ. C. '12 Section 4143; Civ. C. '02 Section 3038; G. S. 2380; R. S. 2495; 1869 (14) 223.

SECTION 29-5-370. Persons against whom lien may be enforced when debtor dies or conveys his interest.

If the person indebted dies or conveys away his estate or interest before the commencement of a suit on the contract, the suit may be commenced and prosecuted against his heirs or whoever holds the estate or interest which he had in the premises at the time the labor or materials were performed or furnished. Or, if a suit is commenced in his lifetime, it may be prosecuted against his executors, administrators, heirs or assigns in like manner as if the estate or interest had been mortgaged to secure the debt.

HISTORY: 1962 Code Section 45-287; 1952 Code Section 45-287; 1942 Code Section 8763; 1932 Code Section 8763; Civ. C. '22 Section 5675; Civ. C. '12 Section 4145; Civ. C. '02 Section 3040; G. S. 2382; R. S. 2497; 1869 (14) 223.

SECTION 29-5-380. Executor or administrator may enforce creditor's lien.

If a creditor dies before the commencement of the suit, the suit may be commenced and prosecuted by his executor or administrator or, if commenced in his lifetime, it may be prosecuted by them as it might have been by the deceased, if living.

HISTORY: 1962 Code Section 45-288; 1952 Code Section 45-288; 1942 Code Section 8764; 1932 Code Section 8764; Civ. C. '22 Section 5676; Civ. C. '12 Section 4146; Civ. C. '02 Section 3041; G. S. 2383; R. S. 2498; 1869 (14) 223.

SECTION 29-5-390. Suits begun by one creditor may be prosecuted by another.

If it appears in any stage of the proceedings that the suit was commenced by the petitioning creditor before his right of action accrued or after it was barred or if he becomes nonsuited or fails to establish his claims the suit may be prosecuted by any other creditor having such lien in the same manner as if it had been originally commenced by him, if the circumstances of the case are such that he might then or at any time after the commencement of the original suit have commenced a like suit on his own claim.

HISTORY: 1962 Code Section 45-289; 1952 Code Section 45-289; 1942 Code Section 8765; 1932 Code Section 8765; Civ. C. '22 Section 5677; Civ. C. '12 Section 4147; Civ. C. '02 Section 3042; G. S. 2384; R. S. 2499; 1869 (14) 223.

SECTION 29-5-400. Allowance of claim and costs of petitioning creditor.

If the suit is commenced by the petitioning creditor before his right of action accrues, his claim may nevertheless be allowed if the suit is carried on by any other creditor, as provided in Section 29-5-390, but he shall not in such case be entitled to costs and he may be required to pay the costs incurred by the debtor or such part thereof as the court may deem reasonable.

HISTORY: 1962 Code Section 45-290; 1952 Code Section 45-290; 1942 Code Section 8766; 1932 Code Section 8766; Civ. C. '22 Section 5678; Civ. C. '12 Section 4148; Civ. C. '02 Section 3043; G. S. 2385; R. S. 2500; 1869 (14) 224.

SECTION 29-5-410. Costs.

The costs, in all other respects, shall be subject to the discretion of the court and shall be paid from the proceeds of the sale or by any of the parties to the suit, as justice and equity require.

HISTORY: 1962 Code Section 45-291; 1952 Code Section 45-291; 1942 Code Section 8767; 1932 Code Section 8767; Civ. C. '22 Section 5679; Civ. C. '12 Section 4149; Civ. C. '02 Section 3044; G. S. 2386; R. S. 2501; 1869 (14) 224.

SECTION 29-5-420. Civil action not barred.

Nothing contained in this chapter shall be construed to prevent a creditor in such contract from maintaining an action thereon in like manner as if he had no such lien for the security of his debt.

HISTORY: 1962 Code Section 45-292; 1952 Code Section 45-292; 1942 Code Section 8768; 1932 Code Section 8768; Civ. C. '22 Section 5680; Civ. C. '12 Section 4150; Civ. C. '02 Section 3045; G. S. 2387; R. S. 2502; 1869 (14) 224.

SECTION 29-5-430. Recording discharge or release of lien.

When a debt secured by such a lien is fully paid, the creditor, at the expense of the debtor, shall enter on the margin of the registry where the statement is recorded a discharge of his lien or shall execute a release thereof, which may be recorded where the statement is recorded.

HISTORY: 1962 Code Section 45-293; 1952 Code Section 45-293; 1942 Code Section 8769; 1932 Code Section 8769; Civ. C. '22 Section 5681; Civ. C. '12 Section 4151; Civ. C. '02 Section 3046; G. S. 2388; R. S. 2503; 1869 (14) 224.

SECTION 29-5-440. Suit on payment bond.

Every person who has furnished labor, material, or rental equipment to a bonded contractor or its subcontractors in the prosecution of work provided for in any contract for construction, and who has not been paid in full therefor before the expiration of a period of ninety days after the day on which the last of the labor was done or performed by him or material or rental equipment was furnished or supplied by him for which such claim is made, shall have the right to sue on the payment bond for the amount, or the balance thereof, unpaid at the time of the institution of such suit and to prosecute such action to final execution and judgment for the sum or sums justly due him.

A remote claimant shall have a right of action on the payment bond only upon giving written notice by certified or registered mail to the bonded contractor within ninety days from the date on which such person did or performed the last of the labor or furnished or supplied the last of the material or rental equipment upon which such claim is made. However, in no event shall the aggregate amount of any claim against such payment bond by a remote claimant exceed the amount due by the bonded contractor to the person to whom the remote claimant has supplied labor, materials, rental equipment, or services, unless the remote claimant has provided notice of furnishing labor, materials, or rental equipment to the bonded contractor. Such written notice to the bonded contractor must generally conform to the requirements of Section 29-5-20(B) and sent by certified or registered mail to the bonded contractor at any place the bonded contractor maintains a permanent office for the conduct of its business, or at the current address as shown on the records of the Department of Labor, Licensing and Regulation. After receiving the notice of furnishing labor, materials, or rental equipment, no payment by the bonded contractor shall lessen the amount recoverable by the remote claimant. However, in no event shall the aggregate amount of claims on the payment bond exceed the penal sum of the bond.

No suit under this section shall be commenced after the expiration of one year after the last date of furnishing or providing labor, services, materials, or rental equipment.

For purposes of this section, "bonded contractor" means a contractor or subcontractor furnishing a payment bond, and "remote claimant" means a person having a direct contractual relationship with a subcontractor or supplier of a bonded contractor, but no contractual relationship expressed or implied with the bonded contractor. Any payment bond surety for the bonded contractor must have the same rights and defenses of the bonded contractor as provided in this section.

This section shall apply to any payment bond, whether statutory, public, common law, or private in nature, that is issued in connection with a construction project or other improvements to real property within South Carolina when such payment bonds are not otherwise required or governed by any other applicable section of the South Carolina Code of Laws.

For the purposes of this section:

(1) "Statutory bonds" or "public bonds" means bonds that are either:

(a) provided because required by statute and in accordance with the minimum guidelines set forth in this section; or

(b) contain either express or implied reference to the provisions of this section.

(2) "Common law bonds" or "private bonds" means bonds that are either:

(a) not required by statute, such as a bond voluntarily provided to meet a contractual agreement between parties; or

(b) required by statute but that specifically deviates from the statutory requirements to provide broader protection.

HISTORY: 2000 Act No. 240, Section 1; 2014 Act No. 264 (S.1026), Section 1, eff June 6, 2014.

National Association of State Contractors Licensing Agencies
NASCLA Membership Information

Membership Benefits

- Networking Opportunities with Industry Experts and Representatives
- Complimentary Copies of the Annual Membership Directory, Newsletter, Model Legislation, and *Contractor's State Licensing Information Directory (CSLID)*
- Reduced Registration Fees for NASCLA Annual Conferences & Training Seminars
- Access to the NASCLA Members Only Website *(*for State Members Only)*
    - ***Member Reference Library*** which includes consumer publications, NASCLA Model Legislation and other information
    - ***Track Bills & State Legislation*** NASCLA has partnered with a nationwide legislative tracking platform that tracks legislation across all 50 states and congress
    - ***Top Regulatory Cases*** affecting the construction industry and regulatory agencies
    - ****Toolkit for Contractor Regulators*** provides a variety of best practices from other states which state members can use to customize your very own programs without reinventing the wheel. Some of the highlighted programs include Elderly Abuse Prevention Program, Disaster Response Program and Understanding the Board's Role in a Legislative Environment to name a few!
    - ***Community Forums*** are available for *Executive Directors, Attorneys, *Public Information Officers, *Enforcement/Investigators, *IT Personnel, and Contractors. Communicate and engage with your counterparts nationally.
    - ***Active Member Directory Search*** allows you to search contact information for any NASCLA Member

To Apply for NASCLA Membership, please visit the following link: www.nascla.org

NASCLA's MISSION

"The National Association of State Contractors Licensing Agencies (NASCLA) promotes best practices and license uniformity for agencies that regulate the construction industry."

NASCLA®

NATIONAL ASSOCIATION OF STATE CONTRACTORS LICENSING AGENCIES

23309 N. 17th Drive
Building 1, Unit 110
Phoenix, Arizona 85027

Phone: (623) 587-9354

Fax: (623) 587-9625

www.nascla.org

APPLICANT INFORMATION

To become a member, please return this form with a check made payable to NASCLA at the address listed above or you may visit our website at www.nascla.org to register online for membership.

If you have any questions, please call NASCLA at (866) 948-3363.

MEMBERSHIP CLASSIFICATIONS

Please read the classifications below and check the box that best describes your membership classification.

- ☐ **Associate Member:** Limited to contractor trade associations, contractor firms, construction material suppliers, individual contractors, and regional (county, city or municipal) contractor licensing agencies.

  $125.00 Annual Membership Fee.

- ☐ **State Member:** Limited to states that have enacted laws to regulate the business of contracting.

  $475.00 Annual Membership Fee.

- ☐ **International Member:** Limited to regulatory agencies from other nations, countries or states other than the 50 United States of America and its territories.

  $475.00 Annual Membership Fee.

- ☐ **Business Member:** Limited to firms whose business is related to the construction industry. These members shall not use the name of the association and its logo or in any manner refer to NASCLA in advertising, selling or soliciting.

  $750.00 Annual Membership Fee.

- ☐ **Affiliate Member:** Limited to former employees and board members of state contractor licensing agencies who are not actively engaged in the contracting business.

  $50.00 Annual Membership Fee.

Name: ______________________________

Title: ______________________________

Company: ______________________________

City, State, Zip Code: ______________________________

Phone: ______________________________

Email: ____________________ Website: ____________________